A Not-So-Nice Jewish Boy Faces World War II

A MEMOIR BY
Norman Beim

For Dr. Sheldon Cohen, best wishes!
Norman Beim

NEWCONCEPT press, inc.
New York New York

copyright c by Norman Beim

NEW CONCEPT PRESS
425 West 57th Street
Suite 2J
New York, New York 10019
212-265-6284   Fax: 212-265-6659

All rights reserved. No part of this publication can be reproduced without written permission from the author.

Library of Congress Control Number: 2012914599

Beim, Norman
A Not-So-Nice Jewish Boy Faces World War II

ISBN: 978-0-931231-20-9   O-931231-20-5
1. Jewish immigrants. 2. Childhood   3. World War II
4. Post War England/ Wales

Title: A Not-So-Nice Jewish Boy Faces World War II

Special thanks: Marty Beim, Larry Erlbaum, Frank Bara, Francine Trevens

Front Cover Design: HOMER GUERRA, New York City

Printed in The United States

10 9 8 7 6 5 4 3 2 1

BOOKS BY NORMAN BEIM

MEMOIRS
A No-So-Nice Jewish Boy Faces World War II

NOVELS
Touring With Stalin
Zygielbaum's Journey
Hymie And The Angel

PLAYS
Behind The Scenes, Plus 2 Comedies & 2 Dramas
Bitter And Sweet: 3 New Musicals
The Wrath Of God, Plus 5 Additional Dramas
Six Ironic Comedies
Three Dark Comedies
Women Laid Bare
Comedy Tonite!
Infamous People
Giants Of The Old Testament
My Family The Jewish Immigrants
Plays At Home And Abroad
Six Award Winning Plays

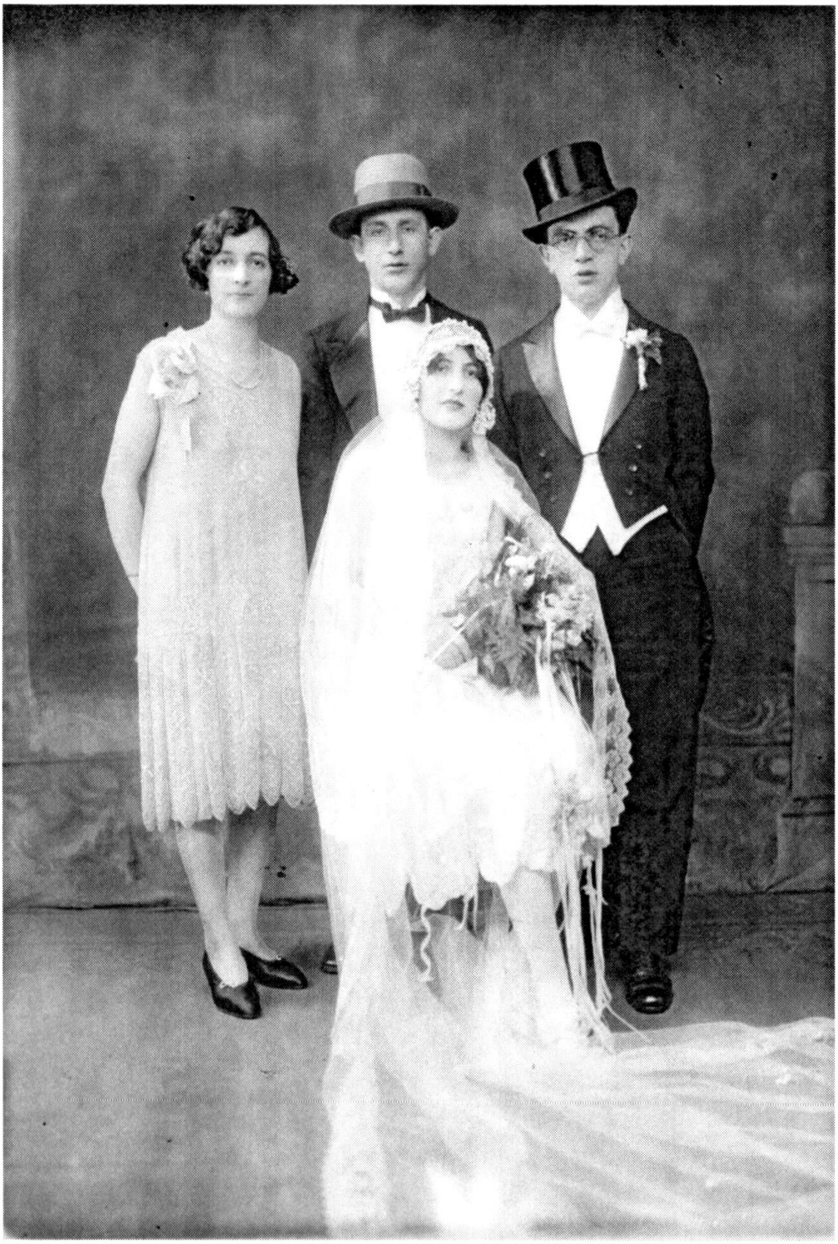

BOOK ONE

A NOT-SO-NICE JEWISH BOY

BOOK ONE

A NOT-SO-NICE JEWISH BOY

PART ONE: CHILDHOOD

Chapter 1: My Mother . . . . Page 7
Chapter 2: My Mother & My Father . . . . . Page 13
Chapter 3: I Enter The Scene . . . . Page 19
Chapter 4: The World Around Me . . . . Page 25
Chapter 5: My Education Begins . . . . Page 30
Chapter 6: So Much For Bravery . . . . Page 33
Chapter 7: My Horizons Broaden . . . . Page 37
Chapter 8: My First Love . . . . Page 41
Chapter 9: A Portrait Gallery . . . . Page 45
Chapter 10: The Dynamo . . . . Page 49
Chapter 11: An Incipient Romance & An Overactive Imagination . . . . Page 54
Chapter 12: The World Of Books . . . . Page 59
Chapter 13: Neighbors, Close Friends & The Library 62
Chapter 14: First Orgasm . . . . Page 67
Chapter 15: I Set My Sights On Carnegie Hall . . . . Page 70
Chapter 16: My Teachers . . . . Page 77
Chapter 17: The Pursuit Of Romance . . . . . Page 81
Chapter 18: The Movies!!! . . . . Page 85
Chapter 19: Encounters With Death . . . . . . Page 93
Chapter 20: I Cast My Lot . . . . Page 100
Chapter 21: Uncle Jack . . . . Page 108
Chapter 22: I Become "A Beast In The Field" . . . . Page 117
Chapter 23: My Father, My Mother & Me   Page 126
Chapter 24: I Develop A Social Conscience Page 135
Chapter 25: I Am Deeply Humiliated . . . . Page 140
Chapter 26: Today I Am A Man . . . . Page 146
Chapter 27: My Shining Hour . . . . Page 153
Chapter 28: A Trip To New York City . . . Page 160

Chapter 29: Early Angst . . . . Page 165
Chapter 30: The Real World . . . . Page 171
Chapter 31: The Day Of Departure . . . . . Page 178

PART TWO: COLLEGE

Chapter 32: Arrival . . . . Page 188
Chapter 33: Two Disastrous Sexual Encounters . . . .
. . . . Page 195
Chapter 34: America Goes To War . . . . . Page 203
Chapter 35: Changes . . . . Page 210
Chapter 36: I Discover A New World . . . Page 216
Chapter 37: I Get In Deeper . . . . Page 222
Chapter 38: I Get A Job In A Defense Plant . . . . . .
. . . . Page 230
Chapter 39: A Ghost, A Defeat & A Triumph . . . . .
. . . . Page 235
Chapter 40: Hail and Farewell . . . . Page 243

PART ONE
CHILDHOOD

CHAPTER ONE

MY MOTHER

That's my stepfather, said my mother.
Oh?
My father died when I was three.
I was helping my mother organize a family album.

Her stepfather was a husky, imposing looking man in a black suit and large black hat and a long dark beard. Beside him sat her mother, my grandmother, a woman I never met, nor would I ever meet. She was a stocky, stern looking woman dressed in black, wearing a "sheitel," a wig that covered her shaved head (a ritual practiced by orthodox Jewish women even today.)

What was he like, your stepfather?, I asked.
He was very strict.

I sat studying this stern looking couple. What were they really like, I wondered. They looked awfully grim.

There were also pictures of siblings, cousins, friends, aunts and uncles...relatives I'd never met, with strange, exotic names. Soocha. Yossel. Gittel. My mother seldom spoke about the fate of the family she left behind in Poland. Children should be sheltered.

That's my sister Malke, she said, pointing to a pleasant looking young woman with wavy hair and a nice figure.

I later learned that, in addition to Malke, another sister, her brother-in-law and their children were hiding from the Nazis. Malke left their hiding place to get some food. She was betrayed by one of her Polish neighbors. She was caught and shot by a German. Her last words were, *If you're going to shoot, aim straight.* The other sister, her husband and children died in a concentration camp. I never knew their names, and they were never mentioned again.

There were three postcard sized photographs of my

mother in the album. One was a formally posed studio photograph; a young woman with a lovely figure, holds in her right hand, what looks like a diploma. The elbow of her left arm is supported by some sort of a tall pedestal and, her head rests on her hand. She wears a long dark skirt and a long sleeved white blouse. The hair is well groomed and the expression on the handsome face is thoughtful, dreamlike.

How old were you? I asked.

I was fifteen.

She looked to be in her twenties.

In the second picture, a snapshot, taken around the same time, a young woman is standing in a field behind a wooden fence. She wears a long dress, a print, and her hair hangs loose, almost down to her waist. The eyes are intense and there's something fiery about this woman's demeanor. This was a wild, passionate creature, a gypsy roaming the countryside.

In the third picture there's a serious looking woman, wearing a rather formal looking dress. It's more like a uniform... and it looks like she's wearing a "sheitel." These three entirely different women were my mother, and I sometimes wondered if I ever really knew her.

******

Though she spoke little about her relatives in Poland, my mother often spoke in great detail about her experiences as a child. Actually, she claimed, she never had a childhood.

She was born on a farm on the outskirts of Brostek, a small town which was on the border between Poland and Austria. Sometimes it was Poland, sometimes it was Austria, depending on the political weather. It was a good sized farm, growing wheat and rye primarily. She worked very hard,

MY MOTHER

rising early in the morning, to help in the kitchen, to milk the cows, to feed the chickens and the livestock. Harvest time was particularly hectic since there were many extra mouths to feed.

She was the oldest of her siblings and, at an early age, was burdened with a great deal of responsibility. One night, after a hard day's work, she was assigned to sit by the bedside of a brother who was seriously ill with cholera. He had a little bell by his bed and he was to ring if he needed attention. She was to give him water and keep him comfortable.

I was working hard all day, said my mother, *and I was very tired, and I fell asleep.*

When she woke in the morning her brother was dead. She was ridden with guilt. Perhaps he'd rung the bell during the night and she hadn't heard. Her brother died a horrible death and the fault was hers! She was convinced of it. No one blamed her. There was no word of reproach, but she was forever haunted by the possibility that if she hadn't fallen asleep, if only she'd remained awake her brother might still be alive.

****

In the winter of 1914 World War I was well underway. The enemy was approaching the farm. There were all sorts of stories about atrocities. Her parents were concerned about the safety of the children. They decided that, until the threat subsided, they would send them all away, except for the baby.

The children were sent to Prague. My mother, being the eldest, was put in charge of her two brothers and sisters.

How old were you?, I asked.

I was sixteen.

The youngest boy was no more than five. She had never been that far from home before and, though burdened

A NOT-SO-NICE JEWISH BOY FACES WORLD WAR II

with many chores, had never been saddled with that heavy a responsibility. The train trip, during war time, was nerve-wracking. The train was crowded. The youngsters were restless and mischievous.

The city of Prague, when they finally got there, was awesome. The buildings, the traffic, the bustling streets. Luckily, after a worrisome search, they were able to find a furnished room they could afford. It was winter, a bitterly cold, harsh winter. The blankets on the two beds were paper thin, and the children kept complaining about the cold.

Jack, the oldest of the brothers, stayed with the children while my mother went shopping for extra blankets. She stepped into a nearby dry-goods store. It was a rather elegant looking establishment and, when she examined the price tags, she heaved a sigh. Everything was so expensive.

She was about to leave when a rather impressive looking, middle-aged gentleman with a dapper mustache approached her.

Can I help you?, asked the gentleman.
I was just looking.
What were you looking for?
Blankets.
You're not from the neighborhood, said the gentleman.
No.
Where are you from?
Brostek, said my mother.
You must be refugees.
My parents sent us here, my brothers and sisters and myself. It's dangerous now where we live.
And who's in charge of your little group?
I am.
Well now, let me see, said the gentleman. *Here's a nice*

MY MOTHER

blanket, the one you were looking at. It's half price, you know. That particular one's on sale. Will this do, do you think?

Well, if it's on sale... Are you quite sure?

I'm the proprietor, said the gentleman. *Is there anything else you need?*

Well, actually we need two blankets.

Well, why don't we throw in an extra one at no additional charge? We are overstocked with this particular model. Was there anything else? Some mufflers, perhaps. That's all right. You don't have to pay right now. Let's wait and see how your budget holds out. My name is Fischel. Karl Fischel. And yours?

Frieda. Frieda Thau.

The mufflers are right over there, Miss Thau. Why don't you pick out one for each of you. It's perfectly all right. Go on, go on.

My mother walked over to the table that contained the mufflers, and Mr. Fischel went and spoke to the lady at the cash register. The conversation seemed rather animated, on the part of the lady at any rate, who turned out to be Mrs. Fischel. My mother, carrying the blankets and the mufflers, approached the two of them apprehensively.

This is my wife, Miss Thau, said Mr. Fischel, *and we were wondering if you and your little family would be available for dinner this Friday evening.*

That's very kind of you.

It would be our pleasure, said Mrs. Fischel rather formally.

Say six o'clock? said Mr. Fischel.

That would be fine., said my mother.

She paid for the blankets and left the store with her bargain. Suddenly Prague was no longer so frightening, and it wasn't so cold outside.

A NOT-SO-NICE JEWISH BOY FACES WORLD WAR II

During their stay in Prague they had dinner once a week with the Fischels and, occasionally, twice a week. When, in the Spring, word came from home that it was all right for the little brood to return, Mrs. Fischel packed a generous lunch for them to eat on the train. Mr. Fischel slipped my mother a pair of lovely wool stockings. She promised to write them as soon as they got home.

The trip back was even more hectic. The Spring air seemed to bring out the naughtiness in the younger children, and they were more rambunctious than ever. There was one frightening moment when, at a train stop, Froyim, the youngest, was nowhere to be found. He turned up just as the train was ready to pull out. He'd gone to urinate in a field nearby.

**MOTHER'S MOTHER
STEPFATHER AND FAMILY**

MOTHER'S MOTHER

MOTHER'S STEPFATHER AND STEPSISTERS

MOTHER - IN COMMAND

MOTHER - THE GYPSY

MOTHER - THE SCHOLAR

CHAPTER TWO

MY MOTHER & MY FATHER

When they arrived home my mother was relieved to find that the house and the farm had been left unharmed. The enemy had helped themselves to some of the livestock but luckily they had left the horses, which were needed for the plowing.

There had been one terrible moment when one of the soldiers threatened to shoot my grandmother who was holding the baby in her arms. The soldier, who was drunk, was persuaded by his comrades to spare her.

My mother had hoped to continue with her schooling but she was needed at home. This was a great disappointment since Jews were so limited in the education that they were allowed. She wrote a long letter to the Fischels telling them about the trip back home and the situation on the farm. She received a letter in return. It was written in German (My mother was able to speak Polish, German and Yiddish) and Mr. Fischel included a photograph of himself. He is seated, dressed in an army uniform, looking rather stern with a large mustache. There's a copy of the letter in the family album. Roughly translated it reads:

"Prague, 11 September, 1915

Dear Fraulein

We have received your welcome letter of the fifth of this month, the contents of which we have much enjoyed. And we hope that, by this time, your mother is enjoying perfect health. We think of you often and of your parents who are so lucky to have a daughter who, in difficult times as a refugee was so self-sacrificing and brave, looking after her brothers and her sisters, and we often point to her as an example for others.

Next year, God willing, we intend to travel through Galicia, visiting most of the area. Perhaps we can pay a visit to you.

We wish everything good for you and your parents and have prayed for this on your behalf.
Karl Fischel and Wife

(Unreadable) promised to send us a signed photograph of you. We would be very grateful for this."

She never did see Mr. Fischel again.

When my mother approached marriageable age there was a young lieutenant who was starting to court her and, apparently, she was quite smitten.

There's a picture of this slim young man, rather dapper looking in his uniform with a little mustache and elegant monocle. Her stepfather however, put a stop to this incipient romance. A soldier, apparently, was not good husband material. My mother turned to my grandmother for support. My grandmother was noncommittal. Without her mother's support the battle was hopeless, so Mother reluctantly gave up the idea of being a soldier's wife. At times however she would dream about what that marriage might have been like, what romantic adventures she might have encountered as the wife of a dashing lieutenant.

There's a picture of another beau, a rather nondescript looking young man in a shirt, tie and suit with a long jacket and hat, holding what looks like a cane or an umbrella. I gather there wasn't much interest on my mother's part, and his suit was not successful.

******

MY MOTHER & MY FATHER

On a nearby farm lived the Beim family. Two of the girls, Tillie and Beatie, were friends of my mother. Beatie, a lovely girl, and the younger of the two, was especially close. Their brother, Hymie, was a shy young man, with a rather wry sense of humor.

As a young man growing up on a farm, one of Hymie's chores was to feed the chickens. Hymie's father noticed that the chickens were behaving very oddly, staggering about, making strange noises. In addition to that they weren't laying any eggs. He decided to investigate. One morning Hymie's father watched surreptitiously as Hymie distributed the feed, and then the father noticed that the young man was adding something to the water. It turned out to be vodka. Then Hymie sat on the fence, laughing hysterically, as the chickens stumbled about. Hymie's fun came to an abrupt end.

Hymie, it appeared, was smitten with my mother, but he was so abnormally shy that he actually hid under the covers when she came to visit Beatie and Tillie. Encouraged by his sisters, however, he eventually became bold enough to court my mother. Her stepfather put his foot down.

A farm boy with nothing in particular to recommend him, said her stepfather, *out of the question!*

My mother was his favorite and, apparently, no one was good enough for her. This time my mother stood her ground. Her stepfather, however, was adamant. Mother defied him and began to meet Hymie on the sly.

They would take long walks in the countryside. She did most of the talking since Hymie didn't really have too much to say. Eventually he did dig up the courage to propose. Mother consulted my grandmother who, this time intervened, and gave her approval.

There's this wonderful sepia picture of my father as a young man. The photograph is oval in shape and laminated

A NOT-SO-NICE JEWISH BOY FACES WORLD WAR II

onto a metal base. Straight and tall in his soldier's uniform, he stands in a field in front of a tree, his left hand on his hip, his right hand hanging loose, holding a cigarette, and sporting a trim mustache. There's another picture taken in Poland. This one's a studio portrait. He's seated, wearing a dark suit, white shirt and tie looking handsome and suave, a regular Rudolph Valentino.

Before the marriage took place, however, my father was drafted. This was World War I. He fought in the Polish infantry, in the trenches under fire. His younger brother, Wolf, was blown to bits in front of his eyes. My father ended up in a hospital in Vienna with pneumonia. My mother took another train ride through war-torn Europe to be by the side of her fiance. She herself became seriously ill on that trip and almost died.

At the end of the war my father returned home. He and my mother were married. Her stepfather did not attend the wedding.

******

My parents were quite poor when they started married life. The house they moved into actually had a dirt floor. Their married life, barely begun, however, was cut short when my father received notice that he was to report back to the army. Poland was now going to war with Russia.

By this time Tillie, his older sister was settled in America, in East Orange, New Jersey. One war was enough for my father. He got in touch with Aunt Esther, his father's sister, who had acted as Tillie's sponsor. Aunt Esther brought him over as well.

I remember Mother speaking of Aunt Esther with great respect, and I remember, as a boy, visiting Aunt Esther in

MY MOTHER & MY FATHER

East Orange. There was this feeling of elegance in the way she carried herself. There was this fancy living room with a grand piano with an exotic shawl on top of it. She seemed like royalty.

My father sailed to America on a boat called the Europa. This was in 1921. He went directly to Newark, New Jersey. At this time there was a large Jewish community in Newark, and Uncle Sam, his father's brother, lived there.

Uncle Sam had a tavern "down neck" in the working section of Newark. He gave my father a job tending bar. And thus my father, to Mother's eternal regret, was inducted into the "saloon business." Even as a young man, Daddy, apparently, enjoyed his liquor, and tending bar was a job he took to at once.

He roomed with the Zimmermans, a Russian-Jewish family who had an apartment on Bergen Street, a main thoroughfare in a primarily residential section in Newark. He attended night school and picked up English rather quickly. He saved his pennies and, the following year, he was able to send for my mother.

Leaving Poland was a wrenching experience for Mother. She was convinced she would never see her family again and, though she corresponded with them regularly, she never did.

On Thursday, November 16, 1922 she traveled to America on the S.S. Kroonland which sailed from Antwerp to New York. The fact that she was accompanied by her sister-in-law, Beatie, was a great comfort to her.

The trip was a harrowing one. The two attractive young ladies on board were very popular, but my mother spent half the trip seasick in her bunk. She couldn't even look at the apple one of her admirers brought her, much less the elaborate menu:

A NOT-SO-NICE JEWISH BOY FACES WORLD WAR II

BREAKFAST MENU

S.S. Kroonland. November 26, 1922

Honeydew Melon

Rolled Oats   Corn Flakes   Fried Plaice, Meuniere

Grilled Lambs Liver and Bacon

Broiled Dorset Sausages

Mashed Potatoes

Eggs: Fried, Turned and Poached

Breakfast Rolls   Milk Scones

Marmalade   Preserves

Coffee   Tea   Cocoa

    Entering America was an awesome experience. The entrance into the harbor, the first sight of the Statue of Liberty, and then the landing to be followed by the nerve-wracking confusion, the crowds, the checking of the passports and the visas. And then the doctors examined you. If you had any health problems you could be sent back. Luckily Mother was healthy. She was admitted. Daddy was able to bring her with him to the Zimmermans, while Beatie went to live with her sister, Tillie, in East Orange.

**TWO REJECTED
SUITORS**

**DAD FIGHTING
WORLD WAR 1**

DAD THE LUCKY DEVIL

THE YOUNG MARRIED COUPLE

MOTHER, DAD, SISTER MOLLY AND BEAU

**MY PARENTS
IN AMERICA**

CHAPTER THREE

I ENTER THE SCENE

I was born at the Beth Israel Hospital in Newark a year or so after my mother arrived in America. The birth certificate, sent to my parents by the city clerk, gives the date as October 2, 1923. My name is listed as Nisel. I was named after my mother's father. There's an elegant gold seal on the bottom of the document. The certificate was accompanied by a letter:

"Dear Friends: It is with pleasure that I enclose herewith a birth certificate of your new born child.

This certificate has been issued so that you have an official record of the birth of your child, and also to insure absolute accuracy in our statistical data.

The information contained in the birth certificate is submitted by the professional attendant at the time of birth. It is suggested that you read the certificate over carefully. In the event of error, will you kindly make a notation on the enclosed blank, sign and return same; or you may call at this office, so that correction may be made and a new certificate issued.

It is the desire of the official of the City that the birth record of your child be correct, and your co-operation is solicited establishing same.

With best wishes for the welfare of your child, I remain,

      Very truly yours,
      W. J. Egan (Written signature)
      City Clerk."

Eventually my Yiddish name was anglicized. At first I was to be called Nathan. How I ended up with Norman, I shall never know.

My parents took me from the Beth Israel Hospital to

A NOT-SO-NICE JEWISH BOY FACES WORLD WAR II

the Zimmermans, their temporary home. That's where I spent a good part of my first year on earth.

Mrs. Zimmerman was a calm, quiet woman, warm but stern. Mr. Zimmerman was short, stocky and rather bow-legged. He had a large mustache and smoked a pipe...continually. I remember it's strong, aromatic odor. As a matter of fact, Mr. Zimmerman smelled like a pipe even when he wasn't smoking a pipe.

The Zimmermans had two sons. These men led very busy lives in the workaday world, and in the evening they took out girls. Mrs. Zimmerman and my mother would often discuss these girls and, of course, the subject of marriage. The Zimmerman sons would date gentile girls, which seemed to me very natural since they looked like square-jawed policemen and didn't seem Jewish at all. This, however, seemed to upset everyone. The boys eventually married these gentile girls.

Since my mother knew no English the first language I spoke was Yiddish. I vaguely remember the rattling and the clang of the trolley cars passing by, and being frightened by a marching band. Music, apparently, had a very strange effect upon me at this period of my life. As a matter of fact, it brought on hysterics.

I was cautioned by friends who read an early draft of this memoir that the following was an unpleasant detail and that no one would care to hear about. I, however, think my bizarre and rather puzzling behavior at this time rather interesting.

Apparently, as an infant I had a taste for excrement. I would reach into my full diaper and help myself to a handful. Once I staggered into the street, crawled towards the trolley tracks and was about to gather up a fistful of horse manure. Luckily that feast was short-circuited by someone. I'm not sure exactly who. This, of course, is all hearsay, but I don't have

I ENTER THE SCENE

any reason to doubt this report. I can only assume that babies are not very bright, and they assume that everything within reach must be a source of nourishment. I'm happy to say I've become somewhat more knowledgeable.

I was also told that I was, as an infant, extremely active. Once I crawled onto the window ledge of the Zimmerman apartment, which was on the second floor. The window was wide open. There were no guard rails, and I could easily have fallen to the sidewalk below. Luckily my mother, panic stricken, crept up slowly behind me and pulled me to safety. Perhaps there is such a thing as destiny or fate. Perhaps it is written somewhere how long we're to live, and how and when we're to die, and perhaps I was destined for adulthood...a state one strives to attain, but more often than not, I suspect, simply manage to grow older.

As a little boy I was very wild. Friends and relatives dreaded my mother's visit because nothing in the house was safe from my destructive little hands. This is hard for me to picture since, as far as I can recall, I was, I would say...too well behaved.

******

The first apartment our little family had to ourselves was in a six family brick building down the block from the Zimmermans on Bergen Street. I remember looking out the kitchen window at an alley, and across the alley a wooden fence that surrounded a big lumber yard. Lumber yards were gentile and rather menacing.

I remember being acutely aware of the climate. I preferred the dark, dismal days; a hill nearby on a cloudy day with a grey house, and across from it an empty lot, desolate and intriguing or a little synagogue with a stained glass

A NOT-SO-NICE JEWISH BOY FACES WORLD WAR II

window and three cement steps leading to the front door, or a row of houses on the other side of the street on a rainy day with the light breaking through the clouds. These images set the imagination a whirl, offering hints of mysterious goings on. Exactly what? That was the question.

I didn't particularly care for sunshine. Sunshine represented happiness, and happiness was rather frightening. After all, how long could it last? An attitude, I'm sure, I absorbed from my mother.

At the age of five or six, my impression of my mother was that of a handsome giant, so it came as quite a shock when I entered the darkened living room late one afternoon to find her sitting in the gloom by the window looking out onto the street, dissolved in tears. It seemed unthinkable that grown-ups should cry, and for no good reason.

Don't worry, Mama, I said. *I'll take care of you.*

She kissed me and held me close.

Eventually I learned that my mother suffered from depression.

On the nearby corner from our first apartment, was a butcher store. The lusty proprietor, Mr. Shtrulovitz, and his wife were friends of the family. The butcher store seemed to me a busy, noisy place with sawdust on the floor. I remember being alarmed by bloody pieces of raw meat lying on a wooden table and displayed in a large glass case, and the strong, acrid smell of the raw flesh which permeated the shop. There were chairs about on which people could wait their turn and sit and gossip...among themselves or with Mr. Shtrulovitz as he went about chopping up the raw flesh and conducting sales.

Mr. Shtrulovitz was a religious man and somewhat of an authority. My mother would sometimes consult him about the fine points of religious law.

I ENTER THE SCENE

Near the butcher store was a grocery. Mother was very friendly with the grocer and his family. Mr. Fine, his wife and two daughters were chubby and rosy and had rather prominent noses. There were often little crises in the flat behind the store, where the family lived. The children ran about with runny noses, and the girls' dresses never seemed to be clean.

There was some sort of incipient romance between myself and the eldest daughter. We were both around five at the time. The possibility of a liaison seemed to meet with favor on the part of both families. Despite her nose, the girl, as I recall, was not unattractive, especially when she put on a clean dress and combed her curly hair, which was always rather messy. Nothing ever came of this hoped for alliance.

The grocery featured myriad cans of food, open barrels of sour tomatoes, sour pickles and sauerkraut. There was smoked fish and lox and cheese and bagels and bread and, behind the glass enclosures, there were metal containers of herring, and all sorts of exotic smelling foods which were ladled into little cardboard containers or wrapped in wax paper.

I remember watching with fascination as the customers came into the store, chose their wares, handed over their money and then strode out the door with a paper bag in the crook of their arm.

The Fine family made a great deal of noise. Sometimes they screamed at each other and sometimes they expressed affection for one another, kissing each other or putting their arm around one another and calling each other by pet names.

My mother and father never put their arms around one another or called each other "honey." The only time anyone kissed in our house was when one said good night and went to bed, or came into the house after an absence. And that was a rather perfunctory kiss.

A NOT-SO-NICE JEWISH BOY FACES WORLD WAR II

My sister, Rose, was born in this house. I had wanted a brother or a sister to play with, and was delighted with her arrival. I remember seeing her for the first time, a pink little bundle, and bending over the crib and kissing her.

Do you love your little sister? someone asked.

Yes, I answered shyly.

What a stupid question, I thought. She's a little baby and she's my sister. Why wouldn't I love her? I remember my mother, just back from the hospital, looking lovely in a pea green housecoat oozing warmth and love.

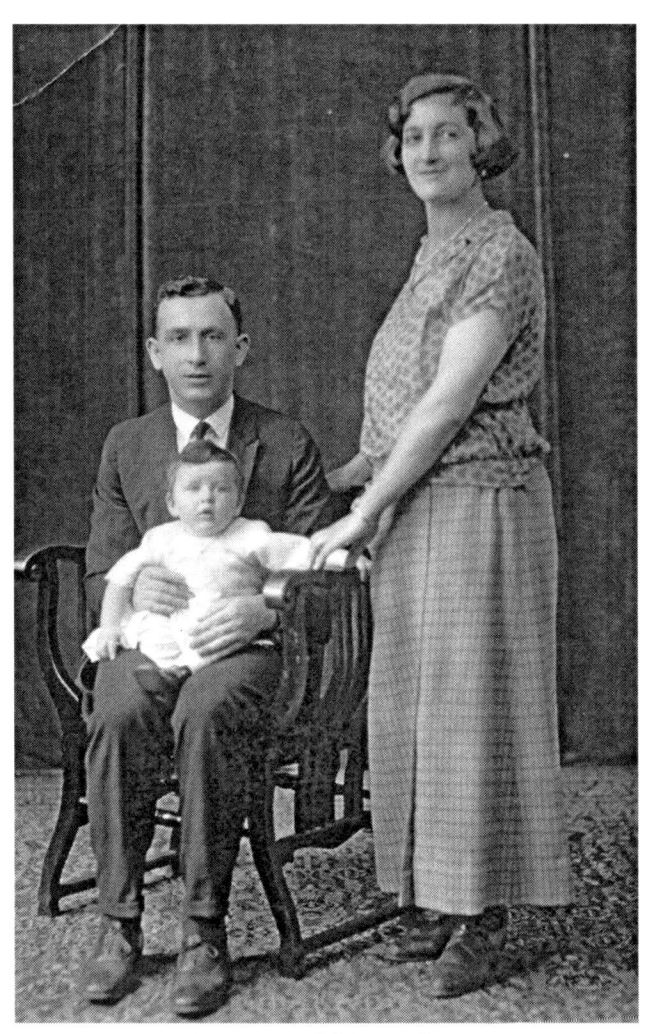

MY PARENTS' FIRST
BRILLIANT PRODUCTION

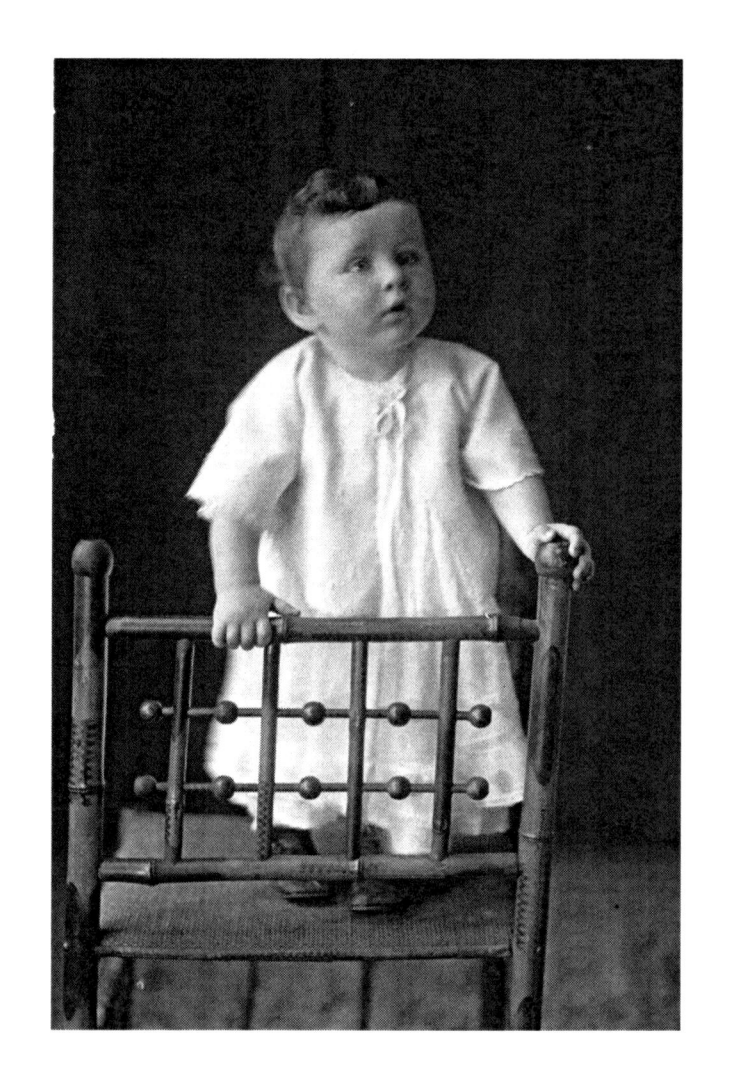

ME AT NINE MONTHS

YES, IT'S ME AT TWO YEARS

ME AT 6

ME AT 8

ME AT 9

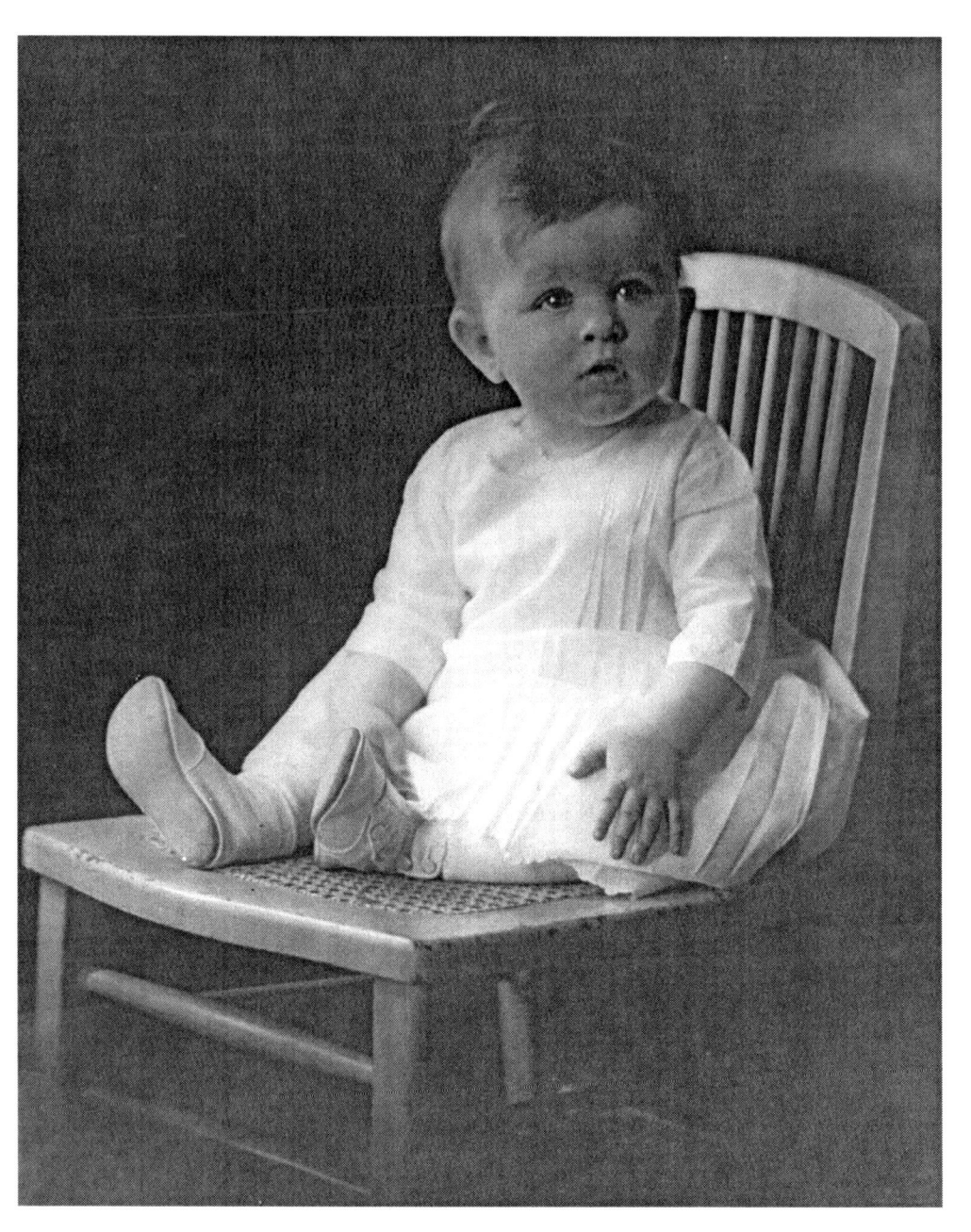

ROSE - 6 1/2 MONTHS

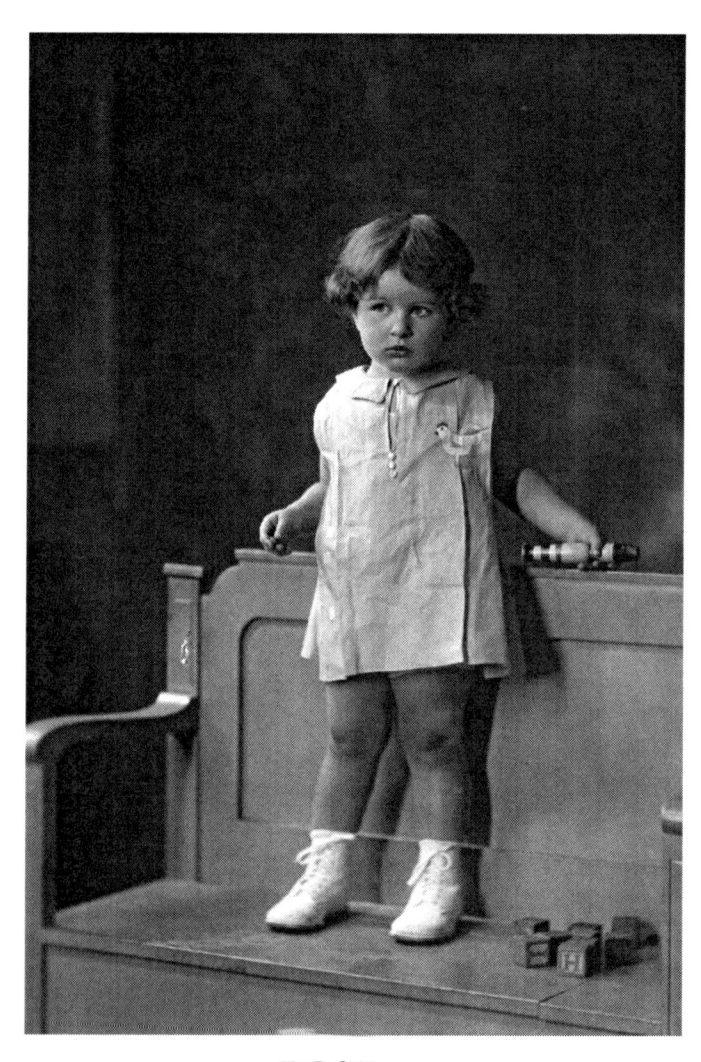

ROSE

CHAPTER FOUR

THE WORLD AROUND ME

I was about seven or eight when we moved to 94 Wainright Street, a four family wooden house on a shady, tree-lined avenue. The house was painted green and there were two large wooden benches on each side of the small porch in front of the house. I played "Pirate" in the backyard with the neighboring children. That consisted of running up and down the slanted cellar door, and climbing up and down the telephone pole next to the garage shouting "Ahoy!" and things like that.

There were no barriers between our yard and the yards to the left, so that there was a large area where one could run a long distance or, in the winter, go sledding. To the right of the house was an empty lot with lots of weeds and wild flowers and grasshoppers and butterflies and even an occasional praying mantis. It was a veritable jungle ripe for exploration, especially in the summer. Except, of course, one had to look out for the bees.

My father would often bring home from work interesting things like pies and assorted foods he received from various customers.

Once he brought home some pigeons, live pigeons in a wooden crate. Since my mother had had her fill of animals, working on a farm and wouldn't hear of having a pet in the house, my sister, Rose, and I were absolutely delighted with our new found friends.

From time to time we would go into the parental bedroom, where the pigeons were kept in a crate. We stood and marveled at these fascinating little creatures. We were even allowed to feed them some bird seed. We would watch them peck at the food and make it disappear. They made these clucking sounds and their heads bobbed up and down so charmingly.

A week or so later, when we went into the bedroom to visit our pets, we were devastated to find that they were nowhere to be found. The crate was gone. The space was empty. I went to my mother to inquire about this mysterious disappearance.

Your father took them back, she said.

Why?, I asked.

There was no answer.

That Sunday roasted birds appeared on the dinner table. They were too small for chickens, I thought.

What are they? I asked.

My mother hemmed and hawed. Finally, to my horror, she admitted that those roasted birds on the plate in front of us were actually our darling pigeons. I refused to eat them. So did my sister. We both watched, dismayed and nauseated, as my mother and father devoured the remains of our former pets.

Human beings are really barbarians, I concluded, feeding on those sweet, innocent creatures with whom we share this planet. This conviction was further driven home by another barbarous act I was to witness around this time.

The father of the family across the hall, was a dark, burly man with hairy arms who spent hours tinkering with his car. He seemed to me to be a brute of a man.

One day my impression of him was altered. I discovered that this barbarian kept pigeons in a coop on top of the garage. Anyone who made a home for those darling little pigeons couldn't be all bad. Then one morning, to my amazement and disgust, I saw him on the roof, thrusting his hand into the pigeon coop, scooping up several eggs, puncturing a hole in the eggs and actually stand there and drink its contents.

The mother of this family wasn't much of an improvement. She was blond and loud. The younger child was a boy, with a rather mild disposition. He was younger than I was, and not very interesting. The older child was a girl my age and, for some reason or other, we didn't seem to care for one another.

I don't remember exactly how it started but we would indulge in a rather spiteful little game. One of us would lock the glass door in the front lobby and prevent the other from entering the inner hallway. As time passed the game grew more intense. It took longer and longer for permission to be granted to enter.

One afternoon I held the door shut for a very long time. The girl grew furious, thrust her hand through the glass. The arm was badly cut. She was rushed to the hospital where she received several stitches. I was chastised by my parents. However, I felt no guilt or shame whatsoever. I was sorry the girl was hurt but, obviously, she was an idiot. What sane person would shove their hand through a glass door?!

The relationship between our two families, which had never been that congenial, was rather strained after that.

******

I was deathly afraid of dogs, especially when they barked and snarled and showed their teeth. I couldn't understand why these animals were allowed to wander the streets, endangering respectable peoples' lives. Cats, on the other hand, seemed rather harmless and were fascinating to watch in spite of or, perhaps, because of their seemingly independent air.

A NOT-SO-NICE JEWISH BOY FACES WORLD WAR II

As a matter of fact, in some ways, animals were just as interesting, perhaps even more so, than human beings. It was fun to watch the squirrels dart from tree to tree and then scamper up into the branches, or watch the birds perch quietly on a telephone wire or fly twittering onto a tree and then soar away in pairs or sometimes in a formation, a whole group of them.

But most fascinating of all were the horses hitched to the peddlers' wagons. They were awesome creatures...urinating and defecating in the street for everyone to see; noble animals, pitiable and vulnerable in their innocence. The only thing that seemed to upset the horses were the flies in the summer. They would swish their tails at the flies and they would twitch and shudder in the oddest way, and they would clop, clop, clop down the street, blinders on each side of their eyes, drawing large wagonfuls of fruits and vegetables.

The peddlers themselves were a rugged lot, out in the streets in all sorts of weather, rain or shine or even snow. They were often unshaven, or seemed to be. They wore old clothes, and would call out their wares as they entered our block. Most of the time their calls were garbled and unintelligible, but apparently they served their purpose. The housewives would come out, choose their fruits or vegetables and place them in the scale that hung at the side of the wagon. The women in the neighborhood and the tradesmen seemed to be old friends. While business was conducted, they would exchange family news, jokes and small talk. These men intrigued me. I wondered whether they had families of their own and what their wives and their children were like, especially when some of them would seem to flirt with a housewife.

On the other hand, the ice cream men, in their immaculate white uniforms, were totally devoid of character.

THE WORLD AROUND ME

They would drive slowly down the street in their white vans, bells chiming the presence of delectable treats to come. They were of interest only in relation to the products they sold. There were Eskimo pies (vanilla ice cream sandwiched between two soft chocolate cookies), chocolate covered popsicles with vanilla ice cream inside, and Dixie Cups containing half vanilla, half chocolate ice cream which you ate with a little wooden spoon, and ice cream cones, sugar or plain, with or without sprinkles. These you couldn't eat too slowly because the ice cream would drip down the side and it got too messy. And there were Melorolls, a vanilla ice cream popsicle encased in orange ice. These were a double treat.

CHAPTER FIVE

MY EDUCATION BEGINS

At about the age of ten or so I became aware of the fact that, except for my father, most of my male relatives stopped kissing me. They continued to kiss my sister, however, and they kissed other little girls and they kissed women of any age, but they stopped kissing me. At the same time I noticed that women kissed men, and women kissed one another, but men didn't kiss one another. If that was the way they wanted it, it was okay with me, but I thought it was kind of silly, and rather discriminatory. Why couldn't everyone be nice to each other?

I had heard the word "fuck" and seen it written on the sidewalk and on walls a number of times, but I had no idea what it meant. One day when I was playing in the alley with some of the boys next door I noticed that strange word on the side of the house. I asked one of them what it meant. He explained it to me in very graphic terms.

At first I thought he was joking. He was making it up. What a ridiculous idea! For one thing, this unbelievable act was a gross invasion of one's privacy. And, for another, how could this one little organ do such an obscene thing? It just didn't make any sense. It also seemed impossible that babies could come out of a woman where they were supposed to come out. I assumed the boy was just teasing me. Then again...

Well, I certainly couldn't consult my father about this nonsense. One never discusses anything with one's father. And I was just too embarrassed to discuss this very personal matter with my mother. Not only did it seem illogical but, if true, the whole system seemed to me very unsanitary, especially for women. I finally decided to file this report away for future reference. After all, this preposterous state of affairs was no

MY EDUCATION BEGINS

concern of mine. And even if, when I did grow up, I found out that people actually did behave in this ridiculous manner, I doubted seriously that I would ever indulge in such foolish shenanigans.

******

I have no recollection whatsoever of kindergarten. I do remember my sister, Rose, crying a great deal on her first day at school. In the first or second grade I remember sitting at a desk, drawing a bird's nest with a black crayon, and getting a great deal of satisfaction in making it blacker and blacker. I also vaguely remember around Christmas time drawing a reindeer leaping into the air and making that blacker and blacker as well.

Bragaw Avenue grammar school was a new one, and only a couple of blocks away from home. The boys and girls had separate entrances. I would line up with the other boys in the morning and then, when the bell rang we'd file into the building and go to our classroom.

There was one older boy who used to bully me when I was waiting on line to enter the school. Sometimes he would accost me in the hallway. He threatened to beat me up and stop me from coming to school. I couldn't understand why. I hadn't done anything to him. I didn't even know the boy. I didn't even know his name. I was afraid to leave the building after class. That bully would be out there waiting for me. I dreaded going to school in the morning. My life became a nightmare, and I was afraid to tell anyone.

One time I stepped out the door at the end of the day and there was my nemesis. He had a big black dog with him. He said he was going to sic the dog on me. In abject terror I ran back into the building. I hid in the hallway. After a little

A NOT-SO-NICE JEWISH BOY FACES WORLD WAR II

while I peeked out the door. He was still there. I ran back inside. This time I waited a long while before I investigated. Thank God, the bully and the dog were nowhere in sight. I hurried down the street. I was certain that I would be attacked at any moment. I heaved a great sigh of relief as I stepped into our hallway. When I came into the kitchen my mother looked very upset.

Where have you been? What took you so long?

I finally told her about the reign of terror I'd been subjected to. My mother said nothing. After that, however, to my amazement, the boy never threatened me again.

I could only assume that my mother must have spoken to someone at school.

CHAPTER SIX

SO MUCH FOR BRAVERY

When my father opened his own tavern in the factory section of Newark, he went into partnership with Mr. Hochhauser, another Jewish immigrant. The partnership was short lived, but the two families remained close friends even after the partnership was dissolved.

The Hochhausers lived quite a distance from us. Twelve blocks or so, at this time, seemed quite a distance, and a visit to the Hochhausers amounted to a minor excursion. During these visits I looked forward to playing with their son, Irving, who was my age.

At the time of this one visit, Irving wasn't home. I was told that he was down the block with some of the boys in the neighborhood. I found him in a rock-strewn lot next to the local synagogue. There was a forked tree which several boys were climbing. Irving was one of the most nimble. He clambered up and down the tree with ease. I became envious. If Irving can climb up and down that tree, why couldn't I? It's true I was afraid of heights and that tree did look pretty high, but that in itself was a challenge.

I'm gonna try it, I said.
Maybe you shouldn't, said Irving.
Why not?
You might get hurt.
You didn't get hurt.
There was no reply.

I began to resent the implication that I was so fragile. I became determined to prove how brave I was. I stepped right up to the tree. I wedged my right foot firmly in the fork of the tree, which wasn't too high from the ground, and proceeded to hoist myself up. When I tried to pull my right foot free, I found it was stuck. Setting my left foot back on the ground I pulled and pulled. I yanked and pulled. When the leg wouldn't come loose, I twisted as hard as I could. Suddenly I heard a snap. I felt a sharp stabbing pain. I had this sinking feeling in the pit of my stomach. Something was wrong. I must have injured myself somehow. I stood there, not knowing what to do next.

Finally one of the boys untied the laces of my shoe and loosened the shoe. I slipped the right foot out easily. When I tried to stand on the right leg, there was that sharp stabbing pain again. Uh oh!

Irving managed to pull the shoe out of the wedge in the tree and, with his help, I hopped on my left foot slowly down the street to the Hochhauser home. I was more concerned about what effect this would have on my mother than I was about the leg. It didn't take very much for her to get hysterical. As I hopped into the kitchen I eyed my mother anxiously. She turned white.

I was helped to the kitchen table. My mother examined the leg. Mrs. Hochhauser scolded Irving, blaming him for the mishap. A cab was called. I was rushed to the emergency section of the Beth Israel hospital. An intern examined me. An x-ray was taken. It turned out to be a simple fracture. I was fitted with a temporary cast. The following day the leg was put into a plaster cast which reached almost up to my hip, and I was laid up for three boring weeks.

******

At this time I received three books which helped somewhat to allay the boredom. There was "King Arthur And The Knights Of The Round Table." On the cover was a wonderful picture in color of knights in shining armor and ladies in long, flowing gowns, and the colored illustrations

SO MUCH FOR BRAVERY

inside were very dramatic. The chapters, however, were much too long and I never got into the stories.

Then there was "Grimm's Fairy Tales." The cover, in color as well, had a picture of Hansel and Gretel. I dipped into some of the stories and found one or two somewhat amusing.

The third book, slightly larger, was entitled "Great Moments In History." The cover was black with a small black and white drawing in the center. It didn't look nearly as impressive or interesting as the other two. The inside, however, was a different matter entirely. Each page described tersely a different historical event...The Crossing Of The Red Sea By The Israelites...The Invention Of The Steamboat...The Finding Of The Rosetta Stone...Napoleon's Defeat At Waterloo...all accompanied by striking black and white illustrations. These drawings were quite dramatic and, together with the text, they set my imagination awhirl.

I read and reread these momentous events over and over again. I stared at the pictures and tried to imagine what it must have been like to have been present at these historic occasions. I marvelled that I belonged to this odd, fascinating species, called man. We were capable of such fantastic feats...inventions, miracles, scholarship, discoveries, explorations.

There was the Spanish Inquisition, and Cortez discovering Mexico, and Balboa calmly viewing the great Pacific Ocean, and Eli Whitney inventing the cotton gin, and the Wright brothers creating an aeroplane, and the French Revolution, and the signing of the Magna Carta in the shade of this large tree. Even wars seemed engrossing and somehow bloodless and romantic, pictured so vividly on the printed page. I would have liked to memorize the entire volume.

The discovery of books, somehow, more than made up for the pain and all the inconvenience.

A NOT-SO-NICE JEWISH BOY FACES WORLD WAR II

When I was finally equipped with a walking cast, I reluctantly returned to school. I was allowed to leave each class a little earlier, so that I could hobble down the empty hallway to my next class.

I sorely missed those fascinating adventures, roaming through the history of mankind.

CHAPTER SEVEN

MY HORIZONS BROADEN

Three or four doors down, in the direction of the grammar school, was Danny's house. Danny lived with his grandmother. I don't remember if his parents were alive or not. I know I never met them, and I don't remember how we struck up a friendship, but I do remember that I had never met anyone so pleasant, so uncomplicated, so nice to be with. Danny's grandmother was very nice too and was very nice to me. And Danny, amazingly enough, was gentile.

Danny's house looked, smelled and felt differently. There were white lace curtains in the kitchen. They sort of hung there, grey and rather skimpy. The kitchen was cool and redolent with the odor of damp earth. It was as if the smell of the garden in back had penetrated the whole house. Even the garden behind the house was different somehow, and yet I was made to feel at home there.

I tried to understand what made Danny and his home different from other people and other homes I was acquainted with. For one thing, everything was so much more easy-going. The relationship between Danny and his grandmother, for example, was so relaxed, so matter of fact.

In some ways, I thought, that was good. But then again, if they were so casual with each other, maybe they didn't realize how precious life was, and maybe they didn't love each other very much. If there's love there had to be scolding and nagging and just a little hysteria...didn't there?

I knew Danny liked me, and yet I always had the feeling that he thought of me as someone rather strange and exotic. I felt embarrassed by all the emotions that seemed to seethe within me. I was so much...so much...**more**. I was only aware of this intensity when I compared myself to Danny who was so easy going. Up until that time I had always thought of myself as a rather placid person. But next to Danny I was a seething inferno. So, much as I liked Danny, there was always some sort of a barrier between us, a difference in temperament, which was not as pronounced as between Irving and myself, for example. Was it because Irving and I were both Jewish, I wondered.

******

The first family car that I recall was a red Chevrolet. It must have been new when my father bought it, but I remember it as a shabby, beat up old car. Every year or so we'd pile into the old Chevy and visit Aunt Gertie and Uncle Morris who lived hundreds of miles away in Windber, Pennsylvania.

We'd get up...it must have been around five o'clock in the morning, or even earlier. I know it was dark when we climbed into the car. There was a bag full of sandwiches and a thermos bottle full of coffee on hand. Riding in the dark through the empty streets and roads I witnessed the sun come up and daylight reveal the world at large. My eyes were glued to the window as we traveled through valleys and hills and mountains, the old Chevy huffing and puffing.

We might stop along the way to buy soda or to use the bathroom at a gas station. We wouldn't arrive at Aunt Gertie's (the house, of course, always belonged to the woman) until that evening.

On these journeys to Aunt Gertie and Uncle Morris we were sometimes accompanied by Aunt Rose and Uncle Sam. Uncle Sam, you may recall, had a tavern, and it was he that my father worked for when he first arrived in America. Uncle Sam was a tall, thin, somber man...distinguished looking with a face that seemed sort of haunted. He was always quiet and

MY HORIZONS BROADEN

considerate. Aunt Rose was pretty, vivacious and quite glamorous. She could have been a movie star, she was so pretty and so lively with this deep, husky voice.

Aunt Gertie was my father's middle sister. I often wondered how she ended up in the wilds of Pennsylvania. She was a warm, gentle soul, baked wonderful pies...(my mother baked, but she never made pies)...and was an excellent cook. Uncle Morris was a hearty man who liked to fish and go to baseball games...and also, according to my mother, *loved to hear himself talk*. He was an expansive and generous man and made you feel right at home.

It was interesting to compare the two of them to my parents. Uncle Morris seemed to be the dominant one in the house, whereas in our house, Mother seemed to be the vital force and Daddy...well, he was the quiet one. Not that my mother talked a lot. She just had a rather authoritative air about her, and when she talked, she meant business. Not that Daddy was a wimp. He didn't have too much to say, but when he spoke it was, eventually, quite clear that he was the one in charge.

Aunt Gertie and Uncle Morris had three children, two girls who were about my age, and a boy. Helen, the older girl was serious and lady-like. Esther, the younger girl was pretty and lively. We seemed to enjoy each others company, as I recall. The boy, Billy, was much younger than myself and my recollection of him at that age is rather vague.

Windber was a small town located in a coal mining district. You had the feeling that it rested rather precariously on top of this mountain, and all the buildings seemed to be on top of each other. It seemed to me, at that age, to be a gentile town...the people, the houses, the streets, the stores. I don't know why. Maybe, at that time, everything and everyone outside of the family, everything strange was gentile. Even

A NOT-SO-NICE JEWISH BOY FACES WORLD WAR II

Aunt Gertie and Uncle Morris seemed to be just a little bit gentile. Maybe it was the way they talked. Their accent was different, more American somehow.

The stay in Windber was a pleasant one. Everyone seemed to be so happy to see one another. But what was most memorable about these visits was the journey itself, my first venture into the world at large, a world of wide open sky, sometimes cloudy, sometimes clear and blue; and tree covered mountains and forests and winding roads and lakes and bridges and, along the highway, stone boulders reaching way, way up.

I became aware of the fact that I lived in a country that was immense, a country that had endless farms and fields with cows, and so many different kinds of houses, large and elegant ones, small and shabby ones, old and quaint ones; a country that had railroad tracks and gas stations and restaurants and picturesque little towns and many other large cities like the one I lived in.

CHAPTER EIGHT

MY FIRST LOVE

Beatie was my father's youngest sister. She was the one with whom my mother came to America. When she arrived, as you may recall, she went to live in East Orange with her older sister, Aunt Tillie. They didn't get along very well. Beatie claimed that Tillie kept after her all the time.

You should do this, you should do that. It was about time that you got married, etc, etc.

Beatie got along better with my mother. She claimed to be closer to her than her own sister. So she came to live with us...and I adored her.

Beatie had a graceful figure, a low, musical voice, large dark eyes, an impeccable complexion and dark brown, wavy hair. She was so gentle and sweet and so loving. She worked in a pocketbook factory.

My sister, Rose, and I would hop into the back seat of the old Chevy around five o'clock in the afternoon, and my father would drive us down to pick her up after work. We'd sit in the car waiting for the whistle to blow, then watch the girls stream out of the factory. When we sighted Beatie we'd wave frantically and jump for joy. She would come running to the car, hop in and kiss us both, looking absolutely breath-takingly beautiful, and she would hold our hands.

Beatie promised to take me to a movie downtown. I waited anxiously for weeks for her to keep her promise. I was sure she'd forgotten all about it. I complained to my mother.

Beatie promised to take me to a movie downtown, I told her. *I think she forgot.*

She didn't forget. She'll take you. Don't worry.

One evening, a day or so later, Beatie told me to put on my best suit, and we took the bus downtown to the Paramount Theatre on Market Street.

A NOT-SO-NICE JEWISH BOY FACES WORLD WAR II

We saw an Al Jolson movie. I don't remember much about the story, but I do remember him tearfully singing "Sonny Boy" with a sob in his voice, and his eyes all moist. For years that remained the most memorable evening of my young life.

Beatie had several beaus. I bristled at the thought of these strange men holding her hand or even, heaven forbid, kissing her. Aunt Tillie claimed that Beatie was too particular. I, on the other hand, dreaded the possibility that she would find someone, get married and desert us.

The current beau was a dapper young man who dealt in jewelry. This young man must have really been taken with Beatie since he even took the trouble to give me, her nephew, a gift...a ring, which I promptly lost. We combed the lawn again and again. The ring was nowhere to be found. I hated to lose it because I'd never had a ring before and, besides, I felt guilty. I wasn't too fond of this interloper, and people might think that I lost it on purpose.

As a matter of fact, no one cared very much for this young jeweler. He was rather glib and sort of oily. I guess Beatie herself wasn't too fond of him either since, eventually, she stopped seeing him.

She was left without a serious suitor until Uncle Jack, Mother's brother who lived in New York City, came up with Izzy Singer, a colleague of his. Izzy worked with Uncle Jack in New York, cutting fur. He was a pleasant looking man, affable and somewhat cultured. I mean he even liked operatic music.

There was something a little sad about Izzy, but he certainly seemed nice enough, and everyone liked him at once and, despite the fact that there was the possibility that he might take Beatie away from us, I liked him too. Beatie and Izzy were soon engaged.

MY FIRST LOVE

    The wedding took place on a Sunday afternoon at Aunt Tillie's. She lived in a two family building at 52 Hilton Street in East Orange. We went there early so that my mother could help out. On that momentous day, we climbed the shiny wooden stairs to Aunt Tillie's second floor apartment.

    In the dining room the imposing china closet and the bureau and the chairs looked newly polished. The large table in the center of the room was covered with a white table cloth. Silverware and napkins had been set out for the meal which was to be served buffet style.

    As the guests arrived I noticed that the women looked particularly elegant and the men, who never looked very impressive, dressed in their dark suits and white shirts and tie, looked almost handsome.

    The ceremony took place in the front room with its bay window. I stood on a little balustrade situated between the dining room and the front room, holding onto a wooden pillar, to get a good view. Beatie wore a light blue dress and the bridesmaids were dressed in pink and blue. I remember the canopy being held up and the ceremony taking place underneath, and Izzy stamping on the cloth covered glass.

    Mazel Tov! Mazel Tov!

    And she was gone. Lost to me forever! Dear, dear Beatie! She and Izzy were now a pair. They were going to live in New York City, not far from Uncle Jack and Aunt Molly. New York, of course, wasn't that far away but it might as well have been another planet. I knew she would never forget me. But she would be a wife and a mother now. She would soon have children of her own. They would come first, of course. After the ceremony I consoled myself by stuffing myself with the deviled eggs. There was fried chicken as well, but that seemed too complicated and messy.

    Izzy soon gave up cutting fur and opened a grocery in

A NOT-SO-NICE JEWISH BOY FACES WORLD WAR II

a rather poor section of Orange. We visited Beatie and Izzy there from time to time.

That first visit gave me quite a jolt. I didn't mind the apartment so much. It was behind the store, and rather pedestrian, and there was nothing particularly tasteful about the furnishings. As a matter of fact the place looked rather dreary. But what did it matter? I was here to see Beatie. She was in the store. I hadn't seen her in a while.

I stepped into this rather ordinary grocery store. And there she was, my beloved, behind this counter, wearing this dreary looking sweater. Her face looked fuller and there were these little lines under her eyes. She was a little heavier, now. And why didn't she comb her hair? She was looking at me with this loving look in her eyes. And it broke my heart. Dear, dear Beatie, I love you so, and you're just an ordinary looking woman now, frowzy and tired looking. What happened to you? What's happened to my beloved? I was ready to cry. Then a customer came in.

Can I help you? she asked.

And there was that cold, business-like smile, a look I'd never seen before. And she was so obsequious. These people are your inferior! Why do you kowtow to them like that? Is this what life does to people? Cooking and cleaning and taking care of the house and working in a store? Is this to be your fate? How cruel!!

And Izzy, too, so sweet and gentle. Why are you so servile to this riffraff? He was so touching, asking me if I wanted something in the store, some candy perhaps. *Help yourself. Anything you want.*

I was heartsick. This was not the way it was supposed to be. Life was supposed to be wonderful and glamorous and full of joy.

**AUNT BEATIE,
MY FIRST LOVE**

BEATIE, IZZY AND PHYLLIS

CHAPTER NINE

A PORTRAIT GALLERY

Originally our family was, for the most part, immigrants and, because of the experiences they had shared in Europe, because of the adjustments they had to make as strangers in a new land, there was an openness and a warmth so tangible you could almost touch it.

Growing up I felt part of a huge extended family, and it gave me a feeling of great security. Even though much of the conversation was rather mundane, I would still become engrossed in all the lively talk about business and family troubles and relatives back in Poland and food and shopping and recipes and clothes and sports and current events and the prices of everything.

Whenever we had company I had the feeling that people expected me to speak up, but I saw no point in saying anything unless I had something really important to say and, I couldn't for the life of me, think of anything important enough to say, so I just kept silent. It wasn't that I was shy which, I was...with strangers. It was just that I was too busy taking everything in, absorbing the various personalities I came in contact with, cousins and aunts and uncles, and people close to the family, friends and neighbors, and I was quite content just to sit and listen and study their faces. I wondered where they came from, what their life was like before, what their everyday life was like now, and what they were really thinking as they spoke.

There was Edna, Beatie's close friend. I wasn't sure how they met, whether they both worked at the pocket book factory, or they knew each other from Poland. Edna had a round, mobile face, and a bubbly, effervescent manner. She always seemed so enthusiastic, so full of life. It was fun just to be in her presence! And there was Frank, her dark, rather

A NOT-SO-NICE JEWISH BOY FACES WORLD WAR II

handsome husband. What a good looking couple they made! He was sort of dashing and sportsman like and was out there in the business world.

My mother pointed out to my father how successful Frank was, and how much money he made. My father pointed out to my mother that when Frank waited on customers (he had a butcher shop) he surreptitiously put his finger on the scale. He actually cheated his customers! I was appalled, Frank was no longer very handsome.

When mother's cousin, Gittel Maltz, came to see us from New York I was fascinated by her wraithlike figure and the soft-spoken voice. She had long, white hair which she wore piled high on top of her pale, gaunt face. She seemed so vulnerable, so fragile, as if a soft wind would just blow her away.

I tried to imagine what terrible suffering she had undergone, what tragedy lay behind those haunted eyes and that soft, quiet voice. She seemed to float rather than walk. Since our parents were so protective of us children, and tried not to burden us with past experiences that might have been harrowing or unpleasant I never did find out what her story was, nor was I privy to the background of all these fascinating people, but I would study them and wonder.

I also sensed something ineffably sad about Anna Hollander, a friend of mother and Beatie, who was so warm and loving, who spoke with this lilting soprano voice which had this emotional tremulo. Her all-embracing endearments were welcome, yet sort of embarrassing, they were so effusive. *Look at that face, that beautiful face! What a 'punim'! A blessing "uff deine koppele."* And there was a squeeze and a hug and a kiss, and another kiss. *Oh! I could eat him up, the both of them.*

Minnie was Mother's best friend. She was an excellent

A PORTRAIT GALLERY

seamstress. She was a sweet, gentle creature and always so solicitous in a very quiet way. My mother tried to fix her up with her brother, Uncle Jack, but Minnie found Uncle Jack's intensity rather alarming. She ended up marrying a saloon-keeper, like my father. I only met the man a couple of times, but he came across like a tough, crude gangster. I wondered how this delicate creature was able to get along with him. And I wondered why she married him since they were so unalike.

There was one woman, an exotic cousin called "Soora" who was always dressed beautifully, her long hair arranged in a bun behind her head. She came to America from Poland with her husband years after my parents did. She wore dangling earrings and looked so sophisticated and continental, a woman of the world in appearance and yet quite simple and down to earth. Her husband seemed rather courtly and gracious, yet the two of them gave birth to two sons who were rather blunt, and appeared to be without any social graces. Their daughter, on the other hand, was rather gracious and resembled the mother. The men earned a living as "peddlers." I'm not quite sure what that meant, whether they sold directly to households or sold to stores.

And, finally, there was one rather elderly cousin who, occasionally, came to stay with us for a day or two at a time. She was a rather majestic woman with a deep bass voice and sounded like Sophie Tucker, an entertainer of that day who sang suggestive songs in a tough, husky voice.

This woman was quite elegant and *expected to be waited on hand and foot,* my mother complained. She would rise rather late in the morning, after we'd all had our breakfast, and expect to be fed as if *she were in a hotel.* Apparently she'd served her time as mother and wife, and was now a woman of leisure. She now amused herself by visiting various family members. I wondered why she didn't spend more time

A NOT-SO-NICE JEWISH BOY FACES WORLD WAR II

with her children, instead of visiting relatives like ourselves, who were not that close.

All of this extended family, the aunts and the uncles and the cousins, the husbands and the wives, were all of them so unique, so colorful. None of them typically American. All of them special in one way or another.

AUNT GERTIE, UNCLE MORRIS, HELEN, THEIR FIRST

EDNA, FRANK & FAMILY

CHAPTER TEN

THE DYNAMO

Of the immediate family, the most vivid, the most dynamic of all was Aunt Tillie, Daddy's older sister who lived in East Orange. To me she was a mythic creature, a force of nature, a colossus that bestrode the world. She had this resonant contralto voice that rang from one end of the house to the other, a business woman par excellence.

Nothing could stop Aunt Tillie, certainly not Uncle Morris (Aunt Tillie, like Aunt Gertie in Pennsylvania, was also married to a Morris) a mild mannered man who lived in her shadow. His fumbling attempts to confront her were mere formalities. He usually ended with a muttered withdrawal when she vilified him as a *goddamned Communist.*

All right, all right.

It's true, isn't it?

I'm not a Communist, he would mutter, barely audibly.

They had a clothing store in Orange, on Main Street. Aunt Tillie had devised a suit club, an arrangement where you paid a fee every so often until you had enough put aside to buy a suit or a coat. She would climb into her car (they had two cars, mind you) and would make the rounds.

When she visited us she would sit at the kitchen table, commandeer a cup of coffee and a roll.

Frieda, I'll have to teach you how to make a cup of coffee. And listen, pick me up a dozen rolls the next time you come. I can't get rolls like this in Orange. I'll pay you.

All right, all right.

What a day!

So, what happened?, asked my mother.

And Aunt Tillie was off and running. *Senator Case said to me, Tillie...he calls me Tillie...you're a born politician. Why don't you run for Assembly? If only he knew. I can't even*

A NOT-SO-NICE JEWISH BOY FACES WORLD WAR II

write my name. (She had to commandeer relatives or friends to help her with her correspondence.) *But I can talk.*

That you can do, Mother agreed.

Listen, I'm not afraid of anybody. A senator goes to the bathroom just like everyone else. The other day Senator Case said to me, "Tillie, I'm thinking about running for governor. What do you think?" "Why not," I said. "If you lose, you can always run again." And they all belong to my suit club...the politicians, the police chief, the firemen. I don't miss anybody. If only I had time to go to school.

You're needed in the business, said my mother.

"Senator," I said, "I never went to college, but I know that two and two make four."

I was rather skeptical about her political connections until, one day, she exhibited a picture from the local paper. The caption read "Shown above are those who attended a political party for Clifford Case held at the home of Mrs. Tillie Kaufman" And there was Aunt Tillie standing next to a table full of food. Standing nearby and sitting around the table were senators and congressmen and local politicians.

Irving had to make a speech the other day. He comes to me for advice. I said, "Irving, I'm not that educated." "But you've experienced life," he said, "and you've learned more than you would in college."

That's true, said my mother.

Aunt Tillie loved to boast about Irving, the older son. He was going to be a doctor and he was *the smartest in his class.* The teacher said that she was *a lucky woman to have such a son.* She would regale my mother with how she ran the store, how she bore the burden and conquered all, despite all those handicaps.

Uncle Morris had been in a car accident. His leg had been badly mangled and there were numerous operations. He

THE DYNAMO

limped about and was continually in pain, so she had to take on the major share of the business responsibilities. This was in addition to looking after the house and cooking, though she did have someone come in to clean, Mother pointed out. And she managed somehow to get to the beauty parlor, at least once a week, to get her hair done. She even managed to squeeze in a weekly bridge game. This dynamo was the most American of everyone in the family. As a matter of fact, it was hard to think of her as Jewish, she seemed so brusk, so businesslike.

According to Aunt Tillie, Uncle Morris would go into New York to buy stock and he would spend the whole day there doing *I don't know what.*

He's doing business, said my mother.

Yeah. But what kind of business?

Aunt Tillie usually gave me a shirt, which she took from the store, as a birthday present.

Don't say anything to Morris. He doesn't have to know.

And he didn't have to know about the clothing she would gather surreptitiously from the store to give my mother to send to Europe.

Often on a Sunday we would hop into the old Chevy and drive to East Orange to spend the afternoon with Aunt Tillie and Uncle Morris. My sister, Rose, and I would sit in the back of the car watching the familiar landmarks fly by. Aunt Tillie usually prepared a dinner for us, but she assured us all that she was not as good a cook as *Frieda.* (My mother had the reputation of being the best cook in the family.) Aunt Tillie did make good apple pies, though, which my mother seldom made. Her house, somehow or other seemed a little impersonal though. Everything was in its place. It looked as if nothing had ever been moved, or disturbed.

Coming back home in the evening on winter nights,

A NOT-SO-NICE JEWISH BOY FACES WORLD WAR II

my sister, Rose, and I would count all the Christmas trees we passed. One year, strangely enough, Aunt Tillie had a Christmas tree. But we were assured that it wasn't really a Christmas tree...it was a Hanukkah bush.

******

I was very impressed with Irving, Aunt Tillie's handsome older son who played tennis and was musical, a self-assured figure in his white tennis outfit and his rather witty sense of humor. At dinner one time he made me laugh so hard that the spaghetti I was eating came out of my nose.

Irving became a psychoanalyst, a very successful one, teaching at a university, and giving lectures all over the world. As part of his training, he himself was psychoanalyzed. His face changed. It became rather puffy, and his charming, outgoing personality became dour and withdrawn. Irving married a lovely young lady, a doctor as well, who played the violin. They both played as a matter of fact...duets together.

Herb, Aunt Tillie and Uncle Morris' younger son, and I are immortalized in a snapshot taken when we must have been around eleven or so. We're standing in the street in front of our house on Nye Avenue, the stairs leading to the stoop rising behind us. Herb is nice looking and well groomed, wearing a suit and tie. I, on the other hand, am wearing short trousers with long stockings held up by elastic bands. My hair is disheveled and I look rather disreputable and bewildered.

I was not quite sure whether I liked Herb or not. Compared to Irving, he was decidedly earthbound. He tended to take charge, and I felt intimidated by him and, somehow or other I had the feeling that he was untrustworthy.

Occasionally Herb and I did play some rather interesting games though. There was one in which we were

THE DYNAMO

Indians. This was on the old sofa in the dining room. We would each take turns being captured and being transformed into an Indian maiden. No clothes were removed. No sexual contact was made. Sexual organs were replaced in pantomime. It was an odd ritual, to say the least, but a perfectly innocent one.

Herb was a bit of a gossip and would pass on to me all sorts of interesting little tidbits, which I took with a grain of salt. For example: my little brother, Marty, who was born when I was twelve, wasn't really planned for. He was an accident. I didn't really want to know all this...but that was an interesting bit of news, if true.

And then came a shocker. A female cousin had confided in him that she had lost her virginity. This last I was extremely skeptical about. Not that the young lady had experienced this mysterious thing called sex, but that she would actually confide this earth-shaking detail to him, to anyone as a matter of fact. One didn't discuss such things.

And finally there was this little bombshell; my mother had left my father for a time. Earth-shaking, if true. Why did she leave him, I wondered, and for how long. And why did she come back? And how did Herb know all this? Was he just making this up in order to upset me?

I racked my brain, trying to remember if such a thing ever happened but, for the life of me, I couldn't recall any such rift. Of course, that was no reason to rule it out completely. I might have been very young at the time.

I was tempted to ask my mother about it, but I never did have the courage, and I never did find out the truth. However I didn't think Herb had that great an imagination to make up a story like that, and I did know that my mother was dissatisfied with her life, and my parents certainly did have their quarrels.

**AUNT TILLIE
THE DYNAMO**

**IRVING AND LITTLE
BROTHER HERBERT**

HERBERT - 4 YEARS

**IRVING
AN EARLY IDOL**

THE KAUFMAN FAMILY

**HERBERT - THE SPIFFY ONE
ME -- THE SLOB**

CHAPTER ELEVEN

AN INCIPIENT ROMANCE
& AN OVERACTIVE IMAGINATION

Life was pleasant on shady, tree lined Wainright Street. I was no longer troubled by the bully at school. I'd visit with my gentile friend, Danny. After school and on week-ends I played "hide and seek" and "tag" with the neighborhood kids. In the winter we'd take a running start and slide on the ice in the adjoining backyards behind the house, or bring out the sleds and go sledding in this area which was quite extensive. In the summer we'd explore the overgrown empty lot next to the house. This was our jungle with the grasshoppers and the butterflies flitting in the sun.

And then there were those stormy afternoons when I didn't have to go to school, when I stayed at home and watched my mother bake cookies. I'd follow the whole process from beginning to end, from the mixing and the stirring of the eggs and the flour and the butter and the vanilla to the sampling of the final mouth-watering product or, when there was icing on the layer cake I was allowed to lick the spoon and clean out the bowl with my finger.

All this pleasant activity was interrupted by the news that we were going to move. The new house on Nye Avenue was actually within walking distance, but those blocks might as well have extended to another country. I would lose touch with my gentile friend, Danny. But even more important than that I might never see Frieda Sperling again. (Was it just a coincidence that she had the same first name as my mother?)

It was in the fourth or fifth grade, I must have been around ten or so, when Frieda, a confection in pink, with a white lace handkerchief pinned to her dress, walked into my home-room class...and into my heart.

She was introduced to us as a new student, and she was

AN INCIPIENT ROMANCE
& AN OVERACTIVE IMAGINATION

the most beautiful creature I had ever seen (except for Beatie, of course, but then Beatie was an adult). Shy or not, I had the temerity to ask her to accompany me to the movies.

I remember feeding her little brother his oatmeal as he sat in his high-chair while I waited for Frieda to get ready to go to the movies with me. As we walked down the street I reached out and held her hand. It all seemed so natural, so inevitable. And now that we were moving, she'd be living so far away, in a distant neighborhood.

******

Our new house on Nye Avenue, number 124, was on a hill, and a steep one at that. It was a nondescript two family house with a lot of cold cement steps leading up to the stoop. Though there was an interesting little alleyway to the right of the house there were hardly any trees on the block...on our side of the block at any rate. The grass on the little lawn in front of the house was sickly looking, almost barren, and the hedges that surrounded it anemic. The backyard was small and the house itself had no character whatsoever. The new school, Hawthorne Avenue grammar school, was not new at all like the old one on Bragaw Avenue. It was really old. The corridors were painted a dreary brown, and there were ugly pipes visible here and there.

At home in the new house I continued to share the bedroom with my sister. I loved her dearly. I enjoyed teasing her and we often had heart to heart talks, but there were times when I longed to be alone.

The only time I had any privacy was at night, when I got into bed and pulled the covers up close. My bed was next to the window and sometimes a breeze would enter the room

A NOT-SO-NICE JEWISH BOY FACES WORLD WAR II

and seek me out. I could look out the window from my pillow and see the top of a brick wall and the backyard of a nearby house. But I could also see part of the dark sky.

That's when I would commune with the stars twinkling way up there. I would lie there and take stock, contemplate my lot, evaluate my character and my relationship to the world at large.

The truth of the matter was I was a coward. There was no escaping that shameful fact. I was afraid of heights, for one thing. I was a afraid of the dark. I even dreaded going down into the cellar at night to put coal into the furnace. As I closed the kitchen door behind me, all sorts of imaginary creatures would come out from nowhere. They would follow me down the hall stairs and down into the cellar and taunt me.

We're gonna get you, you little pipsqueak!

They would leap out at me from the coal bin as I filled the shovel with coal.

*Aha! Now that you're down here all alone, we've got you! You'll never leave here alive! **Never, never, never!***

As I opened the furnace door they would leap out of the flames.

Aha! You thought I was gone, but I'm still here! I told you I would get you!

As I looked stealthily about while I emptied the coal into the furnace, shapeless creatures with blood red eyes would stare at me from the spooky recesses of the cellar.

What are you looking at, you poor little misbegotten excuse for...whatever you are?! You are dead!

It took all of my self control not to run screaming from the dark recesses of this haunted cellar, and make a dash to safety. Most of the time I was able to keep these demons in check. I would force myself to walk up the stairs with some dignity, like an ordinary human being. There were times,

AN INCIPIENT ROMANCE
& AN OVERACTIVE IMAGINATION

however, when I panicked and raced up the stairs. I'd heave a sigh of relief as I slammed the door behind me and took refuge in the light and the warmth of the kitchen.

And I was furious with myself. *Goddamned fool! What kind of a pitiful creature are you? Afraid of your own shadow!*

And I was, literally...afraid of my own shadow. In addition to that I was afraid of the other boys, of getting into a fight and being hurt. I found it difficult to understand how anyone could get angry enough to use one's fists. A fight seemed sensible enough in the movies, even natural and inevitable, in a Western say, or in a gangster movie. But in real life it seemed to me that there was nothing more ludicrous, more pointless than violent anger. What did it accomplish? Besides, the body is a rather fragile entity, and easily damaged. You could be crippled or blinded or disfigured in some way.

******

I was not too keen on sports either, except for the idea of tennis or swimming or even fencing, none of which I took part in. But at least they were graceful activities.

My friends insisted once that I accompany them to a baseball game. I complied reluctantly. After all, I thought, let's be fair, let's give the game a chance. We went to a local ball park. I munched on a hot dog and, all during the game, I kept making sarcastic remarks.

What good does it do me, I asked, *if someone else hits a home run?*

It was boring, boring, boring to sit there and watch someone saunter up to the home plate, pick up a bat and try to hit the ball. It was all so leisurely. This was a game you could get excited about? I couldn't wait for the game to end. As a matter of fact, the players themselves, as they wandered aimlessly about, seemed to be just as bored as I was. Even football, hectic as it was, had some action...or tennis or swimming.

It's true I would like to have been an accomplished athlete, to be able to win a race or make a touchdown and things like that, but I was inept at games. I dreaded my turn at bat. And even if, by some miracle, I would manage to hit the ball I knew I would never make it to first base. The newly enlarged playground next to Hawthorne Avenue school, with its huge wire fence, held untold terrors. I couldn't fight and I couldn't run fast enough.

And I had little patience with the female world as well. Girls weren't much fun, and their interests weren't mine. Dolls and playing house! What a silly game! I didn't mind playing "doctor and nurse." The role of the doctor was a dignified one, and the game itself gave one a curious satisfaction, but the rest was just nonsense.

CHAPTER TWELVE

THE WORLD OF BOOKS

I guess I was about twelve or so, when the outside world had no interest for me, that I sought refuge in the world of books. Here was a world I could understand. Here life made sense and, if it didn't, at least I could sit and try to figure things out at my leisure. There was no pressure. There were no demands. Here I was master of the situation. Here I was in command.

My taste was eclectic. Best sellers like "Anthony Adverse" and "Rebecca" and "Gone With The Wind", and classics like "Crime And Punishment" and "Jane Eyre" and "Anna Karenina" and "Pride And Prejudice" and "David Copperfield." And there was "A Farewell To Arms" and "The Great Gatsby" and "Of Human Bondage."

Somerset Maugham was a particular favorite of mine. He seemed to be able to tell a story effortlessly. The words just flowed. But the greatest of them all was Dostoyevsky. I really couldn't tell you why but, for some reason or other, his writing somehow stood taller than all the rest. There was something raw and vulnerable about the work of this giant. "Crime And Punishment" for example. It seemed to touch on something profound.

Once sampled, books became the core of my existence. Books made everything worthwhile. Nothing was more precious than a book, not even life itself.

Books were myriad lives. They were not one world, but untold worlds...past, present and future. If there was anything worth dying for, it was a book...even a bad one.

I fingered them gently, sensually. I remember taking one down from the shelf in the library and kissing it. I remember opening it's cover as if I were stripping a loved one. I was a very gentle lover, but I could also be ruthless. Each

A NOT-SO-NICE JEWISH BOY FACES WORLD WAR II

affair was begun with the highest of hopes. If, however, I found my partner dull or unfulfilling...after fifty pages or so...out! There were too many other beautiful creatures waiting in line.

I could forgive anything but dullness, and anything that did not smack of the truth was dull. But if you asked me what I meant by truth I couldn't have told you. Certainly a story did not have to be true to life to be true. It had to have a certain vitality, a reality of it's own.

And it wasn't necessary to understand everything. Truth communicated itself subconsciously, whether in a book by the philosopher Santayana called "The Last Puritan", which I barely understood, or in a mystery story in the pulp magazine called "The Shadow" (alias Lamont Cranston who, though invisible, fought crime), or adventure stories about "The Saint," a wealthy rogue detective.

The best place to read was on the sofa in the living room, or on the front porch, when the weather was pleasant. Stretched out on the beach chair, a book in hand, a glass of lemonade at my side, I roamed the universe.

I was no longer in Newark, New Jersey. I was in Russia, I was in London, I was in India, I was in the slums of New York City, I was in Paris during the French Revolution.

Often I never bothered to come down to earth, even after I'd laid down the book. I was continually in the clouds, aloof, impartial, a god on Mount Olympus. I could smile gently and magnanimously upon ignorant and petty people, peasants who were not inhabitants of my magical kingdom. From that rarified level I could view humanity with compassion and pity.

How could people live without books? How deprived they were, how wanting! If I did happen to sight someone carrying a book, in those days a rare sight indeed, or someone

THE WORLD OF BOOKS

sitting on a bus and actually reading, I felt an immediate kinship. There was a comrade, a fellow traveler. He or she knew what life was all about. They were special, like me.

Real life, as far as I was concerned, was a drag. What exactly did it consist of? Getting out of bed in the morning. That, to begin with, was a chore, to be followed by one chore after another...putting on one's slippers, brushing one's teeth, going to the bathroom, eating ones breakfast, getting dressed and going to school. And then there were such humiliating tasks as taking out the garbage or drying the dishes, or one had to go to the store to pick up a loaf of bread or milk, or getting ice for the ice box, or something dreary like that when one was in the middle of an exciting part of the book. Life was a prison, our bodies were a prison. Books opened the gates and set one free.

CHAPTER THIRTEEN

NEIGHBORS, CLOSE FRIENDS & THE LIBRARY

The Nussbaums upstairs at 124 Nye Avenue had three children, two boys and a girl.

One day Raymond, the younger son who was about my age, came up behind me and pushed me into the hedges surrounding our front lawn. Since it was summer I was wearing short pants and my legs were all scratched and bruised. The damage wasn't serious, but the unprovoked attack came completely by surprise. I couldn't understand it, since we'd hardly said two words to one another. What was it about me that brought about this animosity, I wondered. There was the bully at the Bragaw Avenue grammar school and now this. The world, I concluded, was a dangerous place.

I was saddened that Raymond would do such a foolish thing, and I was confused about how to respond to this violence. Should I approach him and ask him why he did this to me? Then I reasoned that he was the one that ought to approach me...and apologize. I decided to ignore him, eradicate his existence from my mind, so I stopped speaking to him.

This went on for several weeks. A month went by. By this time the resentment had faded, and it occurred to me that maybe I should try to make some sort of overtures. After all, it was ridiculous, not talking to someone who lived in the same house on the floor above.

But he was the culprit, I reasoned. He owed me an apology. After giving the matter a great deal of thought I saw no good reason to resume what was, to begin with, a very tenuous relationship, so I just continued to ignore him. Raymond and I never spoke again.

As a matter of fact the entire family was not a particularly appealing lot. As human specimens, however, I

NEIGHBORS, CLOSE FRIENDS & THE LIBRARY

found them fascinating. They were all rather dark and Italian looking. Actually they looked like swarthy gypsies, and they seemed to me rather coarse...the father, the younger son who'd pushed me into the hedges and the older son as well. The older son must have worked in a garage because I remember him coming home all grimy and greasy. The youngest member of the family, a girl, was the exception. As she grew older she was actually rather poised and graceful, in a gypsy sort of way.

Mrs. Nussbaum, the mother, couldn't stop talking. My mother often wondered when the woman got around to her housework. I would come home from grammar school for lunch, and there was Mrs. Nussbaum in the open doorway to our apartment, her left hand against the wall supporting her, engaging my mother in a non stop conversation. Actually it was more like a monologue, punctuated occasionally by *Am I right, or am I wrong?* Apparently the question was rhetorical since she never did give my mother a chance to respond.

******

My two closest friends at this time were Irving Hochhauser and Harold Schwartz. Harold was a year younger than I, and lived two blocks away from me. He had two sisters. The older sister, who was very poised and rather businesslike, played the piano and gave piano lessons. The younger sister was warm and friendly. Mrs. Schwartz was rather sedate and quiet, while Mr. Schwartz, who owned a leather factory, was charming and outgoing. There was always a twinkle in his eye. He was more like a friend to Harold, or a brother, than a father.

I asked my mother why Daddy never seemed to take an interest in me or my sister the way Mr. Schwartz did in

A NOT-SO-NICE JEWISH BOY FACES WORLD WAR II

Harold. My mother defended my father...rather half-heartedly. *That's the way European fathers are*, she said, not too convincingly.

Mr. Schwartz was born in Europe too, I replied

My mother had no answer.

I vaguely remember her saying to someone...I don't remember to whom, *The house and the children is my job. Did you ever hear of such a thing?*

Despite the fact that the Schwartzes were quite well off they were unpretentious and congenial, and their home was always bright and sunny.

Irving's family, the Hochhausers, the one whose father had been my father's partner at one time, had also moved. They now lived three blocks away from us. Their home always seemed rather dark and sort of gloomy. Mr. Hochhauser was short and stocky with squinty eyes and a rather embarrassed air about him. He always seemed to be making wisecracks, which weren't wise at all or the least bit humorous. His remarks were accompanied by a sly, peasant grin which revealed not very good teeth.

Irving had two sisters. Ruth, the older sister was dark, dignified and rather handsome, despite some pock marks on her face. She married, what was then considered late in life. Her husband was a hearty, handsome man and drove a truck. A few years later, we were saddened to hear that he had a heart attack while driving the truck and died. Well, at least Ruth did have a young child, a little girl, to console her.

Irving's younger sister was an anomaly. Blond, blue eyed and spritely, she was warm and uncomplicated, and seemed to belong to another family.

Mrs. Hochhauser was my image of a simple, good hearted peasant woman. She and my mother were good friends. She was extremely religious and she seemed to be

NEIGHBORS, CLOSE FRIENDS & THE LIBRARY

fond of me, urging Irving, to follow my example (whatever that might be.) She always made me feel very welcome.

Since we moved closer to one another, Irving had become my very best friend. He was dark, quite handsome, amiable and laid back; at times, I felt, too laid back. He was the only person I could confide in completely and openly. Not that we didn't have our differences.

Irving's approach to friendship, to life in general as a matter of fact, was much too casual, as far as I was concerned. He was not an avid reader, nor as intense about the movies as I was. He thought nothing of breaking an appointment, or forgetting about it entirely, which infuriated me. When I complained about this to my mother she said that if I wanted him as a friend I would have to put up with his faults. It was wise advice, which has stayed with me to this very day. After all, how many friends would we have if we rejected everyone that didn't live up to our standards?

Irving and I took many long walks together to nearby parks and unexplored streets. The greatest adventure of all was our trip to the nearby branch library. There were shortcuts, fascinating byways, behind garages, through empty lots...an unexplored wasteland with all the exotic glamor of Africa.

One descended down dark, mysterious paths, stepped over debris and climbed up rocks and odd pieces of cement blocks, up and up till one viewed the neighboring backyards from dizzying heights, and then scampered down the hill.

There was always some new path to take, some new byway to investigate, and the journey was always over too quickly.

But there was the library, waiting at the end of the journey. The library was a two story, ivy covered brick building, elegant, cool and inviting. It was set back from the street and fronted by a large, well cared for lawn and a magnificent shade tree. Separate stone paths led to the two floors. The second floor contained the children's library, and was accessible through a stairway at the side of the building. The children's library seemed rather helter-skelter and was somewhat noisy.

The adult library, much better organized and more formal, was on the first floor, and it was a refreshing change when I became eligible to use it. It was spotlessly clean, breathlessly quiet, and smelled pleasantly of glue and paper. There were always fresh flowers on the shiny, shellacked catalogue case in the middle of the room. There were shiny long tables to sit at and study or read, and stately shelves containing precious volumes, volumes too wonderful for words. There were interesting pictures displayed on the sides of the bookshelves facing the door, and there was a special section for new books and best sellers. The room always seemed sunlit, even on gloomy days, and the atmosphere there was timeless and unchanging.

CHAPTER FOURTEEN

MY FIRST ORGASM

Though Irving and I were great buddies there was one thing we didn't share, and that was my introduction to the mystery of sex. He wasn't around when a friend of Harold's led Harold, myself and two other friends down the stairs into my cellar, and initiated us into the art of masturbation. I felt guilty keeping this remarkable discovery from Irving, but I felt that I really didn't have the right to invite him to join us without consulting the others, even if he was my best friend. In addition to that I felt funny about bringing in an outsider to this rather private ritual of which I was not in charge.

The first time the five of us got together, in my case, nothing happened. I refused assistance. I was afraid of hurting something. It just didn't seem right, abusing oneself like that. As a matter of fact it seemed downright dangerous.

However, I repeated the experiment privately in our bathroom one afternoon. This time I was more persistent and lo and behold... My God! It was almost painful.

I was puzzled and fearful. Maybe something wasn't right. Should I consult someone? Should I see a doctor? There were no serious after effects however. Everything seemed to be in working order and, lo and behold, I had discovered a new and fascinating sport.

The wonderful thing about it was that I could do it any time I wanted, when I wanted and where I wanted...within reason, that is...and sometimes unreasonably and insanely...in a dentists's chair, for example, through the hole in my trousers pocket, while the dentist was called away; in a relative's living room during a visit, while everyone was out of the house, and, of course, in the privacy of my own bathroom, inspired by my image in the mirror.

I abused myself with frightening regularity. Indeed

A NOT-SO-NICE JEWISH BOY FACES WORLD WAR II

some of the things I felt and did were rather alarming, like shaving off my pubic hairs. Everyone really ought to look like a Greek statue, I reasoned.

When my mother went to the hospital to give birth to my little brother it was arranged for me to spend the night with Harold, while my sister would remain with the Nussbaums upstairs. I looked forward to the time when Harold and I would get to bed, and possibly join in in this fascinating new sport. I packed my pajamas and slippers, and walked down to Harold's house expectantly. When we finally did get to bed I reached over to initiate the ritual. Harold pushed my hand away.

I don't do that anymore, said Harold rather sternly.

I was surprised. I was disappointed, and I was hurt. Why on earth would anyone want to give up something that was so pleasurable?

Why? I asked.

It appeared that Harold, uneasy about our sessions, had confided in his father. His father advised him to discontinue this delightful practice. I was puzzled, perplexed, resentful. Why would anyone let one's father tell one what to do? I mean, after all this was a personal matter. This was a free country. Then it occurred to me that this might be a bad thing. Maybe I was a wicked person.

Just then the phone rang. It was for me. It was a neighbor. She was going to stay in my house with me and my sister while my mother was in the hospital. I was to come home immediately. I dressed reluctantly and made my way home, confused and puzzled.

Harold seemed unbearably pure after that and, somehow rather admirable. The end of the sexual episodes had no effect whatsoever on our friendship. Nothing more was said about it.

MY FIRST ORGASM

I kept pondering, however, the morality of Harold's desertion. If Mr. Schwartz objected to it, maybe it was wrong. But I couldn't see why. Why was it wrong? It didn't hurt anybody, and it was so pleasurable. I couldn't think of anything more pleasurable.

There was no one I could turn to to discuss the matter. As a matter of fact I really didn't want to discuss it. I might be told to give it up. So I didn't discuss it, and I didn't give it up, though I did proceed with a little more caution.

CHAPTER FIFTEEN

I SET MY SIGHTS ON CARNEGIE HALL

As I grew older, music no longer threw me into hysterics. As a matter of fact I'd grown to love and appreciate it. We didn't have a phonograph but I heard classical music on the radio, and Harold had a phonograph, and we'd sit in his sun parlor and listen to "Harold In Italy" by Berlioz and Liszt"s "Hungarian Rhapsody."

I'd never been to a real live concert, but in the movies there were scenes that took place in concert halls. How exciting it would be, I thought, to stride out onto the platform dressed in tails, sit down at the grand piano, poise dramatically over the keyboard and then attack the keys and dazzle the audience with stirring chords and beautiful, haunting melodies! I became obsessed with the vision of myself as a concert pianist.

I approached my mother. *Can we get a piano?*

A piano? That costs a lot of money.

They don't cost that much, said I. *I'm sure we can find a second hand piano real cheap.*

All right. Let me think about it.

A few weeks later.

When are we gonna get a piano? You promised me.

All right, all right. Don't pester me.

A few weeks later.

When are we gonna get a piano?

Will you stop with the piano?

You promised me.

Which wasn't exactly true.

This went on for over a year.

Finally I learned of a second-hand piano in the neighborhood that was for sale. I persuaded my mother to take a look at it.

I SET MY SIGHTS ON CARNEGIE HALL

How do we know how good it is? said Mother.
Pearl should know.

Pearl, Harold's older sister, who was an excellent pianist, and gave lessons, agreed to inspect the piano. I waited breathlessly for her verdict. After looking it over carefully, she pronounced it a bargain.

It was still quite an expenditure, but Mother had some money put aside and the purchase was made. The day the piano arrived was a red letter day. It was placed in the living room, against the wall near the windows.

I couldn't believe it. It was just a modest upright, but it was mine, all mine. I actually had a piano of my very own in our very own living room. The kingdom of music lay before me waiting to be conquered.

It was arranged for Pearl to give me piano lessons. At my first session I was told how to position my hands and my wrists. I was given scales and some very simple exercises to work on. I was on my way to glory.

I walked home in a daze, my head in the clouds. But I mustn't get too anxious, I cautioned myself. I must be patient. Rome wasn't built in a day. This is just the beginning. These exercises, it's true, may seem elementary but, after all, even Padarewski had to start with scales. Rachmaninoff had to play simple chords before he gave a concert at Carnegie Hall.

Every afternoon, between grammar school and Hebrew school, I would sit down at the piano and practice. As the months went by I graduated from scales and exercises to Bach fugues, Chopin waltzes and etudes and Beethoven's "Moonlight Sonata", and show pieces like "Malaguena" and "Rustle Of Spring."

The living room rang with my majestic renditions. I filled the entire house with music. I wanted to fill the entire

A NOT-SO-NICE JEWISH BOY FACES WORLD WAR II

world. I wanted everyone to hear me play. Who knows? I just might end up in Carnegie Hall! What's there to stop me?

******

And what a wonderful prop the piano made for my dramatic performances! I created a scenario for a mystery drama. I commandeered the neighborhood talent to help me act it out in the living room. My curly-headed sister, Rose, Irving and Gloria, my "zaftig' friend from across the street, were all assigned roles in this melodrama.

The performance begins:

I am a great pianist, one of the greatest in the world. I am giving this concert at Carnegie Hall. I sit down at the piano and play "Malaguena." This is the final number of this historical recital. (Don't ask me why it was historical. It just was.) After acknowledging all the applause and the bravos, I return to the baby grand to give the audience an encore. I sit down, look thoughtfully into the distance. I rub my hands together and tear into "Rustle Of Spring." Suddenly a shot rings out. I slump over the piano...my arms hanging loosely, uselessly.

The audience rises in horror. (I am now the audience.)
I cry out:
Call a doctor.
My God!
Is he dead?
How awful!
How terrible!

I encourage the rest of the cast to join in the tumult. They just stand there. (Oh, well.)

I continue.

I SET MY SIGHTS ON CARNEGIE HALL

An official announcement is made. The great man is dead. He will never play again.

Cries.
Confusion.
Pandemonium.
Curtain!
Next scene.

I am now a great detective. I must find the madman who committed this dastardly deed. What diabolical fiend would have the cruel temerity to silence this great musician, this legendary artiste?!

I proceed to question everyone.

Where were you on the night of the murder? I ask Gloria, my zaftig friend from across the street, who was assigned the role of the wife of the famous pianist.

I repeat, where were you on the night of the murder?
I don't know, says Gloria..
What do you mean you don't know?
I don't know. I guess I was home. I don't know.

I turn away in disgust.

I approach Irving, who was assigned the role of the artist's business manager. *Where were you at the time of the murder?*

I don't know. I was home? Irving replies, slightly confused.

(Oh, these amateurs! No imagination. No talent.)

I turn to my curly-headed sister Rose, who was assigned the role of the daughter of the dead artist. *Where were you at the time of the murder?*

What am I supposed to say? Rose asks.
Just answer the question.
I don't know what I'm supposed to say.
You love your daddy, don't you?

A NOT-SO-NICE JEWISH BOY FACES WORLD WAR II

Yes.

Can you think of anyone who didn't love your Daddy?
Blank look.

(The child is hopeless...hopeless, hopeless, hopeless. Isn't there anyone on this earth who can act, except me?)

I continue with my investigation as the great detective. With my imaginary magnifying glass I examine the room, from top to bottom. I look under the pillows of the sofa. I look under the sofa, under the chairs. I inspect the drawers in the little end table. I lift the lid of the piano bench and inspect its contents. I lift the top of the piano and peer inside at the strings.

Aha! There it is!

I point to the weapon, a pistol, concealed inside the piano. The instrument had been rigged so that it would go off when a certain chord was struck.

But who? Who knew about that certain chord?
Aha! The artist himself, of course.
Did the man kill himself, by any chance?
Quite possibly?
But why? Why would a man take his own life? Especially a man so talented, so successful? Why would this genius want to kill himself? What was the motive?

I look into the man's background, his recent activities and, lo and behold, I discover that the great pianist paid a visit to his doctor. It turned out that he was suffering from an incurable disease. I come up with the brilliant solution. The great man wanted to go out in style, in a manner befitting his glorious career. He decided to kill himself on stage, in front of his adoring audience.

It was a suicide!! I exclaim.
Gasps!
The great detective has solved the crime!

I SET MY SIGHTS ON CARNEGIE HALL

Curtain.
Bows.
Much applause. The little group is bewildered. Of course they are. They are in the presence of genius!

******

In addition to my career as a concert pianist, I now began to think about composing music as well. If I could sing "The Donkey Serenade" at the top of my lungs, that wonderful song that Alan Jones sang so delightfully in the movie, "The Firefly," as he wooed Jeannette McDonald, it was only one step further to compose a song just as wonderful. What could be more exciting? What could be more challenging?

Then again there were those giants like Gershwin and Kern and Friml and Romberg and Strauss. They were really talented...and intimidating. How could I possibly compete with those true geniuses?

Well, why not? Nothing ventured, nothing gained!

As an initial effort I decided to compose an operetta...a parody based on the Jeannette McDonald/Nelson Eddy musicals. With great trepidation I started to write down snatches of melodies in my music note pad, together with some tentative lyrics. I hadn't gotten very far, when I came to a standstill. My muse seemed to have deserted me. Nothing seemed to come. I looked over what I'd written so far and it seemed to me so...so pedestrian, so nothing. I decided to set aside the project...for the time being, that is. Maybe, in time, the inspiration might return.

Time passed. A week. Two weeks. Occasionally I felt the urge to continue. I resisted it. What I'd written just...didn't seem like very much. Besides, I just didn't have the chutzpah to compete with those wonderful songs that I loved. Thus the

A NOT-SO-NICE JEWISH BOY FACES WORLD WAR II

great American musical lay fallow, and I had to admit that I would never have a career as a composer. Ah, well!

But there was still my career as a concert pianist. I was now beginning, however, to feel a little insecure about that as well. Now I was willing to practice every day, to work diligently till I reached Carnegie Hall, but what guarantee was there that I would reach Carnegie Hall? How was I to know if I had it in me to be the best? And even if I could be the best, even if I was absolutely brilliant, what guarantee was there that I would succeed? The competition must be enormous.

One day, after my second year of study, I took the bull by the horns. After my lesson I turned to my piano teacher.

How good am I? What I mean to say is...do you think I have any future as a concert pianist?

Pearl looked at me wide-eyed. After a moment, she spoke rather hesitantly, *At this point, it's difficult to say.*

This came as quite a shock. This was not what I wanted to hear.

You have no idea?
Why don't we wait and see?

Then again she didn't say no.

So, despite this non-committal attitude which was, indeed, a setback I decided I was not giving up. I continued with my lessons, with a little less enthusiasm.

CHAPTER SIXTEEN

MY TEACHERS

School now seemed to encompass most of my life. I was eager to learn, to acquire as much knowledge as I possibly could. Yet, in spite of my love for books, in spite of my desire to learn, I resented getting up each morning, collecting my textbooks and marching off, like some prisoner, to class, after class after class.

The Revolutionary War and the Civil War, and Lewis and Clark exploring the Mississippi, and DeSoto exploring Florida, and Balboa discovering the Pacific Ocean...that was all very dramatic. It was fascinating to read about ancient civilizations like Egypt and Phoenicia, and to learn that Venice was once the trade center of the entire world, but not when one was forced to bury one's nose in a history book, and memorize all sorts of dates and all sorts of minutiae, not when one had to worry about the test at the end of the term, or the surprise quiz, like the sword of Damocles hanging over one's head.

Even though the classroom seemed like a prison, and homework like slave labor, it never occurred to me to play hooky. As a matter of fact, if I did miss a class, for one reason or another, I became apprehensive about falling behind. When I fractured my leg and was out of school for almost two months I was beside myself about all the work I had missed and, upon my return to school, I hobbled eagerly from class to class. I was even gratified at being allowed to leave each class a few minutes earlier so that I didn't have to contend with hallway traffic.

Despite my mother's encouragement I never seriously considered being a teacher. It was, of course, a vocation that might give one a great deal of satisfaction...if one heard the

A NOT-SO NICE JEWISH BOY FACES WORLD WAR II

calling, that is. But it seemed to me the easy way out. Those who can...do; those who cannot...teach.

I was fascinated, however, by all my teachers and the variety of their personalities. I wondered what sort of person would chose, what might be considered, a thankless profession. I wondered why anyone would want to stand on the side lines and watch the parade go by, year after year, dispensing the same information to the same mixture of dullards and, perhaps, one or two bright minds. I wondered what these creatures were like at home, when there was no class to confront. I wondered if they were lonely and unhappy when the shades were drawn, and I wondered what on earth they talked about during their rest periods in their rest rooms.

In grammar school, for example, there was Mrs. Brendel, a home-room teacher, whose magnificent breasts were usually displayed to great advantage, often in a sweater. This teacher also possessed a rather peppery tongue. I wondered what her husband was like, and if he really appreciated her very special endowments, and how he responded to her rather acid comments.

I also vaguely remember a gentle blond beauty in third grade. She was kind and considerate and I had a slight crush on her. I never did find out if she had a boy friend or not.

In high-school there were two French teachers. Miss Robin was a dark, little woman who was bright and cheerful. She reminded me of a little pigeon. There was a businesslike atmosphere in her classroom, however, and one learned ones syntax. She earned our respect but one was a little in awe of her.

Mr. Strawbridge, the other French teacher was a distinguished, charming gentleman, blond, with a mustache. He was usually dressed in tweeds. He was extremely affable. His classes were conducted very casually and French grammar

MY TEACHERS

didn't really seem that terribly important. One didn't learn much in his class, but the time passed so pleasantly, and we all liked him so much it didn't really matter. Years later I received a letter from him asking me to vouch for his character. Apparently, he'd been dismissed by the Board of Education for dispensing Communist propaganda in class, which was ridiculous. I wrote the letter, of course. I was gratified to learn that Mr. Strawbridge was reinstated, but he gave up teaching.

Miss Halter, our economics teacher was a tall, pleasant woman with a rather...well actually she was almost ugly and it looked like she had a very slight humpback. Maybe it was because she was hunched over a lot when she was at the blackboard. It was rumored that she was a Communist. I listened intently for any hint of Russian propaganda. I was sorely disappointed. It would have made the class much more exciting, since economics was really a very dry subject.

There was this one English teacher in high school, dry as dust Dr. Lewis, who always wore a dark blue suit and was more like a business man than a teacher. He spent a lot of time dispensing no knowledge whatsoever and his class was one great big yawn. Dr. Lewis's brother, however, was a prominent movie producer, responsible for some very interesting films. Every once in a while there were these little tidbits about actual films in the making, or one that had recently been released, like "The Flying Dutchman" with James Mason and Ava Gardner. That certainly did make up for a lot.

A second English teacher, Mrs. Bloomfield, a caustic and rather witty Irish woman was married to another English teacher, Mr. Bloomfield, who was Jewish and more easy going. The union intrigued me. I wondered if they went to "shul" or church. Or perhaps they were agnostics. And how would they raise their offsprings? Did they have any offsprings? They never spoke of any.

The English teacher from whom I learned the most, however, was Miss Wyckoff. She had a prominent nose, buck teeth and an impish gleam in her eye. She went about her business in a no nonsense manner, and we really learned our punctuation and our grammar. Years later I ran across Miss Wyckoff at the Metropolitan Opera, of all places. I had taken my mother to see "Tristan And Isolde" (a great mistake.) I wasn't quite sure if Miss Wyckoff remembered me, but I was gratified to tell Miss Wyckoff how much I learned in her class.

Miss Thomas, the woman whom I found the most fascinating, however, was not a teacher at all. She was a librarian, the one in charge of the wonderful branch library on Osborne Terrace. Her hair, sometimes unruly, was touched with grey and she always had a pencil poised behind her right ear. She would stamp the date in the books, when checking them out or when they were returned, with a decided flair. This woman ruled her domain with an iron hand. Though she seemed brusque on the outside and often looked angry I sensed a tremendous caring and tenderness underneath. Was she a frustrated old spinster, I wondered. Perhaps she'd been forced to devote her life tending to an invalid mother. Perhaps there was an aborted romance from which she'd never recovered, a lover who betrayed her or a fiance who was lost in the war. Miss Thomas became the model for the focal character in the first play that I wrote.

I never did find out anything about the personal life of Miss Thomas, or about the personal lives of any of my teachers, yet I'm sure their personalities had a great deal, in some subliminal way, to do with the shaping of my character.

CHAPTER SEVENTEEN

THE PURSUIT OF ROMANCE

As I approached my teens there was no romance in my life, and here I was getting handsomer by the minute. Well, maybe I wasn't exactly handsome, I reasoned, but I was, what you might call, nice looking with clear blue eyes, wavy brown hair, and a rather patrician nose. Surely I was created to be a great lover, a mysterious Byronic figure, flitting from one affair to another, leaving a path of broken hearts behind.

Exactly when I conceived this image of myself, it's difficult to say. Perhaps it was seeing Charles Boyer, as the mysterious Pepe Le Moko in the film "Algiers", dangerous and slightly sinister with his dark, heavy-lidded bedroom eyes and his seductive Parisian accent, or the dashing, swashbuckling Errol Flynn in "The Seahawk" or the romantic Tyrone Power in "Lloyds Of London."

And then there were those playboys in the Society section in the New York Daily Mirror, that my father would bring home and leave on the kitchen table. These glamorous figures would go to all those sophisticated night clubs and swanky lawn parties. They'd go sailing on their yachts and attend all those charity balls. Let other young men get all sweaty and dirty on the football field. The boudoir, the world of high society...that was to be my milieu!

Marriage, of course, was something to be avoided. Why should the man have to go out and slave while the wife sat at home, eating chocolates, reading movie magazines and listening to soap operas? Why should a man be burdened with the obligation to love one woman for the rest of his life? No love could possibly last forever...unless, of course, you were Charles Boyer in "Algiers" and got shot by a stupid policeman who thought you were trying to get away as you moved closer

A NOT-SO-NICE JEWISH BOY FACES WORLD WAR II

to the edge of the pier while waving good-bye to Hedy LaMarr.

And besides, one read in the columns where so and so was divorcing so and so, and the alimony was absolutely astronomical. My God, one could end up paying alimony for the rest of one's life!

Love affairs were okay though. One met a beautiful woman, like Hedy Lamarr or Irene Dunne or Myrna Loy for example, and you swept her off her feet. One dined at a chic restaurant overlooking Manhattan at night, the lights twinkling in the distance. One laughed a lot and looked deeply into one another's eyes and embraced passionately. "Oh, God, I love you so!" Then you took a ferry ride and ate popcorn and did all those silly little things.

And, of course, there was tragedy somewhere. Maybe she was unhappily married to someone else or worse, she was doomed to die of an incurable disease or, sad to say, a kept woman, eager to break away from her rich patron but afraid, and you would come to her rescue, and save her from a life of sin, because she needed someone stalwart and strong who believed in her.

There had, of course, been Frieda Sperling who I went to the movies with when we lived on Wainright Street. But, since we'd moved, I'd lost touch with Frieda. Once in a while, I did think about her, but I never did get around to making that journey to the other part of town. Fickle, and lazy that I was, I decided, there must be someone at hand who could replace her.

Among the candidates was Gloria, the zaftig girl across the street. She was kind of pretty and lively, and I was flattered by her friendship and seemingly romantic interest but, for one thing, she was stronger than I was. She had demonstrated that once during some altercation. She got me

THE PURSUIT OF ROMANCE

into a neck-hold, and I had to cry *uncle!* before she'd release me. Now how could one possibly get dreamy-eyed about someone who could beat you up?

As I surveyed the possibilities in my class I came up with two prospects. One was Gladys, a dark, attractive girl not unlike Frieda Sperling, well built and pleasant enough. And then there was Hazel. Hazel had wavy, chestnut colored hair, a patrician nose, and a lovely complexion, with a beauty mark on her cheek.

I couldn't court them both, especially since they were good friends. Gladys seemed, somehow, more accessible. Then again, though Hazel was not as pretty as Gladys, in the conventional sense that is (and she was certainly not as pretty as Frieda Sperling) there was something regal about her. (Like my mother, interestingly enough.) In addition to that, Hazel seemed to be more intelligent, more elegant, more refined. As a matter of fact she was so refined, she was almost unapproachable, and I did sort of resent this apparent aloofness. Nevertheless, in spite of her lack of encouragement, I decided to pursue her.

The first opportunity came in my eighth grade English class. I volunteered to adapt Shakespeare's "The Taming Of The Shrew" and direct a reading of the comedy. To my delight Hazel agreed to work with me on this project.

The first session took place in my house. As we sat at the table in our kitchen, side by side, almost cheek to cheek you might say, I became aware of how shabby our furniture was. The radio on the sewing machine looked so old and beat up. As a matter of fact everything in our house looked old and beat up. My mother helped some by graciously serving us some milk and cookies as we worked diligently disemboweling Shakespeare's "The Taming Of The Shrew" so that it could be presented in fifty minutes.

A NOT-SO-NICE JEWISH BOY FACES WORLD WAR II

The second session took place in Hazel's house, around the corner. No wonder Hazel was so snooty. She lived in a one-family house on Goodwin Avenue that even had a breakfast room. Carpeted stairs led to the second floor, a grand piano in the living room, a large well-kept lawn in front. This time the maid served the milk and cookies. Everything in the house was new and expensive looking, and Hazel walked about to the manner born.

After the two sessions we were prepared to make our presentation. There was a hasty consultation in the cloakroom, during which we assigned the various roles to members of the class. Gladys read Bianca, the sweet-tempered sister. Hazel read Katherine and I, of course, read Petruchio.

I remember almost nothing about that performance. It was the preparation, sitting next to that lovely vision, that was so memorable, so warmly satisfying. Which calls to mind my favorite poem:

"Bold lover, never, never canst thou kiss,
Though winning near the goal---yet do not grieve;
She cannot fade, though thou has not thy bliss,
Forever wilt thou love, and she be fair!"
                              Ode On A Grecian Urn
                                    John Keats

CHAPTER EIGHTEEN

THE MOVIES!!!

124 Nye Avenue now felt like home. Though the grammar school was old and ugly it did have character. As a matter of fact it was almost majestic in its ugliness. The front of the building, which faced Hawthorne Avenue, a main thoroughfare, was imposing with its dark brown bricks and formal entranceway. There were little drawings pasted on the windows in front, examples of the younger students' attempt at art, which succeeded in giving the building a touch of humanity.

Across the street from the school was Silvers' Bakery. As you entered through the swinging glass doors the pleasant aroma of the assorted pastries gave one a feeling of warmth and security. There were mouth-watering layer cakes with chocolate and vanilla frosting, and cookies and cupcakes and fruit pies and cream pies. I was often sent to Silvers' to pick up a fresh rye bread, *sliced and without seeds,* and three cupcakes (one vanilla, one chocolate and one strawberry) which I carried home in a white waxed paper bag.

There was a special way to eat a cupcake. First you removed the paper from the bottom then you pulled off the top with the icing on it. But you didn't eat that right away. First you ate the fresh, crumbling bottom with coffee or, on Saturday morning with cold milk (because you couldn't light the gas on "Shabas") to warm up the coffee. After that you ate the icing part. You always save the best for last.

A block down the street from the bakery, was the delicatessen where a tart, spicy smell greeted you as you entered. They sold mouth-watering corned beef and pastrami and hot dogs and potato knishes, all kosher of course. Actually my mother was not so sure how strictly kosher they were, but

A NOT-SO-NICE JEWISH BOY FACES WORLD WAR II

they advertised kosher and she took a chance and bought there occasionally. Delicatessen was a rare and welcome treat.

Across the street from the delicatessen was Tabatchnicks, the dairy store my mother patronized. A popular establishment, it featured sauerkraut and sour tomatoes and pickles. There were tubs of fresh butter and cheeses, smoked fish of all sorts and cold salads. The proprietor was always there and, though he was usually busy, he took the time to kibitz with the customers. As the years went by Tabachnicks flourished and opened branches all over the city.

Two blocks down from Tabatchnicks was the Hawthorne Avenue movie theatre. Now my parents seemed to have no interest in culture whatsoever. My father did read the newspaper regularly and, as I recall, my mother did glance at it once in a while.

Actually I do vaguely remember going to the Yiddish theatre in New York when I was very young. As I recall, there was a lot of hustle and bustle and loud talking. I saw Maurice Schwartz, a great dramatic star, in something, but his vision is rather vague in my mind. He had a commanding presence, I remember that. And I saw a musical about a family and marriages and that sort of thing, with songs and dances. But that was about it, and that was only twice. My parents never read any books and they didn't listen to music. (Though my mother did like waltzes.) So I did think there was some hope for my parents when they managed to get to the movies once a week. They were exposing themselves to, what I considered, culture.

My mother liked the movie star, Olivia de Haviland. (*She's very sweet.*) She had a crush on Otto Kruger, a supporting player who was rather distinguished looking...and, of course, there was the aforementioned Charles Boyer, who mother thought was very romantic.

THE MOVIES!!!

My father was rather noncommittal about the movies. But then one never knew what Daddy thought. I think he did enjoy Westerns though.

Wednesday night was "dish night." That's when my parents usually went to the movies. There were almost two complete sets of dishes in the kitchen cabinet.

I looked forward to the evenings my parents went to the movies for two reasons. In addition to the fact that they were exposing themselves to CULTURE, they would usually return with hot dogs on a roll with mustard and sauerkraut, and either sweet or hot relish..."the works," and sometimes even a potato knish or two. The frankfurters were kosher, of course, since they were bought at Cohen's, further up Hawthorne Avenue, a second, less imposing delicatessen, which was supposed to be **strictly** kosher.

It was past bedtime when they returned, but my sister, Rose, and I would remain awake and, at the sound of the door opening, we would hop out of bed and look anxiously to see if there was a brown paper bag in my mother's hand. There usually was. And then we would all sit around the kitchen table, open the bag hastily, remove the juicy morsels wrapped in white, waxed paper, unfold the waxed paper, remove the rolls containing the juicy hot dogs, and bite into this heavenly treat. There was usually cold soda to wash it all down. And while we enjoyed this feast I would grill my mother about the movie they'd seen.

How was the movie?
How was the acting?
Was Bette Davis good?
How was George Brent? He's not very exciting, is he?
Did you like it?

My mother's responses were rather astute and, sometimes, amazingly sophisticated. She could even tell what

A NOT-SO-NICE JEWISH BOY FACES WORLD WAR II

was going to happen before it actually happened, an ability I viewed with bewildered admiration. How in the world could she tell? She must be smarter than I thought she was.

******

    I myself went to the Hawthorne Avenue movie theatre every Saturday afternoon. I'd get in line with the rest of the kids at least half an hour before the box-office opened with my dime (or was it fifteen cents?) clutched in my fist.
    While you waited you could examine the stills on display in front of the theatre which could only hint at the excitement to come. There was "Murder In The Blue Room," for example, and you could fantasize about the experience that awaited you as you studied the scenes.
    Who was the murderer?
    Who was the victim?
    The door would probably creak open slowly.
    Oh, God!
    What was behind that door?
    Who was behind that door?
    Ahhhhhh! The entire theatre would scream with fright.
    A murmur passes through the eager line in front of the box office. Your reverie is broken. The cashier has taken her place behind the ticket dispenser. She removes the CLOSED sign and opens the window. The line moves slowly and finally one makes the purchase. As one passes through the lobby, ticket in hand, one studies the posters on the walls advertising the coming attractions, large colorful posters with dramatic, overblown pictures of the fabulous stars.
    These were double bills, one major picture and one "B" picture, which changed every three days. On the program there was also a newsreel, a cartoon and perhaps even some short

THE MOVIES!!!

subject. Sometimes there were two major pictures on the same bill. That was an unusual treat. If you consulted a newspaper and checked what was at the Roosevelt Theatre, some distance from us, you could tell what was coming. The Hawthorne received the same bill a couple of weeks later.

I liked to sit quietly, by myself, in the exact center of the theatre, just below the horizontal middle aisle, gazing at the blank screen, waiting patiently in the semi-darkness for the magic to begin. I would sit there anticipating seeing the great stars like Kay Francis and George Brent and Glenda Farrell and Joan Blondell and Ginger Rogers and Clark Gable and Katharine Hepburn and James Stewart and Marlene Dietrich and Henry Fonda and Claude Rains who played "The Invisible Man".

There were sophisticated comedies with William Powell and Myrna Loy and Cary Grant and Irene Dunne, and Westerns with John Wayne and Joel McCrea, and gangster movies with James Cagney and Edward G. Robinson and Humphrey Bogart, and historical epics with Paul Muni replete with beards and wigs, and soul wrenching dramas with Bette Davis and Joan Crawford. Who could forget Bette Davis as the arrogant cockney waitress so mean to Leslie Howard in "Of Human Bondage," snooty at first, then vicious and then pathetic as her lifeless body, looking like a drowned rat, is taken away on a stretcher and Leslie goes off with Frances Dee, who was the nice girl?

There were the Saturday afternoon serials with Flash Gordon and his girl friend Dale (or was it Wilma?) and Buck Rogers in the twenty fifth century (maybe **his** girl was Wilma) battling the merciless Emperor Ming, and young Frankie Darrow involved in breath-taking car chases along treacherous mountain roads and exploding buildings which left you wondering if anyone would survive, and "The Last Of The

A NOT-SO-NICE JEWISH BOY FACES WORLD WAR II

Mohicans" with Harry Carey and the good and the bad Indians. You couldn't take them seriously, of course, but you had to admit the suspense was unbearable.

I usually went to the movies with a couple of friends, but sometimes they made so much noise I had to move. I was furious at all the stupid chatter when such fantastic things were happening right there in front of us bigger than life! I left the movie completely drained.

It was so depressing to return to real life, to a real house, to a real dinner at the kitchen table. What a let-down! Life should be like a movie. One should suffer and laugh and cry and love like they did on the silver screen. Life should be unexpected and exciting. Sidewalks should fly and one should be able to reach up and touch the stars. If only one could come face to face with Rosalind Russell or Constance Bennett or Ann Sheridan.

Even if they'd seen it, I would regale my friends with highlights of the latest picture, playing all the parts. I would be the hero, the heroine, the villain, the sidekick. An old red cloth coat of my mother's with a black fur collar was the standard costume. It served as a uniform, a costume, a tuxedo, an evening gown...whatever the scene called for. My most triumphant moment was the entrance I made from the pantry with tears streaming down my face. I later admitted I had resorted to the aid of a sliced onion.

The greatest punishment imaginable, for what I considered some trivial misbehavior, was to be deprived of my Saturday matinee. The threat alone was too terrible even to contemplate. It was enough to make one sick to one's stomach. One tried to maintain ones calm through lunch, but it was extremely difficult.

You're really not going to let me go?
You heard me.

THE MOVIES!!!

Why not?
You know why.
No, I don't.
Silence.
Mother?
No answer.

I bided my time and finally, tense and white-faced, I argued and cajoled and begged. How I hated my mother! To wield such terrible power...so cruelly. Sometimes, after a long, protracted, heartfelt plea, I won out. There were times, however, when she was adamant, and I hated her even more, if that was possible.

All right, I'll ask Daddy.
Go ahead and ask him.

And that's when I knew I was lost. Daddy would never contradict her. And besides, his punishment would mean the strap.

The minutes ticked by.

They were actually lining up in front of the theatre right now, this very minute.

This couldn't be happening...to me.

I sulked from one room to another. I looked out the window. The box-office was going to open up any minute now. It might be opening up right now, this very second.

The cashier was entering the booth. She was removing the CLOSED sign.

She was actually opening the box-office window.

The first person in line was handing in his dime.

Mother, please!
I said no.
I'll never do it again.
That's what you said the last time.
But this time I mean it.

A NOT-SO-NICE JEWISH BOY FACES WORLD WAR II

So do I.
If hate could kill she would have been dead a thousand times.
I cried inside. Oh, God, oh God!! Was she actually going to keep me home?
It's getting late.
And then I wept...openly, unashamedly. The tears streamed down my face.
A twelve year old boy, crying because he can't go to the movies.
I don't care if I'm a hundred.
The movie was actually starting and I wasn't there.
How unbearable! How ironic! I who understand, who feel everything so much more deeply than anyone else, to be deprived of seeing the great works of art. I will never forgive her, never, never, never!
Of course, there's always next week. I'd better not let her know how much I hate her. So I swallowed my resentment. It was painful. It was unfair, but it was over and done with and one day I'll be rich and famous. I might acknowledge my parents...and then again, I might not...especially her!
I emerged from this great suffering old and exhausted, hating myself most of all for caring so much, for suffering so deeply, for being such a goddamned fool.
What's one movie more or less?
It's all a fake.
It's all fiction.
It's just make believe!
But in my heart I knew it was not.
In my heart I knew that the movie was the only reality.
Everything else was fiction.

CHAPTER NINETEEN

ENCOUNTERS WITH DEATH

We were just beginning to come out of the "Great Depression." America was a huge, empty land to be wandered through at night, nursing some deep, dark secret; like the movie stars on the screen, John Garfield or Humphrey Bogart, world weary and lonely, yet hopeful somehow, roaming the highways to the accompaniment of a train whistle in the distance or a harmonica played by some hobo in a passing freight car.

My mama done told me
When I was in knee-pants,
Son, a woman's a two-faced,
She'll give you the glad eye,
And when her sweet-talkin's done...

There was nothing I enjoyed more than taking a walk all by myself and giving vent to my imagination. I would see myself as a starving musician or artist or writer, walking along a country road, stopping for food at an empty, desolate diner and ordering apple pie and coffee, because that's all I could afford, from a rather sad looking, pretty blond waitress that looked like the movie star, Priscilla Lane. Or maybe I was Leslie Howard, the world weary intellectual in "The Petrified Forest," ready to end it all, and pass the dream on to a young and vital Bette Davis.

The only one who didn't interfere with any of my moods was Irving. He seemed to know when to be silent, and when to speak. He seemed to believe that all my dreams would come true. There was no such thing as failure. The difficulties that lay ahead were only trials to strengthen one for future combat. The more one suffered the richer one's emotional life, and the more there was to draw on.

As far as illness was concerned there were the

A NOT-SO-NICE JEWISH BOY FACES WORLD WAR II

inevitable diseases like chicken pox and the measles, unpleasant but not life threatening. Of course, there was the occasional pain, like going to the dentist.

When I was about five or six I was taken to have a tooth pulled. Well, I wasn't exactly taken, I was dragged. When they finally did get me to the dentist's office and into the chair, I broke out of the chair, ran out of the office, ran down the stairs and was halfway down the block before I was finally captured. It then took several people, to hold me down so that the dentist could get the tooth out. So pain was real. It was something one might have to deal with. Death, however, was an abstraction, something that happened to old people or people one didn't know. That's what I thought...until my early teens.

******

My first experience with death, though second-hand, was one that was both shocking and cautionary. We read in the papers one morning about the discovery of the corpse of a young girl on the lawn of Weequahic High School. It appeared she'd been the victim of a botched abortion, and had bled to death. We were horrified and heartsick to learn, as we read on, that the girl was actually the lively younger daughter of a respected Jewish family to whom we were related. My heart ached for the girl and for the family. It also drove home a very important lesson. Not only could one catch a disease from having sex, but you could also get a girl pregnant!

My second experience with death, in addition to being deeply disturbing, had rather complicated ramifications. Jerome was a thin, dark boy and very affable. I was fond of him, and I considered him a friend. Jerome was enamored of Gloria, the zaftig girl across the street, but Gloria had a crush on me. I wasn't aware of how serious Jerome's feelings for

ENCOUNTERS WITH DEATH

Gloria were until one afternoon when she called me on the phone.

This was unusual, since she lived across the street and never called me on the phone. Apparently Jerome had accused me of taking part in some sort of nefarious goings on in the cellar with some other boys. I was flabbergasted. How could he possibly have found out? And why would he bother to pass this information on to Gloria? What a mean-spirited thing, for a so-called friend, to do!

Our phone was in a little alcove right next to the parental bedroom, where my father was taking his afternoon nap. I hemmed and hawed trying to keep my voice down. *"No, I don't know what he's talking about, whatever that might be."* With trembling hands I set down the phone. I had managed to get rid of Gloria without giving anything away. I dreaded my parents finding out about these disgusting goings on. What would my mother say? What would my father say? What would I say?!

When my father came out of the bedroom, he asked me if anything was wrong.

"No. Nothing's wrong."

Nothing more was said.

I was terribly hurt that Jerome would resort to such underhanded tactics. In addition to that I had no interest in Gloria whatsoever, romantic that is. I went about with a heavy heart, deeply disappointed in this betrayal, and gravely concerned about someone discovering my disreputable secret.

A few days later Jerome was riding his bicycle in the street, and was hit by a truck. His liver was punctured and he died shortly after the accident. All sorts of thoughts crowded into my head. Had Jerome been punished for his act of betrayal? I didn't really believe that, of course...yet in the back of my mind was the persistent thought that God may have punished him for his deceitful behavior.

Jerome's family owned a fruit and vegetable store on Clinton Place, nearby, and they lived above the store. Harold, Irving and myself put on our best suits and, sick at heart, we slowly climbed the stairs to the apartment to pay our last respects. The family was hysterical. Jerome's mother clutched me to her bosom.

He's dead. My baby's dead, she moaned, rocking back and forth, and she sobbed uncontrollably.

I felt guilty that I was alive, and that her son was dead. I was sure she resented my existence. I tried to console her, but I felt helpless. I didn't know what to say. The coffin was actually there, in the living room. I walked over to the open, silk lined coffin and looked down at Jerome lying there. He wore a skull cap and a prayer shawl, which I thought rather odd since he hadn't been the least bit religious. My friend looked so peaceful, so serene...so pale, so waxlike. It was hard to believe that Jerome would never open his dark eyes again and smile his crooked smile and greet me warmly as he had done so often. I wondered if he had suffered much pain.

I looked around at the tear-stained faces of his sisters. They all looked so foolish somehow in their grief. This whole event seemed so ridiculous, so pointless. Why should he die so young, so innocent? (Except, of course for that betrayal. Yet, in spite of that treachery, I wished that he was still alive.)

For a long time after that, I would think of poor Jerome. I would conjure up a picture of the accident...the truck bearing down on my friend. I would picture him lying in the street next to his broken, twisted bike, writhing in agony or perhaps he was unconscious slowly bleeding to death. I would see him lying there, so young, so still in that white lined coffin. How final death was! How painful! How sad.

ENCOUNTERS WITH DEATH

******

My third experience with death around this time hit even closer to home. One Spring day, I must have been thirteen or fourteen, I was playing across the street with some friends, when news came that there had been a suicide in the neighborhood. The suicide had taken place in an apartment building around the corner. That was the building that housed my Uncle Sam, the man who had taken my father under his wing when he arrived in America, the one who had accompanied us to Pennsylvania, with his pretty wife, Aunt Rose.

Then I learned that the man who'd *taken the gas* was actually Uncle Sam, that quiet, gentle man, so dignified, so grave. I couldn't believe it. I remembered he hadn't been well, and that he always carried a rubber cushion about with him, but he'd always seemed so stable, so sensible. I assumed he'd taken his life because of his illness. Apparently the pain had gotten to be unbearable.

I dreaded going home. I expected to find my mother in a state of collapse, but it was getting dark and close to dinner time. I delayed going home as long as possible. Finally I crossed the street and entered the house.

When I came into the kitchen I found Mother quietly talking to some of the neighbors. To my surprise, she seemed rather calm. I wondered if she'd heard the news. If she had she would surely be hysterical or carry on or something. I was afraid to ask. Finally I broke the ice and I asked very quietly.
Did you hear about Uncle Sam?
She nodded.
Poor Aunt Rose, I said.
We'll have to pay her a visit, she replied.
Nothing more was said about the tragic event, but

A NOT-SO-NICE JEWISH BOY FACES WORLD WAR II

Mother seemed very gentle with everyone that evening as she served our dinner.

After Uncle Sam's death Aunt Rose went to live with her sister in another city, and we seldom saw her. I liked to remember that one summer afternoon when Aunt Rose and Uncle Sam dropped by the house and took my sister, Rose, and myself for a ride in Weequahic Park. They were childless, Uncle Sam and Aunt Rose, and I seemed to sense their need for children. I tried, somehow, to fulfill that need. I wasn't their son, of course, but maybe for that one afternoon, for these few hours, I could be.

We walked together, the four of us, Aunt Rose, Uncle Sam, my sister, Rose, and myself, through the garden of flowers in Weequahic Park. Everything was so pleasant that enchanted afternoon. The sun was so warm, the blossoms were so pretty. I loved my sister dearly, and I felt so close to Aunt Rose and Uncle Sam.

Somber, dark, gentle Uncle Sam. Where was he now, I wondered. He'd loved his wife deeply, and she was so pretty and so lively. And if he had loved his wife how could he have left her like that? How could one reach that terrible state of mind where one was capable of taking one's own life?

And what happens after death? As far as the deceased are concerned that's the end. That's what I believed, at any rate. I didn't see any reason to believe otherwise. They were gone, forever. But what about the living? How did Aunt Rose feel after Uncle Sam was gone? She was alone, after all those years. How did she face the future? It must have been awfully painful, awfully lonely.

And then there was Jerome's family...they would continue to grieve for the rest of their lives. Was there any way to avoid this terrible pain, this aching emptiness that would probably be endless? There was one solution, I

ENCOUNTERS WITH DEATH

concluded, not to get too emotionally involved with other people.

Play it safe.

But was that really possible?

CHAPTER TWENTY

I CAST MY LOT

When we lived on Wainright Street, before moving to Nye Avenue, we used to patronize the drug store on the corner. They gave out green stamps with every purchase, and if you accumulated a certain amount of green stamps you could redeem them for all sorts of things, like games and toys and tools, etc, which were displayed most tantalizingly in the window.

In addition to these items, there were all sorts of costumes like an Indian costume and a cowboy costume; and uniforms, a soldier's uniform, a fireman's uniform, a policeman's uniform. I never acquired any of these outfits but, at about the age of ten or so, I would stand in front of the drug store window and imagine what it must be like to be a cowboy on the range rustling up cattle, or a fireman rescuing people from the flames, or a policeman protecting peoples' lives.

My dream of being a concert pianist had gone the way of all flesh. Despite the evasive response from my piano teacher in regard to my prospect as a professional pianist, I had plodded on with my classical repertoire. Actually I had become more adept. I could play loud, there was no doubt about that. If the window was open, I could be heard all the way down the block, and I could play...fairly accurately; but delicately and with nuance...well, that I wasn't quite sure about.

If I wanted to make it as a concert pianist, if I wanted to be able to make my fingers do exactly what I wanted them to do, I realized that I would have to concentrate on my music to the exclusion of everything else. I would have to practice night and day. And was I really that talented?

Though my teacher was hesitant to encourage me, she

I CAST MY LOT

could be wrong. There were many classic examples where artists were told that they were absolutely hopeless, and went on to great success. And even if I was that talented, what assurance was there that I could make it? The competition must be staggering.

Mrs. Schwartz was sometimes in the other room when her daughter gave me my lessons, and she had been rather complimentary about my progress. I confided in my mother that I was seriously thinking about a career as a concert pianist. It was obvious, however, that I had qualms.

My mother, aware of my indecision, decided to consult Mrs. Schwartz. I wasn't too keen about that. I was curious, however, to hear what Harold's mother would have to say, so I made no objection. Mother paid Mrs. Schwartz a visit, and then reported back. Apparently Mrs. Schwartz said nothing at all about my ability. All she did was point out to my mother that the path to a concert career was a long and arduous one. It involved...in one word...MONEY! The door to the concert stage was shut for good.

And I was really angry. No one had ever given me one ounce of encouragement, I kept telling myself. If someone believed in me I could have made it. I did have the talent. I did have the vision. I just had to work at it. All those months of practice! Years actually! All those dreams! What a waste! However, I had to be honest with myself. I had to admit, that if I really wanted to be a concert pianist, nothing would stop me. If I had the courage to pursue the dream, my family would not desert me, I knew that. Let's face it, I said to myself, you just don't have the guts. And well, maybe, deep down inside, you really don't want it badly enough.

I tried to console myself with the fact that music was just a pleasant whim, a pipe dream, one that I had never really taken seriously. But dreams do die hard and, from time to

A NOT-SO-NICE JEWISH BOY FACES WORLD WAR II

time I could still see myself strolling onto the stage in tails, sitting down at the keyboard and lamming into the "Warsaw Concerto" or Rachmaninoff's "Piano Concerto," and then bowing majestically to the shouts of bravo. I could actually hear the overwhelming applause.

It was pointless, however, to mourn a musical career that wasn't destined to be, and as the prospect of high school was approaching, the time had come, I decided, for me to bite the bullet, and think seriously about the future. I was not a playboy, like I read about in the Society Column in the Daily News. I was not destined to lead a life of leisure in the lap of luxury. Eventually I would have to earn a living and, if I was going to have to work to support myself, I reasoned that I might as well work at something I would not resent getting out of bed for. After all, practically speaking, one did spend most of one's life at one's job.

******

So one summer day, I sat down on the beach chair on the porch and, with pencil and paper. made a list of all the possibilities. Next to each profession I drew two columns, one pro, the other con.

TEACHER

Pro	Con
Satisfaction of passing on knowledge. Ugh!	More school.

DEFINITELY NOT

SCIENTIST

Helping humanity. Fascinating	Do I have the patience or the temperament?

I DON'T THINK SO

I CAST MY LOT

DOCTOR
Save Lives.   Am I into blood and guts?
I DON'T THINK SO

POLITICIAN
Not into politics
Don't have the stamina or the personality
DEFINITELY NOT!

LAWYER
Fight for the underdog.   Could I defend the guilty?
Trials exciting.   Law research dull and dry.
Lots of competition.
Not an easy profession.
NO

WRITER
Love books   You'll be writing, not reading
Easy life physically   Might have to do lots of research
Freedom to work anywhere   Depend on sale of books
Self expression   Self expression? Oh, really!
Influence others   Influence others? How pretentious!
Writers starve to death.
May take long to be a success.
May never be a success.
Hard uncertain life. You'd have to be a fool!
IS THIS WHAT YOU REALLY WANT?
I THINK SO

And the debate began:

CON: You're not really talented. You don't have the

A NOT-S0-NICE JEWISH BOY FACES WORLD WAR II

skill of a...Somerset Maugham, for example. You don't have the stature of a Dostoyevsky. And what is a writer? What is any artist in America? They're second class citizens.

PRO: I can think of nothing nobler than creating a book. A book cannot only entertain. A book can contain ideas, and ideas can change the world. And besides, even if I'm not that talented, I can learn to write well. I'm willing to learn.

CON: Let's be practical. You should be a teacher. You would make an excellent teacher. Even your mother thinks so. But what you really should be is a scientist. To find a cure for cancer, for polio, for the common cold. To find the secret of life itself.

CON: You're much too high strung. IF you like to read, why don't you be a critic?

PRO: Now there's a pointless profession, passing judgement on other people's work.

CON: You're a fool!

PRO: I don't care. I want to be a writer. Besides I can always change my mind. I'm going to be a writer. That's it! End of argument.

When I made the formal announcement, my mother was very disappointed. She kept hoping I would change my mind. She really had her heart set on my being a teacher.

******

Now that I was going to be a writer, a novelist primarily, I had to prepare myself. In taking stock of my qualifications I came to realize that I actually did possess what I considered unique powers. For example, I was able to analyze myself coolly, like a scientist, both my assets and my defects. I was able to examine the people around me

I CAST MY LOT

objectively. I felt that I could sense their thoughts, their emotions, their motivations. I did have a future as a writer!

And with this conviction I experienced great exhilaration. I contemplated the magnificent career that was in store for me. I became a giant, looking down at the world from above, giddy at the very thought of what I might accomplish. And there were times when my imagination took flight.

One night I stood on the porch looking up at the sky. A soft breeze caressed my face and my whole body seemed to leap into space. It was an out of body experience.

And then suddenly I was plagued by vague unanswered questions, and even though I wasn't quite sure what these questions were, I felt somehow that I had once known the answers and had simply forgotten them. They hung out there in the cool night air, the questions and the answers, just beyond my grasp.

Then it occurred to me that these passionate visions, these periods of exaltation might have sexual origins, and the fact that I couldn't identify their source disturbed me deeply because, after all, I did have an analytical mind. Why couldn't I understand what was going on inside of me?

I became apprehensive. Where would it lead, this strange feeling of uniqueness? This bold journey of the imagination into the unknown? Could it lead to madness, perhaps? Well, I would just have to risk it.

I would walk down the street early in the morning and suddenly be engulfed by the aura and the mystery of life...of the universe...of a house I noticed in passing. I would be flooded by an awareness of a world that reminded me somehow of Eugene O'Neill. And then these dreams, these aspirations became unashamedly venal. I dreamt that at the age of twenty-five I would be a world-wide celebrity. I would

A NOT-SO-NICE JEWISH BOY FACES WORLD WAR II

win the Pulitzer prize, and then go on to win the Nobel prize. At the age of thirty-five, after I had drunk deep from the cup of Life, I would probably be living in a penthouse, married to some breathtakingly beautiful movie star, like Hedy Lamarr. One died around sixty-five anyway, so there would only be about thirty years of enforced domesticity.

After my announcement that I was going to be a writer there seemed to be a myth growing up around me, that I was actually destined for great things. My mother doted on me. My sister looked up to me. Irving and Harold both assumed that I would be a great success. Beatie, and Aunt Tillie and Uncle Jack...everyone was now waiting for me to set the world on fire. Even my father, I sometimes felt, looked upon me as someone special, though no one really knew what Daddy thought.

I became uneasy. I, personally, was convinced that I was destined for greatness, but I wasn't so sure that I wanted others to buy into this glorious picture. Suppose I wasn't a great success? Suppose I was an abject failure? I, myself, might be able to take the disappointment, but I would hate to disappoint others. In addition to that, I was confused by the dichotomy in my personality. I knew very well that there were people much smarter than I, and probably much more talented, and yet I had this feeling of arrogance, of superiority. Yet I didn't really feel superior. It was just that my goals appeared to be higher and more demanding than most of the people around me.

There was no turning back however. Writing was to be my mission in life, my reason for existence, and if I didn't fulfill that mission, if I didn't scale the heights...well...it was a frightening thought, a drastic step perhaps...but I could always end it all. It was an awful thing to contemplate, but it seemed to me that we were here on earth to make some sort

I CAST MY LOT

of a contribution to civilization, and what was the point of living, what was the point of taking up space, if one had no contribution to make? Besides, suicide was not something to think about seriously...for now, but it was, after all an alternative.

CHAPTER TWENTY ONE

UNCLE JACK

There was one thing that steeled my determination to fulfill my dreams. That was the example set by my Uncle Jack, my mother's brother, who arrived in America on the day that I was born. We both considered that some sort of an omen, and there was some sort of special bond between us. Maybe I could do the things he hadn't been able to do.

Uncle Jack was certainly the most intriguing member of our immediate family. When he held forth on current events, on philosophy, history, social science, art, Jewish dogma, the Talmud, biology...any subject under the sun...he was spellbinding. And this in spite of a speech impediment, a sort of stammer, where the words seemed to struggle to emerge from the very depths of his being and finally...erupt. But what did it matter? Didn't Moses himself stammer? He even needed his brother Aaron, as his spokesman.

I could listen to Uncle Jack for hours. His intellectual vitality seemed boundless. He spoke with such authority, such brilliance. He was unchallengeable. He would vanquish any contradiction with such a tirade that his opponent would be drowned in a tidal wave of words, and retreat, cowed and defeated. He questioned the heavens, the earth and God himself, if there was such a thing as God. Nothing was sacred. He even challenged Aunt Tillie once...and no one ever challenged Aunt Tillie. It began with a crack about her weight.

She came right back. *I don't want to tell you what you look like, with that thing over your lip.* (Uncle Jack wore this little Hitler mustache.) *If I were your wife I would take poison.*

If...y-y-y-y-you were my wife...I would g-give it to you.

My mother and Uncle Jack were very close. He adored her. He often came in from the Bronx to visit with us, for nourishment, both bodily (he loved my mother's cooking) and

UNCLE JACK

emotional, since his marriage was a troubled one, fraught with quarrels and anxiety. He lived in the Bronx surrounded by his wife's family.

Where's Molly? Mother would ask.

M-m-m-molly? M-m-m-molly's busy with the b-boy. She's k-k-k-killing that child.

Maybe if you paid more attention...

W-h-h-hat are you t-talking about? The woman sleeps in the same b-bedroom with the b-b-boy, and he's not a b-baby anymore.

That's not right.

W-what can I tell you?

We would sometimes journey on a Sunday up the West Side Highway in Manhattan to his apartment on East 206th Street near Mosholu Parkway. I can still see him standing there in front of his building to greet us...his receding curly hair, his Hitler mustache, the suit that never seemed to fit, the thick white socks and the heavy shoes that were specially made because he had trouble with his feet.

W-what t-took you so long? he would ask my mother.

There was a lot of traffic. Where's Molly?

She's upstairs...w-waiting for you.

You coming up?

F-for what?

We've come to visit you, Jack.

S-so you'll visit. Go, sh-she's waiting for you. It's stuffy up there. I c-can't breathe.

Jack...

G-go, g-go. I'll be up l-later. I n-need some air. Hymie, c-come. We'll t-take a walk in the park. And then he turned to my mother. *At least y-you can give me a k-kiss.*

And Mother would sigh and kiss him, and we would

A NOT-SO-NICE JEWISH BOY FACES WORLD WAR II

climb the stairs to the second floor where Aunt Molly would greet us at the door.

Come in, come in. How was the trip?

We would sit around the apartment, and there was gossip about the family, about the various crises that would arise in connection with daily life. Uncle Jack would join us eventually, but he could barely sit still. He would sit in his easy chair, nervously tapping his feet or drumming with his fingers.

So th-that's the way...it is.

Above the bookcase in his living room there hung a large framed photograph of Uncle Jack in Arab garb, cradling a rifle behind his head, looking like...like Lawrence of Arabia. He stands surrounded by two men, a woman and a child, also in Arab garb. From Brostek, Poland, where he spent his childhood, Uncle Jack had traveled to Palestine, and lived there for a while. This was in the early nineteen twenties. In Palestine he had actually counted among his friends David Ben Gurion, one of the founders of the state of Israel and its first prime minister.

There's also a picture of Uncle Jack in the family album, looking very debonair, with his younger brother, Froyim, sitting in a Paris cafe. I'm not sure whether the trip to Paris came before or after Palestine. At any rate he was disillusioned by life in Palestine. It was hard and unrewarding; *The weather, the flies. There was no future there.* And that's when he decided to come to America.

Uncle Jack, as a youth, had been extremely orthodox, wearing the traditional skull cap and side curls. He would sit in the synagogue all day, reading and debating the scripture. In Palestine he was derided for his orthodox beliefs, and there he went through a radical transformation. He now had nothing but contempt for organized religion.

UNCLE JACK

The Jews in Poland, at least in Brostek, had limited access to public schools but somehow or other (I don't know where...probably on his own) Uncle Jack had acquired a vast fund of secular knowledge. In the living room of his apartment I remember peering through the glass doors of the large book case and being impressed at finding Tolstoy and Dostoyevsky, an encyclopedia, even plays by Bernard Shaw.

I learned that my uncle had had an article published in the Jewish Forward. I asked him why he hadn't gone on to become a journalist. He responded that he wasn't that secure about his command of English. Besides he had a family to support.

Is a family that important? I asked.

A man needs a woman, he said sternly.

Was he trying to justify his not following through, I wondered, or maybe Uncle Jack really had a strong sexual drive. How interesting! Was this brilliant man, this man with a brain that never stopped, was this man dominated by his physical desires, I wondered. He had courted Minnie, Mother's best friend, but she found him frightening, so she stopped seeing him. On the rebound he had married Aunt Molly, an intelligent, attractive woman. Their son, also named Norman, a chubby youth, bright and sweet-tempered with large watery blue eyes was also afflicted with a speech impediment similar to his father.

Uncle Jack labored in the workaday world as a fur cutter to support a child whom he had little access to, and a wife whom he antagonized incessantly, a wife whose life centered about their son. Their quarrels were usually about the boy. According to Uncle Jack she would run to the doctor so often that the doctor told her to stop pestering him.

In the medicine chest in the bathroom of their apartment Uncle Jack had enough bottles to supply a

A NOT-SO-NICE JEWISH BOY FACES WORLD WAR II

drugstore. He lived on pills and complained continually about his nerves. This giant of a man, this learned savant wallowed in misery.

So what does the doctor say? my mother asked.
T-they say th-there's nothing wrong.
So if there's nothing wrong...?
Wh-what do doctors know? Th-they know how...to take your money. Th-that's what they know.
I told him he should see a psychiatrist, Aunt Molly said.
Y-you should see a psychiatrist. N-not me. Ag-gain with the psychiatrist.
All right Jack.
So...t-that's the way it is.
He takes all these medicines. He doesn't even know what they are, said Aunt Molly.
I know w-what they are.
Some day he'll overdose and he'll end up in the hospital.
S-so I'll end up in the hospital. And t-that'll be the end of it. And not soon enough.
If you're so miserable why don't you kill yourself?, said Aunt Molly.
Y-you think I haven't thought about it?
So go ahead. Who's stopping you?
Th-that takes courage.
Oh, Jack, Jack, said Mother.
So, t-that's the way it is.

He would shock people with his brutal frankness, commenting rudely on people's appearance. It was as if he enjoyed insulting them. He told Beatie once that she was placid, *like a cow.* He shook hands with a woman once and squeezed her hand so hard she cried out in pain. The woman's

UNCLE JACK

husband almost knocked him down. The super in his apartment building once complained to Aunt Molly. *Keep your husband away from me, Mrs. Tall, or I'll kill him.*

Friends and relatives refused to come to their apartment.

Why should they come to be insulted, to listen to all that abuse? There was a petition going around the building to have him evicted, Aunt Molly said.

Once he joined us unannounced at a Passover Seder. He kept making sarcastic remarks all during the ceremony. *Annother g-g-glass of wine?! All right. D-drink. D-drink gesuntaheit.*

My father was ready to toss him out of the house but, exhibiting great restraint, said nothing.

Mother would sigh and shrug. *That's Jack.*

I'm ashamed to go anywhere with him, said Aunt Molly. *We go to a restaurant. He's too cheap to leave a tip.*

Th-that's their job. Th-that's what they're paid for.

Jack, they depend on those tips. There's no use talking. Anyway, when he walks away I have to put down some money. I mean how can you live like that? And yet he'll take a taxi at the drop of a hat.

It's my money. I'll spend it the way I want. I d-don't give you money for the house?

I have to beg.

Because you spend it like water.

It's no use. There's no talking to him.

S-so stop talking.

You have to listen to reason, Jack, said Mother.

You're not there. You don't know what's going on, so don't interfere.

All right. I won't interfere.

So th-that's the way it is.

113

A NOT-SO-NICE JEWISH BOY FACES WORLD WAR II

Uncle Jack bought his son, Norman, a tricycle. Norman fell off the bike and suffered a deep cut just above the eye. He was left with a large scar.

He could have been blind! I told him, said Aunt Molly, *I begged him. Don't buy the boy a bike. What does he need a bike for? You think he listens to me?*

During our visit in the Bronx sometimes my father and I would take a walk with Uncle Jack in the nearby park. He loved to walk, and would often take walks all by himself. During our walk my father, quiet and reserved, and Uncle Jack cynical and sarcastic, would talk about business or the stock market or politics. But there was one thing Uncle Jack didn't want to talk about, didn't want to discuss, didn't want to hear...bad news like death or a serious illness.

P-Please, I don't want to hear about it.

You live in the world, said my father.

I-It's a sickness. Nerves. I have it. Frieda has it. Th-that's the way it is. What c-can I tell you?

In the late afternoon, before our trip back home there was usually a dinner in the kitchen. Since the kitchen was so small, there were two shifts, first the adults and then the children. The dinner usually consisted of tuna fish salad and bagels.

If I knew ahead of time you were coming I would have prepared a real meal, Aunt Molly would say.

C-come on! H-how much t-time do you need to make a steak?

Jack, please!

That's all right. Tuna fish is fine, said Mother.

As we drove away I would look back to see my uncle standing in front of the apartment building waving good-bye and looking sort of lost.

Eventually Uncle Jack had to give up cutting fur

UNCLE JACK

because of an allergy and he decided to go into business for himself. He took a loan and opened up a grocery store in Harlem. There was a meat department and he had to hire a butcher...again and again and again. None of the help would stay around for very long.

He insults everybody. You think people want to put up with his nonsense?! said Aunt Molly.

For my birthday he gave me some shares of stock and included a poem.

> "To Norman, my beloved nephew
> close to my Spirit and Heart
> In spite of our "Superficial Differences
> You are of me an integrated part!
>
> Please accept enclosed certificate
> as a 'nest egg' for a future 'Rainy Day.'
> It will come in handy when you reach
> my age, when the Body is feeble and the hair turns

gray.

> Though it's value now is low
> it's potential Growth is great indeed
> as it takes a 'wise man' to put
> 'Springtime' in the ground the seed.
>   With
> Greetings, salutations and Love to back
> With heart and soul your Uncle Jack."

He presented both my sister and myself with two lovely portable typewriters, expensive ones which we both used for years.

Growing up, to me Uncle Jack was a giant, and his

A NOT-SO-NICE JEWISH BOY FACES WORLD WAR II

knowledge seemed uncanny, his mind fearless. I had only dared to think some of the cynical thoughts Uncle Jack uttered so bravely. I watched and listened in awe as my uncle pronounced heresy after heresy in a clarion voice. But this brilliant man, this fountain of knowledge and wisdom, had no outlet for his creativity, and that was why everyone within earshot was scathed by his fury, this anguish that raged inside of him and seemed to tear him apart.

I understood his pain. Other people were either disgusted with him or found him offensive. I was amused by his shenanigans. I seemed to sense what was going on inside of him, and I empathized. And I vowed that I would not be as miserable as Uncle Jack. What ever became of me, no matter how many defeats I might meet, no matter how difficult the path, no matter how crushing the blows, I would not live my life the way he did.

Uncle Jack sent his beautiful books out into the air...into the living room, into the kitchen, into the dining room at the dinner table. People would sit and listen to him in awe. But that was not enough for me. I wanted the world to be my audience.

I was sitting on the porch of our house on Nye Avenue when I made the decision to be a writer. The point of my pencil broke as I wrote my list. I needed a knife to sharpen it. Gloria, the zaftig girl from across the street, was sitting at the bottom of the stairs. I asked her to lend me her penknife. She refused. I begged. I pleaded. *Okay,* I said, *if you lend me your penknife, I will dedicate my first book to you.*

Is that a promise?
It's a promise. I swear.
Okay. Remember.
And she handed the penknife to me.
That clinched it. Now I would have to be a writer.

**UNCLE JACK IN PALESTINE
(LAWRENCE OF ARABIA)**

UNCLE JACK AND UNCLE FROYIM IN PARIS

**UNCLE JACK AND
AUNT MOLLY**

COUSIN NORMAN

CHAPTER TWENTY TWO

I BECOME A BEAST IN THE FIELD

I was around twelve or so when my mother sent me to a drugstore several blocks away from our house to pick up a prescription. On the counter there was a container filled with gold covered chocolates. The gold tinfoil was in the shape of a large coin. The temptation was irresistible. While the druggist's back was turned, I helped myself to a handful. On the way home I ate one of the chocolates and threw the tinfoil away. My conscience must have bothered me because, when I got home, I displayed my ill gotten loot.

Look what I have, I boasted.
Where did you get them? Mother asked.
At the drugstore.
Did you pay for them?
Silence and, after a moment, *No.*
How did you get them?
I took them.
Take them right back.
Silence.
You wanna go to the movies on Saturday?
All right, I'll put them back.
You'll go back there and you'll give them back to the druggist.
Why can't I just put them back?
You heard what I said. All right. Forget about the movies.
All right, all right. I'll go.

What could I do? I was not about to give up my Saturday movie, the only real, unadulterated joy in life.

My mother took me by the hand and marched me into the drugstore. She watched while the tear-stained culprit handed the chocolates to the druggist and confessed to the

A NOT-SO-NICE JEWISH BOY FACES WORLD WAR II

theft. The druggist accepted the chocolates, looked at the desolate penitent and offered him a chocolate. I looked at my mother. She shook her head. I handed the chocolate back to the druggist.

No, thank you, I said.

My mother took my hand and escorted me out of the store.

Now I had great admiration for my mother's integrity. She was right, of course. I suppose I had to be taught a lesson. But I did think she was a little hard on me and, it seemed to me, the world at large was not that scrupulous.

For example: One sunny Autumn day my friend, Irving, and I took a long walk up Nye Avenue. We were strolling along the curb, kicking the dead leaves in the gutter. Lo and behold a ten dollar bill appeared, a shiny green ten dollar bill resting among the dull red and brown leaves. This was alongside the curb in front of a barber shop. I had never even seen a ten dollar bill. I shouted with delight and waved the glorious find at Irving.

We were standing in front of the shop debating how to spend this fortune when out came the barber.

That's mine, he said. *I lost it this morning.*

Dumbfounded and crushed, without a word, I reluctantly handed the bill over to the barber. One didn't argue with adults. We watched, broken-hearted, as the barber returned to the shop, opened his register, placed the bill in the drawer and slammed it shut.

Both Irving and I were furious. We knew the bill didn't belong to the barber. We discussed the incident with our respective families. Everyone agreed that the money belonged to us, but no one was willing to do anything about it. Finally my mother made up her mind. She marched Irving and myself up to the barber shop and confronted the barber.

I BECOME A BEAST IN THE FIELD

That money belongs to the boys, she said.
The money's mine, he said. *I lost it this morning. All right.* He reached into his pocket and pulled out a quarter. *Here.*

I was about to take the quarter, when my mother took it from my hand and handed it back to the barber.

You keep it, she said, contemptuously. *You may need it.* And she turned to us. *Come on,* she said, and we followed her as she strode out of the store. From then on, Every time Irving and I passed the barber shop we stuck our tongues out at it.

******

I often wondered who or what determined our sense of morality. How did we know what was right and what was wrong? The decision had to come from somewhere. Were the standards of our behavior derived from our religion? Did God have anything to do with it? Which started me thinking about religion.

My mother, according to Aunt Tillie, was the "rebetzen" of the family. She kept a kosher house. She lit the candles on Friday night. She refused to cook, turn on a light, ride or write on the Sabbath. It seemed to me, however, that she performed these rituals only because she was taught to perform them, not because she, herself, believed in them.

Why do you light the candles every week?, I asked.
That's what you're supposed to do.

I never bothered to ask her why she never went to "shul" except on the important holidays. I was sure she would find some vague excuse, but it set me to thinking. What, after all, did all that rigmarole have to do with the love of God? And besides, God is love, is he not? At least that was my impression and, if you believed in God, shouldn't you love all

A NOT-SO-NICE JEWISH BOY FACES WORLD WAR II

your fellow creatures, even the Gentiles. Yet Mother mistrusted them so.

But they're people, just like you and me, I argued.

The Jews killed Christ, and they'll never forgive us, was her response.

But Mother was an infidel next to Irving's mother, Mrs. Hochhauser. Her gloomy home oozed religion. She was an authority on all sorts of obscure laws and, if she didn't know something, she would run to the rabbi. Did this really make Mrs. Hochhauser a better person, or did she live her life under the influence of darkness and superstition?

And Mr. and Mrs. Schwartz, Harold's parents, were equally religious, but in a more relaxed and casual manner. Mr. Schwartz attended synagogue every Saturday morning, and sometimes even on Friday evening. Oddly enough, he seemed to enjoy it. He made very generous contributions to the synagogue. He was a pillar of the congregation...and Mr. Schwartz was a charming man with a whimsical sense of humor and a twinkle in his eye. This certainly said something for the Jewish religion.

Observant or not, all my relatives showed up at the synagogue on Rosh Hashanah and Yom Kippur. Aunt Tillie, for example, who seemed to me almost gentile, made it a point to attend services on the high holidays. She would buy tickets for herself, Uncle Morris and "the boys."

As for myself, I'd been indoctrinated into the mysteries of Judaism at any early age. Even before I attended Hebrew school Mother hired a rabbi to tutor me privately. It was an expense the family could ill afford, but my mother was determined that I grow up a good Jew.

The rabbi, an elderly man, came to the house. We would sit at the dining room table and he would attempt to teach me to read Hebrew (ancient Hebrew, that is). He had a

I BECOME A BEAST IN THE FIELD

huge red beard and, as he leaned over me while I read my Hebrew lesson, his foul breath nearly made me gag. Sometimes, mercifully, he would fall asleep during the lesson. Apparently, he was as bored as I was. Sometimes I would try to hide when I saw the rabbi coming. Once or twice I was actually able to escape his clutches. I did have the good grace to feel guilty about it though.

My mother finally gave up on the rabbi. I was enrolled at the Hebrew school at the synagogue on Osborne Terrace, which was a few blocks away. I attended Hebrew school three times a week after public school. Weekly attendance at the Sabbath services in "shul" was mandatory. On Saturday morning Irving, Harold and myself would walk along the tree lined streets, say good-bye to the sun and the blue sky and the fresh air, and enter this musty, claustrophobic establishment.

We'd file into the synagogue, sit down on the wooden bench, usually toward the rear of the room, remove the prayer book from the rack on the back of the bench in front of us, try to find the place, and intone the prayers along with the rest of the congregation. I had been taught to read Hebrew, it's true. I was even beginning to translate the Bible from Hebrew into English, but I never did get anywhere near mastering the language. The words I was muttering half aloud, half to myself were, for the most part, meaningless.

******

The Biblical stories, however...that was another matter entirely. Reading them in English, they seemed so vivid, so theatrical, so fascinating. There was the venerable Abraham who, at God's command, prepared to sacrifice his own son (What kind of God was that incidentally? And what kind of a father was that?) And then there was Esau selling his birthright to his brother Jacob for a cup of lentil soup. (What a sly one that Jacob was!) And then there was Moses in the bulrushes, raised as an Egyptian prince, killing an Egyptian overseer, defying the pharaoh and leading the Hebrews out of Egypt, and then going up the mountain to commune with God, and then descending Mount Sinai carrying the tablets containing the ten commandments, his eyes on fire with holiness, and his grey locks blowing in the wind, and then dashing the holy tablets against the rocks in a fit of anger because the people, during his absence, had built a golden calf and started to worship it. He may have been a great religious figure, but he sure was human!

And then there was the great lover, King David, the most romantic, the most glamorous of all, a legendary warrior, a poet, a skilled musician, his friendship with Jonathan and his illicit affair with Bathsheba. Oh, he was not all goody, goody! After impregnating a married woman he actually conspired to have her husband killed. And what a magnificent enigma, King Saul, the first king of the Israelites was! What went on inside the mind of that wonderfully moody man as he sat on his throne, clutching his spear and staring into the darkness? Why did he suddenly throw his spear at David and try to kill him? And why did he try to kill his own son, Jonathan? And Joseph and his brethren, that fantastic tale of jealousy and forgiveness. Could his brothers really have been so envious and so cruel as to sell Joseph, their own brother into slavery? Such sublime drama, such colorful legends!

These stories were handed down from time immemorial, these great epics with characters larger than life that set the imagination on fire. But did these things really happen? And even if they had, they were probably embroidered along the way by the various scribes that recorded them. I was also skeptical about the supernatural

I BECOME A BEAST IN THE FIELD

elements in these magnificent tales, the parting of the Red Sea or Daniel perfectly safe in the lion's den. Of course, there might have been a perfectly reasonable explanation for all these so-called miracles, if they really occurred that is. Nature does present us with all sorts of inexplicable phenomena. Electricity, for example. The radio. The automobile. Those were things that I didn't understand. But, what did it matter if these stories were true or not? They were wonderful!

But praying in a foreign language to a god I couldn't comprehend, who had nothing to do with the world as far as I could see...what was the point of that? Why not pray to the sun or the moon or a tree or a stone or fire or water or air? And what was the real origin of religion? Fear! Fear of the unknown, fear of death, fear of what came after death. Out of fear we create some sort of superhuman figure to reassure us...a father figure, an image we're accustomed to turning to.

And when it came right down to it, I wondered whether I'd ever really prayed. Reciting meaningless words to some vague entity, was that really praying? "Do unto others as you would have them do unto you." Well, that seemed like a very practical philosophy, one that I could live by. It was the basis for both the Jewish and the Christian religion. But what did that have to do with God?

******

I was standing next to my father in the synagogue one afternoon. I believe it was Rosh Hashanah, the new year. I was about fourteen or so. We were both muttering Hebrew words and swaying back and forth...and suddenly I stopped. Why am I doing this, I wondered. Do I really believe in these so-called prayers, all this mumbo-jumbo, or am I just going through the motions because it's expected of me? I looked about...and it was as if my eyes had suddenly been opened. I looked at my father, deep in so-called prayer. I looked at all the men in the synagogue, mumbling and shaking and rocking back and forth and singing and intoning. It was a farce. None of these men really meant the words they were uttering. It had all become a habit, like brushing one's teeth, or washing ones face. If there was a god he was certainly not in need of all this meaningless ritual. I should think that this unctuous flattery would actually be an insult.

And when did people really and truly pray? When they wanted something. And what entitled anyone to special favors? All this whining and begging was just humiliating. Humiliating to the penitent, humiliating to the omnipotent spirit, if there was one. This sort of toadying was certainly easy enough to see through. And what about self respect?

And then there were those who would go to "shul" on Saturday and then on Monday, go out and commit all sorts of sins, like putting their finger on the scale while selling meat at their butcher shop; like claiming a ten dollar bill belongs to them when they know perfectly well that it doesn't. And how many wars have been started in the name of God! How many people have been murdered in the name of religion?!

If there was a god, he was in charge, wasn't he? And by this time he or she or it ought to know what he, she or it was doing. If we go about our business here on earth, God, if there is a god, would go about his or hers or its, and it seemed to me that man's relationship to man was the important thing, the thing we here on earth should give all our attention to.

I could find no reason to continue with my so-called prayers, so I just stopped. If there was a god, I thought, I would find my own way to him...or her...or it.

At first, because of this heresy, I was convinced that I was doomed to instant destruction. A bolt of lightning would

I BECOME A BEAST IN THE FIELD

strike me down. I would be enveloped by a ball of fire and go straight to hell. (And that's another thing. Is there really a heaven up there in the sky among the clouds? And is there really a hell down there with brimstone and fire? Actually we never discussed this in Hebrew school, but I assumed we Jews were supposed to believe in heaven and hell. And what a lovely fairy tale that was!)

At any rate, days passed, weeks, months...almost a year...and nothing. I took this as a sign that I was right. That I would not go up in smoke or be struck by lightning.

During dinner one time, I happened to mention quite casually to my father my doubt about the existence of God.

What? You're going to live like the beasts in the field?, was his reply.

This came out of the blue, and his vehemence surprised me. Though he seemed to observe all the rules, went to "shul" on the holidays and all of that, I never thought of him as being particularly religious. The food he served to the customers at the tavern certainly wasn't kosher. Whether he himself observed the dietary rules away from home I really didn't know. I suspected that he didn't. And he did work on the Sabbath, and hardly ever attended Sabbath services.

Then again there were those, like Mr. Schwartz, who really appeared to believe, who did seem to derive a certain amount of peace from this whole business. And...well maybe they were right, even those who just went through the motions. Maybe it was better to play it safe...just in case. After all, one never knows, does one?

But this was just a passing cynical thought. Though the seeds had been planted early, my exposure to organized religion was not one that bore fruit.

CHAPTER TWENTY THREE

MY MOTHER, MY FATHER & ME

With my private rejection of religion I contemplated a rebellion. No more prayers, no more Hebrew school, no more yarmulke (skull cap) at the Sabbath meal. I would ride on Saturday, and write, and turn on the lights, and do as I pleased.

But suddenly I was faced with the realization that I was not a free soul. I was not entitled to do as I pleased...not only as I pleased but even as I believed. This house that I lived in wasn't really mine. It belonged to my parents. I was in debt to them for the clothes that I wore, for the bed that I slept in, for the food that I ate.

To put it bluntly, I was a parasite, a nonentity, a mere reflection of those that created me unless, of course, I was ready to strike out on my own, to support myself and create a home of my own which, of course, for someone approaching his teens, was ridiculous. I was not yet ready to face the world. So, if I wanted to continue to receive these necessities of life, I just had to bite my tongue, swallow my pride and do as I was told.

How unfair, I fumed. We have a mind of our own; we can think for ourselves and yet, intelligent as we are, we're subject to these giants that rule the world. As an infant we have to laugh and coo with joy as they toss us up into the air and treat us like toys. As a child we have to run to keep up with these ogres as they stride down the street on legs which are bigger than our entire bodies. We have to wear the clothes they choose for us, eat the food they place in front of us, whether we like it or not; go to bed when we're told, whether we're tired or not, take a bath, whether we're dirty or not.

And yet it seemed to me that children were far more rational and, actually, more fit to run the universe. But, as it

MY MOTHER, MY FATHER & ME

is, we were virtually inmates in a prison overseen by emotionally unstable guards, monsters subject to inexplicable behavior, whose minds are dominated by strange moods and impulses. The madmen are in charge of the asylum!

My mother, for example, had a tendency to get hysterical. For, what seemed to me, some minor infraction she would chase me around the dining room table, brandishing a wooden ladle, because every time she spanked me with her bare hand she would hurt herself and start to cry. On rare occasions, when she was overcome with anger and frustration, she would relegate the spanking to my father, who would chase me around the table with a leather strap, and then I would really get it. My father seldom got angry, but when he did, watch out!

To be absolutely fair, I suppose, one could say that the jailers are the jailed as well. We are, after all, an ever-present burden. We have to be fed, clothed, toilet trained, taught manners, etc. If the parents want a social life they have to see to it that someone's there to look after "the children." If they go on a trip they have to take "the children" along and be prepared to spend time with them and pay attention to them.

I tried to imagine my mother without "the children." Motherhood seemed to be her mission in life, the very core of her existence. And yet, in spite of her obsession with motherhood, there seemed to be an emptiness in my mother's existence. She had a tremendous amount of energy, plus a keen intelligence, and yet she had no completely satisfactory outlet for what she had to contribute.

She offered to help out in the tavern. My father rejected the suggestion adamantly.

What are you gonna do, serve the drinks? Work behind the bar?

I could help out in the kitchen. It must be a mess.

A NOT-SO-NICE JEWISH BOY FACES WORLD WAR II

The kitchen is fine. You don't have enough to do at home?

Mother hadn't had much schooling. She hadn't been exposed to much culture, yet she had these vague dreams that had never been fulfilled. She would have loved to go out dancing, for one thing. My father never took her dancing. As a matter of fact he didn't dance. Besides which he spent most of his life in the bar, and was rarely available for any sort of social life. Mother was a romantic. (A Jewish Madame Bovary, perhaps?) Yet, oddly enough, despite her longing for a social life, she would get upset if you spoke about taking a voyage of any sort, a pleasure cruise for example or, God forbid, take a plane.

Let's talk about something pleasant.

Mother, they're going on a vacation. What could be more pleasant? More people are killed in automobiles...

All right. That's enough.

It's a little scary at first...

I said, that's enough!

If you tried it once. A plane trip is quick and it's over with before you know it. You step off the plane refreshed and ready to enjoy yourself.

You wanna make me sick?

She also had this phobia about cemeteries. She would go to a funeral parlor but absolutely refuse to set foot in a cemetery. I never found out why.

I was deeply troubled by the fact that my mother was missing out on so much, that she made no use of her fine mind. She was a handsome woman, with an excellent figure. She had an innate regal quality. She could be absolutely charming and gracious when she wanted to be, and all of this was going to waste, slaving in the kitchen, dealing day after

MY MOTHER, MY FATHER & ME

day with household chores, washing and ironing and cleaning and shopping.

I tried to encourage her to read, to take an interest in the world outside the house. I wanted her to share my love of literature just as my sister, Rose, did.

You know, Mother, some day we're gonna be gone. Rose and I are not gonna live here forever. What are you gonna do then? You should have some outside interests. Read books. Listen to music.
You're right. I know. You're right.
Why don't you take some courses?
Like what?
I don't know. Cooking. Sewing.
I need courses in cooking and sewing?
Literature.
You have to be educated for those things.
Mother, that's why you take courses, to get an education.
You have to have a head for those things.
So you're gonna sit home and feel sorry for yourself. You're an intelligent woman. You can do anything you want to.
I know you mean well.

She was charity minded though. There was always a "pishka" in the house, a little tin box into which she dropped spare change to be donated to the Jewish National Fund. Sometimes a rabbi would come by and Mother would always make a donation.

******

And then there was my father.

At about the age of seven or eight I watched my father

A NOT-SO-NICE JEWISH BOY FACES WORLD WAR II

shave one morning. I sat on the closed commode and observed with interest this daily ritual. I found it absolutely fascinating. Why I should have been reminded of a box of chocolates I'm not quite sure, but oddly enough that's what came to mind as I watched him lather his face, and then remove the lather with this metal contraption, and then shake it in the water in the basin. I felt close to my father for that one brief moment...while I watched him shave.

I empathized with my mother and, for many years, I harbored a secret resentment against Daddy. I blamed him for Mother's unhappiness. Besides which, Daddy didn't seem to take any interest in me whatsoever. He didn't seem to care what I did, what I thought, what I felt. But it wasn't only me. My sister and, I found out later, my brother, Marty, concurred.

Of course, he was never really there to take an interest. He was always in "the place." In addition to that, when he took his afternoon nap on the old sofa in the dining room his feet smelled. And his table manners were atrocious. I was embarrassed as I watched him hunched over the table stuffing food into his mouth. And why did he eat so much meat, I wondered. It couldn't have been very healthy.

And sometimes he acted rather strangely; an odd comment, or his balance didn't seem to be that steady, and one day I actually smelled alcohol on his breath. Well, well, well. Daddy drinks, I said to myself. Well, at least, there's something interesting about him. Though it never did seem to incapacitate him in any way, it did upset my mother.

I especially remember there was one night when he never came home. My mother was panic stricken. He finally did show up in the morning. Apparently he was so drunk that he was unable to drive. He had parked the car somewhere and fell asleep, and that's where he spent the night.

If the customer offers me a drink, what can I say?

MY MOTHER, MY FATHER & ME

And, of course, Daddy was always ready to offer guests a drink, *if I can find where she hid the Scotch.*

Growing up I knew so little about the man, what he thought, how he felt. I felt shy about trying to sit down and having a talk with him, and besides there was no real opportunity since he was hardly ever home. He was interested in baseball, I knew that, and he'd fought in World War I and, through my mother, I did learn a little something about what he went through in Poland.

Another thing that really bothered me about him was that he was really sort of a wimp. He would actually come to my mother and ask her which shirt to wear, which tie, and then, to top it all off, where he could find the shirt and the tie. Witnessing this childish request from a grown man, I was humiliated for him.

The shirts in the dresser. The white one. I just washed it. And change your pants. How long have you been wearing them?

All right, I'll change my pants.

I will say, however, there was one time he did redeem himself, and I was actually proud of him. As a matter of fact he was a real, true life hero. There was an article in the local paper to attest to my father's bravery.

He'd just withdrawn $1,200 from the bank. He was parking his car in front of the tavern. A man approached him with a pistol.

This is a stickup. Give me the dough, the man said.

Instead of handing over the money my father punched the man in the nose. The man pulled the trigger twice, luckily without any results. The thief then jumped into a nearby car and fled the scene. He was later apprehended. My father identified him and the man was convicted. To make this feat

A NOT-SO-NICE JEWISH BOY FACES WORLD WAR II

all the more glorious, the man turned out to be a professional boxer.

A policeman on the force was a good friend of my father and saw to it that he wasn't harassed. As a matter of fact, Daddy was very popular with his customers, with good reason too. He was a pretty soft touch.

I very rarely set foot in the bar. I'm pretty sure my mother had something to do with that. I do think my father would have welcomed my presence, and that of my brother. The first time I did visit Fifty Bar I saw a different person, a charming, gracious man who smiled, was warm and outgoing and, in addition to that, he actually had a roguish sense of humor. Amazingly enough, he seemed to have a completely different personality at his place of business. Now, why couldn't he be like that at home?

******

The relationship between these two guardians of my fate, at least the part of the relationship that I was privy to, was not exactly an inspiring one. Maybe it was the Depression, since that was the period in which I grew up, but so many of the exchanges between my parents seemed to be about money.

You know what day it is? my mother would ask.
What?
It's the first of the month.
Silence.
Where's the money for the rent?
All right, all right.
What does that mean, "all right"?
Tomorrow.
That's what you said yesterday. I don't like to owe

MY MOTHER, MY FATHER & ME

money. You know that.
I said 'all right.'
What's that money you've got in your pocket?
What money?
You know what money.
You went into my pockets? That money's for the store. I have expenses there, too.
I can't take it anymore.
And then there were tears.
I found out later that my father was somehow involved in the "numbers" game.

My mother was always scrimping and stretching her household allowance to cover all the necessities. Food, however, was never scanted. There was always enough, and it was always of good quality.

Aunt Tillie would sometimes borrow money from my father, surreptitiously, but Mother would always find out, and it made her absolutely furious. According to my mother, Aunt Tillie and Uncle Morris made much more money than my father did, and *they lived*, while she had to sew and darn and make do on pennies. He was too generous to his customers. He cared more about them than he did his own family. Was it necessary to spend day and night in the "place"? He had a partner, didn't he? And another thing, the partner was always taking advantage of him. He was more concerned about what other people thought, and to hell with his family.

He had to put up this big front when it came to presents, wedding and "bar-mitzvahs."

Do we have to give that much?, my mother asked.
It's a first cousin. How would it look?
I haven't bought a dress in over a year.
So buy a dress.
With what? On what you give me?

A NOT-SO-NICE JEWISH BOY FACES WORLD WAR II

Here! And he handed her some bills.
With that I can buy the sleeve.
You have money for everyone else, except for your own family. A colored nun came into the "place" and you gave her two dollars. (How my mother found out about the nun was a complete mystery.) *Is that colored nun gonna to take care of you when you can't work anymore? Other men make good money in the saloon business.*
Other men water their drinks.
You have to be everybody's friend?
All right, all right.

There was one thing positive that my mother did have to say about this man she was chained to, and she would say it with pride. *He never looked at another woman.*

I remember asking my mother if she loved my father. I don't recall her exact words, but the answer, as I recall, was rather noncommittal. But then she did defy her stepfather to marry him. There must have been love of a sort to begin with; and I did have the feeling that my father loved my mother.

And I wondered, what love really was. It couldn't be just sex, though I assumed my parents did have sex. And if there was no money did love fly out the window? Of course, money was important. It was a necessity. But it shouldn't really dominate one's life, should it?

My parents were married, and they stuck it out. Was it because of "the children"? Was it fear of the unknown? Was it a sense of duty? Was it devotion? Or was it that a commitment was made, and that was it?

**HYMIE BEIM
THE SALOON
KEEPER**

Cabbie faces quiz on holdup attempt

Frank Metzker, 35-year-old cab driver and ex-prize fighter, is going to get visitors today—the Newark police. Detectives are scheduled to visit Metzker in his current living quarters, a New York jail cell, and question him concerning an attempted $1,200 holdup of a Newark tavern owner last Friday.

Metzker is accused of trying to hold up Herman Bein, 50, of 71 Walcott ter., operator of a tavern at 50 Hermon st., after Bein left an Ironbound bank Friday. The cab driver, who fought professionally under the name of Kid Metz, came off second best, though, when Bein, instead of turning over his $1,200, punched him in the nose.

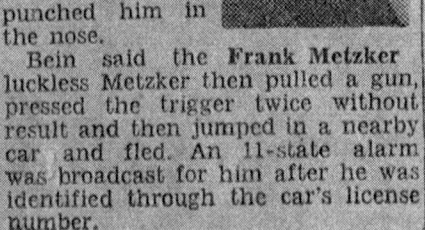

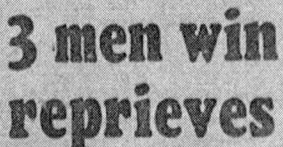

Frank Metzker

Bein said the luckless Metzker then pulled a gun, pressed the trigger twice without result and then jumped in a nearby car and fled. An 11-state alarm was broadcast for him after he was identified through the car's license number.

3 men win reprieves

Clarence Smith, Robert Jellison and Frederick Bunk, slated to die in the electric chair at State Prison this week for the murder of a Newark tavern patron last summer, won automatic reprieves yesterday because their appeals from the death sentence are still pending in State Supreme Court.

No trial date has been set for Thomas "Rocky" Yannuzzi, Newark ex-fighter, also charged with participating in the slaying. Yannuzzi, a fugitive for more than seven months, was picked up in Texas after Smith, Jellison and Bun had been found guilty by a jury of killing Peter Newcomb during an attempted holdup of the Penn Tavern last Aug. 8.

No date has been set either for the appeal hearing of the three convicted men. Yannuzzi has pleaded innocent.

CHAPTER TWENTY FOUR

I DEVELOP A SOCIAL CONSCIENCE

In the nineteen thirties my neighborhood in Newark was predominantly Jewish. There was but one Negro boy in my class at the Hawthorne Avenue Grammar School. This boy visited me in my house once or twice but, for some reason or other, we never became fast friends, though he certainly seemed nice enough and, to my amazement he behaved just like everyone else. Didn't he know that, after a certain age, he would not be welcome in the homes of most of his classmates? My God, he might marry someone's sister! Didn't he know what life had in store for him, the rotten hand he'd been dealt just by being born dark-skinned?

Though I lost track of my black classmate, I often wondered what became of him. When I passed a Negro on the street I tried to look into his or her eyes. I tried to detect some sort of identity, some sort of personality, but there didn't seem to be any vitality there. These people seemed to be walking zombies, dead men without life or hope. When I spoke to my mother of the intolerable lot of the Negro she tried to change the subject. Of course, it was unfair, but what was the use of talking about it?

I wondered what would happen if, one day, the Negroes would suddenly wake up to their humiliating situation. Wasn't there a revolt of the slaves during the history of the Roman Empire? And indeed, I often thought that America bore a strong resemblance to the Roman Empire.

My mother never spoke about the persecution of the Jews in Poland, but I knew she was bitter about it. I tried to challenge what I considered her prejudice against the gentiles.

Doesn't the Jewish religion teach us to love our fellow man?

What do you know? Have you been out in the world?

A NOT-SO-NICE JEWISH BOY FACES WORLD WAR II

They're people just like us, even if they aren't Jewish.
And she would say again, *The Jews killed Christ, and they will never forgive us.*

Since we lived in a Jewish community I, personally, was never aware of being discriminated against. I did know that Jews were sometimes treated unfairly. My cousin Irving, Aunt Tillie's older son, had applied to medical school but had to wait a year to be admitted because the Jewish quota had been filled for that year. I was incensed that there should be a quota for Jews. Why? Shouldn't a person be judged on his merits rather than his ethnicity?

******

In regard to this business of prejudice, it seemed to me that when jobs are scarce and people are hungry and frightened, there's got to be someone to blame. There's got to be a scapegoat. Perhaps if there were no poverty there would be no lynchings, there would be no pogroms. But down through the ages poverty has always been with us. There must be some sort of solution. Man is an intelligent animal. Is it merely a matter of economics?

I sometimes saw derelicts in the streets downtown, on the outskirts of the main shopping area, and I wondered how they lost their way, and what drove them to give up hope. Why did some men live in mansions, surrounded by comfort and luxury while others had nothing? Why, for example, was Mr. Schwartz so successful and my father, who worked so hard, so poor? Was every man really born equal?

When I heard it rumored that my Economics teacher was a Communist I was prompted to look up the word Communism. I was surprised to find that Communism, real Communism, did not exist anywhere in the world. It was an

I DEVELOP A SOCIAL CONSCIENCE

ideal, something on paper, an economic and social system that was only feasible in a small community. What they had in Russia was a form of Socialism.

And even here in America we had Socialism, to some extent. Weren't there certain public services that were run by the government? So what was all that fuss about?

As far as Capitalism was concerned, and free enterprise, what I found objectionable was all the waste. Did we really need all those different kinds of cars, and all those different kinds of toothpastes and all those various brands of cereals and soups and so on and so on? And weren't all those ads in the newspapers and magazines and on the radio...those interminable commercials, some of them singing no less...wasn't all of that a waste of time and money and effort?!

But when I tried to solve the problems of the world, when I tried to wrestle with economic ills and political theories, I gave myself a headache. I knew nothing about Economics or Politics, and I was not about to try to figure it all out. I was going to be a writer and that would certainly be a full time job.

******

But could I dismiss so cavalierly the world of politics and governments? There were those awful rumors, for example, of camps in Germany where Jews were sent never to reappear. And there was the war in Europe. Most people seemed to think that eventually America would be caught up in it. Who knows? I might one day become involved in that war.

The very thought of men setting out to butcher one another filled me with a cold fury. I mean one man killing another was bad enough, but how could entire nations

A NOT-SO-NICE JEWISH BOY FACES WORLD WAR II

deliberately set out to destroy one another? What madness! This war was, at bottom, from what I could gather, a result of greed and subterfuge, a conflict of economic and political agendas, one pitted surreptitiously against the other. If everyone were secure financially wouldn't there be peace in the world? Money again! Was that the answer to everything?

It seemed to me that the only solution for the human race was to have faith in one another, to trust one another. The difficulty lay not in politics, not in economy but in human nature. Any system of government, any system of economy could be made to work if people were honorable. No system, no matter how perfect, could work as long as people were greedy.

Newspapers never printed the truth, the whole truth. How could they? No one actually knew what went on behind closed doors. And certainly people in public life never told the truth, because no one was perfect, and who was willing to admit their faults, to admit their mistakes publicly? Politicians would say anything to get elected. Who knows what they really thought, what they really believed? And did these ambitious men really have ideals that they were dedicated to, and were willing to fight for? In order to get elected, in order to get anything done didn't one have to compromise? I did have tremendous respect for Franklin Delano Roosevelt whom I thought was personable and intelligent and did his best for the country, until I learned that the president, though he was aware of what was happening to the Jews under the Nazis, did nothing. Even when a boatful of Jewish refugees sought asylum in America, he stood by, while the boat was turned away, and the passengers were sent back to die.

I came to realize, early on, that I was a born skeptic. I accepted everything that I read and heard with a grain of salt.

I DEVELOP A SOCIAL CONSCIENCE

In facing the future, I developed a two part philosophy; hope for the best and be prepared for the worst.

And, as far as my social conscience was concerned, I did have the good grace to feel guilty that I did nothing to improve the world, just as I felt guilty about the fact that I ate my fellow creatures when, if I had any real integrity, I would be a vegetarian.

CHAPTER TWENTY FIVE

I AM DEEPLY HUMILIATED

The first radio we had, the first radio I remember at any rate, was a console model...a lot of wood containing a little radio. We could only get a few stations and there was a lot of static. One day, my father brought home a small portable radio which was placed on top of the sewing machine next to the kitchen table. This one had great reception and was in constant use.

My father's prime interest was the news, and many memorable moments were heard over this table model...the Duke of Windsor's abdication, Neville Chamberlain's announcement of the Munich pact with Hitler, Franklin Delano Roosevelt's fireside chats, the progress of the European War. It was a remarkable experience to hear history being made on the spot, to be in direct contact with the entire world as one sat around the kitchen table.

But current events were only one small facet of that magic box. There were educational programs like "Information, Please" and "The Quiz Kids" and "The March Of Time." There were the crime shows like "Gangbusters" and the hour dramatic programs like "The First Nighter" and "Lux Hollywood Playhouse" hosted by the great movie director, Cecil B. DeMille himself. The Playhouse presented hour long versions of popular movies with major movie stars. And then there was "The Witches Tale" which began with the creaking of a rusty door and the cackle of a witch, and went on to tell hair raising stories of the supernatural.

Saturday morning there was "Let's Pretend" and "The Singing Lady," two programs that dramatized fairy tales. And, of course, there were the stalwart dramatic serials like "Jack Armstrong, The All American Boy" and "Buck Rogers," hero of the twenty fifth century, and the romantic sagas like "Myrt

I AM DEEPLY HUMILIATED

And Marge" and "Mr. Keen, Tracer Of Lost Persons" and "Helen Trent" and spunky "Little Orphan Annie."
Who's that little chatterbox,
The one with all the curly locks?
Cute little she,
It's little Orphan Annie.

And "Amos And Andy" representing the Negro community and "The Goldbergs" (*Yoohoo, Mrs. Goldberg!*, neighbors call out through their windows and gossip) representing the Jewish community. There was the rustics, "Lum And Abner," and the comedians like Eddie Cantor who joked about his wife, Ida, and sang songs, and Fred Allen, wry and witty, accompanied by the eccentric characters in "Allen's Alley," and George Burns with Gracie Allen, who was delightfully addled, and the ventriloquist, Edgar Bergen with his wise-cracking dummy, Charlie McCarthy, and Jack Benny who was so stingy that when someone stuck a gun in his back and said, *Your money or your life!*, he took this long pause and finally said...*I'm thinking, I'm thinking!*, and everyone winced as Jack scratched out "Love In Bloom" on the violin. (The truth of the matter was, he could actually play quite well.) And there was Mildred Bailey who sang songs while sitting in her rocking chair, and Arthur Tracy, The Street Singer who sang romantic ballads.

Of course, those radio serials were all a lot of nonsense and one didn't take them seriously, but they did sort of get to you after a while. Even my mother became addicted to the saga of "Myrt And Marge" and "Mr. Keen, Tracer Of Lost Persons". And all this was free, except for the fact that one had to put up with those interminable commercials, singing ones at that.

On Saturday afternoon there was the broadcast of the opera direct from the Metropolitan Opera House, if one cared

A NOT-SO-NICE JEWISH BOY FACES WORLD WAR II

to sit through it all. Some of it was laughable, the screeching soprano and the melodramatic bass. You couldn't make out one word, and even if you could it was a foreign word. But every now and then there were these glorious arias, and it didn't matter what the words were because the music was so beautiful; and there were the baseball games...if you were into that sort of thing. Uncle Morris (Aunt Tillie's Uncle Morris) and my cousin Herb were great baseball fans, as was my father.

The radio became so pervasive that sometimes it interfered with one's daily chores. There was one evening when I had to study for a test to be given the following morning. Several friends were at the house and they wouldn't leave until the end of "The Witches Tale" and its hair-raising story of the supernatural. The show came on rather late, and I didn't get much studying done that night. I barely passed the test the next morning.

But the miracle of radio never ceased to amaze me. How did they do it? The human mind, what a wonder!

******

The busy week ended on Friday evening, when my mother lit the Sabbath candles, placed a cloth over her head, covered her eyes with her hands, said the "brucha" (the blessing), and then waved her hands over the lighted candles. That was when the magic of the week-end began. I usually got together with several of my friends on Friday evening, either at my house or at Harold's.

The Schwartz's dining room was rather elegant and the living room, with its deep Persian rug was absolutely luxurious, but the sun parlor was informally furnished, and there one could relax. That's where they kept the piano. And

I AM DEEPLY HUMILIATED

Harold had a phonograph there, and we would sometimes listen to popular music like Artie Shaw's swinging rendition of "Frenesi" with its magical clarinet solos, and Benny Goodman's wild, rhythmic "Sing, Sing, Sing" and the liquid, melting "I'll Never Smile Again" sung by Frank Sinatra and "Amapola" and "Green Eyes", sung by Helen O'Connell and Ray Eberle. Ray Eberle would sing the song first as a romantic ballad and then Helen O'Connell follow it up with a jazzed up version.

The music called up visions of success and romance, especially in the elegant surroundings of the Schwartz home. Even the lawn and the trees viewed from the sun parlor seemed particularly lush.

We taught each other to dance. Irving was an excellent jitterbug, and I became quite proficient myself, except that I developed the habit of flinging my partner out and returning with rather frightening force, my right hand extended like a spear. My friends kidded me about it, and I startled the neighborhood girls I danced with, but I was a good jitterbug, and had an excellent sense of rhythm.

In Harold's cellar there was a ping pong table. Ping pong was popular at this time. I was not the greatest ping pong player, but there were some triumphant moments when I became inspired and rode a winning streak. It occurred to me that skill in sports demanded a certain kind of concentration which, apparently, I was not able to maintain. There was also Monopoly and checkers and chess, which Harold taught me to play, and I found especially challenging.

Occasionally there were mischievous phone calls to local merchants. *Have you got Prince Albert in a can?* (Prince Albert was a popular tobacco.)

Why, yes... came the answer.
Well, let him out.

A NOT-SO-NICE JEWISH BOY FACES WORLD WAR II

And then we hung up.

Once the group decided to taunt one of the boys at school who was a bit of a sissy. I was against the idea. However I did tag along. I stayed in the background, feeling very uneasy. My friends stood under the boy's window and shouted out.

Oh, Mary! Yoohoo! Mary!
Oh, Nancy!
Come on out, dear.

The boy's sister, a classmate of mine, came out of the house. She sighted me, despite the fact that I tried to be invisible. She walked right up to me.

You're a nice boy, Norman. Please ask your friends to leave my brother alone.

I blushed and nodded, and we all slunk off shamefacedly.

Sometimes we'd take long adventurous walks. A walk to Weequahic Park, for example, which was quite a distance, was considered a real trek.

The city was magical at night, with lights shining in the homes, and the air smelling crisp and fresh in the Autumn, balmy and full of promise in the Spring. The avenue facing the park was lined with large, rather imposing apartment buildings, which seemed to me rather elegant and full of successful people. There was a railroad track nearby, and a hot dog stand on the side of one of the roads leading into the park. If I had some extra money I would join with some of the others to treat myself to a hot dog there with mustard and sauerkraut. (They were probably not kosher, but then my mother didn't have to know everything.) There was a large lake in the park and all sorts of fascinating terrain to explore about the lake, all sorts of hills and valleys.

One evening, I was in junior high at the time, we

I AM DEEPLY HUMILIATED

returned from the park rather late. As we approached my house a front window flew open. My mother stuck her head out and proceeded to scream hysterically.

Where have you been? Why are you coming home so late? Do you know what time it is? And then she turned to some of my friends. *Why did you keep him out so late?* And then back to me. *You know I worry about you. You wanna kill me?* And then she slammed the window shut.

My friends departed silently.

I entered the house, seething with anger. Here I was, almost a high school student, and I was being treated like a child. An argument ensued.

How could you insult me like that in front of my friends?, I said. *I'll never forgive you.*

You'll never forgive me? What are you doing out so late? You know I'm nervous. I was worried to death about you. I thought something happened to you.

I'm not a child anymore. Embarrassing me in front of my friends like that.

Some friends, to keep you out so late.

We went to bed furious with one another. I remembered the incident as one of the most humiliating experiences I had ever endured. I wouldn't have minded it so much, but there were girls present. It was about this time that I strengthened my resolve that, if I did decide to go to college, it would certainly be one far away from home.

CHAPTER TWENTY SIX

TODAY I AM A MAN?

Somehow or other I managed to skip a grade in grammar school. I liked to think it was because of my great intelligence. Actually the school was over-crowded and, since we were scheduled to be graduated in the middle of the school year instead of in June, I suspected they were just trying to get rid of us.

We all lined up for the class picture. And there we were, rows of blank little faces staring into the camera. There I was, standing in the second row gazing dreamily into the distance. I wasn't really that pretty, was I? What was I thinking about? I looked like a girl!!

Along with my diploma I received a testimonial for good grades, my third as a matter of fact, and my grammar school days were over.

No longer would I stroll those three blocks to Hawthorne Avenue Grammar School, half asleep, half awake. No longer would I pass the candy store where I used to gaze at the various delectables clutching a penny or two in my hot little hand, trying to choose between the bubble gum with the trading cards enclosed, the fruit jellies, the chocolate kisses, the nut bars, the black and red licorice sticks and other delights too numerous to take in all at once. I stored in my mind the smell of the damp wood, and the sight of the newspapers on the stand outside, and the six family yellow brick house next door with its garden that contained a pool in which, one day, there was actually a real live turtle, and then the ice house where I would pick up a block of ice and wheel it home in a wagon, and next to the ice house the large wire-enclosed school playground which had held such terrors for me.

The large ugly school was no longer a part of my life.

TODAY I AM A MAN?

The teachers, the recess periods, and all those little crises that had seemed so overwhelming at the time, were over and done with. "This too shall pass"...like the fight I had with my mother to finally shed my knickers, and be able to put on a pair of long trousers.

While all my friends were scheduled to attend Weequahic High School, shiny and new and at a reasonable distance from my home, I was being banished for one year to Madison Junior High on the far side of town, and I mean far. It boggled the mind. Apparently my house was on the wrong side of the street, and I was in the wrong district. It took me almost an hour (well, close to forty five minutes) to walk to Madison Junior High, and I was most uncomfortable at this dreary school.

The only compensation for that interminable trek was that it took me through tree-lined streets I'd never seen before, and there were all these impressive rich-looking homes fronted by well kept lawns.

Though the school itself and its immediate surroundings were depressing, I did have a locker of my own, and I did get to eat lunch away from home for the very first time. So, in spite of it all, I had to admit my horizons were broadening. As a matter of fact, I was now allowed to attend a second movie house, farther away from home.

The Roosevelt Theatre on Clinton Avenue was larger and more elegant and, in addition to receiving the movies earlier than the Hawthorne Avenue Theatre, it wasn't as crowded. It was at this theatre that I saw that epoch making film, "Algiers", with the romantic Charles Boyer and the breathtakingly beautiful Hedy Lamarr. Gloria, my zaftig friend, persuaded me to go there with her on a week day afternoon, which, in itself, was rather daring.

I had some puzzling dreams at this time. Several

A NOT-SO-NICE JEWISH BOY FACES WORLD WAR II

involved the Roosevelt Theatre...either getting lost in its cavernous interior, or not being allowed to enter or waiting for someone who never showed up, and coming in after the movie had started, which was an unforgivable sin.

There was one other dream that was quite persistent. The old Chevy would start off on a trip with my family inside, and I was left behind. I would run frantically after the speeding car. I finally was able to catch hold of a bar which protruded from the back of the car. I clung to this bar as the car sped along, my feet flying in the air behind me...and that was the end of the dream. I was sure this dream had some significance but, for the life of me, I couldn't figure out what.

When referring to Madison Junior High to my friends, I would joke good-naturedly about being sent to Siberia. And that's what if felt like.

******

The year, however, passed quickly and, before I knew it, my exile was over. I was scheduled to enter the brand new high school...and suddenly I became apprehensive. My studies would be more difficult but, more important than that, one began to date girls in high school, and do all those suave, sophisticated things.

You had to learn how to treat a lady. One opened the door for them, I knew that. One took off one's hat in a lady's presence, but then I never wore a hat. One walked on the outside when strolling down the street and, of course, there was the business of paying the bill and leaving a tip when you went out on a date. But I didn't have any money, to speak of, that is. My allowance was a pittance. I couldn't afford a date, and who knew when I'd be able to?

A child's life may have been difficult, but a teenagers

TODAY I AM A MAN?

fate was even worse. We're given all these desires, all these urges and how was one to satisfy them? And this business of sex. I was certainly capable of it. There was no doubt about that! But would I have the temerity to pursue it? How did one embrace a girl or kiss her or feel her breasts, and make it all seem natural? It was all so awkward and so...literally...beastly. Did one really do those animal things with those sweet, delicate creatures? I couldn't imagine making physical love to Hazel, for example. She was so refined and so intelligent. I was sure she'd be repulsed by the very idea. There were girls I could imagine having sex with, but they were certainly not the kind of girls one would want to spend any time with.

Weequahic High School was a large, impressive building. Just walking up the entrance way and looking up at the modern stone front, with its doors of steel and glass made one feel proud. Everyone seemed to take pride in this brand new school, everything was so bright and shiny. As a matter of fact it was so new that the building and the grounds were still in the process of being completed. The principal of the school, Mr. Max Herzberg, was rather illustrious. He'd edited several books and written a number of articles. He looked very dapper and very important.

******

There were a number of clubs I would like to have joined, like the debating club or the French club or the dramatic club, but I had no time. After class there'd been piano practice and homework and Hebrew school, with extra study now in preparation for my bar-mitzvah. I had to learn to chant in Hebrew my "haftorah," a section of the Bible scheduled to be read on the day of the ceremony. There were these little figures under the Arabic lettering that represented

A NOT-SO-NICE JEWISH BOY FACES WORLD WAR II

different grace notes which gave you the tune. This was tricky, to say the least, especially when you didn't even understand what you were chanting.

Bar-mitzvahs, as a rule, took place on Saturday morning, and were usually witnessed by a large congregation. The ceremony was followed by a respectable repast of cakes and wine and schnapps. This was during The Great Depression, and bar-mitzvahs were not the elaborate affairs they are today.

My bar-mitzvah turned out to be even more anti-climactic, if that were possible, than my dismal grammar school graduation, which was more like a dismissal than an important event. For that ignominious event we marched onto the stage, one by one, were handed a diploma in front of a handful of attendees, and that was it. My landmark Jewish ceremony took place not on the Sabbath, mind you, but on a pedestrian Thursday morning.

Mother took to her bed. She was losing her baby. My father, the only family member present at this momentous (?) occasion, escorted me to the synagogue. I was called to the altar and went through my "haftorah," intoning it rather shakily, and then I gave my speech, first in Yiddish.

Liebe elteren und verte fersalmelte...

I repeated the speech in English.

Dear family and worthy assembly...

Afterwards there was some schnapps and a sponge cake which my mother had baked.

This was one of those rare occasions when I did feel close to my father, walking surreptitiously down to the synagogue, as if we were involved in some sort of secret conspiracy, and strolling home with him afterwards. For the first time I felt that Daddy actually took some pride in me.

Unfortunately my bar-mitzvah was not the end of my

TODAY I AM A MAN?

religious enslavement. Unlike most boys, who stopped going to Hebrew school after their bar-mitzvah, I was to continue my Jewish indoctrination. In addition to that, now that I was a man, it involved "laying t'fillin."

Every morning, there was the tedious routine of donning the phylacteries and reciting the so-called prayers. The phylacteries were contained in this beautifully embroidered velvet bag, and had been sent to me from Poland by my grandparents.

Even though I'd never met them, and knew very little about them, I would often receive little gifts from my grandparents. These gifts were accompanied with their well wishes, written in Yiddish. I could read Yiddish with some difficulty, I could still speak it haltingly, and understand it when spoken, but writing extensively in Yiddish with its Arabic lettering was beyond me, so I responded to these thoughtful gifts with my thanks in English.

One rather charming gift which I still possess is a small gold-plated, wrought iron stand, formed in the shape of my initials with little hooks to hold an old fashioned wooden pen, with a little bird carved at the end of it, and a letter opener with a large carved bird as its wooden handle. For my bar-mitzvah they had sent me an ornate prayer book, a beautifully embroidered skull cap, a prayer shawl and those phylacteries.

The laying of the "t'vilin" was an extremely complicated affair. There were these two black leather contraptions, each consisting of two long straps attached to a small lacquered cardboard box which contained holy scripture. I placed one box on my forehead with the straps dangling down, reciting a prayer in the process. I placed the second box on the biceps of my left arm, with the straps bound around my left arm, hand and finger, and I intoned the meaningless prayers as fast as I could, skipping through as many sections as I could get away with, and getting through this ridiculous farce as quickly as I possibly could.

I kept complaining to my mother about this pointless ritual, but she was adamant. It was obvious that my case was hopeless, for the nonce, so I retreated and bided my time. This cannot go on forever, I reasoned.

I absolutely refused, however, to continue with Hebrew School. It was just too much...school and homework and piano. And besides, I pointed out, all the other kids stopped going to Hebrew School after their bar-mitzvah. Mother seemed to be immovable at first, but I could feel her weakening. I persisted. She finally, and very reluctantly, gave in. It took another full year, however, till I was able to lay aside the "t'vilin." I was now finally able to visualize the land of the free in the not too distant future.

CHAPTER TWENTY SEVEN

MY SHINING HOUR

A friend of mine called and told me that a band was looking for a pianist. This was before I'd given up my dreams of Carnegie Hall.
Have you got a phone number?, I asked.
He gave me a phone number.
My heart in my mouth I dialed the number.
I understand you're looking for a pianist, I said.
Right. Great. Can you read music?
Oh, yes. (They didn't ask me how well.)
Fine! Can you be here tomorrow evening at six?
Yeah. Sure.
I was given the address, and I hung up. I didn't know if it was an audition or a rehearsal or what. Actually, I had the feeling that the job was mine. They seemed to need someone pretty badly.

Now I was familiar with the popular songs of the day, and I was able to bang out a few of them, a very few, and rather sloppily at that. There was a piano in the back room of my father's tavern and in my rare visits there I had entertained some of the customers with my renditions of "Bei Mir Bist Du Schoen," a current favorite, which I had learned from the sheet music, and "The Isle Of Capri" and one or two others which I had picked out by ear. As a matter of fact the entire family spent one New Years Eve at the tavern, and that evening I was prevailed upon to sit down at the piano and play for all the guests. People gathered around, and I pounded through my rather limited repertoire. I was roundly applauded for what, I had to admit, was a rather ragged performance. I was well aware that the applause was for the boss's son.

Pop songs were not my strong point. I knew that and

A NOT-SO-NICE JEWISH BOY FACES WORLD WAR II

why, I wondered, had I been foolish enough to take on this...this...audition?...or whatever it was.

I began to dread the ordeal. By the time I arrived at the address I was given, I was a nervous wreck. I stood hesitantly, in front of the apartment door trying to steel myself for the upcoming fiasco. Finally I summoned up enough courage. I knocked on the door. The door was opened. I was invited in and introduced to the members of the band, which consisted of a saxophone, a drum, a clarinet and, of course, a piano. In sort of a daze, I shook hands all around. The faces were all a blur. If I had met them on the street the next day, I wouldn't have recognized one of them.

I sat down at the piano, perspiring profusely. I looked at the music placed in front of me.

That didn't look too difficult.

Then again it didn't look that easy.

Well, I might as well get it over with.

I took a deep breath. My hands, somehow or other, found their way to the keyboard. I proceeded to play, if one can call it that. I sweated clumsily through the first number, hitting quite a few wrong notes...and sounding generally...inept.

There was an embarrassed silence. A second number was placed in front of me. I started to fumble through it then stopped. It was obvious to all and sundry that this was a big mistake.

If I had the music to work on...
Right, right.

They thanked me politely, and I couldn't get out of the room fast enough. I heaved a great sigh of relief as I closed the door behind me.

I didn't expect to be invited back and, of course, I was not. I tried to erase the nightmare from my mind. And, that

MY SHINING HOUR

I'm afraid, was the end of my career as a piano player with a band. But what did it matter? I was going to support myself as a journalist, while I wrote the great American novel, and I soon had the opportunity to test my journalistic skills.

******

Toward the end of my junior year in high school I took a job as an usher at a downtown movie theatre, the RKO Proctors. Actually I was hired as a standby. I would report for work and they used me only if one of the regulars didn't show up. My mother was furious, because I would often take the bus ride downtown, sit around the locker room for an hour or two, and then take the bus back home, not having earned a single penny, and having spent precious carfare for nothing.

But I didn't care. I was working in a movie theatre! And there were a number of evenings when I did actually work, wearing a rather snazzy blue uniform with gold buttons, which gave me a sense of importance. From my post on the balcony, I saw "The Mark Of Zorro" with Tyrone Power and Linda Darnell over and over and over again. I could recite some of the scenes verbatim. It was not the best movie ever made but it was fun, and movies were, after all...MOVIES.

"No, No Nanette" was the next film scheduled to play at the Proctors Theatre. It starred Anna Neagle, a beautiful blonde British movie and stage star who appeared in musicals and dramas as well. I saw coming attractions of her dancing and singing and I was enchanted. When I learned that she was to make a personal appearance in connection with the film I decided that here was my opportunity. I must overcome this ridiculous shyness. If I was to be a reporter, I must be able to approach the greats of the world with aplomb, even a star like Anna Neagle up there on the screen like a gigantic goddess.

A NOT SO-NICE JEWISH BOY FACES WORLD WAR II

When I came to the theatre that night my hands were ice, and my forehead was damp. I decided to come early. I sat in the locker room trying to decide exactly how to conduct this absolutely mind-bogglingg event. I should have a list of questions. That's it! I made a list of nine questions (that's all I could think of) which I wrote down in the little notebook I had brought along.

Now how was I going to meet the great lady? Maybe I ought to present myself in my usher's uniform? No, that wouldn't do at all. An usher interviewing a movie goddess?! I decided to present myself in my civilian clothes, since I had worn a nice jacket. Maybe I ought to be a reporter for the school newspaper. That was it! "The Calumet" was the school paper. As far as Miss Neagle was concerned, I was its representative (self appointed perhaps...but no one had to know that).

In sheer terror I found my way backstage. I hoped the man in charge of the ushers wasn't watching me. There were a number of people waiting to see Miss Neagle. A very dapper middle-aged man approached me. It turned out to be Herbert Wilcox, the star's husband and producer.

Yes, young man? What can I do for you?

I'm from Weequahic High School. I'm on the school paper, The Calumet...and I'd like to interview Miss Neagle...if that's possible.

Wait here.

He disappeared.

I sat down on a nearby metal folding chair and waited and waited and waited.

This was madness.

What was I doing here?

Should I go?

Should I stay?

MY SHINING HOUR

This iron chair is very uncomfortable.

Why not make a dash for it? The door's not too far away. That would solve everything, and no one would be the wiser...except for myself, of course.

Why was I perspiring so?

Too late. Mr. Wilcox was approaching.

Will you come with me, please?

Petrified, I rose and followed him. He ushered me into the dressing room and departed, closing the door behind me.

And there I was.

I was on!

And absolutely tongue-tied.

I was sure I looked an utter fool.

Won't you have a seat? Oh, that lovely, lyrical voice!

Gradually she came into focus. Yes, there she was! Anna Neagle herself! That screen goddess! She looked a little smaller. She was dressed in a black velvet suit with a black velvet hat which had tassels along the brim. Beneath a layer of paint there were these chiseled features, and there was the long blond hair. Was that dandruff on her shoulders or flecks of gold?

I looked about.

There was the chair in front of her.

I sat down.

Where was my notebook? I thought I had it in my hand. No, it was in my jacket pocket.

I quickly fished out the notebook. I flipped it open and hastily fired the first question.

Do you prefer the stage or the screen?

She answered very cordially. I don't remember what, but I did jot it down. I remember that.

Do you prefer musicals or plays? Which do you like better, comedies or drama? Do you find the United States

A NICE JEWISH BOY

much different from England? How long will you be in America? Do you plan to appear on the stage here?

I fired one question after another and wrote frantically as she spoke, keeping my face buried in my notebook. Barely giving her time to finish her sentence, I rushed through my nine questions, afraid to remain silent for one moment, afraid to look her in the eye, afraid that she might find out what a phony I was. Miss Neagle remained very gracious through the barrage. When I had run through my nine questions, she asked me if there was anything else I'd like to know.

No... Thank you.

I looked about for the door, eager to escape. There it was. I opened the door. Mr. Wilcox appeared from nowhere. He led me to the stage door and thanked me for coming.

I mumbled something incoherently. I didn't know what I was saying. I walked, or rather floated, out the stage door into the night air. I stood in the alleyway quaking and triumphant.

What a memorable moment!

What a victory!

I had passed the test.

There was nothing I couldn't do!

The next day, in an euphoric haze, I wrote up the interview. After class I marched proudly into the office of the school paper. I went up to the editor and held out the interview.

I interviewed Anna Neagle yesterday and I've written it up.

The editor took the paper from me with a puzzled look on his face. *Thank you,* he said.

I don't know if he believed me or not. Maybe he thought I was making it all up. I didn't care. I left the room triumphantly. I did it, and they can do what they like with it.

MY SHINING HOUR

I scanned the next edition of the paper. The interview wasn't there. I looked for it in the following edition. It wasn't there. The interview was never printed.

I was disappointed, of course, but I certainly wasn't going to beg them to print it. Besides the important thing was that I had done it. Nothing could take that away from me. In the moment of truth, I had come through.

I had what it takes!

And one day I would conquer the world!

CHAPTER TWENTY EIGHT

A TRIP T0 NEW YORK CITY

My heart skipped a beat when I saw this ad in the Newark Ledger. Ushers wanted for a series of summer concerts to be given at the baseball stadium just outside the city. The series was to feature great classical artists both instrumental and vocal. If interested one was to report to the Paramount Theatre on Market Street that Saturday morning between ten and two.

Here was an opportunity to hear great music...symphonies, concertos even operas (the arias that is) and get paid for it. On Saturday morning I took the 114 bus downtown to the Paramount Theatre. There was quite a crowd waiting and I got in line. Finally my turn came.

Have you ever ushered before?

Oh, yes.

Do you have a white shirt, white pants, and a black bow tie?

Yes! (Actually I had a white shirt, but I didn't have a pair of white pants or a black bow tie.)

Report here next Saturday at six o'clock, in uniform. You get paid one dollar for each concert. After everyone is seated take any empty seat available. Next.

I was hired!

The bow tie turned out to be no problem. My father had one in the dresser drawer. My mother, to my relief, made no objection to buying a pair of white pants. I might need a pair anyway. Nothing had been said about the color of the shoes. I kept my fingers crossed since mine were black.

Four thirty on Saturday I got into my uniform. I took the bus down to the Paramount Theatre. There was someone there checking us in. Nothing was said about my appearance. Apparently I passed inspection.

A TRIP TO NEW YORK CITY

There were buses in front of the theatre. We were herded onto them, and were driven to the stadium. There was much confusion when we arrived. I was finally assigned to the bleachers, which was quite a distance from the stage, but I couldn't complain. All that music, and there was that dollar besides.

I familiarized myself with the numbers on the seats and took my post. As the people drifted in, there were some occasional mixups, but I managed to carry out my duties quite efficiently. I actually enjoyed running up and down the stairs, guiding people to their seats. As a matter of fact I felt quite important executing my responsibilities so well.

When the concert was about to start I was able to find a seat closer to the stage. I was too keyed up to concentrate on the music, too full of the event, the crowd, the excitement, but it was pleasant sitting in the cool evening air, the breezes blowing across the vast open expanse, and there was that satisfaction of a job well done.

There were three concerts in all. After the initial excitement I was able to give myself over to the wonderful sounds emanating from the stage. There was Brahms Third Symphony, a Bach Concerto, the Tchaikovsky Violin Concerto, Beethoven's Fourth Symphony, Strauss Waltzes. My spirit left my body and floated along with the magnificent music, and all sorts of glorious dreams about the future opened up before me.

The most memorable evening of all was the one where Lily Pons, a famous operatic soprano who had even made some movies, appeared. When she sang her encores I rushed forward with the mob and stood right in front of the stage. I could look up at the great star. I was so close I could see the make-up and the little lines around her eyes, but oh she was

A NOT-SO-NICE JEWISH BOY FACES WORLD WAR II

beautiful and glamorous in that expensive looking pink evening gown.

The Bell Song from "Lakme" rang in my ears as I rode home on the bus in a daze. Maybe I ought to be a concert pianist after all. The thought was quickly dismissed.

******

However, it did occur to me that I really ought to improve myself culturally. I mean, here I was, a short distance from New York City, and I had never even seen a Broadway show. Sixteen years old and I hadn't seen any of those great stars on the stage that I'd read about in the Daily Mirror like Katharine Cornell and Helen Hayes and John Barrymore and Judith Anderson and Alfred Lunt and Lynn Fontanne. Why I hadn't even seen the inside of a Broadway theatre. I decided to save up enough money to buy a ticket to a Broadway show.

It took several months but I finally had enough to send away for two Saturday matinee tickets. My sister, Rose, was going to join me. The family was going to pay for her ticket.

Rose and I were soul mates. We shared the same interests, books and music. Her standards, like mine, were of the highest. Only perfection was acceptable. I was so proud of her, her intelligence, her sensitivity, her goodness, and she was the only one in the family who really understood me. She would come to me for advice, and I came to feel that her development was really my responsibility. I sometimes loved to tease her. She was quite chubby as a child, with a head full of wavy hair. But now, that she was growing up she was beginning to lose weight. As a matter of fact, she was almost a young lady, and I looked forward to sharing this adventure with her.

I settled on a new historical extravaganza called "The

A TRIP TO NEW YORK CITY

American Way." It was an epic production about an immigrant family starring Frederic March, a big movie star who also appeared on the stage, and Florence Eldridge, his wife. The reviews hadn't been that great, but it was a spectacle, and if I was going to spend all that money I wanted to get my money's worth. Besides I might never see another Broadway show again, so it might as well be a spectacular one. In addition to that, it was playing in the Century theatre, a new theatre in a newly built complex.

I wanted to make a day of it so I also ordered two tickets to that evening's showing of Walt Disney's groundbreaking movie, "Fantasia", an animated film set to classical music, which had opened recently at the Broadway Theatre on Broadway to great acclaim.

Dressed in our best, Rose and I walked two blocks up to Clinton Place and took the bus downtown to Pennsylvania Station. From there we took the 107 bus to New York. We went early enough to give us time to explore the city. We walked up and down Fifth Avenue, taking in all the elegant shops and gawking at the tall buildings. We then found our way to this large complex which contained the Century Theatre. It really looked brand new, and it had all these plush seats you sank right into.

"The American Way," which unfolded at quite a distance from us, had a big cast, and a lot of marching up and down. The plot was rather pedestrian, a sort of a family saga, and there was all that flag waving. Well, it was a spectacle, and that's what I had ordered.

After the show we had dinner at Toffenetti's, an Italian restaurant on the corner of 43rd Street and Broadway, "in the heart of the theatre district." There were large glass windows through which you could watch the passing crowds as you dined on Italian food. And then it was onto the Broadway

A NOT-SO-NICE JEWISH BOY FACES WORLD WAR II

Theatre, a massive auditorium with a mammoth screen, to see "Fantasia." Some of "Fantasia" was quite imaginative, I thought, but I thought most of it was rather silly, a high class cartoon, more fit for children.

In order to preserve this momentous occasion, on the way back to the bus station, we stepped into Woolworth's Five And Ten Cent Store on Broadway. We entered a photography booth, and dropped a quarter into the slot. We sat cheek to cheek in front of this automatic camera which produced a strip of four little pictures. And there we were, captured for eternity, two excited, dreamy eyed youngsters staring into the future.

On the way home, I studied the four little pictures thoughtfully. What did the years hold in store for the both of us, I wondered. If only one could tear aside the veil and take a peek at what was to come!

Were we going to be successful and happy?

Or were we doomed for tragedy and failure?

ROSE AT 15

**BEATIE, FRIEDA, HELEN
ROSE, PHYLLIS, TILLIE**

CHAPTER TWENTY NINE

EARLY ANGST

I was now in my junior year at Weequahic High School and, though the junior prom was no big deal, I thought it might be good preparation for the big one...the SENIOR PROM. I decided to attend. Hazel was spoken for, or so she said, and so was Gladys. I settled for Loretta Galarno, a girl I wasn't particularly interested in. She was nice, attractive, had a very nice figure...and she was available.

And she was Italian!

And probably Catholic!?

You couldn't find a Jewish girl?

No, I couldn't. It's just a date, Mother. I'm not gonna marry her.

Nothing more was said, but I could feel the tension.

A corsage, of course, was mandatory, and an expense I could ill afford. But what the hell! How many proms would I be attending? And this was to be my first real date.

I put on my best suit, my heart beating a little faster. I tried not to make a big deal of it, but I couldn't avoid the fact that this was an important night. I made my way to the young lady's house. I rang the bell. She answered it and invited me in.

I became very well aware of the fact that she was slim, attractive...and she was dressed very nicely. But so was I. I mustn't feel intimidated. I felt stiff and awkward and kind of silly handing her the corsage.

We started out for the school gym where the dance was to take place. Luckily she lived close enough so I didn't have to order a taxi. As we walked along it was hard for me to think of things to say. It would be stupid to talk about school. But what else was there to talk about? Why did we have to talk at all? Anyway I started talking about the tests and the teachers, feeling very pedestrian. Why couldn't I think of clever things to say, funny things, witty things. Anyway, at least there wasn't that deadly silence.

And then there was another thing to be considered. Should we hold hands? Or would that be presumptuous? Then again, I did hold hands with Frieda Sperling when we went to the movies. But that was different. I really cared about Frieda Sperling. I couldn't make up my mind...so I did nothing. It was all so phony. I had to watch my manners. I had to make conversation. Why couldn't we just be ourselves?

The music started as we entered the gym. We automatically headed for the dance floor. I put my arms around her waist. How far away should I hold her? If I hold her too far away it's awkward. If I get too close she'll think I'm trying to get fresh.

The band played "Stardust" and "Deep Purple" and "Blueberry Hill".

I found my thrill on Blueberry Hill,
On Blueberry Hill, where I found you.

I held the fragile creature in my arms, feeling very self conscious and perspiring profusely. I felt her breasts against my chest. (Oh, Lord!) As we danced, my hand on her back came in contact with the straps of her bra. She wasn't really that fragile after all, was she? Maybe I was the one that was fragile. What was she thinking? What was I thinking?

On the way home I was in a quandary. Should I try to kiss her good night? It didn't really matter one way or the other, did it? I mean, after all, it's just a kiss. I just want to do the right thing. I'm not really interested in this girl, romantically I mean. I mean, it isn't as if we're going to have sex right there and then in the doorway. We were approaching her house. Make up your mind! Now's the time! What are you

EARLY ANGST

waiting for? I held out my hand automatically and we shook hands. Coward!!

Obviously I was not Charles Boyer.

But at least I had my first official date. I had gotten my feet wet and was ready for the big event. Or was I?

******

THE big event, the SENIOR PROM was to be followed by a visit to The Top Hat, a nightclub in nearby Jersey City. An added expense, a long taxi ride. To my surprise I was given the extra money without any fuss. And, even more surprising, it was my father who gave it to me. I just hoped it would be enough.

I asked Hazel again. Again she had a date. Her friend, Gladys, however was available. Good. That might teach Hazel a lesson. She wasn't the only pebble on the beach. I felt a little more at ease with the corsage, with holding the door open, with being on the outside when walking down the street. (I did know that much.) It was a little awkward, though, changing sides when you crossed the street.

On the dance floor I held her reasonably close. It wasn't such a big deal after all. After the prom a large group of us piled into several taxis and drove to The Top Hat. All the way to Jersey City I was thinking of the cab fare piling up...mile...after mile...after mile. And then there was much consultation about how much to tip the cab driver.

The nightclub was rather dark, and you had to check your coat...and the girl's as well...another expense...one I hadn't counted on. We ordered drinks and things to nibble on. The drinks weren't cheap. As a matter of fact, the entire evening was getting to be much more expensive than I had

A NOT-SO-NICE JEWISH BOY FACES WORLD WAR II

planned, and I felt guilty about spending my father's hard-earned money on such frivolity.

When we got the bill there was much consultation again about splitting it, and how big a tip to leave the waiter, and then there was also the maitre'd. Apparently one had to be concerned about the feelings of the waiter, the feelings of the head waiter, the feelings of the cab driver and all those people that were supposed to be concerned about you, which seemed to me rather topsy-turvy.

******

My graduation took place in February instead of June...again. (I was doomed to be dismissed unobtrusively.) My mother attended the ceremony in the high school auditorium, accompanied by Aunt Tillie, who gave me a shirt as a graduation present. Uncle Jack gave me money. My parents gave me a watch. Beatie gave me a sweater.

My grades were above average, and I made the top third of my class, placing twelfth, which came as a pleasant surprise. I thought I was reasonably intelligent, but I certainly didn't compare with the class whiz, Charles Jacobs and Charles' friend, who was even smarter. But then they were rather prissy, and there was some talk about them, and besides artists shouldn't be too brainy anyway.

And suddenly it was over. It was good-bye to more than a decade of dreary classes. It was good-bye to getting up in the morning and, books in hand, trudging to prison; good-bye to coming home day after day to do homework, or some other dreary chore like Hebrew school or sitting down to practice piano. (Yes practicing piano, I must admit, was sometimes a chore.) Good-bye to twelve years of drudgery, twelve years of endless routine.

EARLY ANGST

And, strangely enough, there was now this big empty space in my life. There was nothing now to stand between me and the world at large. And wasn't that a frightening thought?! Was I really ready to face the world, to weather the storm, to start out on my career? Was I really ready to be a journalist, a reporter on some newspaper, while I wrote the great American novel?

No I was not. I had to admit it. And, coward that I was, I decided to go to college...and my self respect received quite a blow. I was not as brave and as forthright as I thought I was. I was not too thrilled about attending more classes, but I just was not prepared to face the rocky road that lay ahead. I needed more time to gird my loins, so to speak, to steel myself for the hard knocks that were to come. And besides a degree would certainly help...if I was going to be a journalist, or a reporter or whatever, would it not, I asked myself, knowing full well that it was mostly fear that propelled me to hide behind those ivied walls.

I applied to a number of universities and was accepted by three: New York University, the University of Missouri and Ohio State University. My mother couldn't understand why I would want to leave home when there were all sorts of excellent colleges nearby. I insisted that only the University of Missouri and Ohio State University had really first rate journalism departments, which was actually true, from what I gathered. In addition to that these were state universities so the tuition was the cheapest. I glossed over the fact that there'd be additional travel and living expenses.

I really wanted to go to the University of Missouri. For one thing, it was further away. I ended up choosing Ohio State. It was a compromise. It was closer to Newark and I thought that might bolster my case.

All this, of course, was discussed with Mother, and

A NOT-SO-NICE JEWISH BOY FACES WORLD WAR II

Mother, very reluctantly, finally gave her consent. There were rumblings up until the very end, but the world-shaking victory had been won. The die was cast. The ship was soon to weigh anchor. My father, as usual, said nothing.

CHAPTER THIRTY

THE REAL WORLD

Since I graduated Weequahic High School in February, and wouldn't start college until September, I had almost seven months to make the necessary expense money. I hated the idea of getting some sort of ordinary job, something not connected with my career, but if I was going to go to college I had no choice.

I reluctantly consulted the help wanted ads. I wasn't that good a typist. I couldn't take shorthand. I was really qualified for nothing. There were ads for stock-clerks/cashiers in super markets which required no skills whatsoever. That seemed like the logical way to go. There was a supermarket within walking distance. They had an ad. I walked in. I was interviewed. I was offered the job...and I took it.

Thus it came about that my initial foray into the world at large was as a cashier and stock clerk at the local Big Bear. I stood by the register, rang up the purchases, bagged the sales and collected the money. When I wasn't on the register I would be on the floor, opening boxes and putting the goods on the shelves. It was quite a comedown to the potential heir to Dostoyevsky, Dickens and Maugham.

In order to wipe out the reality of this dreary, daily grind my imagination worked furiously. It worked so furiously that I often made mistakes on the register. How could one actually concentrate on something as mundane as ringing up groceries, bagging them and making change when there was a glorious future waiting to be won? What a wasteful way to spend a day!

Up until that time being poor was just the way things were, inhibiting perhaps, but no big deal. Now I saw poverty as a crushing burden. Thirteen dollars a week was what I earned. From that was deducted the shortages on my register. My mother was indignant.

They're paying you nothing, said my mother, *and they're taking money out of your salary? It's ridiculous!*

Mother, what can I do?

It's not right. Talk to them.

Mother, I am responsible for the losses. That's what I was told. I agreed to that.

Then find another job.

Where am I gonna find another job?

It was bad enough working at this lowly job. Looking for another one would have been even more degrading. Besides, time was of the essence, and I had no idea how long it would take to find another job and, after all, it was only temporary. Together with the money that had been put aside I should have about six hundred dollars in the bank by September and, with a part time job at college, I should be able to get through my first year.

To my chagrin, Mother insisted on coming down to the store and having a talk with my boss. I cringed with embarrassment when she showed up and asked me to point out the man in charge. I watched her approach the gentleman. I watched the exchange from the distance, wishing I was anywhere but there. I felt like an idiot, having my mother fight my battles for me. Despite Mother's angry plea the supervisor remained adamant. The deductions continued.

Actually I enjoyed working on the floor, unpacking the boxes and placing the cans on the shelf. It was physical exercise, for one thing. Besides which, I didn't have to concentrate on what I was doing. I could give my imagination free reign.

I dreamt vaguely about the epic novels I would write, sweeping and grand like "War And Peace" and "David

THE REAL WORLD

Copperfield" and "Crime And Punishment," the greatest of them all. But I could dream for just so long and the dreary days seemed endless. Mother was an excellent cook, but, surprisingly, the sandwiches she made for my lunch were dull and dry.

Sometimes my friend, Irving, would meet me at the store in the evening and walk me home. If he came early and I was on the floor emptying boxes, he would hand me the cans from the box so that I could finish more quickly.

On the way home I would tell him about my dreams for the future, my hopes for literary greatness. I would pass judgment on books I'd read, on movies I'd seen and Irving listened respectfully. I was grateful for his support and I tried to improve him culturally, telling him what books he ought to read, which movies were good, which were not so good, which actors were brilliant etc. I would miss him when I went away to college.

******

By this time I had made some tentative start on my writing career. I became literary editor of my high school yearbook, which certainly bolstered my confidence. I composed the class poem for the yearbook, describing the members of our English class rather cleverly, I thought. I doctored some of the other students' contributions to the yearbook, and Miss Bloomfield, the teacher in charge, seemed to respect my judgement.

In addition to that, I had written a rather melodramatic composition in which a maid, working in the Schwartz household, was dying of some disease, unspecified. This poor, downtrodden Negro woman was slowly rotting away amid all

A NOT-SO-NICE JEWISH BOY FACES WORLD WAR II

this luxury, all this wealth. I empathized with the woman and felt that her fate was an unjust one.

I had written a composition describing the movie star, Kay Francis, in the movie "Confession," when she makes her appearance in a cabaret. Apparently she'd come down in the world and was now a gaudy blond. I describe her entrance...how the curtains part and this cheap looking woman with dyed, frizzy hair and bright red lipstick slinks onto the scene and begins to sing in a low, sexy voice.

I stood in the kitchen one morning and was suddenly engulfed by the vision of the works that I would create. Life was overwhelming. What a gift it was! I vowed that I would record every moment of my existence exactly as it happened. I would leave nothing out. I would immortalize every second of this glorious experience. I would record every cloud that passed by, every breeze that had ever caressed my cheek, the happy days, the sad days, the rain, the snow, the smell of wet grass, the clothes I wore, the food I ate. I would leave nothing out. How could I? Life was such a miracle! I tried to decide on the subject for my first novel. It would be blinding in its scope and power. It would be unlike anything that had ever been written.

Yes, but what will it be about?

I don't know.

It takes time to write a novel, years maybe. Don't you think you ought to get started?

I will, I will.

When?

When I'm ready.

When will that be?

When the time comes.

Or are you afraid to face the fact that you're simply

THE REAL WORLD

lazy? Or worse yet, you're really not that talented? That you have nothing to say?
    I'll get started. Don't worry.
    When?
    When the time comes!!
    And when will that be?
    When I'm good and ready!!!

******

And at this early stage of my career, a career that hadn't even gotten underway, I received two set backs, setbacks that sent traumatic shockwaves through my entire system.

One incident that left a deep scar had taken place during an English class at Hawthorne Avenue Grammar School. I submitted a composition which I thought was absolutely brilliant. I described the coming of the snow, how beautiful and fresh it was when it fell, and then how dirty and unattractive it became later on. I poured my heart and soul into that little piece. It was unique and original. When the papers were returned I was shocked to see that I'd received a "C." I couldn't believe it.

After the graded compositions had been returned the teacher asked if there were any questions. I raised my hand and asked why I had received such a low grade. The teacher asked me to read my composition to the class, which I did rather defensively. The teacher then asked the class why they thought she had given the composition a "C." The only comment came from Charles Jacobs, the class genius, who stood up and said that the composition was too subjective.

So what, I thought. I saw no reason why writing could not be subjective. However, I said nothing. What was the

A NOT-SO-NICE JEWISH BOY FACES WORLD WAR II

point in arguing? I returned to my seat deeply troubled. How successful could I be as a writer, when I earned a "C" in a class composition?

The second incident was just as troubling, perhaps even more so. One Saturday afternoon I decided to take a trip to the library on Bergen Street, quite a distance from my house. It was an adventure to another part of town. I entered the library with reverence and awe...the same way I entered every library. I picked up a book called "The Man On The Flying Trapeze." It was the first work of a young Armenian writer called William Saroyan. I had read some praiseworthy comments about it somewhere. The book was relatively new. I was delighted to find a copy.

I hurried home eager to dip into my find. Back home I dragged the beach chair onto the porch, poured myself a glass of lemonade. I sat down to enjoy a new and refreshing experience. As I read I became sick to my stomach, literally sick to my stomach.

This man, this William Saroyan, had written **my book**. He had said all the things I wanted to say. Reading this book was like looking into a mirror. I went around in a daze for a week. My career as a best-selling novelist was over before it had even begun.

If you're not going to be a novelist what else is there?

Maybe you ought to be a teacher. You'd please your mother at any rate.

No! I want to be a writer.

After several days of deep depression, I began to pull myself together. Saroyan, after all, is Saroyan, and you are you. He grew up in California. You grew up in New Jersey. He's Armenian. You're Jewish. Your backgrounds are completely different. Your experiences are completely different. Maybe you can find things to say that Saroyan

THE REAL WORLD

hadn't thought of. Little by little I gained back my confidence. But that encounter left me shaky, very shaky indeed.

In addition to that, I still couldn't get over the fact that my brilliant, imaginative little composition about the snow received a "C."

Was this what I would have to contend with?

CHAPTER THIRTY ONE

THE DAY OF DEPARTURE

How do you do.
(They'll introduce themselves and I'll reply.)
Norman Beim.
(We'll shake hands, and they'll ask me where I'm from and I'll reply.)
Newark.
(They'll ask if I mean Ohio.)
No, New Jersey.
(They'll ask me if I know a certain Beim in Newark and I'll reply.)
No, I don't. There are lots of Beims in Newark.
(They'll say that this Beim is in a certain business and I'll reply at length.)
No, my father's a saloon-keeper, uneducated but reasonably intelligent. He works behind a bar in the poorer section of the city, wearing a large white apron, serving beer to factory workers, to neighborhood denizens, and probably a couple of barflies. He's a nice looking man with a receding hairline, and he's beginning to put on weight. My Aunt Beatie, my father's sister, was a great beauty at one time. She is now, dressed in a shabby sweater, waiting on customers in a grubby grocery store in the seedy section of Orange (that's Orange, New Jersey) demeaning herself by buttering up customers in order to sell food staples. She has two children, she's beginning to lose her looks, and her occupation I would say is housewife. My mother is a regal beauty with no education to speak of. She's a great housekeeper, very conscientious. She places newspapers on the kitchen floor after it's been scrubbed in order to keep it clean. Don't ask me to explain. She's an excellent laundress, seamstress and cook.

THE DAY OF DEPARTURE

Her roast chickens are fabulous. She makes her noodles from scratch as well as her gefilte fish. She keeps a kosher home and is a slave, so to speak, to Jewish rituals, though she's highly intelligent. In addition to that, she's frustrated and neurotic, to put it mildly. My Uncle Jack, her brother, is a brilliant, bitter man, highly articulate despite a vocal impediment. When he isn't cutting fur, he's busy alienating friends and relatives and making life generally miserable for his immediate family. I come from a family of immigrants, you see, Jewish immigrants from Poland. Strange country, strange language, strange customs, you see, so it's been very difficult for them. Why yes, I suppose there are some immigrants who've made it, who've become rich and famous. As a matter of fact it just so happens that my Aunt Tillie, Tillie Kaufman, my father's older sister and her husband, Morris Kaufman, have a very successful clothing store on Main Street in East Orange...that's New Jersey. In spite of her lack of education, in spite of a crippled husband, my aunt has forged a place for herself in the business world. Not only that, it just so happens that she deals with mayors, senators and all sorts of local officials and people of distinction. And in reference to my father, he does have a way of taking charge of things, a way of handling his customers, of dealing with laborers and peons on their own level and still maintaining his dignity. And it just might interest you to know that he's something of a local hero. That's right. There was this time that a hold-up man came up to him with a gun in front of the tavern..yes, well ...he does run a tavern. All right, so it's a bar. As I was saying, this gangster came up to him with a gun and said, *This is a holdup,* and my father punched him in the jaw and the guy tried to shoot him and he ran away and he was caught

A NOT-SO-NICE JEWISH BOY FACES WORLD WAR II

and he turned out to be a professional boxer. As a matter of fact, there was actually an article in the local newspaper about my father. As you can see, my father is actually something of a celebrity. It's true that maybe my father and I are not that close, but he is supportive in his own limited way. There's always food on the table, we're always well dressed if not, perhaps, in the latest of fashion. And his presence, I must say, does give one a sense of security. He's always there, sometimes in the morning when I get up, and in the afternoon, taking a nap on the daybed in the living room. And maybe his feet do smell, but he is on his feet all day. In addition to that he often comes home with extra goodies like pies and things, and the New York Daily mirror which he leaves on the kitchen table for us to read and he takes us places in the car. And sometimes there's even some sort of brief personal exchange between us, when we're both tired or, perhaps, when my mother's asleep or away somewhere. And, I must admit that it was difficult leaving them all behind like that. My mother does dote on me so, and my sister Rose, a charming girl, bright and sweet and vibrant, is at a rather crucial age, and she seems to rely on me for advice. I've done my best to try to make her think for herself, to be independent, but I'm not so sure that I've been entirely successful, and I sometimes wonder whether she's capable of making her own decisions, the right ones that is. We'll correspond, of course, but it's not the same. And, of course, there's my little brother, Marty, a child of five, sweet and affectionate. Actually I tremble for him when I think back to my childhood, and how awful it was to be at the mercy of those ogres called adults. At the moment, the boy seems quite content with his lot. But what about a few weeks from now? A few months from now? He does have a mind

THE DAY OF DEPARTURE

of his own, and sometimes is a little difficult to control, and there's always these little emergencies. At a street-corner, for example, he let go of my hand once and dashed headlong into the street. Thank God there was no oncoming traffic. And there was that one time when I took him to a neighbor's house and we were sitting around, chatting when suddenly there was a loud clatter and the child let out a yell. The heavy door of the radio cabinet had come off somehow and fallen on the boy's foot, and when I removed his little shoe and sock I was horrified to see what looked like a white splinter protruding from one of the tiny toes. I finally managed to quiet the child, and told him to say nothing at home since I didn't want to upset my mother. Nothing serious came of the injury, but I worried about it for days. And then when I had my friends over to the house on a Friday evening, he would crawl out of bed and insist on joining the group. My friends got a kick out of the child, but eventually, I had to usher him back to bed, and here I am, leaving behind this unformed creature in need of guidance. It does make one uneasy. And people do change, you know, and when you're apart your life moves forward and so do the lives of those you leave behind...on separate paths, n'est pas?

As you can see I was in a bit of a turmoil as the day of my departure approached. Insecure, to put it mildly. I began to realize how sheltered my life had been so far. I began to get some sort of perspective...on myself, on my family, on my surroundings.

How would others see me?
What would others think of me?

******

A NOT-SO-NICE JEWISH BOY FACES WORLD WAR II

This was all brought on, I suppose, by the visit of a representative of Alpha Epsilon Pi, one of the fraternities on the campus at Ohio State...a Jewish fraternity, of course.

The young man was casually elegant, yet down to earth, and he won my mother over completely. I tried to let him know, as quickly as possible, that financially, a fraternity was out of the question. Besides I was against fraternities on principle. There was something snooty about fraternities, exclusive in a bad sense. I didn't go into all of that with the young man, who was anxious to have me as a guest for the first few days. I explained to him that I would have to get a part time job, just to see my way through. The young man insisted on extending the hospitality anyway, so I accepted the invitation, especially since I was told that, one way or another, there would be a job for me at the fraternity house.

There was something called orientation week. Freshmen had to come to school a week early to register and get settled. A week before the big departure I quit my job at the Big Bear. What a glorious day that was! I walked out of the store hoping to hell I would never see that place again.

Hour by hour the big moment approached. I began to say my good-byes to friends and relatives. I visited Aunt Tillie and Uncle Morris. I visited Beatie and Izzy. I said goodbye to Uncle Jack and Aunt Mollie, all the while collecting going away presents...clothes, a pen and pencil set, money. I said goodbye to Irving and Harold and Gloria across the street. There was a flurry of last minute shopping. I got a new suit at Aunt Tillie's and Uncle Morris's clothing store. Harold's father, Mr. Schwartz, owned a leather factory and I was going to buy a suitcase from him. I assumed we could get it at cost price or close to. The payment was refused. I felt rather awkward about it, but they insisted.

THE DAY OF DEPARTURE

No, no, no. It was meant to be a gift, said Mr. Schwartz, *a going-away present.*

And last, but certainly not least, we bought a trunk, which added a very final note to the preparations.

There was six hundred dollars in my bank account. If I got a part time job I could just about make it through my first year at Ohio State.

******

Finally, unbelievably, the day arrived.

The moment is now.

I'm all packed and ready to go.

And here we are, leaving the house, walking down the steps of the porch, the three of us, my mother, my father and myself.

Here we are, piling into the car and driving down familiar streets, streets I wouldn't be seeing for almost a year. Before I know it we're riding down Broad Street, downtown. We're riding down Market Street. We're approaching Penn Station. We're pulling up at Penn Station.

My mother and I get out of the car and wait while my father parks. I hold on tightly to my black leather suitcase, the gift from the Schwartz's. And suddenly I panic. Where's my trunk? At home, of course. My parents are going to send it on to me as soon as I got settled.

My father joins us and we inquire at the information desk where to get the train to Columbus, Ohio. We then make our way up the stairs to the platform.

On the platform we wait for the train.

And wait.

And wait.

My parents are strangely quiet. My mother seems to be

A NOT-SO-NICE JEWISH BOY FACES WORLD WAR II

a little too composed, which is actually a relief. I expected hysterics. My father, as usual, is stone-faced.

Finally, at last... I thought it'd never get here...the train steams into view.

It moves closer and closer.

You'll write, says my mother.

Yes, of course.

As soon as you get in.

Yes, Mother.

I kiss my father.

There is a tense embrace from my mother. I can sense the maddening restraint underneath.

I kiss her.

The train comes to a halt right in front of us.

The train doors remain shut.

Why don't they open?

What in the world is the matter?

Another delay!

What's holding things up?

The doors open...finally.

I step onto the train. I am actually on my way.

Well, not quite, but very soon.

I sight an empty seat and stow my suitcase on the rack above.

I sit down and look out the window.

I wave to my parents.

They wave back.

My mother sure seems calm. Tight faced, but calm.

Why don't we start?

What are they waiting for?

Suddenly the train gives a jerk and starts to move.

I wave again, disturbed by the sight of my mother's pale face.

THE DAY OF DEPARTURE

The train jerks again and we are off.
We are actually moving.
I could have sworn I heard a snap.
It was, of course, the umbilical cord.

MARTY

BIG BROTHER, LITTLE BROTHER

ROSE AND MARTY

MARTY

MARTY

PART TWO
COLLEGE

CHAPTER THIRTY TWO

THE ARRIVAL

The train sped across the vast continent and our hero, eyes glued to the window eagerly, drank in the varied scenes of America as they flew past; the rural country side, the villages, the towns, the magnificent panorama of this crude giant of a country, barely emerged from its cradle. The wheels of the train turned and clicked...clickety click, clickety click, clickety click. The fields once inhabited by red-skinned aborigines, where wigwams and tribal fires once burned, now inhabited by monstrous factories belching smoke into the ozone, whizzed by. Prim white puritanical churches now stood sternly where once colorful totems reached upward toward the happy hunting ground.

The daylight faded slowly and the dusk turned into night as the train hurtled into the future. One by one lights came on in the majestic office buildings in the metropolis, in the elegant homes in suburbia, in the little windows of a farmhouse whizzing by in the distance already part of the past. Stars twinkled in the immense dark blue arc above. A crescent moon revealed a scarecrow in a cornfield trembling in the cool night air visited, perhaps, by the ghost of some wandering spirit seeking sanctuary from his eternal wanderings.

Out there in the darkness what fate awaited our young hero as the world spun crazily in its off-kilter orbit? Where was it heading, this tiny planet, in this minor galaxy in the unfathomable universe? And our hero, that raw, innocent youth, drinking in the passing scene tried vainly to envision the days, the months, the years to come, to tear aside the curtain that concealed his karma.

Hold it! Just a minute!

THE ARRIVAL

What? What is it?
You are not Thomas Wolfe.
Oh? Who am I?
Whoever you are, whatever you are, dear boy, you have got to be yourself.
Easier said than done.
Oh?
I'm fresh from the womb, a vulnerable, impressionable piece of protoplasm, a slate that has yet to be written on. I've experienced nothing...absolutely nothing except a rather placid, uneventful childhood. I haven't witnessed a murder or a robbery or been rescued at the very last minute from a firing squad like Dostoyevsky.
As a matter of fact, you haven't even experienced sex yet! Have you? Well? Have you?
Well, no, not exactly.
You are a nonentity, dear boy.
True.
Well, this is ridiculous! Are you, or are you not...a male? You've got to do that, at least. Get it over with.
How? When?
The best place is in a bed.
No kidding.
There's also the back of a car.
That must be very uncomfortable.
And don't try to be clever, because you're not. And you've got to have some sort of a personality, some sort of an image to present to the world, one that will intrigue the beholder, one with an essential, mysterious quality that will fascinate and cast a spell. You've got to be a "mensch," for God sakes!
I suppose I could be charming and suave.
That's one possibility.

A NOT-SO-NICE JEWISH BOY FACES WORLD WAR II

Or perhaps I could be cold and mysterious.

Or dashing and romantic on the order of Lord Byron, let's say.

Oh really!

Well, why not?

Lord Byron?!

I have it. Honesty! That will be the keynote to your personality. You will shock people with your directness. Everyone will marvel at your no-nonsense piercing perception.

Suddenly, out the window, there were rows of houses, city streets, parked cars. My train of thought was interrupted by the icy grip of reality. We were actually approaching Columbus. It was early morning, and we were passing through the suburbs. And my heart beat faster as we pulled into the station.

I took my suitcase down from the rack and made my way into the waiting room. It was much larger...and much shabbier than I'd expected. As a matter of fact, it was almost grimy. As I walked through the waiting room I felt a sudden surge of excitement. Despite the heavy suitcase, despite the disappointing surroundings there was a bounce to my step. My feet hardly touched the ground. For the first time in my eighteen years I was experiencing Life. I was facing the future.

This was it!

The adventure was about to begin.

Suddenly I stopped. I felt weak in the knees. I felt defenseless. I set down my suitcase. I looked around. Here I was in a strange city, in the middle of nowhere. The hundred dollars I had in my pocket was all that stood between me and poverty.

No matter what happens, you will never starve to death.

THE ARRIVAL

Relax. This is America. No one starves in America. Onward and upward! I took a deep breath, picked up my suitcase and walked on. I decided to take a cab. I hated to spend the money but I didn't trust myself to public transportation.

In the cab I looked eagerly out the window at this alien city. Where were the tall buildings, the elegant shops? As we rode on we came to the main street. I slowly came to the conclusion that Columbus, Ohio, where I was about to establish some sort of identity, was not very impressive; provincial, actually, after New York City. I tried to reserve judgement. Besides, the more backward these surroundings were, the more confidence it would give me. One might even say that I was a sophisticate from back East. How do you like them apples!

The main street went right past the campus. There were the campus gates and beyond the gates there were the green lawns and great expanse of walks and there were the buildings where the classes would be held.

The cab turned right and drove up Iuka Avenue, which became a winding tree-lined thoroughfare as we came to where the large, classy looking fraternity houses were located.

Alpha Epsilon Pi, the fraternity house where I was to spend my first day, was most impressive. It was a tall, white building fronted by a large well-kept lawn, like one of those mansions on a Southern plantation. Tara in "Gone With The Wind." I was glad I was able to step out of a cab. How elegant can you get?

I was greeted by the young man who had come to recruit me. Somehow he didn't seem as friendly though. Maybe he was just too busy. After all, he did have lots of people to look after.

There was an elaborate breakfast of pancakes and eggs and biscuits and rolls and pastries and cereals, both hot and

A NOT-SO-NICE JEWISH BOY FACES WORLD WAR II

cold, and coffee and tea. And bacon? A Jewish fraternity? I resisted the forbidden food. Let's take it one step at a time.

There was much laughing and joking and giddiness on the part of all, new students and old, which I found rather difficult to relate to. What was so funny? I simply didn't see the joke. Was it possible that all these young men were just plain silly?

Or maybe it's you. You're too serious.

I do have a sense of humor and if something's funny I laugh.

You've really got to lighten up.

I quickly came to the conclusion that I would not be very comfortable living in, what seemed to me, a very phony atmosphere.

Several of the freshman planned to join the fraternity. They were assigned to a bedroom. I was to sleep on the sofa in the living room, which was all right with me since I felt guilty about accepting all this hospitality anyway. I was anxious to get settled. But since I had been assured that there would be some part-time work for me at the fraternity house, I was eager to clear that up, so I had no choice but to spend the night there. Actually, until I spoke to my councilor at the university, there was no place else for me to stay.

The next morning I walked down tree lined Iuka Avenue to the campus. My feet seemed barely to touch the ground, I was so full of the sense of freedom and adventure.

The campus was huge, yet many of the buildings were rather pedestrian, without any personality whatsoever, which was a let-down. The front part of the campus was a large grass-covered oval with a number of diverging paths, and one large tree. Actually it seemed, somehow, flat and empty. Why aren't there more trees, I wondered. Towards the rear of the

THE ARRIVAL

campus, however, there were little hills and a bridge and a stream.

As I walked across the bridge the steeple bells rang out. I stopped and looked around. What a charming scene! The quaint bridge, the trees all about, the stream beneath. It was like being in a movie.

This first day was chaotic. There were many new students and no one seemed to know what to do or where to go. Eventually things straightened themselves out. I finally enrolled and met my councilor. With his assistance I chose my curriculum. Actually there wasn't much of a choice since there were so many courses that were required; English literature, a foreign language, philosophy and, since this was a State university I was saddled with R.O.T.C (Reserve Officers Training Corps), which I did not look forward to. As a matter of fact, the classes themselves seemed to me to be the least of all this.

The dorms were filled. Besides which I was not particularly interested in living in a dormitory. It might have been an opportunity to make friends, but there wouldn't have been much privacy. I was looking forward to the luxury of privacy.

In spite of my eagerness for privacy, however, most of the single rooms were beyond my means, and I ended up sharing a room in a private house with another freshman. The house was located behind the campus, which pleased me no end, since I would have to cross the little bridge over the stream in order to get to my classes. Every morning I'd be able to pause in the middle of this charming bridge, and look about and drink in the beauty of the scene.

My roommate was a dark, rather sober looking young man from Gary, Indiana who planned to be an engineer. He was quiet, for which I was thankful, and he wasn't exactly

A NOT-SO-NICE JEWISH BOY FACES WORLD WAR II

unfriendly, but he wasn't particularly friendly, and he seemed to be somewhat moody. His reserve made me a little self-conscious. I began to wonder if I wasn't too enthusiastic, too eager. Was I expecting too much? What exactly was I expecting?

As a matter of fact why, on earth, was I here in the middle of nowhere? I didn't really want to go to college. I should be out in the world...facing reality.

CHAPTER THIRTY THREE

TWO DISASTROUS SEXUAL ENCOUNTERS

The young man from the fraternity kept his word, and there was a job for me at the fraternity house. I was to help with the dishes in the kitchen, stacking, washing, drying...for which I got two meals...lunch and dinner. Which meant that all I had to buy was my breakfast. I bought a pocket-sized notebook in which to enter my daily expenses. Since I was forced to live on such a limited budget, I thought it wise to keep a detailed account.

The freedom of being on my own was rather alarming; being responsible for paying my rent, for paying for my meals, for taking care of my own laundry. No longer did I sit down at the kitchen table and wait to be served. No longer was there a fresh shirt in the drawer waiting for me. Not that I had much time to ponder these things, what with classes and homework and my job at the fraternity kitchen.

Of course, my social activities were limited because of my financial situation but, if I was really careful, I could actually afford one or two dates. I even had money enough to buy a season ticket to the football games, the home games, that is, which were played in the huge arena near the campus. I was determined to experience it all. I would learn to like footfall if it killed me. Or, at least, tolerate it. As a matter of fact I had attended a local football game back in Newark once and, to my amazement, I got so caught up in the excitement I heard myself shouting, *"Come on, come on!"*

I had received in the mail back home a little brochure from the Hillel Foundation, a Jewish organization which had chapters on many college campuses. It was advertised as *"a home away from home."* The organization had an entire building all to itself, and it was rather cozy. Though I resented

A NOT-SO-NICE JEWISH BOY FACES WORLD WAR II

the idea of polarizing groups of any kind, this building was sort of a beacon of warmth in an alien world.

The first open house at Hillel was to welcome all the new students. I wandered about feeling comfortable and strange at the very same time. I wasn't a good mixer, but all these people were Jewish, after all. That should have made it easier, but it didn't really.

In the library I came across a young lady on a ladder, arranging some books. From the back she looked rather interesting. Long brown hair and a stunning figure, legs and all. The figure was even more stunning when she turned around. A simple grey woolen dress seemed to downplay most pleasant curves. The face, unfortunately, was marred by an unusually large nose. Though she did have lovely eyes, cat's eyes, and nice cheekbones. We smiled at each other and spoke briefly. Her name was Virginia, she lived in Columbus and was going to major in social work. She seemed to be extremely shy, and I could understand why. That schnozola! What a pity!

I continued to wander about exploring the various rooms, and smiling at strangers...a nod and a brief hello. Events like these made me feel rather lonely. All these people, but somehow I felt unable to communicate with any of them. What was there to say? Where are you from? How prosaic! I mean, what difference did it make where you were from? When I was alone I had no trouble carrying on a conversation with myself. In a group, however, one made small talk, and I hated small talk. And with all these people around, I was too distracted to be able to carry on a conversation with myself, which was usually quite stimulating.

I continued to visit Hillel regularly, and it was there, one evening, that I met my first would-be romance. Toni was a product of the Midwest, one of the most un-Jewish girls I'd

TWO DISASTROUS SEXUAL ENCOUNTERS

ever met. She was short, solidly built, sloe eyed and dark, a striking looking girl who filled a sweater very nicely but, what was even more exciting about her was her dynamic personality. She was so vibrant and full of energy, she fairly glowed. We got to talking and agreed to meet for a "coke" later in the week at the campus hangout. I thought of her as a "real bitch," that is to say, a nice, earthy girl I could see myself having sex with.

I thought about her a lot, her sparkling eyes, her hearty laugh, her fantastic energy. Actually, she was so vigorous, if it came to a fight, there was no doubt about it, she could probably beat me up. And yet I was completely captivated.

At our first encounter I had the feeling that the attraction was mutual. After our second date, however...I guess you might call them dates, we just met for "cokes" at the campus hangout...it was quite apparent that she was totally disinterested...and she was, at times, annoyingly masculine. I began to suspect her femininity. She was just too tough, and she even had a boy's name, though she did spell it differently. I debated whether it was worth my while to pursue her. And then, one evening, I ran into Toni accompanied by another student, a big bruiser, a member of the football team. I couldn't believe my eyes. This was not the Toni I knew. She was soft and feminine and hung disgustingly onto the boy's arm.

Well, if that's what turned her on, muscles and beef, she was certainly not my kind of girl. She was much too hyper anyway, and she really was on the stocky side, sort of chunky. As a matter of fact, she didn't know what she was missing!

******

A NOT-SO-NICE JEWISH BOY FACES WORLD WAR II

I was becoming desperate about my love life...it's non-existence, that is. I mean, here I was in college and I was still a virgin. Granted there were other joys in life: just walking down the street on a cool autumn day, strolling across the campus in the evening, dreaming all sorts of dreams. Just sitting in a barber chair, getting a haircut and thinking. But that was it! My life was confined to dreams, dreams and thoughts, thoughts and dreams.

One of the boys working in the kitchen of the fraternity house told me about a prostitute who was very popular with the boys on campus. Her name was Marjorie, and she charged twenty dollars. Now twenty dollars was a lot of money, especially for a tight budget. However it was certainly a cheap price to pay for one's manhood.

So one cold, bleak day in February, weeks after I'd been given her name and number. I screwed up my courage, so to speak, called Marjorie, and made a date with her...or an appointment...or whatever one made with a prostitute.

It was a bitterly cold night and my teeth chattered uncontrollably as I walked down a very respectable street, stopped in front of a very respectable looking two-family house, walked up the stairs of the front porch and rang the doorbell.

No answer.

I rang again.

After a while I heard the rustling of a blind and, finally, the window opened and a woman stuck her head out.

What do you want?

I'm Norman Beim. I have an appointment, I managed to stammer through my chattering teeth

Go round the side door. That's where you're supposed to come in.

I walked around the porch to the side door. The woman

TWO DISASTROUS SEXUAL ENCOUNTERS

let me in. Apparently she had very nosey neighbors. The living room of the apartment was comfortable and cozy, but my teeth couldn't stop chattering. The woman led me through some sliding doors into a rather lushly furnished bedroom. Everything seemed to be pink and very feminine. There was no cover on the bed. The blanket and the satin coverlet had been folded back.

Marjorie was all ready for business. She was dressed in an attractive, quilted housecoat, wore orange lipstick and, when I was finally able to pull myself together and get a good look at her, I found myself staring at an extremely good-looking lady, probably in her early thirties. She had lustrous brown hair and when she took off her housecoat she revealed a magnificent body, full breasted and voluptuous.

The first order of business was the twenty dollars, which I handed over to her. She told me to undress and left the room for a minute. I took off my clothes, and hopped into the bed, pulling the cover over me.

The woman returned, got into bed with me and went to work with her hands. She was very business-like, not the least bit affectionate. My hands were still cold. My feet were still cold, and my teeth wouldn't stop chattering. Her ministrations were in vain. I thought about admitting that this was my first time, but decided against it. The woman continued to ply her hands resolutely. I fondled her breasts half-heartedly. This really was ridiculous. I felt nothing, absolutely nothing...except cold and mortified. To top it all off, somehow or other she reminded me of my mother!!

While this disastrous love-making was going on in the bedroom, I heard a noise in the living room through the half open doorway. The manipulation halted temporarily.

Helen?, Marjorie called out.

A NOT-SO-NICE JEWISH BOY FACES WORLD WAR II

A feminine voice responded. It was the woman's dressmaker or a friend of hers, or maybe both.
I've got a customer, Helen.
That's OK. I'll wait.
Well, this finished me.
Marjorie suggested that I come back at another time. She would give me a rain check.
I put on my clothes, my teeth still chattering.
She let me out through the side door.
It was over and done with, and I had no intention of coming back. Twenty bucks shot to hell, and I was still a virgin!

******

My second sexual experience was of another nature, but just as disastrous.
One of my favorite courses was French literature. We studied the French poets Lamartine and De Vigny and Victor Hugo etc. in their original tongue. I enjoyed these sessions immensely.
Sitting in the same row, a few seats down was a rather nice looking boy who wore tight pants. The boy seemed to be pleasant enough but he really was too big for his pants. He kept shifting his leg and foot about all during the lesson. This was really distracting. Then I remembered those interesting sessions with my friends in the cellar, and I became intrigued.
Was this a signal or was the boy just restless?
I began to shuffle my foot in response, rather timidly.
He responded in kind.
This went on for several days. The boy never spoke to me. I never spoke to him.

TWO DISASTROUS SEXUAL ENCOUNTERS

Finally I decided to clear the air so that I could concentrate on what I was in that class for.

How to go about it? Should I approach the boy or not. I had a great deal of thinking to do.

The words of my friend, Harold, rang in my ears. *I don't do that anymore.*

And I remembered that Harold's father, did not approve of such hanky-panky.

Was it wrong or not? No one ever spoke about sex between men, and I had never actually heard it condemned.

But then again no one had ever dared to say that it was acceptable.

Apparently this sort of thing was not officially sanctioned.

Then again, it did go on. And it certainly wasn't a crime, was it?

One evening I stood on the little bridge over the stream, the wind caressing my face, and I communed with myself, or my conscience or...whatever. If I was to be a great writer, I must be open to everything. I could not reject Life, no matter what form it took...and sex, sex of any kind was LIFE.

The next day I approached the boy, made his acquaintance and suggested that we study together. The boy seemed indifferent, but interested. We arranged for me to come to the boy's room.

When he opened the door that evening he was wearing the same tight pants. We settled down, supposedly, to study. We sat side by side, books in front of us, vaguely muttering...I don't remember what. I was flustered, and didn't know what to make of it all. I dropped several vague verbal hints and "accidentally" brushed my leg against his. He didn't withdraw his leg, nor did he respond. It was both baffling and irritating.

A NOT-SO-NICE JEWISH BOY FACES WORLD WAR II

Well, I guess I better get going, I said.
He didn't respond.
I rose.
He rose.
You wanna get together tomorrow? I asked.
Okay, he said.

Even though nothing had been accomplished, study-wise or sex-wise, I thought I might as well see this thing through to the end.

At the second session I became a little bolder. Let's get this over with! My hand found its way to the boy's thigh and there couldn't be anymore pretense. He rose. I rose. We adjourned to the bedroom. The boy dropped his trousers. I dropped my trousers. I extended my hand. I waited for him to extend his. He just stood there. He made no overture to me whatsoever. The both of us just stood there. Finally it became obvious that he expected to be serviced in some manner or other, without any response on his part.

I zipped up my trousers, buckled my belt and, seething inside, I muttered something about there being some sort of misunderstanding, and I left...fuming. What gall! To expect to receive pleasure and give none in return.

I was angry at the boy, angry at myself for making a fool of myself and for missing part of a class I really enjoyed; and I was angry at the world in general for making sex so godamned complicated.

The next day in class the boy appeared as cool as ever, in the same tight pants and, believe it or not, there he was signalling again. It was not to be believed! I changed my seat so that the boy was sitting behind me and, regretting the time I had lost, I was able, once more, to get back to French literature... **which was what I was there for in the first place.**

CHAPTER THIRTY FOUR

AMERICA GOES TO WAR

I did meet a couple of girls at Hillel who seemed to enjoy my company. There was Peggy. She was spritely and a good sport, but she was on the scrawny side. I enjoyed dating her, but I considered her more like a friend.

And then there was Anya. Even the name was exotic. Anya had long brown, flowing hair, was slim and glamorous and really classy. She wore this black chiffon dress and had great legs and she was really chic. Sort of like Katharine Hepburn. I took her to a night club once, after a movie downtown. It was "Casablanca" which, at the time I thought rather hokey, and we had a rum and coke and some French fries. I mean we were actually sitting in a bar, sipping a real drink and dipping French fries into ketchup and chatting away like really sophisticated people.

It was an extravagance, but it was really worth it. I was becoming a man of the world. Anya, however, liked to spend money. At least I had the feeling that her lifestyle was a little more luxurious than mine. So, much as I wanted to see more of this classy lady, I felt I really couldn't afford her...very often, at any rate.

I investigated the downtown area of Columbus, and lo and behold the city was actually a metropolis. It had several large movie theatres, a legitimate theatre, a concert hall, night clubs, restaurants etc. and, since romance didn't seem very imminent, I was determined to steep myself in culture.

Columbus had its own philharmonic orchestra and had just taken on a new and exciting conductor. I bought a concert subscription. I sat in the balcony and let the music pour over me, through me, around me. It seemed as if I was discovering the power of classical music for the very first time.

Franck's Symphony in D Minor was my favorite, but

A NOT-SO-NICE JEWISH BOY FACES WORLD WAR II

there was also Brahms and Beethoven and Schubert and Mendelssohn. I bathed in the glorious sounds and my dreams soared and floated up to the ceiling of the concert hall...and far beyond.

There were many first rate touring companies playing the old Hartman Theatre, a large legitimate house off the main street. Some of these productions were actually pre-Broadway tours. I saw Katharine Cornell, a major Broadway star, in a production of "Rose Bernd," a French play translated into English. I don't remember much about the play but I do remember being impressed with Miss Cornell's stage presence. The play, apparently, was not a memorable one since the producers decided not to bring it to Broadway.

I saw the great Judith Anderson and Maurice Evans in an excellent production of "Macbeth." Shakespeare actually came to life with this glorious Lady Macbeth. Her "letter scene", where she prepares to greet her husband and plans to convince him to murder the king, was mesmerizing. She was a small woman, but on stage she was a giant. Her voice rang through the theatre deep and resonant. And her "sleep walking scene"...

Out! Out damned spot!...
Unforgettable!

There was also a stock company in residence at the Hartman. They produced recent hits, in addition to some obscure classics by playwrights like the British playwrights, Arthur Wing Pinero and Frederick Lonsdale, who wrote light comedies. It was interesting to discover new plays by playwrights I'd never heard of. Even the productions that didn't seem to be particularly distinguished still had the advantage of being performed by live actors, the action taking place right there in front of one.

It was exciting just sitting in the balcony of that old

theatre, waiting for the curtain to rise. What was the set going to be like? Was the play going to be dramatic or comic or romantic or sentimental? Perhaps there would be one performance that would be absolutely galvanizing. And the balcony seats were really cheap.

I'd read great reviews for a movie called, "The Maltese Falcon." It was playing at a movie theatre in a distant suburb. Here was a chance to explore this Midwestern city, a city I knew so little about. I found out which bus went to the part of town the movie was playing. I boarded this strange bus, and took this long ride to a section of the city completely new to me. My face glued to the window, I peered into the dusk and revelled riding through these alien streets. Would I get off at the right stop? Or would I get lost and wander about in the dark, stumbling into some dangerous slum area?

I found the theatre without any mishap, and the film was a memorable one, a haunting one, a dark, bitter tale of mystery and betrayal with unexpected twists and turns, and odd, colorful characters. Sidney Greenstreet, that menacing hulk of a man, and Peter Lorre, weasel like and slimy, and Humphrey Bogart cynical yet square shooting and compassionate underneath, and Mary Astor, the mystery woman, beautiful and deceitful, and that unforgettable ending as the elevator door closes on her tear stained face as she heads for prison, because she turns out to be a murderess and even though he loves her, Humphrey Bogart sends her to jail because she killed his partner. And those immortal closing words...*The stuff that dreams are made of.* On the ride back home at night in the dark, through dimly lit streets the air was full of mystery and promise.

******

A NOT-SO-NICE JEWISH BOY FACES WORLD WAR II

There was a four day Thanksgiving hiatus. Aunt Gertie and Uncle Morris invited me to spend the holiday with them. Since they lived in Pennsylvania, and Windber was closer to Columbus than Newark, and time was short, I decided to accept their invitation, and I took the train to Windber, Pennsylvania.

I woke up that first morning in Windber, Pennsylvania, looked out the window, and found the hillside behind the house and the mountainous countryside as far as one could see covered with snow. It was a breathtaking sight. I stood at the kitchen window absorbing the view. My head was in a whirl.

What an adventure!

The world is full of exotic cities and mountains and deserts and rivers. Why within one year I've traveled to Columbus, Ohio and then to a mountain top in Pennsylvania. And then I'll be traveling back to Columbus and then back to New Jersey and then ...who knows where. The future lay unknown before me like that snow-covered hillside and the mountains beyond just waiting to be conquered.

Aunt Gertie called me away from the window and I sat down to an elaborate breakfast. Then I walked down to visit with Uncle Morris at his store. He welcomed me warmly and introduced me to his help. The store was a combination grocery and butcher shop, and I was taken aback by the casual way Uncle Morris, wearing a large white apron, handled the bloody slabs of meat. Afterwards I walked about this picturesque little town on top of a mountain, taking in the stores, the people, the atmosphere.

Beneath this quaint, rather mundane way of life who knows what seething passions lay hidden, what twisted frustrations? What lives lived out in quiet desperation? Some day I must write a novel that takes place in a town like this.

AMERICA GOES TO WAR!

******

Back at school, however, my intellectual life seemed to be at a standstill. My first semester at college was drawing to an end. The courses, for the most part, were uninteresting and unrewarding, except for that one class in French literature. And R.O.T.C. was a drag! I was horrified to be studying war as a science, as if it deserved the same respect as chemistry or physics or mathematics. I mean actually sitting down and measuring the trajectory of a bullet! The glory of man being put to such depraved use. It was hair raising! And then there was my experience with the horse.

As a child I'd admired horses from a distance. They seemed romantic, legendary animals. And now, as part of my ROTC training, I was going to learn how to ride.

Great! I really looked forward to it.

The first step was learning how to saddle a horse. I remembered all those Western stars saddling up and jumping onto their steed and galloping away. I picked up the saddle, which was much heavier than I'd expected, and I approached the beast. He, or she, didn't seem to be very enthusiastic. It just stood there, slowly swishing its tail.

Up close they were rather imposing, and not particularly friendly. Now, maybe it was an accident, and maybe it wasn't. At any rate, just as I was about to place the saddle on its back, the beast lifted up its leg, and started to put its foot down, right down on my right toe. Before the animal came down with its full weight and could do any damage I gave it a shove, and the brute backed off. I stood there, staring at the beast.

What next?

The instructor came by and helped me place the saddle on the monster's back. I climbed onto the animal with additional help from the instructor. Then came the posting. Now, I gathered one was supposed to grip the horse with one's thighs as one rode.

Well, off we went and, I don't know, maybe my thighs weren't strong enough or maybe I wasn't doing it right, but I squeezed and squeezed and, no matter how hard I squeezed, each step the animal took sent a painful jolt up my back. By the end of the day the romance of horseback riding had lost its charm. Apparently I would never be another John Wayne.

Early Sunday evening, on December 7, 1941, I was sitting in the lounge at Hillel, thumbing through some newspapers, when suddenly it became very quiet. There was an important announcement coming over the radio. Everyone gathered around.

The Japanese have attacked Pearl Harbor!

The war in Europe had been going on for almost two years. It seemed inevitable that we would get involved. And there it was!

I was a college student. Maybe I'd be allowed to finish my education. After all, I was taking R.O.T.C. Shortly afterward President Roosevelt announced that the United States was formally at war with Japan.

I couldn't make up my mind how I felt about the war. Never, for one moment, did I doubt that war was insanity. And now my own participation in battle might soon be inevitable. If, as it was rumored, the Germans were actually murdering the Jews, I had no choice. I couldn't not join the army. But, actually killing a man...it was incomprehensible. There was nothing more precious than life itself. To destroy human life, no matter what the reason...was a sin. Even if I killed in self defense I felt I would have committed an unpardonable crime. It would haunt me for the rest of my days.

AMERICA GOES TO WAR!

And what did the Bible have to say about it?

Apparently the sages had a way of hedging their bets. There was "an eye for an eye", and then there was "turn the other cheek" all in the same breath.

The atmosphere on campus was charged with apprehension, the possibility of death...for friends, for relatives, for oneself. The sweetness of life became even more poignant. The appetite for living became even more voracious.

How was one to satisfy one's insatiable desires, except perhaps to live each moment as fully as possible? I thought about how Thornton Wilder had spoken about the simple pleasures of everyday living in his lovely play, "Our Town."

"Good-bye to clocks ticking...and Mama's sunflowers. And food and coffee...Oh, earth, you're too wonderful for anybody to realize you....Do any human beings ever realize life while they live it?---every, every minute?"

How magnificently Thomas Wolfe had captured the passion of it all in his novels, "Look Homeward, Angel," "Of Time And The River" and "You Can't Go Home Again!"

Would I ever get the chance to try my own luck at achieving immortality, I wondered.

CHAPTER THIRTY FIVE

CHANGES

My first semester at Ohio State came to an end. I seemed to be standing still on a fast moving treadmill. Life was suddenly rushing on, and I had no control of what was happening. There I was on the train again, on my way back East on my Christmas break, and suddenly I was home with my family and friends.

The streets were still the same. The trees, the houses were still the same, but something was different. I felt like a stranger. Not that I didn't feel welcome, but things had gone on at home that I hadn't been part of. My relationship to Irving, my very best friend, was completely altered. We were no longer an integral part of each others lives. We both had experiences that we hadn't shared. I was also alarmed by the fact that there was a gap in the relationship between my sister and myself, for the very same reason.

Most amazing of all was my new relationship with my mother. I was no longer the favored child. The crown had been passed to my little brother, Marty. There, apparently, the umbilical cord had not been severed. It was a rather frightening feeling, cut loose like that.

I'd been too busy for the repercussions to really sink in. Now I suddenly became aware of the fact that I was no longer nourished by the maternal blind faith I'd been accustomed to. Where was that special affection I'd grown up with...that, apparently, I'd grown dependent upon? I was out in the cold world...on my own. I did have ties elsewhere, I suppose, but they weren't really ties. They were just new and different acquaintances, nothing to hold on to. Was it possible that I was really an adult now? Is this what it felt like to be grown up? It was scary.

Peggy, the spritely girl I'd dated back in Columbus,

CHANGES

lived nearby in New York City. I had her telephone number. I called her and made a date. I took her to the Persian Room in the Plaza Hotel. It was one of the most elegant night clubs in one of the poshest hotels in Manhattan. I wore my navy blue suit, a white shirt and tie. Peggy wore a long dress, and seated in this famous club, we watched Hildegarde, the ultra glamorous chanteuse...long white gloves, upswept hairdo, and elegant gown. She made her entrance singing her signature song.

Darling, je vous aime beaucoup.
Think of me a little, too...
It was all so very continental.

Another time I went to the Pennsylvania Room at the Pennsylvania Hotel, across from Penn Station in New York City, and heard Jimmy Dorsey, one of the popular bands of the day. This time I took the svelte, elegant Anya, who also lived in New York City. I was really getting to be a man about town.

At home, I received my grades. They were dangerously low. As a matter of fact, I'd received a couple of "D"s, almost a failing grade. I had been warned that the first year of college was usually very difficult since there were a lot of adjustments to be made. In addition to that, I had not been very enthusiastic about my curriculum in general and, apparently, it had affected my work. My primary purpose, after all, in going to college, in spending all that money and all that time, was to get an education. I did enjoy my visit home, but I was really glad when it was over. For the first time in my life I really had to concentrate on improving my grades.

******

A NOT-SO-NICE JEWISH BOY FACES WORLD WAR II

Back at Ohio State I was faced with finding another room. My current roommate was leaving school and going back to Gary, Indiana. It was family business. Or was it the army? I wasn't quite sure. He was close-mouthed as usual. If I wanted to keep the room the rent would have been doubled, and I did want a place of my own. I consulted the housing list that was available, and found a room at the foot of winding, tree-lined Iuka Avenue, not too far from the fraternity house where I worked. The room was actually a double room. Luckily, I was allowed to have it all to myself.

The personality of the Midwest hit me more forcibly on my return. The people in Ohio seemed to be so much more friendly and more open than they were back East...on the surface, at any rate. It was always *Hi* and a bright, cheerful smile. It wasn't important whether they really meant it or not. It was heart warming. It was attractive and it was refreshing. I decided I would adopt an all American Midwestern personality. So from now on it was no longer the reserved, thoughtful Norman. It was *Hi* and a big smile, no matter what was going on inside. This was a new me. A little phoney perhaps but, actually, when people asked how you were, they didn't really mean it. They didn't really want to know how you were feeling, what you were thinking. So what was the point in wearing your heart on your sleeve? Give 'em what they want.

I also became acutely aware of my New Jersey accent. That wouldn't do at all. I went about deliberately changing my speech pattern. It was no longer "cawfee" for coffee or "ant" for aunt. It wasn't easy, and it wasn't the Norman that grew up in Newark, New Jersey, that nice, shy little Jewish boy, but it was a bright, cheery personality that one could present to the world at large. I was now a clean-cut, wholesome Midwestern WASP, American as apple pie.

CHANGES

I also became more aware of diction in general. Years ago, during my first years in grammar school, I had had difficulty with my "th's" and my "s's." It had been necessary for me to attend a remedial speech class. I realized now that speech was an indication of what sort of a man you were. I became more aware of my diction.

With this new personality of mine I also became acutely aware of my posture. I had a habit of craning my head forward when I walked. As a matter of fact, my friends back home used to call me "goose neck." I tried to stand more erect.

My first day in the new house I met Mel Josephs. Mel had the room across the hall from me. As I was unpacking he called a greeting through his open doorway. I came into his room. There was Mel reclining on the upper bunk of a double-decker bed. He was long and slim and somewhat Semitic looking. He wore a long flannel nightgown. His right leg was raised and his genitals were completely exposed. I was taken aback for a moment. However, since Mel behaved very matter-of-fact about it, I did likewise and I conducted the conversation as casually as if we were in a coffee shop, sitting and talking over a coke. I kept wondering if the exposure was deliberate. I decided that it was.

Mel seemed uncommonly interested in me. I was extremely flattered by the interest, since the man seemed absolutely brilliant. I assumed that Mel was more interested in men than in women. That was his business, I decided, and it needn't concern me. I often spoke to Mel after that. His door was always open and I enjoyed the conversations immensely.

Mel was older than I was and more sophisticated. He was related, somehow, to a Hollywood starlet, which made him rather special. He spoke of a previous college and referred vaguely to an emotional breakdown. He was witty

A NOT-SO-NICE JEWISH BOY FACES WORLD WAR II

and fascinating and a most stimulating friend. I envied his volubility. Why couldn't I be that clever?

Mel's main interest was dramatics. He urged me to audit one of the acting workshops. I wasn't particularly interested. I thought acting was frivolous, and a waste of time. Nevertheless it was intriguing. There had been, of course, my grammar school experience with "The Taming Of The Shrew." Also in grammar school there had been my encounter with pantomime.

In assembly class the teacher had asked pupils to volunteer to get up on the large stage in the auditorium and act things out without words. I had raised my hands several times, eager to try my luck. I don't know if it was deliberate or not, but the teacher seemed to ignore me. Finally, reluctantly it seemed to me, the teacher called on me. My heart thumping wildly, I stumbled onto the stage and raced through the assigned exercise. When I took my seat, there was complete silence. I waited for some sort of evaluation. None was forthcoming. I assumed I was just too awful to discuss, and I was slightly crushed, but flushed with excitement. I may not have impressed anyone, but I had fought the good fight and, for one brief moment, conquered my shyness.

And then there was my theatrical experience in Hebrew school. That, comparatively speaking, had been a victory. The teacher there had suggested that someone write a play dramatizing the story of Purim (the Jewish Feast Of Lots)...the story of how Esther, a Jewess, had saved her people from destruction by Haman, the scheming Prime Minister. The story took place a long time ago in the days of ancient Persia. I wrote the play and rehearsed it with members of the class and the teacher's assistance. I also played Ahasuerus, the Persian king. My mother sewed a very elegant costume for me with a purple cape and gold pantaloons and a gold cardboard

CHANGES

crown. We gave our performance for the students and teachers at the Hebrew school. This was on the dais in the synagogue. I had no recollection of how well the performance went, but the experience had been a fulfilling one. I did remember that. So, merely out of curiosity, I decided to sample a session of the acting workshop.

CHAPTER THIRTY SIX

I DISCOVER A NEW WORLD

It was with mixed emotions that I sat in the back of the darkened little auditorium and watched the advanced acting students rehearse several scenes. Somehow I felt it was a dangerous thing for me to do. There was something too tempting about the theatre, too seductive. I planned to be a serious writer. Theatre was really rather frivolous.

The first scene to be rehearsed was from Moliere's "The Imaginary Invalid." It was being played by Mel and a talented young woman by the name of Eileen Heckart. Mel played the hypochondriac and Eileen played his saucy maid. They seemed to be having a lot of fun working out the scene, deciding where they would stand, how they would react to one another. It was fascinating to watch the process. And when the scene moved along it was like watching two pros at a tennis match, and it was very funny. Eileen was especially enchanting. No matter what the future held for this young woman...this was an actress, as accomplished as anyone could be.

Next there was a scene from "Rosmersholm," a play by Henrik Ibsen. The mood was completely different. A former clergyman and his housekeeper are in love with one another, but they're haunted by the suicide of the clergyman's wife. The girl playing Rebecca, the housekeeper, seemed rather pedestrian. Somehow I felt she should be more attractive or more sensual or something. But it was interesting to watch the two actors discuss their roles and try to make the scene work.

Having seen the rehearsals I was curious to follow through and witness the formal presentation of these scenes in class. I asked permission and I was allowed to audit the class. I sat back, waiting eagerly to see how the scenes turned out.

I DISCOVER A NEW WORLD

The scene from "Rosmersholm" was the first to be performed. It was a revelation.

In rehearsal the girl had been wearing old jeans and a T shirt and worn her hair in a braid. In performance she wore a long, brown velvet gown and earrings, and put her hair up. Suddenly she was Rebecca. She was glamorous and seductive and somehow the scene seemed to catch fire. Whether it was the costume or a change in her performance, I couldn't tell, but the transformation was truly remarkable.

The scene from "The Imaginary Invalid" was hilarious. There was much laughter and, at the end, hearty applause.

This whole business of make-believe...it was like entering another world, a world with a language and a heart of its own. There was glamor. There was excitement, even something to chew on. It seemed to be an enchanting life, the life of the theatre. The love for the stage seemed to eradicate all barriers, all social levels, gender differences, social formalities. Communication was heartfelt and direct, no nonsense and, as I watched these actors talk to one another, there seemed to be this wonderful sense of camaraderie. How pure and beautiful this love of the theatre was! If only the entire world could share it. There would be no wars, no destruction, no killing. There would be only innocence and make-believe.

******

The Strollers was the main dramatic group on campus. I attended a Strollers production of "Ladies In Retirement," a murder-suspense melodrama by Reginald Denham. It was a period piece that took place in the English countryside. Eileen Heckart played the leading role of Ellen, the take-charge older sister who committed murder in order to protect her two

A NOT-SO-NICE JEWISH BOY FACES WORLD WAR II

demented siblings. Eileen seemed to own that stage. At her very first entrance, you sat up and took notice. Her lines were spoken with such authority, in that throaty voice which seemed so unique. Here was someone to watch! Even her exits were somehow special. There was a certain flair about everything she did. As a matter of fact her entire performance was amazing. I couldn't stop marveling at her talent.

I debated for a long time whether I should take an acting course. I was there to get an education. The world was coming apart. My future was highly uncertain. Was this a time for make-believe, for playing games, for frivolity? It would be a sinful indulgence, wouldn't it? Finally, I thought, to hell with it. I might be dead in a year or two. When I ate a cupcake, I used to save the icing, the best part that is, for last. Well, I might not be around long enough to eat the icing. When it came time to choose my curriculum for the next semester, I signed up for an acting class.

At my first class in Basic Acting I found that there was to be little discussion of theory, and no boring exercises to endure, which suited me fine. Why sit around and talk? One learned by doing. We were told to pick a partner, rehearse a scene and present it in class. There was one familiar face in the class, the girl with the large nose and the beautiful figure, the one I'd met at Hillel, and seen there several times since. Virginia and I greeted each other like old friends. Neither of us knew anyone in the class, and we happily agreed to work together.

We met the following afternoon and debated what scene to work on. We wanted one that would give us both a meaty role. We decided on a scene from Maxwell Anderson's "Elizabeth The Queen," the final meeting between Elizabeth and her favorite, Lord Essex. Essex is condemned to death for treason. Elizabeth offers him a reprieve if he promises to give

I DISCOVER A NEW WORLD

up his ambition. He refuses and goes to his death. Elizabeth is left alone and loveless.

We rehearsed, sometimes in the corridor near the little auditorium and, when we could, which was not very often, on the stage. At our first rehearsal we spent most of the time getting acquainted. We talked about our background, our future and life in general.

Ginny's family...she preferred to be called Ginny... was quite poor and, as a matter of fact, was against her going to college. Since Ohio State did not charge tuition to state residents, and she lived in Columbus, she managed to persuade her father to let her go. However she had to work at Hillel part time to pay for her living expenses. She wanted to be a professional actress, but she had to promise to major in social work, so that she'd have a real profession to fall back on. I told her about my meager theatrical background, and that I hoped, someday, to be a best-selling novelist.

Ginny was very quick and very creative, and we had this wonderful rapport. First we read the scene through, and talked briefly about our characters. We then discussed the staging, where to put the furniture, where to enter, where to move etc. I made suggestions, she made suggestions. We worked unselfishly, concerned as much with each other's performance as our own. After we blocked out the movement we found, as we rehearsed, that the emotional conflict seemed to get deeper and deeper and, somehow or other, it seemed so easy, so natural to express our innermost feelings. It was exciting to feel the scene grow bit by bit, so exhilarating when the scene seemed to take off and have a life of its own. We felt we had something special.

The day of the presentation I was pretty nervous. When our turn came, we got up on stage and set up our furniture. Actually we just used one chair to represent Elizabeth's throne.

A NOT-SO-NICE JEWISH BOY FACES WORLD WAR II

I was completely numb. Ginny sat on the chair. I went off stage to prepare for my entrance. I wore a white shirt open at the neck. To me it was my costume as an Elizabethan lord. Suddenly I was panic-stricken. There were actually people out there that were going to watch Ginny and myself exchange very deep felt emotions. How I was going to get through this...this nightmare I had no idea. Ginny seemed to be ready and waiting for me to enter. I took a deep breath. My legs seemed to take on a life of their own. They took me into the scene and I spoke my first line.

You sent for me. Or so they said. (My voice sounded so unnatural, so constricted. Why was I so tense? It was just Ginny and me.)

Yes, said Elizabeth.

It would have been kinder to leave me to my thoughts till the axe came down and ended them. You spoil me for death.(I sounded a little more human.)

Are you so set on dying? (In contrast to rehearsal, Ginny seemed much more secure than I was, and that made me a little more secure.)

I can't say I care for it....

The scene seemed to go quite well, some moments more truly felt than others. But I did feel like a lord up there, yet sort of naked and exposed. The people in the audience seemed to be able to look into my very soul. They knew what I was thinking, they knew what I was feeling. I could hide nothing. They know all about me. Was there anything I should feel guilty about? And, incidentally, it did flash through my mind that I was rather dashing, wasn't I. And Ginny actually did seem crushed and old as she let her lover go to his death. She seemed so alone and so desolate. I marveled how her voice became harsh and dry. Before I knew it I was saying

I DISCOVER A NEW WORLD

my last line and making my exit, reluctantly. I wanted the scene to go on, but it was over.

Applause.

I thought it sounded pretty healthy. Ginny and I came to the front of the stage for the critique. When members of the class looked up at me, I felt slightly uneasy. They seemed to know all about me...personally. What did they see, I wondered.

I was too full of the experience to digest the assessment, but I gathered our work was good. I was exhilarated...and somewhat concerned. I was enjoying this too much. I'm going to be a writer not an actor!

CHAPTER THIRTY SEVEN

I GET IN DEEPER

Our next assignment in the acting class I signed up for was to work on a scene from a Greek tragedy. Ginny and I chose one from Euripides' "Medea," the final encounter between Jason and Medea.

Medea, a foreign princess with magical powers, betrayed her family and her country for the sake of her husband. Jason, however, is ambitious and later deserts his wife for a Greek princess. In revenge, Medea sends his bride-to-be a poisoned dress which consumes her, and then she slays the children she bore with Jason, which I thought a little extreme. After she murders her children, Medea boldly faces the crowd, and Jason. She's immune, she tells them, because she's protected by the gods. Jason curses at her and rants and raves.

In some ways this scene was simpler because the emotions were quite straightforward, mostly anger. The language, however, translated from the Greek, was stilted, the phrasing awkward. But Ginny was so full of fire as she taunted the accusing crowd that it was easy to summon up the anger. The more Ginny taunted me the more furious I grew, and actually it was great fun battling with each other and working oneself into a fury.

As we dug deeper and deeper into the relationship between this bitter couple, we began to feel like a team, a really good one. When it was all said and done, I think the scene was much more fun to act, than it was for the audience to watch...and what a great way to get rid of all one's frustrations.

I became aware of the fact that this wonderful rapport between Ginny and myself could easily ripen into love, but that big nose was really a turn off, much as I castigated

I GET IN DEEPER

myself for being so superficial, so shallow. And she seemed so insecure, so helpless, and she really didn't know how to dress, and yet she was so talented. I sometimes felt like her father. I came to take a very personal interest in her career, in her ambitions. Gradually I became less and less aware of the nose.

I was friendly with some of the other students in my acting class, but I never really got close to them. There was one cute little girl, Shirley Berger, cuddly and rather forward. She wore this white angora sweater which she filled very nicely and was rather sexy. She seemed to want to come between Ginny and myself, but she didn't have the excitement, the class that Ginny had.

I dated Ginny a couple of times. Once I took her to a nightclub. I picked her up at her home and, as I waited for her in the living room, I met her parents. They seemed to be untutored working class people, peasant types. Ginny came into the room in this godawful polka-dot dress which, though it showed off her figure, was not becoming at all. It looked cheap. I had the feeling that she'd bought the dress especially for our date. Later in the evening she asked me what I thought of the dress. I told her as tactfully as I possibly could, which may not have been that tactful, but I had to be honest, didn't I? What I mean to say is she would have wanted me to be honest, wouldn't she?

******

Whether I liked it or not, I was beginning to get hooked. In addition to The Strollers there was The Hillel Players, and the drama department gave one or two productions a year. In the Hillel newsletter I read that The Hillel Players were presenting the Capek play about robots

A NOT-SO-NICE JEWISH BOY FACES WORLD WAR II

called "R.U.R." The plot didn't sound very interesting. However I managed to get a copy of the play and read it. I didn't feel right for any of the roles but here was an opportunity to audition, and the experience might stand me in good stead. Ginny and I consulted one another and, though she wasn't too keen on the play either, and neither of us felt too hopeful, we decided to audition anyway. Neither of us were cast, and neither of us was really disappointed.

The Strollers' next production was a psychological suspense mystery by the British playwright, Emlyn Williams called, "Night Must Fall." I hadn't bothered to audition for it. I thought that I really should take a breather. Theatre was becoming too important.

Ginny was cast in the role of the old lady who gets murdered. I was delighted for her. It was quite a coup. I didn't get to see much of her during the rehearsals. She didn't seem to be too happy about the way it was going, but I attributed that to her insecurity, because I knew how good she really was.

I attended the opening with great anticipation. And there she was up on that stage, the old lady in the wheelchair. Her makeup was quite good and she really did look old in that grey wig as she maneuvered about the stage in her wheel chair. But maybe it was me, I don't know, but she did seem a little self-conscious. And her voice was rather tight, as if caught in her throat. I wasn't sure whether it was nerves or maybe she was trying for old age. I felt very uncomfortable for her. I knew how anxious she was to be good, and I was so anxious for her. She could be ruffled so easily. I wanted so to instill in her the confidence I felt she should have had. I was tactful enough not to criticize her when I went backstage. And she really was quite effective when she got hysterical, just before she got murdered.

I GET IN DEEPER

Ginny also got to play Queen Elizabeth in a production of "Mary Of Scotland" by Maxwell Anderson. This was presented by a group off campus but, for some reason or other, I never did get to see it.

******

The Strollers were next presenting an old-fashioned melodrama in the main auditorium on campus. Neither Ginny or I were cast in the production. We were both disappointed. I suggested that she work with me on a duet for the olio to be presented during intermission. I had no idea whether I could sing or not.

There was only one way to find out, I said.

And Ginny did have a lovely voice. It took a lot of persuasion and she finally did agree. We chose "A Bicycle Built For Two" as our introduction to the world of song and dance. We raided the costume department. Ginny found an old fashioned dress. I found a period blazer, a straw hat and a cane. We rehearsed the song, doing our own staging, which we kept very simple. Ginny, however, felt unhappy about the progress of the number. I tried to allay her fears.

It'll be fine, I said. *Don't worry about it.*

But she did, and she wanted to show it to Nancy, one of the instructors in the English department, a bouncy, droll blond woman with a wonderful sense of humor, to ask her opinion.

Why do we need someone else's opinion? We ought to know what we're doing, I said.

She insisted however.

I was perturbed that Ginny didn't trust my judgement, but what could I do? *Okay, okay,* I said.

We went through the song for the instructor. She and

A NOT-SO-NICE JEWISH BOY FACES WORLD WAR II

Ginny conferred. Apparently, the feedback was not good. Ginny decided not to go through with it after all. I felt betrayed and hurt. I was determined, however, to go on, even if I had to go on alone.

I chose another song, "Hello, My Baby," and worked on it by myself, with appropriate gestures. Nothing could be more glamorous, nothing could be more exciting, than to be a song and dance man with a straw hat and a cane, and nothing was going to stop me. After learning the new song, I approached the director of the melodrama.

I have this song I'd like to do during the intermission, as an olio, I said.

The director looked at me for a moment. I waited, apprehensively.

Okay, she said.

I couldn't believe it. I was walking on air. I was gonna be in the show, after all. It was too late to be listed in the program, but what difference did that make? I was in the show, and that'll show Ginny!

Came performance time, there I was backstage in my striped jacket, straw hat and cane, petrified but eager and ready.

Intermission came.

I stepped out onto the stage, in front of the curtain.

I did my number as rehearsed. People were not prepared for the olio. They got up from their seats and moved about, talking among themselves. I was disturbed by this, but I couldn't let that stop me. I plowed on. I didn't know whether I was being heard or not. I didn't know whether I was good or not. It didn't matter. What mattered was that I was out there, doing my best. I had not backed out like that coward, Ginny. I came off the stage trailing clouds of glory.

I had done it!

I GET IN DEEPER

By God I had done it!

One had to dare and dare again or one would never achieve anything!

I was really furious with Ginny. What was she afraid of? Why was she so timid? She was the one that was dedicated to the theatre. She was the one who wanted to be a professional. How was one to learn if one didn't expose oneself? If I was bad, so what? The next time I'd be better. Maybe one had to be bad before one could be good. Ginny made no comment. I was really concerned about her.

And now I was really hooked.

******

One of the professors had written an historical play about the war of 1812. The play was to be presented in the small auditorium used by the drama class. I auditioned, and I was cast in the bit part of a sailor. I came on, made some sort of announcement, I forget what. I do remember it consisted of three short lines, and then I exited. I wore this white uniform, the trousers of which were rather tight which made me a little self-conscious. At dress rehearsal, as I came off the stage, I was aware of giggles and whispers on the part of a couple of the girls backstage, and, of all people, that traitress, Ginny. I asked her what they were laughing at. Apparently my behind wiggled when I walked. I became even more self-conscious, and very insecure. That wouldn't do at all.

During the performances I tried to walk more slowly. I asked Ginny to watch and see if I still wiggled. Ginny conceded that there was some improvement. I still detected a rather suspicious smile.

However I had a part in, what was for me, a major production. This was definitely a step upward. I decided it was

A NOT-SO-NICE JEWISH BOY FACES WORLD WAR II

pure jealousy on the part of the girls, and maybe Ginny, too. I was in the play and they were not. Anyway, from now on I had to make sure my behind didn't wiggle. Maybe I had to be sure that I was standing tall.

But being on that stage and giving a performance really was a precarious feat. One had to watch one's speech. One had to watch one's movement. One had to remember one's lines. One had to relate to the other people on stage. In addition to that one had to be aware of the people out front and make sure that they heard you. It was like walking a tightrope, an irresistible challenge, a test of one's metal. Maybe I was a physical coward but...MORAL COURAGE...that's where one's virility lay.

But what I was really concerned about at this time was immortality. I wanted to create something that would live after I was gone. So much as I enjoyed acting, much as I felt challenged by it, lured by it, seduced by it, fulfilled by it I did not seriously consider acting as a profession.

Acting, after all, wasn't really an art. What did an actor do but parrot the words that had been written for him? Duse and Bernhardt...what was there left of them, in contrast to Shakespeare and Dostoyevsky?

And that was another thing. Wasn't acting really a woman's profession?

Of course, there was John Barrymore. And Stanislavski was a man and he, supposedly, was the father of the modern actor. The exceptions to the rule.

The dream, of course, was fame, wealth and a beautiful woman to love, in that order. But whether that dream should include the theatre in some way or other I couldn't decide.

Behind the campus was the Olentangy River. I took walks along the river on week-ends, usually alone but sometimes with Ginny. I remember sharing with her a glorious

I GET IN DEEPER

orange, red and gold sunset, the vivid colors reflected in the water.

Also behind the campus was the barn where the cows and livestock were kept. The university had an agricultural college as well as a college of arts and science, which reminded me that this was the heartland of America, that there were farms across this great country of ours as well as large cities.

In this bucolic setting I dreamt of leading a simple, uncomplicated existence in tune with nature. At the thought of tilling the soil I felt a certain strength flow through my veins. I saw myself as a gentle giant in soiled working clothes with large, calloused hands and the body of an oak tree, rising at dawn from a warm bed, my woman breathing softly at my side. I saw myself tilling the soil, eating simple meals and enjoying the elemental pleasures of life. What a wonderful way to grow old!

If only I hadn't been cursed with an over-active imagination!

CHAPTER THIRTY EIGHT

I GET A JOB IN A DEFENSE PLANT

My first year at college was now nearing it's end and the war hung over the campus like a dark cloud. The word was that seniors would definitely be allowed to finish their schooling, and maybe the juniors. As far as the freshman were concerned...it remained to be seen.

It was early September when I'd left home for the very first time, and I tried to figure out what I had accomplished during these past nine months. Sexually I'd been a dismal failure. Yet both encounters had somehow assuaged my curiosity, for the time being that is. There was still a big question mark in my mind about the propriety of sharing sex with another male, but that was really of secondary importance.

I had attended several major league football games. It had been thrilling to sit in that huge oval stadium bundled up against the cold, to see the band parade about the field followed by the cheer leaders, and then to join in the cheers. And then to see our team march out on the playing field, line up...and then the game was on, fast and furious, and I found myself shouting with the rest of the crowd. I experienced, I had to admit, a sense of pride, corny and fleeting as it was. And it occurred to me that an athlete's career was even more ephemeral than an actor's. As far as my courses were concerned, I had encountered some beautiful French poetry, and that was about it.

With my future so uncertain, I began to think of my life on campus as a thing of the past and I wondered if, in years to come, if there were years to come, I would remember the details of my days here at Ohio State. Would I remember the coffee shop on the corner where I bought my breakfast? Would I remember the student hangout where I stopped for a

I GET A JOB IN A DEFENSE PLANT

coke? Would I remember the different buildings? Would they still be standing, the old ones especially? And the chiming of the clock in the tower as I crossed the campus? Would I remember the bookstore where I bought my textbooks, the down town movie house where I saw "Casablanca", the ride through the dark streets to see "The Maltese Falcon", the balcony of the old Hartman Theatre where I spent so many enthralling evenings? And if I did survive the war, would my dreams survive as well?

As I packed to leave on my summer hiatus there was this feeling of regret. I regretted leaving my school life behind. I regretted leaving Ginny behind, though I tried to downplay the relationship. I looked forward to seeing my family, but I also looked forward eagerly to my return to college, hoping against hope that I would be able to return.

******

Back home there was now the question of a summer job. I had managed to get through my first year on the six hundred dollars I had put aside, with even a little left over. In the two upcoming months I was hoping somehow to earn enough to pay for my second year. My father knew someone connected with a defense plant in a nearby town. Because of my father's connection, I was hired on the spot. I was assigned to the night shift, seven in the evening to three the next morning.

I had mixed feelings about taking the job. For one thing, the trip to the factory was a long and complicated one involving two buses. I didn't mind the trip out there, but I didn't look forward to taking two buses in the early hours of the morning when I'd probably be dead tired. In addition to that, there was the decidedly unpleasant prospect of menial

A NOT-SO-NICE JEWISH BOY FACES WORLD WAR II

labor, standing in front of a machine for eight long dreary hours. The pay, however, was excellent and that, after all, was what really mattered and, besides, it was only ten weeks, and I would be doing my bit for the war effort.

After my second day (rather night) at the plant I made the acquaintance of one of the workers who lived not far from my home. The man had a car and was kind enough to pick me up in the evening, and drop me off in the morning.

It was certainly odd going to work at sunset, just when you felt like relaxing. All night long I stood in front of a drill press boring two holes into small, round metal discs. Oil poured automatically over the discs to prevent them from overheating. My fingers were covered with warm oil. My feet grew tired, my back ached, and the hours dragged on endlessly. I tried to keep reminding myself that I was "doing my bit" for the war effort, in addition to the fact that I was making good money.

I tried to occupy my mind with something, anything, to shut out the boredom, but that was dangerous. I had to keep alert. If I didn't, if I started to dream, I could easily have an accident. The nights were endless, and by one in the morning I found myself in a sort of daze. I'd get home at sunrise, and found it hard to get to sleep.

******

There were no more leisurely hours on the porch, immersed in a book. As a matter of fact I didn't feel very much like reading. I was either too tired, or too on edge and, because of my odd hours at the factory, I was not able to see my friends very often. Not that there were that many to see. Irving and I did manage to get together a couple of times, but it wasn't the same. And we managed to get together at

I GET A JOB IN A DEFENSE PLANT

Harold's house once, but that, too, was somehow less satisfying, overshadowed by what the future held.

Gloria, my friend across the street had moved. The family who now lived in her apartment were not as forthright or as uncomplicated. The parents were meek and very religious. Jewish, of course. There was a quiet little boy whom I seldom saw, and his older sister, Ruth. Ruth was a wonderfully foolish girl, naive, gossipy and easy to tease. I enjoyed baiting her in a good natured sort of way, but she didn't have the energy and the joy for living that Gloria had. And Ruth, silly girl that she was, had a crush on Irving.

I was now a sophomore, a travelled one at that, and I was even more aware of the schism that had grown up between me, my family and my friends. In addition to that I seem to have lost touch with life in general. I had no anchor. I was a ship that had been loosed from its moorings, and was drifting out to sea, and a stormy sea at that.

And the war was ever present. That's all one read about. That's all one heard on the radio. And, if you went to the movies, the newsreels brought it home in very graphic terms. Soldiers, wounded and dead. Hordes of refugees evicted from their homes trudging down dusty roads, bombed out buildings everywhere. And the news reports from day to day continued to be more and more alarming.

NAZIS WIPE OUT THE ENTIRE CZECH VILLAGE OF LIDICE!

JAPANESE SUBMARINES BOMB AN AREA NORTH OF OREGON!

POLISH GOVERNMENT IN EXILE REPORTS 700,000 JEWS SLAIN IN POLAND!

FIRST USA CASUALTIES: 44,143 WOUNDED. 4,801 DEAD!

Madmen were in charge of the asylum, and I was truly

A NOT-SO-NICE JEWISH BOY FACES WORLD WAR II

ashamed of belonging to the human race. I wanted to hide somewhere, to block out the horror that seemed to be inescapable.

On June 30th young men, eighteen to twenty, were required to register for possible draft. I reported to the draft board. I was classified as One A. My return to college was now really up in the air.

Soon my manhood would be tested. But I was a coward. I was the first to admit it. I don't think I would run away if I were faced with the enemy, but neither could I shoot a gun. Or could I? If someone was shooting at me, I guess I'd return their fire. But suppose I came face to face with the enemy? Hand to hand combat?

In the ten weeks that I worked at the plant I had managed to save almost twice as much as the six hundred dollars I was aiming for, more than I had saved in my seven months at the supermarket. But what was the point of going back to school when I might be called up at any moment? Then again what was the point of just waiting around, waiting for the axe to fall? I decided to go back to Ohio State, and let the future take care of itself.

CHAPTER THIRTY NINE

A GHOST, A DEFEAT AND A TRIUMPH

The railroad station in Columbus was just as old and as decrepit as I'd remembered it, but it now had an air of nostalgia. The house I had roomed in the year before was filled up. I found another room, closer to the campus in a charming, old fashioned home. Overstuffed chair with a doily in the living room. A quaint wooden staircase leading to the floor above. I climbed the winding staircase, passing a small lace-curtained window on the landing half way up, and then a few more stairs, and there was my room, private and cozy.

It was sort of lonely after the previous house, and I missed Mel Joseph's lively talks. Other than that it suited me fine. Mel, who had introduced me to acting, was nowhere to be found. Eileen Heckart, whose acting I'd admired so much, had left for New York to make her fortune as an actress. Quite a number of the young men had been drafted. As a matter of fact I was gratified to find that men were at a premium on campus.

My job in the kitchen of the fraternity house was given to a needy fraternity brother. I found a lunch job at the university hospital in the staff cafeteria. The food was delicious and plentiful. There were all sorts of odd culinary treats like escalloped oysters, which I'd never tasted before, and veal marsala, chipped beef on toast...and ice cream.

The ice cream was produced at the dairy on campus. It was rich and mouth-watering, one flavor more luscious than the other...maple walnut and coffee and strawberry and butter pecan and rum raisin. I devoured bowls of it. By the time I got to my first class after lunch my stomach was full and my mind was groggy. I was furious at myself for nodding off now and again because that particular course was the most interesting of all. It was philosophy.

A NOT-SO-NICE JEWISH BOY FACES WORLD WAR II

Philosophy was a new and a fascinating world, stimulating, provocative. There was Hobbes' "Leviathan" and Plato's Dialogues and Descartes and Hume. Some of these theories were hard to digest, but that didn't matter because they were a challenge, and they made me think. I was particularly struck by Plato's imagery of passion, represented by two spirited horses, difficult to keep in check, one pulling one way, one pulling the other. What a brilliant metaphor! What thought-provoking ideas! The conflict between reason and desire! What fantastic minds! And there I was nodding and jerking awake. How humiliating! But the food was so tempting. I gained several pounds that semester.

I also took a course in elementary psychology. I was irritated by the pretentious terms. I left each session fuming at, what I considered inaccuracies, half truths and guesswork. Art was far more accurate and realistic than this so-called science.

I was required to write a thesis for my English class. I chose as my subject Thomas Wolfe. I had read most of Wolfe's novels, "Look Homeward, Angel," "Of Time And The River" and "You Can't Go Home Again." I set about reading the rest of his work. Wolfe had died only two or three years ago, at the age of thirty eight, leaving not a large body of work, and not too much biographical information. The novels themselves, however, were autobiographical, so I didn't feel the loss of factual information about his personal life.

I steeped myself in his writings. I breathed Thomas Wolfe day and night. I came to identify with this brilliant giant from North Carolina, his outsized extravagant personality, his novels, so galvanizing, so imaginative so soaring. If only I could write like that! His colorful family became my own; his penny pinching mother, his giant of a father, his sensitive brother; and I made the journey with him from the rural South to the towers of Manhattan, to his

A GHOST, A DEFEAT AND A TRIUMPH

adventures in Germany. And there was his passionate love affair with Aline Bernstein, the famous stage designer, a married woman who was older than he was.

I experienced vicariously his feverish literary toil. I stood beside him as he scribbled away on his notebooks resting on top of his refrigerator. I accompanied him on his sessions with Maxwell Perkins, the famous editor and I gloried in his triumphant success... and I tried hard to overlook his anti-Semitism.

How disappointing!

Nobody's perfect, I guess.

One evening, as I was coming up the winding staircase leading to my room, I stopped at the landing halfway up to catch my breath. The window was open. A breeze blew the curtain towards me, and I found myself face to face with Thomas Wolfe, his spirit at any rate.

My hair stood on end.

Was this a friendly spirit or was it an angry one?

Was he flattered by my attention, or did he resent it?

Before I could make up my mind, he was gone. Disappeared just as quickly as he had made himself felt.

I stood there in a daze. Why had he manifested himself to me? Was he trying to tell me something?

I continued up the stairs, puzzled and apprehensive.

Finally I decided that he had come to give me his blessing.

Now I am a skeptic. I have always questioned the existence of spirits of any sort. Yet what happened to me on that landing that evening was real.

The thesis on Thomas Wolfe was a labor of love and I was gratified to receive an A plus.

******

A NOT-SO-NICE JEWISH BOY FACES WORLD WAR II

What with the shortage of men on campus I was in great demand in our acting class. I could pick and choose my partners and the scenes I would take part in. I gloried in my popularity and enjoyed working with the different women in the class. For some reason or other I didn't work on any scenes with Ginny during the early part of that semester. I think it was because she was involved with an important production, which I'll get to later.

One treasured moment in our acting class had nothing to do with performing. The professor was out sick one morning and Nancy, the buxom young blond who was his assistant, took over. She was unprepared for the session and decided to read to the class from Stanislavski's "An Actor Prepares."

The class took seats and she opened the sacred text, and started to read from this holy of hollies as Mae West, the sexy and witty actress/playwright, would have read it. All the highly technical terms and discussions took on hilarious sexual overtones. The class roared with laughter for the entire hour. "An Actor Prepares," the so-called actor's Bible, was sacred no more.

The drama department's next major production was going to be "Medea." Ginny was virtually assured the leading role of Medea, since she was a favorite of Professor Bahn, and he was going to direct the play. Since I had worked with Ginny on the role of Jason, Medea's faithless husband, and it had gone well, we both felt that my being cast as Jason was a shoo-in. There was really no one else around that was suitable.

The auditions were in the evening. I had a ticket that night for a concert, the Russian Cossack Chorus. I asked to be taken early. I read well and I knew it. I left for the concert confident that the role was mine. As I sat through the concert,

A GHOST, A DEFEAT AND A TRIUMPH

I was a little uneasy though. Maybe I shouldn't have left that early. Maybe that was a mistake. Then I thought, what difference did it make? I read well. There was no one else around who was as right as I was for the role. I didn't enjoy the concert as much as I would have under ordinary circumstances.

I waited anxiously for the posting of the cast list. Two days later it was tacked to the bulletin board. I raced over and scanned the list eagerly.

Ginny was Medea.

My eyes scanned the list.

Where was my name?

There was Jason...but my name wasn't opposite it.

There must be some mistake. I stared at the sheet in disbelief.

I checked the list once, twice, three times, four times.

How could this be?

Something's wrong.

I was sick, literally sick to my stomach. I thought I was going to vomit.

I staggered around the corner to an empty section of the corridor and tried to pull myself together.

I could easily have passed for a young Greek warrior. Alec, The boy that was slated to play Jason had an awful nasal Midwestern twang, and he looked like a ruddy farm boy, a bumpkin.

Several people came by to console me. I shook them off. Their pity only served to make the disappointment even more painful. I wished I could cry, but I couldn't. It was stupid! Getting this upset because I didn't get a part in a play. What kind of a fool are you? You break down in tears because you can't go to the movies. You practically have a

A NOT-SO-NICE JEWISH BOY FACES WORLD WAR II

nervous breakdown because you didn't get a part in a play. What nonsense! You ought to be ashamed of yourself!

But I couldn't help it. This would have been the chance to play a leading role and, what's more, it would have been opposite Ginny. What a triumph it would have been...for the both of us! And now she had to rehearse and spend time with that idiot! That oaf! Apparently, after I left for the concert, that moron was the only male around, and he read all evening. Somehow or other, he convinced that inept director that he could play the part. I lost my respect for the director who was, supposedly, a Doctor of English. **Dr.** Bahn, indeed! He was not that highly thought of anyway. Pretentious snob!

I followed the progress of the rehearsals with grim satisfaction. I sat in the back of the darkened theatre and watched, eating my heart out. Oh, God, he can't even speak! He's embarrassing. He's awful! Surely they're not going to let him get up in front of an audience. He'll be laughed off the stage. That professor must be out of his mind, absolutely mad!

Ginny, of course, did all she could to console me. But what could she say? In addition to that, I was jealous of her relationship to her leading man. I felt betrayed, even though I knew she was not to blame. But did she have to be so nice to that...so and so? That supportive? That close? And here I thought that she was my friend.

I came to the opening night. I sulked in my seat.

The curtain went up.

Jason was barely adequate, to put it kindly. That helped a little. To be absolutely fair, however, every now and then, he wasn't completely embarrassing.

Despite my frustration, I kept my fingers crossed for Ginny. What did it matter if I wasn't in the show? She was, and I wanted her to shine. To my disappointment, Ginny was not very good. Oh, she had moments, here and there, in which

A GHOST, A DEFEAT AND A TRIUMPH

she was absolutely wonderful, but those were only moments, brief flashes of brilliance. Her performance, for the most part, was flat and empty. She made the gestures, she made the movements, but the performance was hollow. She was just saying words...and she knew it, I could tell.

I came backstage after the opening. She looked at me apologetically, as if to say...I wasn't very good, was I? I tried to bolster her morale. Maybe she was sensitive about her nose.

You looked great, I said. *Like a real princess. No, you really did. Like a classical princess.*

You think so?

And that's a great costume.

She looked at me skeptically. Nothing more was said, and I left. I forced myself to attend a later performance. She was not much better. Alec, however, to my chagrin, seemed to be improving...very slightly. Or maybe I was just getting used to that nasal twang. The pain, the wound itself, lingered for weeks. A short time later, however, I had a minor triumph which made up, in part, for that major setback.

******

"The Silver Cord" by Sidney Howard was chosen as a class production. In this play about a possessive mother one of the sons was solid and down to earth, the other neurotic and completely under the thumb of his domineering mother. Instinctively I seemed to understand both these two young men. I could play either one of them, I thought.

A problem...which turned out to be a blessing. I was the only male in the class. I volunteered to play both roles. The two men were hardly ever on stage at the same time. Those scenes could be cut, I suggested. I was thrilled when I was given the opportunity to undertake this tour-de-force.

A NOT-SO-NICE JEWISH BOY FACES WORLD WAR II

With some judicious pruning, a slight change in costume...and I was cast as both the younger and the older son.

The rehearsals were exciting. I had never felt more comfortable, more self-assured. I switched from one character to the other with the greatest of ease. One minute I was the sensitive boy, weak and pliant. The next I was the more mature son, down to earth and strong.

During the performance itself, I was amazingly confident, and it came off exceptionally well. I was delighted that the performance was witnessed by Dr. Bahn, himself, and, I must say, the man redeemed himself. He critiqued all the performances and when he came to mine, he was highly complimentary. This was unusual, because he was usually very critical. He did question some nervous gestures in one scene where I played the more stable son. I explained that was a choice I made and gave him the reason. He did not disagree. The man did know something about theatre, after all.

And I was really coming into my own as an actor.

CHAPTER FORTY

HAIL AND FAREWELL

My job at the hospital cafeteria became unavailable at the end of the semester. No explanation was given. I wondered if the powers that be resented my eating all that ice cream? But I wasn't the only one.

At any rate, I got a job as a waiter in a restaurant. I worked lunch and dinner. I had to gulp down my food, which wasn't nearly as good or as plentiful. I wasn't even allowed a salad with my dinner. Lunch was a nightmare. The place was mobbed. I was hassled by my employer. *You've gotta be faster.* It was a most unpleasant job, and I was a lousy waiter. This too shall pass, I kept telling myself.

Unfortunately the future was not something to look forward to. My draft notice had been forwarded to me from home. I would be called up in April, which meant that I would be able to finish my second semester...and that was it.

Winter was winding down. The sky was bluer than ever. The cold earth unfroze, and green leaves began to appear on the trees, and Spring was more poignant than I'd remembered it. What had seemed so intimidating at first now seemed cozy and homelike. Those professors, who had seemed stern or withdrawn, now seemed warm and compassionate. College had become my way of life, and it was slipping away from me. Physically I was still there in Columbus, I was still there at Ohio State, attending classes, enjoying the acting, attempting to keep up a social life, but my mind was beginning to focus elsewhere, and I tried desperately not to think about what was to come.

Though I did date one or two other girls, I was closest to Ginny. We were colleagues. We were comrades. There was an unmistakable chemistry between us, and she seemed to grow more and more dependent on me for advice, for encouragement, and I was amazed at my own apparent strength and self-confidence.

******

The next assignment in acting class was to rehearse and present a scene from Noel Coward's comedy, "Private Lives." Ginny and I chose a scene from the second act between Elyot and Amanda, the roles Noel Coward had written for himself and Gertrude Lawrence.

Purely by coincidence a divorced English couple come to the same hotel on the Riviera with their newlywed spouses to spend their respective honeymoons. They come face to face with one another on adjoining balconies, realize that they're still in love, and run off to Paris, leaving behind their bewildered spouses. We chose a scene in the second act between the two lovers which takes place in their Paris apartment. It's both a love scene and a fight scene. They can't live with each other, and they can't live without each other. Sometimes the scene turns whimsical, sometimes childish, sometimes sentimental, but always there was that crisp, witty dialogue.

During the scene Elyot plays the piano, and they sing. I chose a song from Noel Coward's operetta, "Bittersweet"..."I'll See You Again." Actually, one of the reasons I chose it was because it was simpler than the one that was indicated in the script. In addition to that, somehow or other, it felt more appropriate.

There was something so poignant about these two seemingly frivolous people. The dialogue, at first glance, appeared to be brittle and artificial but, as we worked on the scene, we came to realize that, what appeared to be flippant words, originated from something deep down inside, something true and painful and lovely. Each line Ginny and I spoke seemed to come from our very own hearts. We came to understand and identify with this volatile couple. Since we both knew that I would soon be heading off to war there was an air of urgency, of sadness in the air, as we rehearsed.

The scene was an intimate one and, in staging it, Ginny and I seemed to be all over each other as we tried different positions on the sofa. It was a little awkward at times, but it brought us closer together. As a matter of fact, I was a little alarmed as to where the relationship was heading. I was careful not to allow what I was feeling as Elyot to spill over into what I felt for Ginny. At this point in my life I wasn't ready for anything that serious. Besides my feelings for Ginny were still rather ambivalent.

The day of the performance arrived. Backstage I got into a dressing gown, and Ginny got into a fancy housecoat, both of which we borrowed from the costume department. After waiting nervously for what seemed like hours, our turn finally came. I walked onto the stage and moved the piano into place. Then came the sofa and a chair. We took our places, took a breath, and began. As the scene progressed it became obvious that the lines had a resonance beyond the characters, beyond the situation in the play. Ginny and I, two naive Midwestern college students, were somehow in tune with this ultra-sophisticated British playwright's voice. We knew so little about the sort of lives that Elyot and Amanda led, but the words these two elegant people spoke, the relationship they had was ours...and "I'll See You Again." without our even acknowledging it, became "our song." We could feel that the audience, too, was aware of something special going on. We came off the stage in sort of a daze and, perhaps...a little embarrassed.

Our performance was highly praised by Dr. Bahn, and

even by several of our fellow students. I sensed a note of surprise in some of the laudatory words. Obviously there was no hiding what we felt for one another and, in my mind, I could no longer deny the incipient romance. We never spoke about it, but every time we met, accidentally at Hillel, or in class there was a start of recognition, as if we'd come face to face with a part of ourselves.

******

How fragile, how ephemeral...life and people and time and love...and everything, I thought.
Each day that passed was the first.
Each day that passed might be the last.
I would be returning home shortly, and yet it wouldn't be a homecoming at all. It would be a stop-over on my way to war, a pause before I started on a journey from which I might never return. And I asked myself, If I were to die tomorrow what would I look back on with pleasure? What were the highlights of my short life?
And I recalled that fall morning in Windber, Pennsylvania, the vacation I spent with Aunt Gertie and Uncle Morris, waking up to see the ground, the trees, the world as far as one could see covered with snow. And, way back when, in the days of what I now considered my childhood, there were those trips to the Jersey shore, to Bradley Beach and Asbury Park, barely awake in the cool of an August morning, getting into the car, glancing lazily out the window as the day grew warmer and warmer, sighting the boardwalk and the ocean, finding a place to park near the beach, the race to the lockers to change into the bathing suits, bathing in the chilly water and lying in the sun, the sandwiches and soda, walking along the boardwalk eating an ice cream cone and then the

HAIL AND FAREWELL

drive back to Newark. My sister, Rose, and I would joke and play "Ghost," a spelling game, or a game in which you had to guess the name of celebrities given their initials; and we'd stop at a vegetable stand and Mother would buy fresh corn and peaches or apples or plums. In the evening we'd sit around the kitchen table, cheeks still aglow from the rays of the sun, eating fresh corn on the cob with butter and salt and pepper and my mother sitting in a chair paring an apple, cutting the apple into sections, and chewing it slowly, sometimes even chewing the seeds and spitting out the husk.

And the most charming memory of all, the Passover Seder, the table laid out with an elegant tablecloth with the best dishes and silverware, and my father sitting at the head of the table, a pillow placed behind his back, as was the custom for the head of the household, and I would ask the four questions, first in Hebrew.

Mah nishtanu halaila hazeh,
And then in English.
Why is this night different from other nights?

And everyone at the table would drone on and on, reading in Hebrew from the Hagadah, the Passover prayer book, the answer to the four questions. And there were winks and undercover jokes between Rose and myself and, as part of the ritual, one of us would hide a part of a matzo, the "aphikomen," which was later ransomed by my father, since the ceremony couldn't continue without it. And there were all sorts of odd bits of food along the way like "haroses" (a delicious concoction made of ground apples and walnuts and exotic spices) and potato dipped in salt water and eggs dipped in salt water, and greens with horse radish and four glasses of sweet kosher-for-Passover Manishevitz wine, and a full meal consisting of a roast chicken with potato kugel and fresh vegetables and a noodle pudding sweetened with pineapple for

A NOT-SO-NICE JEWISH BOY FACES WORLD WAR II

dessert. And sometimes Beatie and Izzy would join us, or sometimes Aunt Tillie and Uncle Morris or Uncle Jack and Aunt Molly, and if Aunt Tillie was there she would ask for coffee and, with a sigh, my mother would serve her day old reheated coffee, black, of course, since she didn't mix meat and milk, and if Uncle Jack, the heretic, came by himself he would make sarcastic remarks infuriating my father, and after the meal the ceremony would be completed and there was this truly eerie moment when the door was opened so that the spirit of the prophet, Elijah, could pay us a visit, while Rose and I grew tipsier and tipsier; and finally the glorious Passover songs which Rose and I would sing at the top of our lungs. And when the event finally came to an end and my mother was faced with all the washing up, she would cap the evening with her usual. *Now let's open the window and throw out the dishes.*

At college there were no real goodbyes except for Ginny, who wept a little. I was alarmed and gratified by the tears. Somehow or other, whether I wanted it or not, some sort of unspoken commitment had been made. I wasn't quite sure exactly what it was, but it was there. We promised to write one another. I packed my things, and I sent my trunk on ahead to my family's house in Newark.

Suitcase in hand I treated myself to a cab. As we rode down the main street I looked out the window, drinking everything in. Was it only yesterday, arriving in Columbus for the first time, my heart in my mouth, I had stepped off the train, wandered into the train station, looked about at the strange surroundings, thrown caution to the winds, and climbed into a cab?

As we approached Union Station, as I prepared to leave Columbus, Ohio, possibly for the very last time, life was no longer real. It had taken on a dreamlike quality, a mythic

HAIL AND FAREWELL!

quality. I was a character in a novel, a young soldier, reluctantly leaving his college days behind.

Would he face combat?

Would he be wounded?

Would he die on foreign soil?

Would he be buried in some cemetery in France or Germany or Italy? Or would he survive and return, a war scarred veteran, cynical and wise, ready to take on the future, ready to write the great American novel?

What lay ahead for this naive young man as he boarded the train back to Newark, New Jersey, and silently said farewell to his youth?

BOOK TWO

A NICE JEWISH BOY FACES WORLD WAR II

BOOK TWO

A NOT-SO-NICE JEWISH BOY FACES WORLD WAR II

Chapter 1: I'm Introduced To The Army ... 255
Chapter 2: I Take A Giant Step 266
Chapter 3: A Pleasant But Painful Hiatus 278
Chapter 4: A Surprise Visit 283
Chapter 5: We Depart 288
Chapter 6: We Arrive 290
Chapter 7: The Continent 297
Chapter 8: A Pleasant Interlude 307
Chapter 9: The First Casualty 322
Chapter 10: The Hurtgen Forest 329
Chapter 11: A Defining Moment 334
Chapter 12: Another Test 342
Chapter 13: Cold, Waiting & Reflecting 345
Chapter 14: "Just Taking A Stroll" 350
Chapter 15: I Shed A Tear 361
Chapter 16: I Embarrass Myself 367
Chapter 17: I Am A Playwright! 371
Chapter 18: A Minor Tragedy 374
Chapter 19: The Aftermath 382
Chapter 20: A Wild Ride 388
Chapter 21: Making Friends 391
Chapter 22: Getting Better Acquainted 399
Chapter 23: Liege 405
Chapter 24: Next Stop: Wales 411
Chapter 25: The Arrival 417
Chapter 26: Cardiff 422
Chapter 27: I Meet A Young Lady 429
Chapter 28: My First Voice Lesson 436
Chapter 29: I Meet 'The Little Mouse' 443
Chapter 30: An Artistic Photographer 448

Chapter 31: The Dramatic Club 453
Chapter 32: Between The Devil & The Deep Blue Sea 459
Chapter 33: Choices, Choices 467
Chapter 34: Life Is Very Complicated 473
Chapter 35: London! 481
Chapter 36: A Music Lesson 492
Chapter 37: An Act Of Betrayal? 497
Chapter 38: Moliere's "The Misanthrope" .. 502
Chapter 39: Clara Gets Permission 510
Chapter 40: London Revisited 517
Chapter 41: At Last! 524
Chapter 42: Matthew 531
Chapter 43: Uh Oh! 535
Chapter 44: The Outcome 541
Chapter 45: The First Farewell 548
Chapter 46: What Is There To Say? 555

CHAPTER ONE

I"M INTRODUCED TO THE ARMY

I remember reading somewhere that a memoir is no more true to life than a novel. The writer went on to say that an author's job is to take life, which is unruly, and make it serve the story.

Memory is, after all, selective. In addition to that it is not very reliable...so I hesitate to call this book a memoir. You might call it a journey, a journey into the past. Though I lived through the events in this volume, encountering them is as fresh an experience for me as it would be for the reader. I am continually surprised by things I recall. Did I really do that? Was I really that foolhardy? Was I really that astute?

The war coincided with a very crucial period in my life. I was trying to find myself as a man, and as an artist. At the age of nineteen, having led a relatively sheltered existence, my exposure to war was a traumatic one. I'm still not really sure how deeply it affected me.

When the announcement came over the radio that the Japanese had attacked Pearl Harbor everything that seemed so important suddenly became a minor afterthought. What did it matter whether I wrote a magnificent novel or not? Making the best-seller list and becoming a celebrated author seemed so trivial. So I was pushing nineteen and still a virgin. So what? We were bound to go to war. It was now a matter of life and death.

I realized, for the first time, how peaceful, how idyllic my life had been up to then. Growing up in a middle class, primarily Jewish neighborhood in Newark, New Jersey had been relatively uneventful. Though World War II had been going on for two years now, and London had been suffering under the blitzkrieg, and Jews were being exterminated in Europe, here in America it was business as usual. Then came

A NOT-SO-NICE JEWISH BOY FACES WORLD WAR II

Pearl Harbor, "a day that will go down in infamy," said Franklin Delano Roosevelt, and we were now at war.

When I reported to the draft board and was classified as "One A," I seriously considered becoming a conscientious objector. Killing another human being, under any circumstance, I considered a crime.

Where this philosophy, attitude, or whatever it is, came from I really don't know. Certainly not my religious education which, though plentiful, was actually quite superficial. In Hebrew school I learned to read the Old Testament in Hebrew, a Hebrew I never really understood. I don't remember ever discussing morals or ethics or God, for that matter, not seriously, at any rate. But it seemed to me that life, human life, was the most precious thing imaginable. However, having learned that the Germans were slaughtering the Jews, as a Jew I decided that I couldn't just walk away. When I was called up, I would have to go.

During the second semester of my second year at Ohio State I received word that I was to report for induction that Spring. I was able to finish that second semester, and that was it. I bid farewell to Columbus, and returned to Newark to await my call to arms.

At home I was in limbo. Though I loved to read I had no desire whatsoever to pick up a book. I felt restless, uprooted. Now that I was faced with the possibility of imminent death I tried not to think, not to feel. I vaguely remember confronting my mother with the accusation that it was her generation that was responsible for the war. Governments are elected by voters, and the people get what they voted for. The poor woman was to blame for my having to go into battle. Money and greed are the reasons wars are fought. I was bitter, angry and scared to death.

When I reported for duty I was sent to Fort Dix in New

I'M INTRODUCED TO THE ARMY

Jersey. It was there that I received my first army wardrobe. (I guess you can call it that.) It consisted of a dress uniform and work clothes, which were called fatigues...and very aptly named.

In those shapeless green trousers and jacket, feeling like a nonentity, I stood around in the heat of the morning sun with other new recruits, looking as lost and confused as everyone else.

Okay, men, I want you to police the area. I wanna see nothing but assholes and elbows. Understand? I want this place spick and span.

"Police the area?" What the hell could that be, I wondered, and why the hell was he shouting? I learned quickly that sergeants always shout, and that "policing the area" meant nothing more than picking up cigarette butts. Was that what we were there for, to pick up cigarette butts?

I remember the shocking lack of privacy, while sitting in the latrine and taking a bowel movement. Could anything be more humiliating, more shameful? Was there no such thing as human dignity?

Lying on a cot in a long row of cots in a wooden barracks and staring up at the ceiling, I wondered what was in store for me? What dreary, dangerous, back-breaking ordeals lay ahead? Would I survive the grueling training? Physical activity, after all, was not my metier.

******

One day we were marched into the auditorium to be entertained by a contingent from Hollywood. This was a pleasant surprise! The movie star, Jane Withers, who was Shirley Temple's nemesis in one of her movies, headed the bill. Shirley Temple, a number one box office star, was a

A NOT-SO-NICE JEWISH BOY FACES WORLD WAR II

curly headed little moppet who could sing and dance and pout and cry, and be delightfully charming. Jane Withers, was the nasty little girl who was so mean to dear Shirley in one of her movies.

Jane Withers was now a tall, gracious young lady with a Texas accent and a downhome manner. As part of her show she told some jokes and sang some songs for us. Then she held a jitterbug contest. She invited volunteers onto the stage to dance with her. The best dancer was to be awarded a prize.

Now I was a great jitterbug. As a matter of fact, I was a menace on the dance floor. My energy was boundless. Holding on to my partner with my left hand I would whirl her around, and throw her out, and pull her back with frightening intensity. My right hand would be extended like a spear, ready to catch her and throw her out again. This great dexterity, you may recall, came from practicing in my friend Harold's sun parlor with friends, including my best friend Irving, to recordings like Artie Shaw's "Frenesi" or Benny Goodman's "Sing, Sing, Sing."

Confident of my ability, I raised my hand to volunteer as a contestant and dance with Jane Withers.

Come on up, soldier. Yes, you, said Jane Withers..

Surprised at my own temerity, I walked down the aisle, climbed onto the stage and stood next to the other two recruits. The contest began. My turn came. Jane Withers extended her hand and I took hold of it. The band started up and I threw myself into the music. I was inspired by the challenge. I tossed the movie star out and pulled her back, spun her around, whirled her about skillfully, masterfully. My feet hardly touched the floor. When the music stopped, the movie star caught her breath.

Wow!, she said and laughed.

I wasn't quite sure whether that was a compliment or

I'M INTRODUCED TO THE ARMY

not, since some of my friends had made fun of my intensity. However, when she held her hand over the three contestants, I got the most applause. Jane Withers handed me a carton of Camel cigarettes. Amid more applause and pats on the back, I climbed down from the stage, dazed and triumphant. Back at the barracks, since I didn't smoke, I distributed the contents of the carton to my fellow cannon fodder.

After a few days at Fort Dix we were sent to Fort Bragg for basic training, which I somehow managed to survive, most of which I have mercifully blocked from my memory. I vaguely recall running double-time under a blistering sun, a pack on my back, sweating profusely and being at the point of exhaustion. I vaguely remember learning how to load a howitzer and firing it, learning how to load a bazooka and firing it, learning how to take a carbine apart, clean it and put it together again. I'm almost sure I never mastered this last chore, but maybe I did, or maybe I had a lot of help, because I am not mechanically minded. As a matter of fact, KP was a blessed relief.

And then most astonishing, most unbelievable of all, I remember crawling on the dirt under barbed wire while there was live machine-gun fire overhead. That's what we were told. That's live ammunition. I still couldn't believe that they were actually firing real bullets. Were they crazy? Someone could get killed. These people were absolutely insane.

But it wasn't only the physical activity, which was rough enough, it was the inner conflict, this reluctance, this refusal to give myself fully to the task at hand. I could not accept the fact that I was actually preparing myself to take another person's life. It was like a ton weight that I carried around inside of me. It sapped my energy and made me weak, even weaker then I really was.

Since the future was not something to dwell on, and the

present was not exactly a lark, my thoughts, understandably, were often with my family back home. I thought a great deal about my parents, my mother especially, her nerves, and all she'd been through during the last war. As far as my father was concerned I regretted the fact that we weren't as close as I would have liked. I regretted that loss, which now I might never be able to make up.

My little brother, Marty, was twelve years my junior. I was often responsible for him and he could be a cutup. How would he progress without me? How would he turn out?

And then there was my sister, Rose. Rose and I shared the same ideals. Our standards, as far as books and culture in general, was of the highest. As a child she had been rather moody and timid, and I was greatly concerned about how she would fare without my tutelage. She was now preparing for college, and about to face the world. I encouraged her to go to a college far from home, but my mother was putting her foot down. She'd lost her first born too quickly. The same thing was not going to happen again.

"PERSONAL TO MOTHER!

"January 2
Dear Ma,

I want to talk to you about Rose. Ma, I want you to see to it that she goes away to college. I know it's very hard for you to let her go while I'm so far away...I know. I can realize how you feel. But you can take it. You've lived a while and learned to bear things. Rose is soft, very soft. Right now she's at a turning point and it's a bad time to be at such a point. She can flower out into a wonderful woman, or be tied down, sour, unhappy. Ma, keeping Rose at home is like keeping me in the army. No freedom of expression, no room to move. You never had the chance she has now. Don't you want her to

I'M INTRODUCED TO THE ARMY

have it? If you let her go you may feel bad lots of times and low, but you're giving her a chance...and she deserves it. If you love her at all, if you love me at all don't think of any excuses, don't think of any arguments, don't, <u>don't</u> postpone it and make promises. It's up to you and we know it. I would always be miserable if you keep her back. You mustn't.
 Love,
 Norman"

"January 24
Dear Ma,
 Got your letter of January 15. Ma, I'm so glad you're letting Rosie go. I know how hard it is for you and we'll always be grateful. But you're not losing us when you're letting us go, you're first gaining us. I never appreciated you till I left home. Don't think we don't appreciate it. I know you'll help Rose just like you helped me. Some day we'll make it up to you. We'll dress you in silks and diamonds and help you enjoy all the things you've missed and so richly deserved to have. It made me feel so good to hear that Rose is going away.
 Ginny writes four times a week and sometimes more. Her letters are usually pretty long. Please take good care of yourself. Ma, I want to find you just as I left you.
Love,
Norman"

 Back at Ohio State Ginny was the only girl I had really bonded with. I remembered that fantastic figure, those green cat's eyes, the high cheekbones, the good complexion...and that nose! It was certainly the largest nose I'd ever seen on a girl. However, there was this wonderful rapport between the two of us.

A NOT-SO-NICE JEWISH BOY FACES WORLD WAR II

In our drama class, as we rehearsed, we were as much concerned about each other's performance as we were about our own. And then there was that scene from Noel Coward's "Private Lives" that we worked on. The lines we spoke to one another in this love scene seemed to come from the very core of our being. There was no denying it. Our relationship was special. Our being together seemed so natural. Was it love? God no, I thought, then scolded myself for being so superficial, because I did love everything about her. We were like soul mates. But that nose of hers! That's it! I was what I was. A petty, shallow person. So her nose was big. So what? Do you really care? Do you really think about it now that you know her? What you're really concerned about, let's face it, is what other people will think. You may not be handsome, but you are...well nice looking, well, let's say pleasant looking, and you want a...a what?...a wife?...to be equally attractive. You ought to be ashamed of yourself!

But yes, I would keep Ginny abreast of things. I supposed she was waiting for me. There was no verbal commitment but there was some sort of an unspoken understanding, wasn't there? What that was, exactly, I wasn't quite sure. And, at this point, what did it matter? I might not come back, and that would be the end of that. And she certainly should be free to look around...if she could find someone else. There you go again. You're disgusting!

******

After finishing the grueling basic training, to my surprise, to my delight, to my relief, I was given an unexpected reprieve. I was sent to the University of New Hampshire. There was no explanation for the assignment, and I was certainly not about to question it...and there I was in

I'M INTRODUCED TO THE ARMY

Durham, New Hampshire, picturesque New England. The cold, crisp air, the glorious colors in the Fall, and snow covered hills and trees in the winter. What a refreshing change from the heat and humidity of the South!

We were housed in the school dormitory, which was luxurious compared to the barracks at Fort Bragg. None of us young recruits seemed to know why we were there. The conclusion was that the army didn't know what to do with us. Or maybe the war was coming to an end and we weren't needed anymore. Or, maybe because of our educational background we were being primed for officers training. Nevertheless we were assigned a curriculum of studies, science courses primarily.

The courses themselves weren't very interesting; mathematics, which was difficult enough, and physics, which was a mystery, and chemistry which was completely incomprehensible to a mind hungry for literature. I suffered through the classes but, at least, I suffered in comfort. And the company was most congenial.

What a relief to be able to talk to civilized human beings! My cohorts were actually people you could have an intelligent conversation with. What a refreshing change from the yahoos and the rednecks from the wilderness where men chewed tobacco, and then spit it out, and where every other word was "fuck" or "shit" or "getting laid." I made several friends, men I could talk to, men I had something in common with. There was Eric, a rather proper young man who planned to study medicine, and Michael, pleasant and reserved who was an English major and planned to teach.

One of the men had a camera and I had a picture taken with my shirt off, posing with raised fists to show off the magnificent physique I had acquired during my basic

A NOT-SO-NICE JEWISH BOY FACES WORLD WAR II

training...at least that. I sent one copy home and one copy to Ginny.

I hiked to nearby landmarks, Lexington and Concord and the home of Louisa May Alcott, the author of "Little Women." I visited the very room and saw the very desk on which she wrote her classic novel. I visited Boston several times. I took in the historical sights of the city, The Paul Revere House, the Old North Church, Faneuil Hall and the Old State House. I walked across the Common and strolled along the Charles River.

And late one afternoon in Boston I went to a movie theatre where a young singing sensation was making a personal appearance. This skinny young man had all the teenage girls in America hysterical. In Life magazine there were pictures of mobs of screaming bobbysoxers following this idol about. I was curious to see for myself what the hoopla was all about. There was a movie first, which I don't remember. At the end of the movie the house went completely dark and in the blackness a voice came over the microphone

Ladies and gentleman, Frank Sinatra.

There was an explosion of ear-splitting screams which grew and grew till I thought the theatre would burst. The entire building actually seemed to rock back and forth. Finally the lights came up, and down there on the stage was this skinny young man singing into a microphone. You couldn't hear him because of the tearful, frenzied, hysterical clamor which seemed to go on forever. When you did finally hear the man, the voice was pleasant enough, but all that fuss... Caruso he was not. So much for the power of teenage puberty!

I spent a great four months in New England. The only thing to spoil what amounted to a vacation was the sixty four thousand dollar question, where do we go from here? Would we be sent to officers training school? Would we be sent to

I'M INTRODUCED TO THE ARMY

another university. There was also the uneasy possibility that we might just be sent back to camp for more training.

The end of the semester came all too soon and our worst fears were realized. It was back to the army for all of us. I was sent to Camp Pickett to join the 78th Infantry Division. I was assigned to the field artillery.

BEIM, THE SOLDIER

BEIM - WATCH OUT!

IN UNIFORM

**BEIM IN BRUSSELS
WITH A BUDDY**

ROSE AT GRADUATION

ROSE

CHAPTER TWO

I TAKE A GIANT STEP

My encounter with the South, both at Fort Bragg in North Carolina and Camp Picket in Virginia, seemed to me like entering prehistoric times. The barracks was infested with what I considered "godawful country music". I couldn't believe that people actually took that nasal twanging seriously. And, of course, there was the eternal talk about sex..."fuck," "fuck," "fuck." I didn't think of myself as a snob but, if including literature and music (real music) and art in one's life was snobbery then, I decided, I most certainly was.

"June 16
Dear Family,
 You probably are worried by now, but I couldn't help it. I was going to write yesterday but I worked 17 hours, so I didn't have much chance. I got up at five to go to the rifle range early in the morning, so fifteen of us could replace the KPs so they could shoot in the afternoon. It was blistering hot and after we came back we went to work in the kitchen. However there were some compensations. We kept on making ice cold orange-lemonade and drinking. We had about two hours with nothing to do, but wait for the guys on the range to come back and eat so we could clean up. About 9:45 (PM) we were getting finished when there was an air raid exercise. All the lights went out. There was a nice little storm meanwhile, and it was really pouring. We finally finished up at 10:45. I was really dead.
 I don't remember if I told you about Sunday. We went swimming, one of the guys from the outfit and I. Irv was confined to quarters because of his swollen gum. (Irv, my best friend back in Newark, was stationed nearby.) Irv is better now. For the first time since I've been here I had a lot of

I TAKE A GIANT STEP

energy. I kept diving off the raft and swimming back and splashing, etc. The water was very cool, the sun hot... I got a light sunburn. In the eve I went to the movies with a guy from New York whom I ran into here. We saw "Five Graves To Cairo." It was interesting and kept me excited, though it was nothing exceptional. However since I didn't expect much it was OK. I liked Anne Baxter very much, except for her, at times, over-thick French accent.

Nothing is new here except that this place hasn't improved any. It's really hot--and I do mean hot--and when you have to double time under the burning sun it's no picnic. So if I were you I wouldn't complain about the heat.

Marty, do you really want to know who I danced with? There were a lot of girls. There was one pretty one from Florida who was here to visit her brother. There was also a black haired, pretty girl who was a swell jitterbug, whom I also walked home. There were lots of others. Well, maybe not lots of others 'cause there aren't too many girls around.

Today we had cannoneering. We were lucky to have it in the morning when it isn't so hot. In the noon we sweated in the recreation hall where we fell asleep to a movie on motors. It was so funny. Practically everyone was nodding.

I can't wait till the weekend. Friday eve Irv is supposed to come over and we'll see what we'll do.

Please tell me what you've been doing and seeing. You didn't tell me how you felt, Ma. Rose, what are you doing this vacation? Have exams started yet?
Love,
Norman"

"June 17
Dear Family,
    Received your letter of the 15th. I still haven't got paid

A NOT-SO-NICE JEWISH BOY FACES WORLD WAR II

but I just signed the payroll and expect it soon. Tell me how Marty's X rays turned out.

[Marty was having spinal problems. It turned out to be a touch of polio. He eventually had to have a spinal fusion, and spent a number of months in a full body cast. Poor Marty seemed to be plagued with all sorts of problems. I remember my Mother coming home from the hospital in tears. Marty had just been born, and he was confined to a special ward because he had some sort of infectious disease in his throat. He was a sweet child, and never complained.]

Rose, it's quite all right. You can say what you want. But please let me say what I want. Have you sent to the colleges yet? Did you get tickets for a show? Please send me the review of "Those Endearing Young Charms." There should be one in the Daily Mirror. The play ought to be pretty good, and besides Dean Harens, who is one of the leads, is a good friend of my ex-roommate (at Ohio State) so I am anxious to see how he was.

Tomorrow we're going on a hike. I'm on KP and I imagine I'll have plenty to do. However, I'm glad I got it Friday so I won't get it on the weekend. I hope I don't get guard duty on the week end.

I sure wish I was out of this place. Sometimes, when I'm marching I think about the things I could do instead of all this junk. I guess I'll just have to wait.

Ma, maybe I never said or did anything, but it really made me feel bad to see you work so hard, and Dad work so much. I may have been selfish in many ways, but I had always planned to be a great success in my own way and get as much as I could for myself, but always I wanted to help out at home so you both wouldn't have to work so hard. I always had dreams about things I would do. I still have. I

A PLEASANT, BUT PAINFUL HIATUS

can't wait till I can start. I don't know what brought this on. However there it is. I hope you don't read these letters out loud. I should hate to hear the above.

What's going on now?

Love,
Norman"

At the age of fourteen I had decided that I was going to be a great novelist...like Dostoevski or Tolstoy or Dickens. I was going to write books of stature, classics of course, but they would also appeal to everyone, not only the intelligentsia, like...maybe that mind-blowing novel, "The Great Gatsby," by F. Scott Fitzgerald. Here were pages that simply took your breath away, the words were so evocative.

It was the dream of creating great works of literature that was my motivating force in life. I lived, not in the real world, but in a world that had a golden glow, a world of beauty and poetry, untouched by the mundane reality of everyday existence. But ever since my induction into the army my greatest fear was that my poetic nature, my joy of just being alive, would not be able survive the dreariness of army life, the ugly brutality of war. Lines from an ode by Keats seemed to haunt me.

"When I have fears that I may cease to be
Before my pen has glean'd my teeming brain,
Before high piled books, in charactery,
Hold like rich garners the full-ripen'd grain;
When I behold, upon the night's starr'd face,
Huge cloudy symbols of a high romance,
And think that I may never live to trace
Their shadows, with the magic hand of chance..."
............................"then on the shore
Of the wide world I stand alone, and think
Till Love and Fame to nothingness sink."

A NOT-SO-NICE JEWISH BOY FACES WORLD WAR II

My moods vacillated from deep apprehension...I was nineteen years old and I would soon be dead...it would soon be over with and I hadn't even started to live, followed by a state of euphoria. I was still alive. I must make the most of every moment that was left to me. Every day, every hour was precious, and had to be lived to the fullest.

I remembered my classmate, Billy Greenfield. What a delightful friend he was! What a wonderful sense of humor he had. How I admired the mischievous twinkle in his eye! Just being around him made life seem so much more fun. And then, it must have been a year or so after high school graduation, my friend dropped by the house to pay me a visit. Billy wasn't going on to college. He had just gotten himself some menial job.

I can't even remember what sort of work it was, but I do remember being appalled by the change in my dear friend. This was not Billy. This was not the boy so full of fun. This was some colorless, disillusioned old man. Where was the joy? Where was the laughter. What happened to Billy? Who was responsible for this? Is this what life did to people?

I was determined that this was not going to happen to me. I was not going to be ground down by life. I was determined to follow my dream, no matter what. But when? How? I was trapped in the army preparing to fight a war I could not condone, yet accepted as inevitable.

******

And then, at Camp Pickett one day, enclosed in a letter from Rose, I received this newspaper article. A nationwide competition was being held for one-act plays by service men. I'd been postponing my entrance into the literary world up until now. What was the point of being a writer if you hadn't

I TAKE A GIANT STEP

done some living, if you hadn't seen something of the world, if you hadn't experienced LIFE? This was what I told myself, at any rate. I wouldn't acknowledge the sneaking suspicion that gnawed at me, that what I lacked was the courage to face the challenge of achieving immortality. But this was it. It was now or never! I would have to enter that contest!

Whenever I thought about my literary career, whenever I dreamed up something to write about, it was always in the form of prose, a short story perhaps or a full blown novel, an epic work of fiction, a saga that would echo down the corridors of time like the aforementioned "War And Peace" or even "Gone With The Wind."

It's true that in Hebrew school, at the encouragement of the rabbi, I had dashed off a Purim play, the story of how the beautiful Queen Esther had saved the Persian Jews from being massacred by the evil Prime Minister, Haman. In grammar school, in collaboration with Hazel Shaeffer, my second crush after Frieda Sperling, I'd boiled Shakespeare's "Taming Of The Shrew" down to fifty minutes so that it could be read during one classroom period. These ventures into the field of drama, however, I did not take seriously. They were frivolous endeavors, nothing more.

My encounter with the acting classes at Ohio State, however, had been earth shaking. Acting demanded that you expose your innermost feelings for all to behold. Standing emotionally naked on a stage you communicated with an audience waiting to be entertained, to be moved, to be amused, to be taken on a journey. And the gratification was instantaneous, direct and personal.

It followed naturally that playwriting offered the same advantage. Your words reached out immediately to hundreds, thousands, perhaps, all at once. There was no waiting till one person read your work and responded to it in private, and the

A NOT-SO-NICE JEWISH BOY FACES WORLD WAR II

applause was instantaneous. And when you came right down to it who, after all, was considered the greatest writer of all? Who reigned supreme in the world of literature? Why, a playwright named Shakespeare! So why not make, what might be my only contribution to the world of literature, a one-act play?

So one evening, after a long, hot day of dreary chores, after a day of arduous exercise, of soul destroying combat training, I made my way to the camp library.

A library was a haven, whether it was in the wilds of Virginia, or safely back in New Jersey. Here everything was magical and beautiful and full of romance. Here there was no such thing as time. Here the world stood still and there was room to contemplate, to philosophize, to dream. And in this refuge in the desert, in the library at Camp Pickett, in the wilds of Virginia, surrounded by books, which I loved above all else...they were my obsession...I sat down to write my first serious effort, my challenge to immortality.

But what should I write about? Life here at Camp Pickett was miserable. I could barely make it through the day. Why burden people with my dreary, depressing problems? Why not write about a time when the world was full of promise, when you woke up in the morning and you knew that some day your dreams would come true?

There were two places where you could let your imagination fly. There was the darkness of a movie theatre, and then there was that lovely, immaculate haven with its well kept lawn and spreading oak tree, with it's polished tables and fresh flowers on top of the card catalogue, and the shelves, and shelves and shelves of books, books that I would handle lovingly, books that I would caress, even kiss...there was the branch library on Osborne Terrace in Newark, New

A PLEASANT, BUT PAINFUL HIATUS

Jersey...my utopia, my temple. I would now immortalize that childhood refuge.

But a library was an inanimate object. A drama had to have people. Of course, there was the librarian. She would certainly be the focal character. She was colorful enough. Crusty on the outside, but underneath I could sense a nature that was warm and nurturing and, with it all, a worldly sense of irony.

I would start with her. What was she really like? What was she like at home, when she was not checking out books, when she was not in charge of her domain, keeping its objects and its inhabitants in order? Perhaps her young lover had died in the war? Perhaps she had an old mother to look after? She was a living, breathing person, not just an authority figure, a dry as dust old maid.

And then there were the library patrons, mostly young people from the nearby high school. Myself, perhaps. An idealized portrait of myself, a poet in search of the answer to Life. As a matter of fact whom did I know best? Why, myself, of course. Why not take various aspects of myself and turn each facet into a character? A lascivious little boy looking for the "dirty" parts of a book. There was the child emerging into the adult world, represented by a little girl charmed and awed by the new surroundings she was entering... her very first visit to the grown-up library. A young soldier, perhaps, returning for a visit as I had done once when I was on leave. Then, perhaps, my sister Rose as a young high school girl dreaming of love and then another aspect of Rose as another girl, a friend, struggling with school work, burdened by homework and lessons.

But this play couldn't be just an ordinary play with a commonplace thing like a plot and ordinary dialogue. Dialogue was what you heard on the radio in those mundane

A NOT-SO-NICE JEWISH BOY FACES WORLD WAR II

serials and in the "soap operas." I was a poet! This was going to be a poem, not in verse, perhaps. Verse was really artificial. Poetry had to come from the heart, from the soul. Poetry could just as well be prose, if the prose was pure, if the prose was pristine, if each word was a gem. And I wanted to get to the soul of my characters, their innermost feelings, their most private thoughts.

That's it! The words would be their thoughts.

That's it!!! That's what Eugene O'Neill did in "Strange Interlude!"

And the conversation, their communication with one another, instead of dialogue, would be conducted in pantomime. After all, one did whisper in a library.

That's it! The words would be the music and the stage movement would be the dance, the ballet.

I didn't know which character would open the play, what he or she would do or say. I waited and waited and waited.

Finally the Librarian insisted on speaking first. She'd been observing the Poet and her thoughts are verbalized.

LIBRARIAN: *Well, have you found it yet? Yes, I mean you with the patched polo shirt and the lovely long lashes. You've been searching long enough.* (She snaps an elastic band about some cards and lays them aside.) *If you want to know something, why don't you ask me? Librarians know everything.*

And suddenly the Boy looking for the "dirty" parts in a book seemed to want to speak.

BOY: (Reading from a book) *"He closed the door behind him. 'Anne,' he said softly, "Did you mean it?' Anne turned to him. She was breathing heavily."*

And then the Librarian insisted on speaking again, and then the Poet seemed to want to speak. And slowly, slowly I started to write. I wasn't quite sure where I was going, what

I TAKE A GIANT STEP

was going to happen next. It was one step at a time. It was a journey into the unknown, and one never knew what was just around the bend, what he or she would do or think. And the words didn't come from me. They seemed to come from the characters once he or she had come into existence. It was as if the play...it wasn't a play, it was a poem...was writing itself.

It wasn't easy though. It was painful, it was so slow, slow, slow. I found that I couldn't concentrate for more than three hours, three hours at the utmost. And even that was a strain. Maybe just a few words during an entire evening session. Maybe, if I was lucky, an evening session would produce a couple of speeches, maybe nothing, not even one word. But I couldn't rush it. Each word, each sentence had to be spontaneous, had to come from inside myself. Each phrase had to be examined and reexamined and polished till it shone. And everything had to be true and real...and inevitable.

"'Beauty is truth, truth beauty,'--that is all
Ye know on earth, and all ye need to know."

For three agonizing weeks I worked on my one-act play, three hours or so each night. When it was finally finished I heaved a sigh of relief. But it wasn't really finished, was it? I knew it could be better. But I'd gone over it again and again with a fine tooth comb. It was the best I could do, for now. Maybe some day I could make it better but, for now, it was complete.

I approached the young woman in charge of the post library. She allowed me to use her typewriter. (That was the one useful course I'd taken in high school, touch typing.) I sat down and slowly, very slowly typed up my masterpiece, "Inside". That was the title, since it all took place in the mind of my characters. I sent one copy home for safe keeping and sent another off to the contest.

That evening I felt terribly empty. My "child" was out

in the world. My labor was done. This was the way a woman must feel, I thought, after she's given birth. Then I was overcome by the realization that I'd actually created something, something I was proud of. I'd taken the first step, the step I'd dreaded for so many years. One act play or not, I'd actually written what I considered a piece of literature, and no one could take that away from me. I'd written something good and fine, good because it was true, every single word of it. I was a writer now. I was actually a writer! And there was this splendid sense of accomplishment.

Late the following afternoon, I was sitting on my cot in the barracks, this sense of pride surging up within me. The sky outside seemed to darken rather suddenly. It wasn't quite evening yet. There was a loud clap of thunder. A flash of lightning. Another loud clap of thunder and the heavens split open pouring down sheets of rain. I could hear the clatter of the rain on the tin roof.

Impulsively I reached down and unlaced my shoes. As if in a daze, I took off my shoes and socks. I stood up, ripped off my shirt, my trousers, my underwear. Completely naked I ran down the wooden stairs onto the muddy road between the barracks. I looked up at the sky, welcoming the water pouring down on my face. I danced about in the rain, waving my hands about and shouting like a madman, *Wheee! Wheee!* I was at one with the universe. How wonderful just to be alive, to be able to breathe, to be able to commune with Nature.

Gradually the rain subsided. The dark clouds started to drift away and the sunlight shone down on the muddy road. I walked back into the barracks and climbed up the wooden stairs to the room that contained my comrades, who had labeled me odd to begin with. Why would anyone want to bury their nose in a book all the time?

As I entered the room and passed cot after cot, my

I TAKE A GIANT STEP

bunk mates made a point of ignoring me. They continued with their chores, cleaning their carbines, polishing their shoes, writing their letters. Were they embarrassed or were they disgusted? They must now be convinced that I was insane. Who cares, I thought.

I turned to the Redneck in the bunk next to mine. We had absolutely nothing in common. As a matter if fact there was this agreement of mutual contempt, or something like that.

You oughta try it, I said to the Redneck. *It's great out there.* The Redneck smiled and shook his head. I laughed with glee. The Redneck looked up at me. Was there the tiniest glint of admiration?

CHAPTER THREE

A PLEASANT, BUT PAINFUL HIATUS

The day dawned hot and humid. I lined up for roll call. I eyed the captain with a jaundiced eye. What a pretentious ass! Sergeant Murphy, that big lumbering ox, called off our names...not our first names mind you, but our last names.
Barnes?
Here.
Barret?
Here.
Beach?
Here.
Beim?
Present!
I had to have some identity.

This caught the captain's eye, as he strutted back and forth, and I was glad that it did. It was difficult to keep my contempt for that arrogant man out of my eyes. I had the feeling that he felt the same way about me, or maybe it was just my imagination.

After roll call I returned to the barracks and made up my cot, making sure that the sheets were taut and tucked in properly, and making sure the blanket was folded back neatly. This was followed by a breakfast of artificial scrambled eggs and (sinful) bacon, which I loved, and coffee strong enough to stand by itself...and leave one with a sour stomach.

Then there was bunk inspection. Sergeant Murphy, the bully, followed by that toady, Corporal Verano, marched down the aisle, stopped in front of my bed, stood staring at it for the longest time, then moved reluctantly on, after which he returned to his office to sit on his fat ass for the rest of the day. I often wondered what he did to earn his pay.

Then there was calisthenics, after which there was an

A PLEASANT, BUT PAINFUL HIATUS

exhausting morning hike under the burning sun. loaded down with a pack that grew heavier and heavier as the heat grew more and more oppressive.

Hut two three four. Hut two three four.

I wept inside. Not at the rigor of all this physical activity. I wept because my life was slowly slipping away. Hour after hour. Day after day. Week after week. Time that could have been spent creatively was being wasted with all these pointless, mundane, idiotic, soul destroying stupidities.

After lunch, with barely enough time to rest and digest our food, we were lined up and marched out into the field under a scorching sun. Another training exercise with those monster howitzers. I was charged with lifting the tail of the monster and moving it. The monster had to be shifted after a simulated firing.

Fire!

Okay, okay. Move it! Move it! Come on! Move it, Beim! What are you waiting for?

Okay, okay.

I bent down wearily. The sweat was rolling down my face. My entire body was soaking wet. I took hold of the heavy metal and lifted. My hands were wet with sweat. The thing weighed a ton. Suddenly I felt the piece slipping out of my hand. As if in a daze, I watched helplessly as a hundred of pounds of steel fell towards the ground in, what seemed like, slow motion. I heard myself yell as I fell backward. The full weight of the tail had landed on my big toe.

The Redneck, I think it was him, came rushing over with several squad members. They pulled the steel off my foot. For a moment I didn't feel a thing, and then I almost passed out with the pain.

Are you all right? the Redneck asked.

Yeah. I'm okay.

A NOT-SO-NICE JEWISH BOY FACES WORLD WAR II

The pain was excruciating.
The Redneck helped me up.
I let out a yell. *I think the toe is broken,* I managed to gasp.
Can you walk? asked Corporal Verano.
Yeah. I think so.
You better go over to the infirmary. Have them take a look at it. You sure you can manage?
Yeah, yeah.
Careful not to put any weight on the injured foot, I limped slowly, painfully to the infirmary. I sat down and waited my turn. Finally I was called over. I limped toward the orderly and sat down.
What's the matter with you?
I think my toe is broken.
Take off your shoe.
With great difficulty and several yelps of pain I removed the shoe and the sock.
Jesus! How did you do that?
The tail of the howitzer fell on it.
A look of skepticism came over the face of the orderly. "No, I did not do it deliberately!" I responded mentally, looking the orderly in the eye.
A doctor was called over. An x ray was ordered. I was told to wait. The word came back. The big toe was badly fractured. I was sent to the hospital. I was assigned to a bed and given a hospital gown to wear.
I couldn't believe my luck. The pain, the inconvenience, the scorn...what a small price to pay for all this luxury. Nothing to do, absolutely nothing to do, but lay around and read. What to read first? "War And Peace," of course. I admired it because it was considered a great classic and I'd

A PLEASANT, BUT PAINFUL HIATUS

read all about it but, actually, I'd never really read it. What better time than now?

The war was still going on, and there were rumors of peace in the air. The Allies had landed in Normandy back in June. France was free. It was only a matter of weeks, days maybe, before the war would come to an end. The 78th Infantry Division would never go overseas. That was the scuttlebutt, at any rate. A few more months perhaps, a year at most and, a dream come true, I and the army would part company. A sigh of relief would be heaved by both of us.

I opened "War And Peace" and began the journey, a most rewarding journey except for the long description of that battle. Why? Why spend so much time on a battle? And then there was that final section where the story is deserted and the writing goes off on this philosophical tangent. Who wants to read pages and pages about a train and history and stuff? (Dostoyevsky was still my favorite.)

"Anna Karenina" was next. Much, much better. It was easier to empathize with the characters, and the suicide was truly touching.

I finished "Anna Karenina" and was getting ready to delve into Dostoyevsky's "The Brothers Karamazov" when new rumors started to circulate. The division might be going over after all.

Did that mean I was going over with it? How long would I be in the hospital? The toe was still swollen but I could limp around, and it was improving rapidly.

I received the word. I was being released and sent back to my outfit. Corporal Verano came to fetch me.

When I got back to the barracks I was greeted by the fat-assed oaf, big-gutted Murphy. *Okay, Beim. You're coming with us whether you like it or not.* As if I knew, at the time of the accident, that the outfit was scheduled to leave!

A NOT-SO-NICE JEWISH BOY FACES WORLD WAR II

The Redneck greeted me with a twinkle in his eye. *Welcome back,* he said.

Thank you, I replied, ignoring the subtext.

No one in the barracks said a word about the accident, but I was aware of all the knowing looks. Well, fuck 'em, I thought. And then I smiled, amused at myself. Foul language had never offended me. I just thought that there was no need for it. It was merely a sign of bravado. Men cursed to prove that they were tough. I wasn't tough, and I wasn't out to prove anything. Yet those vulgar words seemed to well up so naturally. It seemed to come from a part of my psyche I hadn't been aware of before.

The nasty rumor was fast becoming a reality. Preparations for departure had begun. Equipment was being packed and stenciled. The order came through that all correspondence had to be left open. Mail would now be censored. Personal belongings were to be sent home. Weekend passes were discontinued and everyone was confined to the area. Word got round that the advance party had left already.

One dark, dreary morning, one week after my return to my unit, we packed our duffel bags and hoisted them onto our shoulders. Weighed down with our equipment we climbed onto the trucks. The trucks rumbled out of Camp Pickett. The 78th Infantry Division, nicknamed the Lightning Division, was headed for destination unknown.

CHAPTER FOUR

A SURPRISE VISIT

The first stop, on our journey towards the unknown, was the railway station. There we were herded aboard a train.

When the train steamed out of the station we were still ignorant of where we were heading. Was it East to the Atlantic, or was it West to the Pacific?

As the sun rose bright in the sky, and countryside whizzed by, I was given a clue. Welcome to Maryland. We were going North. We were now in New Jersey.

It was dark by the time the train pulled into a station. We were still in New Jersey apparently.

We climbed down from the train and boarded the trucks that were waiting for us. We were now approaching an army installation. Was it Fort Dix, I wondered. Was I back where I started from? There was a sign. Camp Kilmer. This was not too far from Newark. If we got a pass I would certainly be able to pay the family a visit, a visit that might very well be my last.

We were assigned to barracks.

As I set down my duffel bag I read on the wall above my cot, a message from a previous occupant. "Arrived May 6--Left May 9." Below it someone else had written, "Arrived August 10--Left August 13." Obviously the stay here was going to be a short one.

The next day, after morning calisthenics, we were treated to some films, films for our edification. In one there were dire warnings, with graphic illustrations, about VD. Another film warned us not to mention anything to anyone, THAT MEANT ANYONE, about army affairs. In this film a soldier inadvertently blurts out to a girl he just met that he was shipping out the following day. In the next scene we see a ship at sea exploding. "A slip of the lip could sink a ship."

A NOT-SO-NICE JEWISH BOY FACES WORLD WAR II

If one was captured by the enemy all one was required to give was one's name, rank and serial number.

Gas masks were issued. There was a lecture and demonstration on how to use them. We were lined up for a medical exam. Then we were given inoculations. Maybe we were going to the South Pacific after all.

Three day passes were issued. I decided not to let the family know that I was coming. What a wonderful surprise it would be! I boarded a bus to Newark. On the way, I made up my mind that if I should ever get into combat which, at this point, was very likely, I would never let the family know. Mother was nervous enough as it was, and my sister, Rose, would certainly be upset.

It was odd coming back to Newark. The whole world was in a turmoil, yet everything here was the same. I drank in all the sights, coming up Market Street, turning onto Broad Street. There was the Paramount Theatre, where my lovely, young Aunt Beatie had taken me to see an Al Jolson movie, and there was the RKO Proctors where I'd worked as an usher, and conducted that triumphant interview with Anna Eagle, the beautiful British film star, and there was Bamberger's Department Store, and the Branford Theatre and all the familiar stores along the way, Lincoln Park and then Springfield Avenue and Clinton Avenue and then Clinton Place and Nye Avenue where I got off.

There was the bakery on the corner, which we never patronized. Mother didn't think it was kosher. (Why a bakery couldn't be kosher, I never did find out.) And there was the synagogue where I'd spent so many impatient hours waiting for the service to end, and where I ended up an agnostic. And I was passing Wolcott Terrace. I walked down Nye Avenue to number 124 and up the front stairs.

I opened the door to the foyer and then the front door

A SURPRISE VISIT

into the apartment. I walked quietly down the small corridor leading to the dining room.

Is anyone home? I called out.

Norman?!

Mother came rushing into the dining room, her eyes aglow. Hugs and kisses. God, there was so much love, so much love! So much to catch up on.

The family came home one by one, my brother, Marty, from school. He wasn't a child any longer. He was a young boy. Daddy came home from the tavern for his afternoon nap. And it was so odd. I was part of the family, yet I wasn't. I was something of a stranger in my own home.

In the late afternoon Rose returned from New York. After that battle to gain her freedom, Rose found that living in Ohio was too much of a wrench. She got homesick attending Ohio State. She was now going to New York University. I tried hard not to show my disappointment.

There were questions, of course, about where I was stationed and where I was going.

I don't know. Another camp, I suppose. No, I don't think we're going overseas.

That's all Mother needed. Reflecting on my decision not to let the family know if I was sent into combat, I decided that it was definitely the right thing to do. Mother had all these phobias. She would never set foot in a cemetery. You couldn't talk about traveling. You couldn't talk about this, you couldn't talk about that because it made her nervous. There were those traumatic experiences during her youth in Poland, and now she was confronted with the possibility of her first born going off to another war. If I was killed she would probably have a complete nervous breakdown.

And what effect would my death have on Rose, sensitive as she was? And what memories would Marty have

A NOT-SO-NICE JEWISH BOY FACES WORLD WAR II

of his older brother? If, ignorant of my presence in combat, they were suddenly to learn of my death, it would certainly be a shock. But why put them through the day to day anguish and suspense of not knowing what was happening to me in the midst of battle? No, I definitely had made the right decision.

The next day I visited some friends in the neighborhood. In the afternoon I paid a visit to the library on Osborne Terrace.

There was the librarian, a pencil lodged behind her ear, her grey hair in slight disarray. She remembered me and greeted me warmly. Did she look younger or was it my imagination? I wondered how she'd feel about being the central figure in my one-act play. I decided to say nothing about it. Maybe some day, if I won the prize...

In the late afternoon Daddy drove me down to Bergen Street to visit Aunt Beatie and Uncle Izzy who had a grocery store there. Dear Beatie whom I absolutely adored as a child. She was so beautiful. And then she married and had children and worked in the store and was losing her looks and gaining weight. And Izzy who was so gentle and kind and thoughtful and a little sad looking. *Would you like something? Have some candy. Some chewing gum.*

And then we drove to Orange to visit Aunt Tillie and Uncle Morris who had a clothing store on Main Street. Aunt Tillie, the dynamo, the politician, the giant who nobody dared to challenge, who drove around the Oranges persuading police captains and firemen and senators to join her "suit club", and Uncle Morris with his lame foot who was so quiet.

There wasn't time to travel to New York to visit Uncle Jack and Aunt Molly, so I called them on the phone. Uncle Jack, the nervous intellectual who went out of his way to offend everybody, who, despite his vocal impediment, was so cultured and knew everything about everything, and could

A SURPRISE VISIT

keep you spellbound as he pontificated on the state of the world, on the stock market, on everything, the one who could have been a writer, but was burdened with earning a living cutting fur, and then running a grocery store, the one in the family with whom I most closely empathized, and the one I vowed I would not emulate, I would not lead a life as frustrated as his. I wondered if I would ever see all these people ever again, these people that I loved so much.

I tried to be bright and chipper during the three day visit. Keep it light. Keep it cheerful.

I might get another pass when I get to the next camp, I said. *Who knows?* I tried to make all the good-byes as casual as possible. *I might even be stationed in New Jersey. Who knows?*

CHAPTER FIVE

WE DEPART

On a dark and rainy night, four days after our arrival at Camp Kilmer and my visit home, we packed our duffel bags and boarded another train. This one took us to a ferry. We filed onto the ferry. Full field packs on our backs, rifles on our shoulders and duffel bags lying nearby we stood in silence as the ferry glided quietly along.

It was drizzling slightly as we filed off the ferry. An army band was playing. The dreary music lent a depressing note to an already depressing evening. We lined up in the wet night air. We were at a seaport apparently. In the dark I could make out this huge ship nearby. We stood on the dock and waited, and waited and waited, fretting in silence.

What the hell were we waiting for? Why were we standing there in the cold and the wet? How long would we be exposed to this miserable weather? We'll probably die of pneumonia before we got to the war. How typical! Hurry up and wait. Hurry up and wait.

Red Cross volunteers went up and down the line serving doughnuts and coffee. *Good luck, son. Good luck.* Jesus! That certainly sounded ominous, as if they were saying goodbye...forever.

After being chilled to the bone, after what seemed an eternity, Sergeant Murphy started calling off names. At least he was good for something.

Barnes?
Here.
Barrett?
Here.
Beach?
Here.
Beim?

WE DEPART

Present!
Sergeant Murphy looked up, then continued.
Bernard?
Here.
In the fog I made out the gangplank.
It looked rather steep.
Loaded down with all my equipment and shivering with the cold I plodded slowly up the ramp behind Private Beach. After everyone was aboard we were able to dispose of our bags and open our cots. The idea was to try and get some sleep. Sleep? With that damp, penetrating cold, with the noises of the harbor? Sleep? We still didn't know where we were going. How could anyone sleep?

The next morning there was still that gray, cold mist. The ship was still tied to the docks.

The fog lifted.

The sun came out, and disappeared again.

We were given breakfast... ersatz eggs, mashed potatoes and coffee...then ordered below.

We crowded around the portholes. A loud whistle. The ship slowly started to move. The gray, cloudy day revealed the New York Harbor fading into the distance. The New York harbor! There was the Statue of Liberty growing smaller and smaller.

The Lightning Division was on its way to war. We were crossing the Atlantic. We were going to Europe.

CHAPTER SIX

WE ARRIVE

A few hours later I was standing on deck looking out at the sea. The sky was grey, the ship was grey, the water was grey and it was bitterly cold. An icy wind whipped the waves. In the distance, through the mist, I saw some other ships We were part of a convoy. Well, at least we had protection. But could those battleships stop an underwater torpedo launched by a German U Boat?

Well, war or not, this was a memorable moment, dreary perhaps, anxiety ridden perhaps, but memorable nevertheless, a landmark day in my nineteen years on this planet earth. I was experiencing Life. I mean really experiencing it. I was actually leaving America. I was actually crossing the Atlantic Ocean for the first time in my life. If only I could pierce the fog and peer into the future. What lay ahead? Where would we land? Would I actually see combat? Wouldn't it be wonderful if I survived to write about all of this? Wouldn't it be wonderful if I survived? Period!

During the nine day voyage there were occasional drills and lectures. The drills were not very strenuous and conducted, obviously, just to keep us occupied. Blackout precautions were rigidly observed. I suffered briefly a very mild bout of sea sickness and, except for that, the days passed without any remarkable incidents. And, believe it or not, it began to get boring. Water, water and more water.

There was a brief scare though. Rumor had it that a U Boat had been sighted. It turned out to be a false alarm...or maybe the U Boat was scared away. We weren't quite sure. Word came down that we'd soon be landing.

England! I couldn't believe it! Was I really going to visit (if you could call it that) the home of Shakespeare, Shaw (even though he was Irish) and Noel Coward and Charles

WE ARRIVE

Dickens. The land of Byron and Keats and Shelley, the literary home of the English speaking world.

The convoy began to break up. We were approaching port. The ship pulled in slowly. We saddled our backpacks, collected our gear and slung our rifles over our shoulders. On deck we stood waiting and waiting and waiting. Par for the course. Finally, we began to move. We were approaching the gangplank. I stepped cautiously down. It was tricky going, burdened with my duffel bag and balancing my carbine.

As we set foot on British soil a British band played a Sousa march. This band, at least, sounded a little more spirited. Or maybe it was the fact that it was daylight, and it wasn't raining... and this was England.

There were British officers on hand to welcome us, as we made our way to a train nearby. I climbed into this small quaint compartment. There was just room for four of us. I looked about...the seats the windows, the baggage rack overhead. I was really in, honest to God, England, not only the England of literature, but the England of all those wonderful movies like Alfred Hitchcock's "The Lady Vanishes," most of which took place on a train like this; the England of those cinematic landmarks like "Rebecca" and "Goodbye Mr. Chips" and even a "A Yank At Oxford." I drank in the strange/familiar train compartment. I gazed hungrily out the window as the train slowly began to pull out.

The romantic illusion was suddenly shattered. My eager eyes were greeted by the sight of pillboxes, concertina wire and AA installations. Well, it was wartime! What did I expect? I sank into my seat.

The ride was a short one. We filed out of the train and were met by members of the advance party. We were in Bournemouth, a traditionally popular seaside resort.

As we marched through the town to our billets I tried

A NOT-SO-NICE JEWISH BOY FACES WORLD WAR II

to imagine what the town must have been like on a sunny day before the war. I vaguely recalled a movie in which there was a scene that took place in Bournemouth. I remembered elegant hotels and the boardwalk and the beaches without the barbed wire, without the mines; couples strolling arm in arm and the beach covered by large, colorful umbrellas, and a little orchestra in the bandstand playing popular songs. Or was it Strauss waltzes? At any rate that was not the Bournemouth we were in now. Apparently the army had taken over the town. The hotels and the homes, for the most part, were filled with "Yanks."

******

I was billeted with ten other men in a private house emptied of its occupants. The accommodations weren't fancy, but they were certainly comfortable. But where was the heat? It was freezing! Didn't they have heat in England, or was it just the war?

During the day there were drills and calisthenics. In the evening we were free to do as we pleased. There were pubs and dance halls and restaurants and, believe it or not, there was a real live theatre and a local theatre company was actually putting on plays. My eyes devoured the poster in front of the theatre that listed the coming attractions. There was a play by Terence Rattigan, an English playwright who wrote clever, well crafted plays. There was a play by J. B. Priestly, who wrote novels as well, and there was "Hay Fever" by Noel Coward. There was even a play entitled, "The Brontes."

This was really something to look forward to, a play about Charlotte Bronte, the author of "Jane Eyre," and Emily Bronte, the author of "Wuthering Heights," There was that

WE ARRIVE

unforgettable movie with Laurence Olivier as Heathcliff standing tearfully at the window, holding Merle Oberon as the dying Cathy in his arms... *Don't leave me, Cathy. Please don't leave me!* And then there was Joan Fontaine as Jane Eyre with Orson Welles magnificent as Rochester. And then there was that movie called "Devotion" about the three Bronte sisters and their beloved brother, played by the interesting actor, Arthur Kennedy, the dissolute Bramwell, who died of alcoholism. The charming Olivia DeHaviland played Charlotte and the dynamic Ida Lupino played Emily. This play about the Brontes was something I had to see!!

    The first week in Bournemouth I attended a performance of "They Came To A City" by J. B. Priestly, a play about a motley group of men and women who arrived at an unspecified city. It was supposed to be symbolic or mythical or something. The highlight of the evening, for me, was the actor who played an American, at least the English conception of a typical American. He was dressed in a "zoot suit," the jacket of which had wide padded shoulders, narrow waist and was flared at the bottom, and he wore this wide brimmed hat. He kept swinging a gold watch chain, chewing gum and speaking his lines out of the side of his mouth with the most god-awful American accent.

    Despite the cold and the damp the time passed pleasantly, what with the light training schedule during the day and freedom in the evening to enjoy one's leisure. And, believe it or not, they were actually giving out passes to London. London! Wow! Wouldn't that be something?!

    I approached Corporal Verano. He could be pleasant when he wanted to be, when he wasn't being bullied by that oaf, Sergeant Murphy.

    What are the chances of my getting a pass to London?
    I'll see what I can do.

A NOT-SO-NICE JEWISH BOY FACES WORLD WAR II

A week passed by. I put in another request. *Do you think I might be able to get a pass to London?*
I put your name down on the list. That's all I can do.
Okay, okay.
Another week passed by. *I guess I won't be getting a pass to London. What do you think?*
Verano shrugged. *It's not up to me.*
I was well aware that, as a soldier, I was not that highly thought of, and I certainly couldn't contest the verdict. There were others, of course, much more deserving. I would just have to settle for the pleasures at hand.
Three idyllic weeks went by. The talk now was that we might not be sent to the Continent after all. At the beginning of the fourth week, however, Sergeant Murphy announced that from now on we were not to leave the area. This was the week that "The Brontes" was scheduled to play.
The hell with it, I'm going, I muttered to the Redneck.
We're not supposed to leave the area, the Redneck cautioned.
What are they going to do, shoot me?
You could be shot for desertion. You could be shot for disobeying orders. This is war ya know.
Let 'em shoot me, I said. *I'm not gonna to miss that play.*
After the evening mess I returned to my room and waited. I waited until the very last minute, then quietly walked out of the house. No sign of Sergeant Murphy anywhere. No sign of Sergeant Garrell, my young nemesis, a gung-ho young man from the Bronx. (Garrell and I had had several discussions and agreed to disagree about everything.) And there was no sign of Corporal Verano.
I walked calmly down the street, looking straight ahead, dreading at every moment that I'd be stopped by an officer.

WE ARRIVE

I cleared the area without any problems. I walked quickly to the theatre. I bought my ticket and took my seat. I looked about, fearful that I might sight an unwelcome face. It then occurred to me that there was probably no one in the outfit who would actually be interested in seeing a stage play, much less a play about the Brontes. I heaved a sigh of relief and, though still apprehensive, I sank into my seat, prepared to enjoy the evening.

The theatre grew dark, the curtain went up and I was transported to another world, a civilized world, a literate world. At this point, I don't remember much about the play, but I do remember it taking me out of the nightmare that I was currently involved with. There was no war, no freezing cold you couldn't escape from, no miserable army life, no imminent threat of death to come. There was drama and romance and civilized gentility. There was still some culture in this godforsaken existence! I left the theatre warmed and exhilarated, proud that I'd had the guts to defy military authority. Now there was the problem of getting back undetected. Like the Redneck said, I could, after all, be shot for desertion or, at least punished for disobeying orders.

When I came to our area I stopped and looked about. So far the coast was clear. I started toward the house. Not too fast though, not too fast. You don't want to look guilty. But then again not too slow. That too might look suspicious. I sighted the house. That was our house, wasn't it? They all looked so much alike. Yes, it was. So far, so good. I approached the house. All clear. As I came up the steps to my room, who should I encounter but the fat ass and the big gut.

Where you been? asked Sergeant Murphy.

I looked him straight in the eye. *Out,* I said.

Where?

Just out. Enjoying the air.

A NOT-SO-NICE JEWISH BOY FACES WORLD WAR II

The asshole looked at me skeptically, then walked on without a word. I was convinced the moron knew that I'd left the area, but decided to say nothing, not out of the goodness of his heart, that was for sure, but he couldn't really prove anything.

Could he?

The next day the shipping orders came through. Laden with our equipment we boarded the train. No one seemed to know where we were heading. It was mid November 1944.

CHAPTER SEVEN

THE CONTINENT

Our destination turned out to be Southampton. There we were loaded onto a British Channel Transport. The English Channel! Wow! The legendary English Channel! What history! This was where the English defeated the Spanish Armada, wasn't it? I think. And it didn't seem like a channel at all. It seemed like the open sea. And the water was rough, rougher even than the Atlantic Ocean. The weather was so bad it was four days before the end of the voyage was in sight, and I was slightly seasick.

Chilled to the bone by the biting wind, peering through the fog, we could finally make out France. It turned out to be Le Havre, or what was left of it. As we came ashore, for the first time we received the full impact of the war. The devastation was awesome.

How lucky we've been in America, I thought. And I was again reminded how, by a stroke of fate, I had escaped the concentration camps. Suppose my parents hadn't come to the States when they had? Suppose they had remained in Poland? We would all have been killed by the Nazis!

In Le Havre we were loaded onto trucks. Would the rain never stop? Would we ever be warm again? No matter! This was France! Within a stone's throw, perhaps, was Paris! The Paris of Ernest Hemingway and F. Scott Fitzgerald and Gertrude Stein. Paris with it's Latin Quarter and all those great artists like Renoir and Monet and Degas and Pissaro, the Paris of Moliere and Racine and Hugo and Zola...and Sarah Bernhardt! Perhaps I might actually get to Paris. God, wouldn't that be something?!

I was itching to try out my French. Back at Ohio State, I had read (well, let's say stumbled through) the play, "La Dame Aux Camelias" by Alexandre Dumas, and "Atala" and

A NOT-SO-NICE JEWISH BOY FACES WORLD WAR II

"Rene" by Chateaubriand and "Emile" by Jean Jacques Rousseau and the poetry of Verlaine ("Il pleure dans mon coeur") in the original French no less. I could even put a sentence together in conversational French...sort of.

We rumbled through the ruins of Le Havre...and kept on going. I was hoping that we might be billeted with a French family, but no such luck. Outside the city, we pitched tents in the mud, and that's where yours truly spent his first night in glamorous France.

The next morning we climbed onto the trucks and the convoy rumbled on through the rain. Were we going to pass through this legendary country without even stopping? In the late afternoon the rain finally let up. The trucks came to a halt on the outskirts of a village.

I clambered over the reels of wire and jumped out of the truck. The sun was actually shining. France! I was really here! In France! I was joined by the Redneck.

We sat at the side of the road and ate our rations. I washed the food down with a swig of water from my canteen. The Redneck's canteen was empty. He wasn't interested in going back to the truck and refilling it. He reached over and took my canteen from my hand.

All those pills Verano puts in the water. Tastes like shit.

Thank you, I said to myself, as the Redneck took a healthy swig and handed back my canteen. Great manners!

Looks like we're going to spend the night here. Maybe we can find someone to put us up, the Redneck said.

You think it'll be all right? I said.

Why not?

Maybe we ought to ask Verano?

The hell with him! Besides, you never know, kid, we might luck out. Find ourselves a nice piece of French ass.

I don't know, I said.

THE CONTINENT

Just stick with me, kid.

A middle-aged woman came down the street carrying a loaf of bread.

Filthy country. Just look at the way they carry their bread, said the Redneck as he tossed his empty K ration box on the side of the road. *Why don't we strike up an acquaintance?*

What do you mean?

Do I have to draw you a diagram? Put it to her straight. These French women are easy. Go ahead.

You must be kidding, I said.

Go on. The French understand these things. I'd speak to her myself only my French is kinda rusty.

You speak French?!

My grandmother was French.

Maybe he wasn't a Redneck, after all.

Go on, go on.

I rose reluctantly and we approached the woman. The Redneck nudged me.

Bon jour, I said.

Bon jour.

Comment allez-vous?

Bien.

What'd she say?

She's fine, I said.

Did you ask her?

No. Not yet.

Well what are you waiting for?

Cette ville...?

Soissons.

This city is Soissons, I told the Redneck.

Great.

Que desirez-vous savoir, monsieur?

A NOT-SO-NICE JEWISH BOY FACES WORLD WAR II

What'd she say?
She wants to know what we want?
Well tell her!
This woman is old enough to be my mother, I said.
Well, not mine. Go ahead, go ahead. Don't be bashful.
The woman smiled.
She'll say "no" and it's very embarrassing. Okay, okay.
I turned to the woman. *Ah...ce soldat,* I said, indicating clearly that I was not speaking for myself, that I was speaking for the "gentleman" at my side, *ah...interesse a vous. Comprenez-vous?*

Moi? The woman burst out laughing. *Oh, non, non.* She continued to laugh. *Non, non.*

There, I told you. She said no. I knew she would. This is ridiculous.

Oh, non. J'ai un mari. J'ai deux enfants.
She's married and she's got two kids.
Well, that's not my fault.
Il y a un bistro la-bas.
The woman pointed down the street.
There's a cafe down the block. I turned back to the woman. *Merci. Merci beaucoup.*

Pas de quoi. Bon jour. And the woman walked away and entered a house across the way.

Why don't we check out this cafe? said the Redneck.
Maybe we oughta check with Verano first. We don't know for sure where we're going to spend the night, I said.
She said it's just down the block, didn't she? So what have we got to lose? Relax, kid.
Okay, okay. But if we're gonna stay there for any length of time we'd better check first.
Okay, okay. But I'll tell you one thing. I'm not spending another night in that goddamned truck. Riding all day and still

THE CONTINENT

behind schedule. That lieutenant doesn't know his ass from his elbow. Did you see the way he was studying that map? He doesn't know what the hell he's doing. We'll end up in Germany somewhere in some prison camp.

We started down the road when a middle aged man came running out of the house the French woman had entered.

Messieurs, messieurs.

I think he's calling us, I said.

Messieurs. Suivez moi. Venez, venez chez moi. Un peu de vin. Quelque gateau. Chauffer vos mains au feu.

Repetez.

Chez moi. Un peu de vin. Quelque gateau. Chauffer vos mains.

He wants us to come to his house. Some wine. Some cake. Warm our hands by the fire. Shall we go?

Why the hell not?

Merci, merci.

Venez, venez.

We followed the man into the house and were led into the kitchen. The woman I spoke to on the street came to greet us.

Hello. Hello, she said. *Il fait froid dehors, n'est ce pas?*

Mais oui. She says it's cold outside.

C'est mon mari, ma soeur, mon beau-frere. The woman indicated the man who brought us into the house and a middle aged couple seated at the kitchen table.

That's her husband, her sister and her brother-in-law...I think. Bon jour, bon jour.

Vous allez en les camion qui se trouvent dans la rue, n'est pas?

Repetez?

Les autos dan la rue.

Yes, yes. The trucks in the street.

A NOT-SO-NICE JEWISH BOY FACES WORLD WAR II

Vous allez en Allemagne?
Yes. Yes, we're going to Germany...unfortunately.
Depuis combien de jours allez-vous en camion?
Ah...trois jours. I told her we've been traveling for three days.
Ask her where the kids are?
Les enfants? Ou est?
Le garcon demeure dans une autre ville.
The boy lives in another city.
La fille est alle avec son ami au cinema.
The girl's at the movies with her boyfriend.
The man of the house poured several glasses of wine and passed them around.
Merci, I said.
Mercy, the Redneck said.
A victoire.
Victoire.
Victoire.
To victory, said the Redneck.
And we all raised our glasses and drank.
This wine's not bad. Tell her it's very good, said the Redneck.
Lemme rest for a minute, I said. Trying to dredge up the right words was exhausting.
The sister was discussing me with her husband. He's very young, isn't he? Younger than Robert, the woman was saying. No, no, the husband answered. Oh, yes. I think so, she said and leaned over and whispered to her sister.
Ma soeur demande quel age vous avez?
What'd she say? asked the Redneck.
Her sister wants to know how old I am.
J'ai..ah...vingt ans, I said.

THE CONTINENT

The sister nodded and nudged her husband. See, I told you. Twenty. When Robert was his age he was still in school.

Quelque gateau?

No, no. She's offering us some cake, I said.

Mais oui! said the woman.

Tell her no. They probably don't have enough food themselves, said the Redneck.

Merci, non.

The woman waved her hand, brought out what looked like a coffee cake, sliced two pieces and placed them on plate.

No, no.

We're not hungry lady. We just ate. Had a delicious meal. All full, said the Redneck.

Paris? C'est loin? I asked.

Paris? Quatre-vint kilometres.

Paris is eighty kilometers from here. How far is that, do you know? I think a kilometer is smaller than a mile, isn't it? That means that Paris is less than eighty miles from here.

Never mind Paris. How far are we from Belgium?

The man responded. *Belgique? Deux cent quatre-vingt dix.*

Encore.

Deux cent...

Two hundred...

Et quatre-vingt dix peut-etre.

And ninety.

We oughta be there in a day or two. If that lieutenant can read that map right, said the Redneck.

The film que votre fille aller...le titre?

Je ne sais pas. The woman turned to her sister and asked the name of the film her daughter went to see. The sister shrugged. The woman turned to me. *C'est une filme Americaine.*

A NOT-SO-NICE JEWISH BOY FACES WORLD WAR II

Her daughter went to see an American movie. I turned to the woman. *Le titre?*
J'ai oublie.
What do you know? They have American movies here. Isn't that something!?
Oh, nous avons beaucoup des filmes Americaines et anglaises, said the man.
They have a lot of American and English movies here. Isn't that something?! Avez-vous un theatre ici?
Oh, mais oui, said the woman. *Il est ferme a present.*
They have a theatre here but it's closed right now.
Avez-vous beaucoup des pieces?
Say translate a little.
Qu'est ce qui'l dit? asked the woman.
Il dit qu'il ne peut comprendre.
The woman laughed. *Il faut qu'il apprende de parle francais.*
She says you must learn to speak French.
Yeah, huh
Il faut manger le gateau, said the man pointing to the cake and then to his mouth.
No, no, said the Redneck.
Pourtant nous l'avons coupe, said the woman.
They say they cut it and now it'll get stale.
Maybe we better, said the Redneck.
The Redneck and I helped ourselves to a piece of the cake.
You make this yourself? asked the Redneck pointing to the cake and to the woman and making stirring motions.
Oh, mais oui, said the woman and laughed.
Very bun, said the Redneck. *Very bun.*
Merci.
As we were eating the cake I heard the sister say to her

THE CONTINENT

husband that I had the same hair as Robert, their son apparently.

What's this? Friday night? I turned to the woman. *C'est comme ma maison ici.* And then I turned to the Redneck. *I said it's like my house here on a Friday night.*

There was a tap on the kitchen window. It was Corporal Verano. He motioned for us to come out. We waved at Verano and nodded.

Il devoir que nous allez, I said.
Mais oui, mais oui.
Merci, merci.
Yeah, yeah. Thank you.

The woman nodded. She came over to me and kissed me on both cheeks, then walked over to the Redneck and did the same. We shook hands. We waved to the sister and brother-in-law still seated at the table, and left the house to join Verano.

What do you mean running off like that? We almost left without you.
So what? said the Redneck.
Aren't we gonna spend the night here? I asked.
No we're not gonna spend the night here. Get in the truck!
Okay, okay.

We walked over to the convoy, climbed into the truck and took our seats...and sat there...and sat there.

I thought you said we were leaving, I said.
We are. Any minute now.
Yeah, yeah. Hurry up and wait, said the Redneck.

We were still in France on Thanksgiving. And it was still raining, but there was turkey with all the trimmings and mashed potatoes and lima beans and cranberry sauce and

A NOT-SO-NICE JEWISH BOY FACES WORLD WAR II

pumpkin pie. We sat in the truck eating our feast, the rain beating down on the tarp. Corporal Verano climbed in.

We'll be entering Belgium this afternoon, he said.

Will we be staying there? I asked.

Your guess is as good as mine. And throw your garbage in the garbage bags, said Verano. *Don't forget.*

Yes, sir!, said the Redneck.

That evening we left France and pulled into a small town in Belgium.

CHAPTER EIGHT

A Pleasant Interlude

I don't remember the name of the Belgian town we ended up in. I vaguely remember cobbled streets and the bitter cold. The town had been liberated recently, and the Yanks were looked upon as saviors. I remember the warm reception we received from the people in the town, especially from the family in the house in which Shale and I were billeted. (I'd finally discovered that the Redneck had a name.)

Just as we were ready to turn in Corporal Verano showed up and we were assigned to unloading the truck and laying some phone lines.

Looks like we'll be here a while, said Shale.

Your guess..., said Verano.

Is as good as mine. Yeah, yeah. We know, said Shale.

But, from the way things were settling down, it did look like the unit was here to stay.

Flemish was the official language of the country. French, however, was the fashionable one and everyone spoke a little English, a few quite well.

The house we were in was owned by Albert (that was his first name) a widowed farmer, and his family. After a few days Shale and I began to feel like part of the family. The atmosphere in the house was one of overwhelming joy, verging on euphoria. The town had been occupied for over two years and, according to the townspeople, the Germans had helped themselves to everything...clothes, food, cattle and hadn't paid a cent.

Not one franc, Albert complained. *They broke in the closets. Took everything.*

I hear some people were well off. Got rich under the Germans. Compris? said Corporal Verano. He was billeted in

A NOT-SO-NICE JEWISH BOY FACES WORLD WAR II

a nearby house, but came over to bring his wash for Gertrude, Albert's spinster sister, to do in exchange for chocolate.

Not us, not us, said Albert.

Boche drink all champagne and cognac. Nix champagne. Nix cognac, said Anni, Albert's young daughter.

Well, you're making money off of us, said Verano.

What? asked Albert.

Nothing.

What?

I said souvenir getting expensive, said Verano.

What are you gonna do with all your money? said Shale, coming out of his room after taking a nice nap. (In this homey setting I became acquainted with a side of the Redneck I hadn't seen before. I began to think of him as a human being.) *And stop giving away your chocolate,* Shale continued. *You heard what the captain said. 'Hold onto those bars. Your life may depend on them.'* And he winked at me.

Don't you worry about me, said Verano.

Oh, but I do, I do, said Shale. *And you know what else he said. 'Gonna pull a surprise inspection, he said, and if I find you've been giving away government property I'll have your ass.'*

That's right, I added. I was sitting at a table writing a letter.

And the captain's been trying damn hard to get those stripes away from you, and that's a perfect excuse...giving away government property, said Shale.

Why don't you just look after yourself? said Verano.

I fully intend to, said Shale.

By this time, the two of them were like contentious buddies.

Shale came over to Albert's father and patted the old

A PLEASANT INTERLUDE

man on the shoulder. *Hey, Pop, how ya doin? Phew! That smells awful. What are you smoking?*

Nix goot. Nix goot.

Shale took a pack of cigarettes from his pocket and handed him one.

Here smoke one of these.

Merci, merci.

Hey, Shale, called Albert, and motioned to him. *Here.*

What do you want?

Here.

Shale walked over to him.

What do you want?

Albert motioned to Shale to bend over. He wanted to whisper something to him.

Yeah, what is it?

Give me cigarette.

You bastard, said Shale. He pulled out a cigarette and handed it to him.

You bastard, said Albert and smiled broadly.

Shale, you bad, said Gertrude. She was sitting by the fire and darning some socks. *Full holes in stocking.* And she held up one of Shale's socks.

That's okay. Give you something to do on these cold winter nights. And he winked at her.

You bad.

Albert's grandmother, a spry old lady in spite of her weight seemed to dote on Shale. *Shale, Shale,* she called from her chair by the fire. She motioned for him to sit in the chair beside her.

All right, all right, you old bat, said Shale. He sat down beside her, patted her thigh and motioned to her. *Hey, you. Sit on my lap. Come on.* And he winked at her.

309

A NOT-SO-NICE JEWISH BOY FACES WORLD WAR II

The grandmother laughed hysterically, and said something to Gertrude.

What'd she say? Shale asked.

She say you too old for her. She likes young men, said Gertrude.

Hey, hey! What do you know. Okay, gorgeous, if that's the way you feel.

Anni went into the kitchen and came out, carrying two pails.

Hey, Anni, where you going with those pails? Shale called.

Milch de couw.

What the who?

Milch de couw. Milch de couw.

Oh, milka de coo, milka de coo, echoed Shale.

Ja, milch de couw. You come.

Anni set down the pails and took hold of his hand.

Me, too milka de coo? Shale asked.

Come.

No, it's nice and warm in here. Me stay by the fire, said Shale.

No, no. You come. Milka de coo. Come. Come.

Milka de coo, laughed Albert.

Come. Milka de coo, said Anni and pointed to a pail.

Shale sighed, shook his head and sighed. *What I gotta put up with!* He picked up the pail and followed Anni off as Albert laughed.

Hey, Shale, nix milka de coo.

The opening of the door sent an icy wind through the room.

It sure is cold out there, I said.

Write letter? asked Albert

Yeah.

A PLEASANT INTERLUDE

To parents?
No. Actually I was writing to Ginny.

She'd been writing to me regularly. I was still unsure about my feelings for her. There was no other girl in my life, and I did need someone to think about, to look forward to coming home to. But how did I know that after I'd actually committed myself I might not fall in love with someone else, I reasoned. This whole business of love and marriage was really very complicated. She was in love with me. I was fairly certain of that. Well, I wasn't misleading her, I assured myself. We were friends. Officially no more than that.

The grandmother walked over to the radio and turned it on. An orchestra was playing French songs, and then some American songs. The grandmother returned to her chair and rocked back and forth. Albert and his father smoked their cigarettes. Gertrude continued with her darning. A French baritone was singing "Deep Purple," in French, no less. It was one of my favorite songs.

My mind wandered back to Newark, and I imagined myself with my best friend, Irving and my friend Harold. We were sitting in Harvey's sun parlor teaching each other how to dance. We were playing chess, and Harold kept winning. We were playing ping pong in the cellar, and I was on a roll. We were venturing all the way down to Weequahic park in the cool of an Autumn evening. There was a hot dog stand there and we treated ourselves to hot dogs with "the works," which consisted of mustard and sauerkraut and hot or sweet relish.

I wondered if Irv had left Camp Pickett too. He might very well be nearby. Or maybe he was in Germany by now, engaged in hand-to-hand combat. I tried to picture him with a gun in his hand, coming face to face with the Germans. He was more likely to be exposed to danger than I was, since I was in the field artillery, while he was in the infantry.

A NOT-SO-NICE JEWISH BOY FACES WORLD WAR II

Corporal Verano warmed himself by the fire. "Deep Purple" had been the most popular song of the day when he'd worked in the Colony, a music store on Broadway and forty ninth street. This came as a revelation, and I discovered that, beneath that rather oily, obsequious demeanor, there was a real human being. His wife would come by and join him for lunch sometimes. That's when they were getting along, but the marriage wasn't going as smoothly as he thought it might. The love affair had been rather rocky, and the marriage was supposed to solve everything, I learned. That was what she wanted, at any rate. A child might be the answer, they decided, but so far, they hadn't had any luck. Maybe when he got back...

Gertrude looked up from her darning, and turned to Albert. She was concerned about Shale being alone in the barn with Anni. Albert reassured her saying that Shale was interested in Anni's friend, Trudi, and besides it was cold in the barn. Suddenly Gertrude rose and set aside the socks.

I show you something, she said to me.
What have you got to show me?
I show you. And she went into the next room.

The song came to an end and a newscaster started to give the news in French. The grandmother rose quickly from her chair, walked over to the radio and turned it off. Albert shouted at her to turn it back on. He wanted to hear how the war was going. The grandmother had a headache and refused. An argument ensued. Albert finally got up and turned the radio back on. By this time the war news was finished, and we learned nothing. The announcer was now giving the weather forecast, which was rather grim. Snow and cold.

Gertrude came back into the room with a cardboard box which she placed on the table in front of me.

Christmas cards. They're very nice, I said. I hesitated

A PLEASANT INTERLUDE

about going into an explanation about why there weren't that many people I could send Christmas cards to, and I wondered why. Was I ashamed of my heritage? Why didn't I just say that I was Jewish? I wasn't ashamed of it really, nor was I particularly proud of it. *Are you selling them?* I asked.

You want?

How much?

Three francs...one.

Hey Verano, you interested in some Christmas cards? They're very nice, I said.

Verano came over and inspected the cards.

Three francs, said Gertrude holding up one finger.

I'll take these four, said Verano. *How about a package of cigarettes?*

Goot.

I'll pay you tomorrow. Okay?

Okay.

Verano sat down next to me at the table, took out a pen and started writing out the cards. *By the way, we don't have to pull any guard tonight,* he said.

Hallelujah! Any news about how long we'll be here?

We'll be here for weeks, said Verano.

I hope you're right, I said.

Shale came back in carrying two pails of milk, followed by Anni. They set the pails down on the floor.

Hey, close that door, shouted Verano.

Okay, okay. Take it easy, said Shale.

Hey, Shale, you milka de coo? called Albert.

You bet your ass.

Shale! Shale! called the grandmother.

What do you want, you old bat?

Stay, said Anni to Shale, and she ran off to another room.

A NOT-SO-NICE JEWISH BOY FACES WORLD WAR II

You shoulda seen me milka de coo.
You milka de coo? said Albert.
Anni came running back into the room holding a pair of little wooden shoes.
Pour vous...souvenir, she said to Shale.
Well, what do you know! Just what I needed. Thank you.
Let's see, said Verano as he took one of the shoes out of Shale's hand. *Very nice.*
Yeah, very nice, said Shale and he beckoned to Anni. *Come here. I want to thank you.*
Oh, non. Non, said Anni, and she started laughing hysterically.
What's wrong with me?
You...Trudi, she said, continuing to laugh.
Nix Trudi. Nix Trudi, said Shale, shaking his head.
The family took up the laughter.
Gertrude! called Albert.
More laughter.
Nix Gertrude, nix Gertrude.
Grandmere! shouted Anni, laughing harder than ever.
Nix. Nix. Nix grandmere. Nix Anni. Nix Gertrude.
Qui? Qui?
Da coo. I milka da coo.
Another burst of laughter.
Hey, Shale, Shale! You kiss da coo, called Albert.
Hell, yes! Juiciest kiss I ever had.
How you kiss da coo? asked Anni.
Hell, I just kiss her.
Nix, nix. Show how, Anni giggled.
Like this, said Shale. He puckered his lips, made a smacking sound and rolled his eyes.
Nix, nix.

A PLEASANT INTERLUDE

Come here. You be coo.
Anni screamed and laughed. *Nix.*
Well, I can't show you how?
Yes, yes. Kiss da coo, shouted Albert.
Yes, yes. Kiss da coo, chanted Anni.
Yes, yes. Kiss da coo, chanted Gertrude.
Yes, yes. Kiss da coo, I joined in.
And everyone joined in unison.
Kiss da coo, kiss da coo, kiss da coo.
Aw right, aw right. Wait a minute. Let's see. Now watch. See? Watch carefully. I take her by the ears like this, see? And I lift her head up like this, see?
And we all laughed as he went through the motions.
Then I wipe her chin with my elbow, like this. See? Then I lean over like this, see? Then I grab both ears in one hand, like this, see? And I hold my nose with the other hand, like this, see? And then I move close up and... He puckered his lips. *Shtick oot moo lips and then I kissss.* And he made a long drawn out kissing sound.
Moooooooo, came from Albert and everyone burst out laughing.
Shale straightened up and waited for the laughter to die down. *That's the way the movie stars kiss in America.*
Nix.
Ja, ja.
Ohhhhh, said Anni.
Ja, ja. In kino. Movie stars.
Anni explained to the grandmother that that was the way they kissed in America.
Ahhhhhhh, said the grandmother. *Ahhhhhh.* And she crept up behind Shale and slapped him on the back.
Hey, you old bitch!
Old bitch! Milka de coo, laughed Albert.

A NOT-SO-NICE JEWISH BOY FACES WORLD WAR II

The grandmother slapped Shale on the arm. *Shale, Shale, Shale,* and she returned to her rocker.

After the laughter died down Anni pointed to the two pails of milk on the floor. *Come!*

I don't know, said Shale as he shook his head, picked up the milk and followed Anni into the other room.

The room was quiet again. Albert went to the radio and changed the station. The grandmother went to the radio and changed the station back. Another argument ensued which the grandmother, eventually, won and music again filled the room.

The outside door burst open and a short, blonde young man with an efficient air about him entered the room. His name was Ernst, a young man of many talents.

Goot nacht, he said to all. He walked over to Verano and shook his hand. *Hello,* he said. He then walked over to me and shook my hand. *Hello,* he said. *How are you this evening?*

Good evening. I'm fine, I said.

The door was blown open by the wind and sent an icy breeze through the room. The young man walked quickly to the door and slammed it shut. Shale came back into the room followed by Anni.

Ernst! Just the man I was looking for, said Shale.

How can I help you?

This watch of mine, said Shale. *It's stopped.*

You have the watch?

Hey Gertrude, where's my watch?

Gertrude got out of her chair, walked over to a shelf, pulled down a box from which she took out a watch and handed the watch to Ernst.

I think it needs a cleaning, said Shale.

Did you hit it against something, asked Ernst, and he opened the watch very professionally.

A PLEASANT INTERLUDE

I don't know. Maybe I did.
Let us see, said Ernst.
Both men peered into the open watch.
I don't see anything is broken, said Ernst. *It does need a...ah yes...here. You have bent a spring and a wheel.*
Take long to fix?
When do you need it?
Right away.
I'll have it ready for you tomorrow evening, said Ernst. *Gertrude can pick it up when she comes into my shop tomorrow.*
Okay.
Ernst dropped the watch into his coat pocket and brought out a pack of American cigarettes.
Would you like a cigarette?
No, thank you, said Shale.
Ernst offered cigarettes to each member of the family except for the grandmother. They all pocketed the gift for safe keeping.
Shale, Shale, called the grandmother, and she started to jabber in Flemish. She rose from her chair, approached Shale and continued to jabber.
What the hell is she talking about?
Ernst started to interpret. *She wants you to speak to the cook. Every day he throws out a great deal of food. He wastes food. You speak to him. Save it for us.*
Ja, ja. Cook. And she continued to jabber.
Okay, okay.
Grubbo might not do it, Shale, said Verano.
Sure he will, said Shale. *Gertrude you bring out a pot tomorrow and I'll see to it that they fill it up.*
I don't know, said Verano.
Sure he will. You bring out that pot tomorrow,

A NOT-SO-NICE JEWISH BOY FACES WORLD WAR II

Gertrude. You can't throw away food like that when people are hungry. Hey, Ernst, did you see the shoes Anni made for me. And Shale held up the little gift.

Yes, yes. Very nice, said Ernst. *We sell souvenir shoes in our store like that. Different sizes. Very nice. And we paint them ourselves with anything you like.*

Hey, Ernst, I said. *Will you hold a pair of shoes for me?*

Yes. What do you want me to paint on them?

I'll write it down for you. I wrote down Herman and Frieda, the name of my parents, and handed the paper to Ernst. *One on each shoe.*

Okay. Tomorrow I will have them for you. What sort of work did you fellows do in America?

I was going to school. The university, that is, I said.

And you, Corporal?

I worked in a music store, said Verano. *Had a real classy clientele. All the rich women used to ask for me.*

I'll bet, said Shale.

Knew all the salesmen from the music companies, said Verano. *Used to get free tickets to all the concerts, all the operas.*

Did you really? I asked.

I used to sit in the box like the Rockefellers.

Wow! I said.

And you, Shale, what did you do?, asked Ernst.

Me? I was a gangster.

A gangster? asked Gertrude. *What is gangster?*

You know, said Shale. *I had a mob, like you see in the movies. You don't know what a gangster is? I packed a rod. Right here,* and he patted himself under his left armpit. He then pretended to draw out a revolver and fire it. *Bang, bang! Bang, bang!*

A PLEASANT INTERLUDE

Ernst translated into Flemish for the family.
Anni squealed, *Nix, nix!*
Gertrude let out a surprised, *Ohhhhh.*
Ja, ja, said Shale. *Bang, bang, bang, bang, bang!*
Nix, nix!
Ja, ja. I had a couple of molls back home. Real tough babes. They were so tough they smoked cigars.
Ernst continued to translate.
Ohhhh, said Anni.
Ja, ja.
Nix. And Anni laughed.
I used to be the biggest butcher in Chicago, said Shale. *Used to sling those carcasses around like they were meatballs.* Then he started to talk out of the side of his mouth, and gesture with an imaginary cigar, like Edward G. Robinson, the movie star who often played gangsters. *Now look here, Shale. We want this guy rubbed out, see? We want a nice clean job, see? Then they'd hand me a few grand and I did the job. See? No fuss, no bother. Nice clean job. See? Right through the heart.* And he grabbed his chest, as if wounded, and started to fall over.
Anni squealed, *Nix.*
Ja, ja.
And she giggled. *You mademoiselle...?* And she went through the motions of smoking a cigar.
Hell, yes. All the women in America smoke cigars?
What does he say? asked Gertrude.
Ernst translated.
Ohhhh, said Gertrude. *Nix.*
Ja, ja.
Est-ce vrai? asked Anni.
Yeah, sure, said Shale. *They all sit around and smoke cigars. Nix work.*

A NOT-SO-NICE JEWISH BOY FACES WORLD WAR II

Nix work?
Nix work, said Shale. *They sit on their ass and eat chocolates.*
Nix.
Hell, yes. Nobody works in America. We got machines to do everything. We sit in skyscrapers, you know. Real big houses, ya know. We sit in skyscrapers and eat chocolates.
Quelle sorte des machines? asked Gertrude.
That's right, said Shale. *We push buttons. Machines.* And he illustrated with gestures.
Suddenly Anni burst into gales of laughter and clutched her sides.
What's the matter with her?
Anni continued to laugh and finally blurted out, *Machine kaput.*
And the entire family joined in the laughter.
What the hell are they laughing at?
Hey, Shale, you kiss the mademoiselle with the cigar? Albert called out.
Hell, yes.
Machine kaput, Shale kaput, shouted Anni in between bursts of laughter.
What the hell is she laughing at?
She's laughing at you, you idiot, said Verano.
What the hell you laughing at?, Shale kept asking.
Machine kaput, machine kaput, shouted Anni.
She bent forward clasping her thighs and squeezing them together. She let out a little squeal and ran out of the room. The entire family burst into laughter.
You're nuts, the whole lot of you, said Verano.
There was a short silence, after which Ernst spoke up. *I hear you are leaving us next week. They say in the village that your whole division is getting ready to move up.*

A PLEASANT INTERLUDE

Where did you hear that? asked Shale.

They say your captain is going up to the front tomorrow, said Ernst.

That's good, I said. *Maybe he'll stay there.*

He sure likes to show off, that's for sure, the way he walks around, said Shale, *in those boots of his and that riding crop.*

They say he is to look over positions for your battalion, said Ernst.

Uh oh, said Shale.

Ah, we won't be moving for at least a month, said Verano. *We'll be here till the middle of winter.*

You mean the middle of next week, I estimated.

Yes, that is what they say, said Ernst. *The middle of next week.*

Suddenly the room was not that cheerful. Our haven was not that secure anymore, and fun and games no longer seemed to offer a refuge.

CHAPTER NINE

THE FIRST CASUALTY

The move took place the beginning of the following week. Early in the morning we loaded all the gear onto the trucks, and climbed in after it. Sergeant Garrell, my nemesis, sat down next to me as the convoy started to move. Garrell was from the Bronx. He was about my age, a little shorter than I was. His pleasant features masked a rather aggressive nature, and there was this little private war going on between us.

Ready to kill some Germans? asked Garrell.

Was that supposed to be funny, I wondered, but I said nothing. Since we were in the field artillery, and we were members of the ammunition squad, the prospect of our coming face to face with the enemy was exceedingly slim. Nevertheless the thought troubled me. Along with the sense of guilt at the thought of taking another man's life, along with the fear of being killed, in the back of my mind there was also an oddly impersonal curiosity.

What was I made of?

How would I behave under fire?

Was I really an abject coward, as Garrell seemed to imply, and I, myself, secretly concurred? I couldn't see myself running away, yet I couldn't see myself actually trying to kill another human being.

Certainly my father, in his own quiet way, was "macho," the way he defied that gunman who was trying to rob him, punching him in the nose, and the man turned out to be a professional boxer. Was I my father's son or was I my neurotic mother's son? But then again Mother was actually a pretty gutsy lady. She came through when put to the test during World War I; and when Irving and I found that ten dollar bill in the street in front of the barbershop, and the

THE FIRST CASUALTY

barber came out and said the money was his, and we meekly handed over the money to the man, even though we knew he was lying, and nobody in the family came forward to speak for us, it was my mother who confronted that villain; and she fought for me when she thought I was being short-changed when I worked as a clerk in the supermarket...the way she marched into that store and confronted that supervisor. Come to think of it, I come from pretty sturdy stock, I reasoned.

After a few hours on the road, the convoy stopped for lunch. The sun was nowhere in sight. It was now snowing heavily. Artillery fire could be heard in the distance. *We're in Germany now,* someone said, as we sat in the truck, waiting...and waiting. As the day progressed, it seemed to grow darker and darker.

When the trucks finally started up again we left the road and headed into a forest.

Where the hell are we? I asked.

Exactly, said Sergeant Garrell.

I regretted being so honest with this pipsqueak about my attitude towards war. I turned to him, looked him in the eye and asked, *Are you really looking forward to killing someone? Is that it?*

Garrell said nothing.

At least I had made my point.

The truck rumbled, rocked and jolted on into the darkness. In was December of 1944, the height of the war, when we entered the Hurtgen Forest. The rumble of gun fire was getting much louder. Someone thought it might be our own guns we were hearing because they seemed so close. We sat huddled inside the truck, numb with cold, our rifles upright between our legs, the butts resting on the floor. The truck jerked to a halt. Nervous questions filled the air.

What are we stopping for?

A NOT-SO-NICE JEWISH BOY FACES WORLD WAR II

Is this it?
Who knows?
Fat assed Sergeant Murphy came by. *We'll be stopping here for a while,* he said. He wasn't barking now.
Why are we stopping? someone asked.
Are we there yet?
What's happening?
I don't know, said Murphy. Was this really Murphy? He sounded so subdued. Was he actually scared, I wondered. Was he actually human?
The questions continued.
What good are you?
What do you know?
There's been a casualty, Murphy said very quietly.
There was silence.
Do they know who?
Corporal Oakdale.
Is he...?
Yeah.
Silence.
How did it happen?
I don't know.
To my amazement, I found myself weeping uncontrollably. My body was racked with sobs. I couldn't help it, and I didn't care. I didn't care what anybody thought. Corporal Oakdale...that nice looking, sturdy young man. He couldn't have been more than twenty five. And he was dead. His short life was ended. The only one in the whole goddamned army that had actually shown me a bit of warmth, that had, figuratively speaking, extended a hand to me, the only man in the whole damned army that I actually looked up to.
Even in the middle of my grief, I was aware of the

THE FIRST CASUALTY

respectful silence in the truck. No one made a crack about my display of weakness. No one said a word. Did they actually empathize with me, those cold, callous comrades of mine whom I had such difficulty relating to?

I had never actually spoken to Oakdale. The corporal had never actually spoken to me. Back at Camp Pickett, however, when the noncoms were choosing sides for some sort of an exercise no one wanted me on their team. "Mr. Shakespeare" was not someone you wanted next to you when you were in a foxhole. But Oakdale had chosen me. He hadn't left me just hanging there, all alone, a pariah.

In all fairness, I couldn't really blame the others. My attitude was well known. There was that rather public conversation, or debate if you will, that I had with Sergeant Garrell.

What do you mean you couldn't kill anyone? What do you think you're here for? Garrell said.

Murder is a crime, I said.

This is war. It isn't murder.

What is war? It's mass murder, isn't it?

Suppose someone was firing at you, said Garrell, *you wouldn't fire back?*

Not unless I absolutely had to. I mean, if I had to defend myself, I suppose I would.

If that's the way you feel, said Garrell *why did you join the army?*

I was drafted.

You could have been a conscientious objector, said Garrell.

I was thinking about it. But I'm a Jew and they're killing the Jews.

You know what? You're nuts, said Garrell.

No, I'm not nuts, I said to myself. It's the world that's

A NOT-SO-NICE JEWISH BOY FACES WORLD WAR II

nuts. The world is a madhouse and I'm ashamed to be a member of the human race. Just taking part in this carnage is a sin, I reasoned, a sin that will haunt me for the rest of my life.

And now that we were here in Germany, in the midst of the battle, the debate...or whatever it was...would be settled. I would finally find out what I was made of.

The word came down a little later. It appeared there'd been a freak accident. When fired for the first time the howitzer Oakdale was in charge of had exploded.

We remained in the truck, in the freezing cold, waiting to find out what our assignment would be...waited and waited for, what seemed like, hours. The gunfire continued sporadically.

Put on your helmet, Sergeant Garrell said

When we get out of the truck, I replied.

You're in combat now. You're supposed to wear it at all times.

I'm aware of that.

Garrell shrugged. *It's your head.*

I'm aware of that, too.

I was not prepared to explain that I couldn't stand anything on my head. I found the helmet stifling, and it was giving me a headache.

How far were we from the front, I wondered. The gunfire was certainly nearby. Was there such a thing as the front? This was World War II, not World War I. There was no such thing as trenches anymore. How dangerous was it really? One man was killed already, and we were just entering combat.

We weren't in the infantry, it's true. But being on a howitzer was just as dangerous, apparently, and I would be

THE HURTGEN FOREST

delivering ammunition to the howitzers, probably in the line of fire.

Would I ever be warm again, I wondered. Maybe I ought to keep my helmet on. Oh, the hell with it! And, to top it all off, my fingers were frozen. If I did have to use my rifle I wasn't even sure I could fire it.

After I recovered from the initial shock of Oakdale's death I wanted to go off somewhere and mourn the loss of this friend whom I'd never really met. I wanted to commune with this man who tossed me a bit of warmth in this unfriendly atmosphere. But sitting there, among the rest of the squad, I just couldn't somehow. I needed privacy to let my imagination take flight, to imagine what this man was like, to wonder where he came from, what his childhood was like, what his interests were. Was he just a good-hearted jock, or did he have any cultural interests? And what was his family like? His parents? Did he have any siblings? Did he attend a college? Was he a high school graduate? Where would they bury him? Exactly how did he die? Was it a piece of shrapnel that entered his heart or his brain? Was there much blood? Was there much pain, or was death instantaneous? How did they move the body? Where did they move the body to? Would it be shipped back to the States? I'll probably never know any of this.

You okay? asked Shale.
Yeah, I'm fine.
This really is a bitch. Cold as hell.
Well, I guess fresh air never hurt anyone, I said rather airily. I appreciated the concern, but I wasn't a baby. I didn't need to be pampered.

Besides the question did interfere with my thoughts. I wanted to bury this unknown man who had suddenly become my hero. I wanted to lay him to rest, with honors. I wanted

A NOT-SO-NICE JEWISH BOY FACES WORLD WAR II

closure. I would never forget him, I knew that, but I did have other things to think about.

CHAPTER TEN

THE HURTGEN FOREST

Where were we actually, I wondered, and how long were we gonna be here? Hurry up and wait, hurry up and wait. The whole thing was like a dream. A nightmare rather. I tried to block out the present, the misery, the cold, the danger.

It was really getting dark. Or was it the trees shutting out the light. Was it actually night time, or was it still day?

Everybody out!

This was Staff Sergeant Murphy. I put on my helmet as we climbed out of the truck.

I tried to conceal my contempt for the asshole as I passed by him.

He went back to his truck, and the truck moved off together with the rest of the convoy.

Where were the trucks going, I wondered, and why the hell weren't we going with them? And where, exactly, were we?

Four of us were left behind.

Sergeant Garrell, apparently, was in charge. *Okay, men. This is where we spend the night,* he said.

I looked around at the trees, at the ground covered with snow. *Where?!* I asked.

You got a sleeping bag, haven't you? And dig yourself a foxhole. I strongly advise it.

As if to emphasize the importance of Garrell's advice the gunfire seemed to grow louder and closer.

What are we supposed to dig it with, I asked.

You've got a steel helmet, haven't you?

Yeah, but I'm not supposed to take it off, am I?, I countered.

You got a problem, came Garrell's comeback. (Chalk

A NOT-SO-NICE JEWISH BOY FACES WORLD WAR II

one up for the little sergeant.) *And watch where you step. There are supposed to be land mines all over the place.*

Oh, great! With all this snow on the ground you're supposed to see a land mine?!

And there are booby traps. There may be wires that can set them off.

How interesting! I said.

We'll be standing guard in two hour shifts. I'll take the first shift, said Garrell.

Shale and Verano were assigned the next two shifts. I was assigned the last one.

We set our packs down on the snow, sat on them and ate our K rations.

My fingers are so cold I can hardly feel them, I said.

It might be a good idea to take off your shoes and rub your feet. It's easy to get frostbite, said Verano.

After I finished my meal I did exactly that, and it seemed to help a little.

We oughta start digging our foxholes, said Verano.
Not me, said Shale.
Maybe we ought to, I said.
Go right ahead, said Shale.

I took off my steel helmet, leaving the cloth lining on my head, and started to dig. The ground was as hard as a rock. I scraped and scraped. I wasn't getting anywhere. Finally I stopped. *The hell with it,* I said. *This is ridiculous.*

I unrolled my sleeping bag. I climbed in and luxuriated in the slight bit of relief it offered.

By this time it was pitch black. I couldn't see a thing. I closed my eyes. Now was the time to mourn the death of Corporal Oakdale properly. But the mourning period seemed to be over.

What happened to all that grief?

THE HURTGEN FOREST

Was this it?
Is that what happens to us after we die?
A brief homage and then...nothing?
Oh, God! I had to take a leak.

It was so dark. Where could I go? I might step on Verano or Shale. I might even step on a mine.

Shale? Shale! I whispered.
Yeah? What is it?
I gotta take a leak.
Use your helmet.
My helmet? Oh, Jesus!

I groped around for my steel helmet, pulled it inside, managed somehow to position myself, and I relieved myself. Now what? Was I supposed to step out into the freezing cold to empty it? The hell with it! I set the helmet, with its steamy contents, down next to me, and made a mental note to remember to empty the helmet before I put it on again.

I covered myself up, sank deep into the sleeping bag, and closed my eyes. The forest was strangely quiet. No gunfire. As a matter of fact, it was too quiet. Suddenly someone was shaking me.

Hey, Beim! Wake up! Wake up! It was Sergeant Garrell.
Is it my turn? Already?
We're moving.
Moving? Where?
We're going back to Belgium. To pick up some ammunition.
Now?!
Pack up your things, said Garrell. *And hurry up.*
What time is it?
What difference does it make? Come on. Get your ass moving.
Okay, okay.

A NOT-SO-NICE JEWISH BOY FACES WORLD WAR II

Half asleep, half awake I rolled up my sleeping bag. I put my things together. I picked up my helmet, placed it on my head, and cold liquid poured over my hands and legs.

Oh, Jesus! That was all I needed!

Okay, men, let's go, said Garrell.

Where? I can't see a thing, I said. *Shale? Shale?*

Yeah. I'm right here.

Give me your hand.

I pawed the air. Nothing.

Where are you?

Here, here.

I came in contact with Shale's sleeve. I held on tight. I couldn't see a thing.

Shale started to move. I clung to him, and followed as fast as I could, stumbling occasionally. I was still groggy, still half asleep.

Take it easy. Where the hell we rushing to? I said.

Shhhhh. That was Garrell.

At this point, as far as I was concerned, the danger seemed secondary. I was not about to lose contact with my squad. This was madness. Racing through the forest in the pitch black with the possibility of stepping on a mine or setting off a booby trap. Where were they rushing to? Didn't they care whether I was with them or not?

Hey, hey. Slow down, I whispered.

I stumbled, lost my footing, got up and peered into the darkness.

Shale?

No answer.

Shale?

No answer.

Garrell?

No answer.

THE HURTGEN FOREST

Verano?
No answer.
Shit! Shale? Where the hell are you?
I peered into the darkness.
They were gone, all three of them, gone, and I had absolutely no idea in which direction they'd gone.
Now what?

CHAPTER ELEVEN

A DEFINING MOMENT

I remained standing in the dark, not knowing which way to turn. I had absolutely no sense of direction. I would have liked to have followed the squad, but at this point, I didn't know how. If I kept going I might walk right into a German machine gun nest, or an enemy camp, or, God forbid, I might step onto a mine...or a booby trap. I stood there...debating. Shivering and debating.

Finally I decided. It was ridiculous to wander about in the dark, not knowing what I might run into. The sensible thing to do was to stay right where I was and wait, wait for the daylight. I'd be blamed, of course. I was the fuck up. I was the worst soldier in the outfit, and it was all my fault. But was it, really? I was a subordinate. I wasn't in charge. I was part of a squad. Garrel was in charge, and I was his responsibility. If you're in charge of a squad, you look after your men. He should have made sure that we were all there, that we were all together. I was half asleep when we started out. He should have been aware of that. Well, I was wide awake now.

I stood listening. It was awfully quiet. The rest of the company was probably bivouacked somewhere in the area. Or were they? They could have been miles away.

I sighed and looked about.

Something loomed in front of me in the dark. I looked at it apprehensively. It looked like a tree. A large tree.

I took my fate in hand and approached it slowly. I reached out and touched it. It was a tree.

I looked about. I couldn't make out anything.

I looked down. I could make out the snow around the tree. Barren and cold as they were, the tree and the snow offered some sort of a haven.

I stood there, trying to decide what to do.

ANOTHER TEST

Minutes passed as I stood there, indecisively. I was beginning to feel sleepy, but I was certainly wide awake. This was ridiculous, I decided. I couldn't just stand there for the rest of the night.

I sat down on the snow. I could feel the cold snow through my heavy army coat. I held my rifle in my lap and looked about...and listened.

Nothing.

I yawned and lay down on the snow, assumed a fetal position and snuggled next to the tree, hoping it might offer some warmth, some protection. It was pointless. I was freezing cold and uneasy.

I sat up.

I lay down again.

I stood up and looked about.

I couldn't decide which was worse, standing or huddling next to the tree on the cold snow. Finally, I gave in to the weariness, lay down again and just remained there.

For the rest of the night I lay shivering at the foot of the tree. The cold of the snow penetrated my body. God help my poor kidneys, I thought. Half asleep, half awake, I waited for the dawn, yet dreaded it. Suppose I found myself near the enemy camp? I might get shot. Yet, if I wandered about I might step on a mine. Well, that would solve everything, wouldn't it?

I must have dozed off for a brief while because when I opened my eyes I could see clearly the tree right next to me. I could see the trees around me. I could see the sky above. Suddenly the forest didn't seem that formidable.

Now I had to decide what to do next. I had to go somewhere, but there still were those mines and those booby traps.

I rose and stood shivering. I would never be warm

A NOT-SO-NICE JEWISH BOY FACES WORLD WAR II

again, and my kidneys would never be the same again.

I started walking slowly in the direction from which I thought I had come. Actually, there was really no way of knowing. I thought I saw some smoke not too far away.

I walked apprehensively in the direction of what I took to be smoke. It's got to be our bivouac, I reasoned, it's just got to be.

Or the enemy camp.

One or the other.

Take your choice.

I walked just a few yards, and there was a clearing.

There was a kitchen.

A cook was preparing breakfast. It was our kitchen! I'd spent the night just a few yards away from our bivouac.

I walked into the clearing and who should I almost bump into but my favorite noncom.

What are you doing here? thundered Staff Sergeant Murphy.

I got lost.

You're supposed to be on your way to Belgium, roared the asshole.

I'm aware of that.

You left your squad?

I said I got lost!! The man was obviously deaf.

Murphy looked me up and down. *You left your squad?!*

Stone deaf!

Boy, you are in deep shit. We are in combat, boy. You don't leave your squad in combat, boy. It's what's called desertion.

How could I desert? I'm here.

Boy, you are in deep shit. Come with me?

I couldn't believe it. That stupid ass! What were they

A DEFINING MOMENT

gonna do? Put me up in front of a firing squad and shoot me for getting lost in the snow?
Where are we going?
I'm bringing you to the captain. Boy, you are in deep shit.
Obviously I was in deep shit.
Murphy marched me over to the captain's tent.
Wait here. And I advise you to stay here. Don't move! 'Cause you are in enough trouble as it is. Murphy strode into the captain's tent. He came out a minute or so later.
Come with me. Boy, you are in deep shit. Murphy seemed to be enjoying the situation immensely. Apparently I'd given him something to do, an excuse for his existence.
We entered the tent. I saluted the captain. The captain was in the middle of shaving. Somehow, he didn't look that threatening, with the lather on his face. I looked down at those black shiny boots. They, on the other hand, did not look very friendly. As a matter of fact, they looked downright menacing.
What happened?
I got lost, sir. I was half asleep when Sergeant Garrell woke me up, and I couldn't keep up with the squad. It was dark, and I got lost.
He deserted the squad, Captain, said the asshole.
Wait outside, Private.
Yes, sir.
He deserted the mission, sir.
I said wait outside, Private.
Yes, sir.
I saluted the captain and left the tent. Murphy came out a minute later, trying to look very officious.
Come with me, he ordered.
Where are we going?
Murphy didn't reply and started for the kitchen area.

337

A NOT-SO-NICE JEWISH BOY FACES WORLD WAR II

I followed him.

The asshole stopped in front of a large pit, a sump meant as a receptacle for the garbage. *Get down there and start digging*, he ordered.

Don't I get any breakfast?

You're lucky you're not being court-martialed. Men have been shot for less. This is combat, boy.

I took off my pack and set it down on the ground. I placed my rifle next to it. *What am I supposed to dig with?*

There's a shovel down there. Pick it up and start digging.

Yes, sir! I said, as if I were being given the most important order in the world. I'm sure the sarcasm was lost on this man. He was absolutely dense.

I jumped down into the pit. I picked up the shovel and started to dig, throwing the dirt up to the side of the hole. After digging for a while I took off my coat and placed it next to my pack. I was hungry. I felt weak. I dug slowly, leisurely, stopping every once in a while to catch my breath.

The asshole stood watching me from above. What was that man's function in life, I wondered. I assumed that Murphy was an army man, that the military was his career. But all he ever seemed to do was either sit on his ass or strut around.

Stop gold-bricking and dig, came the order.

I picked up the pace, but I was really weak. What I needed, in addition to a good night's sleep, was a hearty breakfast.

Come on, come on. Get to work!

Suddenly I found myself throwing down the shovel. I looked up at the monster. Never in my life had I felt such anger. All the frustration, all the agony, all the bitterness of the past two years came spewing out from the very depths of my being. *If you don't like the way I'm digging this fucking*

A DEFINING MOMENT

pit, come on down here and dig it yourself, I found myself shouting. I stood there in the pit, my legs spread apart, my hands on my hips, staring defiantly at the asshole. My hair stood on end. I couldn't believe this was happening to me. Never in my life had I used the word "fuck." Never in my life had I been ready, almost eager, to do something violent.

This was the way Daddy must have felt when he defied the thief with the gun. There was no fear of danger. There was no thought of the consequence. It was pure animal behavior. Suddenly I realized that this nice Jewish boy was actually capable of violence.

What did you say?, roared the asshole.
You heard me!

Is this where ones virility lay, I wondered. Deep down inside, waiting to spring forth? This defiance...was it anger? Fury? Disgust?

What did you say? thundered the asshole.
I said, if you don't like the way I'm doing it, come down here and dig this fuckin' pit yourself.
You come up here.

I hesitated. It suddenly occurred to me that I had refused an order. This, after all, as Staff Sergeant Murphy kept repeating, was combat. I could, after all, be shot.

I said, come up here.

I threw down the shovel defiantly. I climbed out of the pit. I was beginning to wonder if this bravado wasn't just a little bit foolish. After all, I did value my life.

Come with me.

Murphy strode off towards the captain's tent. I trailed behind him.

Wait out here. And don't move!

I stood outside the tent trying to hear what was being said. I heard the captain's voice, but I couldn't make out the

A NOT-SO-NICE JEWISH BOY FACES WORLD WAR II

words. Murphy came out of the tent. He didn't seem as all-fired sure of himself as he had been when he went in.

You are in deep shit. Come on. And the asshole strode back to the sump.

I followed him.

Now get down there and start digging, and I don't want anymore lip. You hear me?

I hear you all right, I heard myself saying, *but if you want me to dig that pit you're going to have to give me some breakfast. I'm tired, I'm hungry, and I am weak.*

The asshole stared at me.

It was at that moment that I realized that I had won. The captain had obviously thrown the asshole out of his tent, and the asshole was just trying to save face. The asshole had made an ass of himself. He knew it. The captain knew it, and the asshole knew that I knew it too.

The men were starting to line up for breakfast.

Get over there and eat your breakfast, and then report back to me, he said, trying to sound gruff, but fooling no one, not even himself.

Yes, sir!!

I started to pick up my equipment.

Leave your stuff here.

Yes, sir!!

I tried hard to repress the smile that was forming on my lips, but I wasn't quite sure how successful I was.

I'll need my mess kit, I said quietly, triumphantly.

Murphy said nothing.

I took out my mess kit and joined the chow line.

As I ate my breakfast, I tried to digest the events of the last twenty four hours.

For one thing, I'd discovered that Staff Sergeant Murphy was a hollow man. Even the captain didn't take him

A DEFINING MOMENT

seriously. There was nothing inside that blown up buffoon except hot air and, maybe, even cowardice.

And as far as Garrell was concerned, as a sergeant in charge of his squad, he was the one that had failed, not me. He should have seen to it that all his men were with him. So, the hell with Sergeant Garrell! There was no reason on earth why I should be ashamed of what I felt, ashamed of what I believed in. For the first time, in a long time, I really liked myself.

CHAPTER TWELVE

ANOTHER TEST

What happened to you? asked Sergeant Garrell.

That's a good question, I said, looking him straight in the eye.

Garrell said nothing. He never referred to the incident again, and I sensed a slight change in his attitude. Maybe he wasn't such a hot shot.

How was the trip? I asked Shale.

Fine.

Any problems?

No. We just picked up the ammunition and delivered it, said Shale. *We're going back this afternoon.*

In the daylight, I hope.

What happened to you? Garrell was cursing you all the way, said Shale.

Tough shit!

There were two more trips to Belgium. The first one was uneventful.

Returning from the second trip we stopped at the side of the road to eat our lunch. We sat near the truck in an open field. It was a peaceful, sunny afternoon. Even Garrell seemed relaxed.

Suddenly the air was filled with a deafening noise. Buzz bombs whizzed overhead. One landed across the road, near enough for us to see the flying debris.

It was too dangerous to return to the truck. It was filled with ammunition. It was just as dangerous to sit in the open air. On the other hand, if we sought shelter in the trees nearby and a bomb hit the top of the trees we could be in even worse trouble. There had been a number of casualties caused by falling shrapnel. Nevertheless the trees seemed to offer the only haven available. We ran under them.

ANOTHER TEST

As we sat huddled in the shade the noise grew louder and louder. We could hear the swoosh over head. The tops of the trees swayed back and forth. Verano took some beads from his pocket and started to mumble some prayers. Shale was muttering something, curses or prayers, it was difficult to tell. Garrell knelt tight lipped.

A second bomb landed a little closer than the first. I was as frightened as I'd ever been. "There are no atheists in foxholes," I recalled someone saying.

Should I pray or should I not? The threat of instant death seemed to be getting closer and closer. The tops of the trees rustled more dangerously than ever as the bombs flew overhead.

If we had any sense at all we'd get out of here. But then again, how was one to know which was safer, the open field or the forest?

All right, I said to myself, if there is a god, I hope he gets me out of this. There! I'd said it. Well, I'd thought it anyway. I'd formed that thought in my mind, and there was no way of taking it back. And I was ashamed. But it wasn't really a prayer, I reasoned. It was sort of a half-hearted prayer, an indirect one. Actually it was just a hope. But I had agreed that if I came out of this alive I would be grateful. To whom? To what? I wasn't quite sure.

The noise stopped. It was quiet now. We waited a few minutes and then we came out into the open field.

That was close, said Verano.
It sure was, I said.

I tried to put the incident behind me. I tried to forget my moment of weakness, the moment when I may have compromised my integrity. I was alive. That was all that really mattered. If there was a god he (or she) would understand...and if there wasn't, there was no harm done.

A NOT-SO-NICE JEWISH BOY FACES WORLD WAR II

I was convinced, now more than ever that, no matter what the Bible said, it wasn't God who created man. It was man, out of fear, who created God.

But there was no denying that I had sort of prayed in a left-handed sort of way, and maybe my prayer, or wish...or whatever it was...had been granted. Besides I wasn't an atheist, was I? I was an agnostic. There were lots of things I didn't understand. I didn't understand electricity, I didn't understand radio, I didn't understand how a complicated organism like the human body came into existence.

And what did it really matter? Alexander Pope said it all. "Presume not God to scan. The proper study of mankind is man."

Noel Coward said it, too, in of all things, his immortal comedy, "Private Lives."

Elyot: You have no faith. That's what wrong with you.
Amanda: Absolutely none.
Elyot: Don't you believe in...? (He nods upwards.)
Amanda: No. Do you?
Elyot: (Shaking his head.) No. What about...? (He points downwards.)
Amanda: Oh, dear no.
Elyot: Don't you believe in anything?
Amanda: Oh, yes. I believe in being kind to everyone, and giving money to old beggar women, and being as gay as possible. ("Gay," of course, in the sense of "spirited", not in the modern sexual context.)

My experience under fire did nothing really to change my mind about religion or about God, and maybe Noel Coward's plays were not that frivolous; and we delivered the ammunition safely without any further incidents.

CHAPTER THIRTEEN

COLD, WAITING & REFLECTING

Back in the Hurtgen Forest the snow was deep as we trudged along. We were assigned to laying wires. At night there was guard duty. Sometimes there was nothing to do, except trying to keep warm The snow continued to fall and the shelling in the distance continued as well. Once or twice the shelling came close but, gradually, it became part of the background noise.

There was still the danger of stepping on a land mine or a booby trap. As time passed, the threat seemed to become academic...though there was word of one incident where someone had stepped on a mine, was hospitalized and lost a leg.

I tried to block everything out of my mind, except surviving from day to day. There was no future, there was no past. There was only survival.

Laying wire near a command post one day I came across a group of German prisoners. A sentry stood guard. Was it to prevent their escape or to protect them, I wondered.

I studied them. I said to myself, I am standing face to face with men who belonged to a nation that had slaughtered members of my family, relatives I'd never met, perhaps, but relatives nevertheless. Just a short while ago their task had been to kill me as well.

I stood there, staring at them. They were men, just like me. Most of them were quite young, not much older than I was, some of them probably younger. I didn't hate these men. I wished that I could, but I couldn't. I did, however, resent the fact that they were safe and sound. I resented the fact that the United States Army was now feeding and housing them.

This whole business of war just didn't make any sense. One minute you're trying to kill someone. The next you're

A NOT-SO-NICE JEWISH BOY FACES WORLD WAR II

taking care of them? What kind of business was that? Madness on top of madness.

As I studied the prisoners the love that I felt for my fellow man froze inside of me. I felt an unwelcome animosity, a coldness that was foreign to my nature. But that's why I was there, wasn't it? I was part of a killing machine, an organization dedicated to wiping out one's fellow creatures, and again I felt tainted, tainted by hate and corruption, by the horror that was an integral part of the civilization that I lived in, a horror that I myself was contributing to, and I felt unclean. And there was nothing I could do about it.

The days passed into weeks. Things seemed to be at a standstill. Why were we here? What were we accomplishing?

At times the cold seemed unbearable. My mind became as numb as my frozen limbs. If I was lucky enough to survive this nightmare, would I really want to be a writer? Was it really worth the effort to create something beautiful? For whom? For a world that was this barbaric? Why go through all that agony? For what? What was the point?

******

If only I could get a pass to Paris, I dreamed. I needed to come in contact with humanity, with beauty, with things that made life worth living. There were some passes being issued. As a matter of fact a couple of men in my outfit had received passes to Paris. With my record, however, I did not hold out much hope.

One day in the mail there came a package for me. It was a book. I opened it eagerly. "The Fountainhead," by Ayn Rand. I'd read about it somewhere. It was a controversial book, a popular one. In the fly leaf was written, "To the dearest of brothers, May your novels exceed this one in greatness. Your ever-loving sister, Rose." I was touched by my sister's faith in me. Dear Rose, so sweet, so fragile. If only I could be there to advise her, to guide her.

I opened the book with loving care. Whenever I could find a spare moment I read, and as I read I smiled. Dear, dear Rose, how impressed she must have been by the idealism the book promulgated. Before the war, I suppose, before all this, I, too would have shared her admiration for this author. But now? How naive, and how nice if there were such dedicated heroes, as brave and as incorruptible as Howard Roark, the books protagonist.

But Howard Roark, in my jaded eyes, seemed to be the dream man, the Prince Charming of a dewy-eyed young maiden. All the characters in the novel seemed fabricated, synthetic symbols to illustrate some sort of theory, some sort of philosophy. But underneath this grand idealism there was no real humanity, no warmth, no heart. There was a ruthlessness, an egotism which, if everyone adopted, could be quite dangerous.

I wrote nothing of this to Rose. I didn't want to spoil the gesture. So I wrote that I "enjoyed the book very much. It was fascinating and thank you so much for sending it to me."

I continued to correspond regularly with Ginny. She wrote me faithfully, sometimes three or four times a week. I confided in her, and her alone, about the hardship and the soul searching I was going through.

I realized, perhaps for the first time, how deeply I was involved with her, and how deep her feeling was for me. After much hesitation, after much soul searching I decided to make a formal commitment. I might regret it later on, I told myself. After all, how does one know if one woman is the right one? You might meet someone tomorrow whom you loved even more. But out here in the Hurtgen Forest I was not about to meet anyone else. As a matter of fact, I might never get a chance to meet anyone else. I was stuck with Ginny, and that was it. So her nose was large. So what? Everything else about her was fine and beautiful and we had such a great rapport.

In a ridiculously clumsy letter, I wrote words to the effect that a soldier needed someone to come home to, and I hoped that she would be there waiting for me. Of course, I continued, I'd always dreamed that someone as beautiful as Hedy Lamarr would share my glamorous life (or something to that effect.) It was cruel thing to say, I knew that, especially in a love letter, but I had to be completely honest, didn't I? She'd respect me for that, wouldn't she? I didn't ask her to answer what, in actuality, was, if not a proposal, a definite commitment of some sort. I just assumed that her acceptance was understood.

I finished the letter with a sigh. I'd done it. I might regret it later on but there was no help for it now. I signed it with love and sealed it.

To my family I wrote that I was stationed in England, permanently. There was no possibility of my going into combat. I began to question the decision I'd made. And then I remembered Mother having hysterics that summer evening when I came home late from a walk in Weequahic park with my friends, leaning out the window and scolding me in front of girls no less, causing me no end of embarrassment. No, I decided, I'd made the right decision.

"We're leaving for a rest area tomorrow," Sergeant Garrell said one afternoon.

"How nice," I said.

The next day we climbed into the truck and headed back to a camp in Belgium.

For one day we were housed in tents, given clean

COLD, WAITING & REFLECTING

clothes and were finally able to take a shower. The showers were out in a tent that was not well heated and my teeth chattered as I soaped himself. Standing naked under the water I was able to view my body for the first time in weeks. Lean and mean, a fighting machine! I gloried in the surprising toughness and muscularity of my body. If only I could stay that way!

And I wondered what would become of this fragile, vulnerable entity as the years went by, that is if the years went by. Would it become flabby and ugly and deformed?

And I was again reminded that, technically, I was still a virgin. There was that one failed attempt with a prostitute back at Ohio State. Then again at this point, what did it really matter? I might possibly die a virgin and that would be the end of that.

Back in the Hurtgen Forest the monotony continued. It was now six weeks since we had entered that hell hole. Christmas was a memory. New Years was a memory. Suddenly, the very last day of January the word came down.

"We're moving out," said Sergeant Garrell.

The move was certainly welcome. The question was where, and to what new dangers would we be exposed?

CHAPTER FOURTEEN

"JUST TAKING A STROLL"

The following day we stored our gear in the trucks, climbed in after it. We shook and rumbled our way slowly through the forest. A while later we emerged onto a highway.

I noticed what looked like litter along the side of the road. Looking closer the litter turned out to be bodies of dead soldiers. I couldn't make out if they were Americans or Germans. I didn't think our GIs would be left by the side of the road to rot like that.

It was the first time I'd come face to face with corpses. The sight both appalled and touched me deeply. These were, after all, men...young innocent men for the most part, who would be mourned by their families, their lovers. It was over for them, probably before it had even begun.

We approached a town, or what was left of it. I vaguely remember the remains of a church. Except for the one wall of that church, the town had been leveled. There was no sign of life anywhere, nothing but debris. What happened to all the people in the town, I wondered.

We rolled on. We were approaching another town. There were remnants of some buildings left standing. A civilian here and there was picking through the rubble.

The trucks stopped. We got out our mess kits, climbed out of the trucks and lined up for a hot lunch. As we ate, the artillery fire in the distance seemed to grow louder.

Somehow or other Shale had gotten hold of a bottle of cognac. He grinned triumphantly as he held up the bottle. *All you gotta do is look.*

You gonna drink that stuff? I asked. *It might be poisoned.*

I can't think of a better way to die. Shale uncorked the

"JUST TAKING A STROLL"

bottle which was half empty and took a swig. *Yeah man!* He held the bottle out to me.
 No, thank you, I said.
 It'll put hair on your chest.
 I don't want hair on my chest.
 Sergeant Garrell came by.
 What have you got there?
 Cognac, said Shale. *Have a swig.*
 Get rid of it.
 Yes, sir!
 I mean it, said Garrell.
 Yes, sir!!
 And as soon as you two are finished eating, we got a job to do, said Garrell. *There may be some Germans hiding out in some of those buildings.*
 Or what's left of the buildings, I said.
 What's that? Yeah. You two start right there, with that building behind you. Garrell pointed to a space where a house had been leveled to the ground.
 What building? asked Shale. *There's no building.*
 There's a cellar, isn't there?
 I don't know. I guess we'll have to find out, said Shale.
 Exactly. And get rid of that bottle, said Garrell as he walked away.
 I fully intend to, said Shale, and he took a healthy swig.
 Curiosity got the better of me. *Let me taste it*, I said.
 Be my guest, said Shale as he handed me the rather suspicious looking bottle.
 I took a sip, gagged and spit out the mouthful. I handed the bottle back to him. *That stuff is awful!*
 What do you expect for nothing? said Shale as he took another healthy swig.

A NOT-SO-NICE JEWISH BOY FACES WORLD WAR II

We finished our lunch and washed our mess kits. Shale was still holding on to the bottle.

You're not gonna drink the rest of that stuff, are you?, I asked.

You heard what the sergeant said, 'get rid of it.' And Shale did just that, finishing off the bottle and throwing it away. *There's gotta be more where this came from.*

Where did it come from?

That's my little secret, said Shale.

He was beginning to display the effects of the liquor. He rose unsteadily. *C'mon, let's go. There's work to be done.* And he started to sing. "*I been working on the railroad, all the live long day.*"

What are you, nuts?

What's the matter? Right, right. And he put his finger to his lips. *Shhhhh.*

We approached the remnants of the house Sergeant Garrel had pointed out. There were bits of wall remaining, a few pieces of scrap that had once been furniture, and a battered floor. We discovered a trap door which, we assumed, led to the cellar.

That's where they keep it, said Shale.

What?

The cognac.

Be careful.

Shale approached the trap door, took hold of the ring and pulled it up.

Shale!

What?

There may be someone down there.

Shale removed his carbine from his shoulder and fired several shots into the cellar. *Not anymore.* He then climbed down the stairs. I stood nearby, my carbine at the ready. After

"JUST TAKING A STROLL"

a moment I called out, *Shale? Shale?* There was no answer. I came to the edge of the stairs and peeked into the hole.

Son of a bitch! came Shale's voice out of the darkness.

Shale, are you all right?

Shale climbed out a moment later, covered with debris. *There's rats down there.*

Well, as long as they're not human.

C'mon, let's go, said Shale.

We moved on to the remains of the next house. There seemed to be no signs of any Germans so far. Shale was getting more and more frustrated in his failure to find more cognac.

We approached what looked like a hut, the remnants of a house that had been pieced together to provide shelter. The opening, that had once been a window, was covered with black paper. There was an upright door which looked like it might topple over any minute. It was ajar.

As we came closer we heard a human voice. We stopped and listened. The voice was that of a little girl. Since I spoke Yiddish before I spoke English, and Yiddish sounded very much like a corrupt German, I was able to make out the words.

You must be a good little girl and you mustn't go outside. The airplanes will go boom. You must eat your potatoes. That's a good little girl. Now, now, now. You mustn't eat too fast.

C'mon, said Shale.

Be careful, I said. *There are people in there.*

Where there's people there's bound to be cognac.

Will you forget about the cognac!?

Don't eat too fast, Irma, or you're going to get sick. Good potatoes.

Shale kicked the door open and we peered inside.

A NOT-SO-NICE JEWISH BOY FACES WORLD WAR II

In the dim light I could make out some rudimentary furniture, a table, some chairs and a couple of chests. On the floor, in the semi-darkness, sat the little girl with a rag doll on her lap. She looked up at Shale, who entered the room and crashed about. The girl crawled under the table.

I followed Shale into the room. *There's only the kid*, I said. *C'mon, let's go.*

Are you kidding? said Shale. *Where there's people there's bound to be cognac.*

Where's your mother? I asked in Yiddish, hoping it sounded like German.

In the cellar, replied the little girl.

What'd she say?

Her mother's in the cellar.

Hiding the cognac, I'll betcha. Shale started ransacking the place, pulling out drawers and spilling its contents onto the floor.

What the hell are you doing?

They're hiding it somewhere, the sons of bitches! Goddamned bitches! Goddamned war!

There's nothing here, I said. *C'mon, let's go.*

Don't rush me, boy. Don't rush me.

Mamma is in the cellar, said the little girl.

C'mon, Shale, let's go.

It's in the cellar, that's where it is. That's where they keep the fucking cognac.

Shale started for the cellar door, when suddenly it opened and a figure emerged. It was a woman wearing a long dark peasant dress, her face hidden by a shawl wrapped around her head. She was carrying something folded in her apron.

Ask her where the cognac is, said Shale.

Nix cognac, the woman said.

"JUST TAKING A STROLL"

I'll give you nix, cognac, you old bitch!

As the woman came into the light we got a good look at her face. Her left cheek was swollen twice its size. Half her teeth were gone, and there were scabs on her lips. Her eyes were sunk deep into her face. The skin around the eyes had turned blue and green. Nothing remained of her eyebrows except for two raw red lines, and from what could be seen of her scalp it looked like she'd lost all her hair.

Jesus Christ, lady, what happened to you?

The woman's free hand went to her face.

Nix cognac.

Don't give me that shit, lady. What have you got there?

Shale pulled at her apron and several potatoes fell to the floor. She bent down hastily to pick them up. I bent down and helped her place them on the table.

Shale collapsed onto one of the chairs. *Goddamned war! Goddamned liquor! Goddamned captain's got it all. That's where all the cognac went.*

The woman chattered on in German. *Nix cognac. Other American soldiers were here. Everything is in a mess.*

What'd she say?

American soldiers took all the cognac.

That's her story.

The little girl crawled out from under the table, came to the woman and held onto her skirt.

Is that your daughter? I asked.

Yes. Yes, I am the mother.

Is she the mother of that kid?, asked Shale.

That's what she said.

Jesus. How old is she?

I asked the woman how old she was.

Twenty three, she said and nodded tearfully.

She's twenty three.

A NOT-SO-NICE JEWISH BOY FACES WORLD WAR II

Twenty three? Christ, she looks worse than my grandmother and she's in her nineties.

Yes, that's my daughter, said the woman and she began to weep.

Woman you are gruesome, said Shale.

Yes, yes, said the woman, *I am the mother.*

Don't cry, I said.

Bombs. Airplanes. Many bombs, the woman continued in German. *I was in my house. This is not my house. This is my sister's house. My sister is dead. We were in the kitchen, my mother, my sister and my daughter and the planes came very fast. We ran to the cellar, but we were too late.*

What is she squawking about?

The woman rattled on. I had to listen hard in order to understand. I missed a lot of the words, but I did get the gist of it. Apparently the bombs fell. The whole house fell in. It was horrible. Her mother was dead. Her sister.

The house was hit by a bomb, I translated for Shale..

Yes, yes. Bombs fell. The war is not good. My husband is in the war a long time. In Russia for two years. I haven't heard from him for two years. I don't know if he's alive or not.

What's she blabbin' about?

Her husband's in Russia.

Yeah, yeah. Good for him. Hey, Beim, tell her it's a good thing she's so Goddammned repulsive.

When will the war be over? Can you tell me?, the woman pleaded.

Shale rose from the table and demanded loudly, *Where the hell is the cognac?*

Nix cognac, nix cognac.

Nix cognac, my ass. I'm gonna pull this goddamned joint apart.

"JUST TAKING A STROLL"

Shale stumbled towards the cellar door and fell to his knees. I went over to help him.

Leave me alone, he shouted.

Take it easy, Shale.

Shale rose, made his way to the cellar door and opened it. *I'm going down the cellar. You keep an eye on them.*

I sighed as Shale disappeared into the cellar.

Nix cognac.

I know, lady, I know. He'll just have to find out for himself. He had too much cognac. Do you understand? Too much cognac.

Yes, yes.

I continued, half in English, half in Yiddish. *It's all right, lady. All he can do is break down the house, and there's not very much to break down.*

I haven't any cognac. I haven't any cognac.

I know, I know. I went to the cellar door, opened it and shouted, *Hey, Shale, let's go. It's time for chow.*

Right with ya, right with ya.

Come on, Shale, we gotta get back. The trucks are pulling out.

Awright, awright.

I'll be damned if I'm gonna wait around, I countered. *If you don't come out by the time I count ten I am leaving.*

The woman started to straighten the mess that Shale had made, putting the contents back in the drawers.

I'm starting to count. Here I go, Shale. Here I go. One. Two. Three. Are you coming?

Hey! Hey, Beim, I think I got something.

Four. Five. I'm not kidding, Shale.

Just one more minute. One more minute.

Six. Seven Eight. I'm really going. I mean it. I'll be damned if I'm gonna hang around here.

A NOT-SO-NICE JEWISH BOY FACES WORLD WAR II

You better wait for me, if you know what's good for you.

Niiiiiiine. Nine and a half. Nine and three quarter.

I mean it. You better not leave me. I really found something.

And ten. So long, Shale.

I stepped away from the door and remained silent.

Hey, hey Beim. Hey, I got something. Did you hear me? Hey, Beim. That goddamned.... Beim, you lousy bastard, I'll break your neck when I get hold of you. You goddamned yellow skunk. Wait'll I get out of here! Sonofabitch, lousy goddamned bastard. Shale burst through the opening and looked around. *I knew you didn't go. Look! Look what I got.* And he brandished a bottle.

Nix, said the woman. *Nix.*

Better see what it is, I said.

Shale pulled the cork out of the bottle and sniffed it. He then handed it to me.

I smelled it. *It's vinegar,* I said and I handed the bottle to the woman.

Shale knocked the bottle to the floor. It shattered and the vinegar splattered about.

C'mon, Shale. Let's go.

Wait a minute, said Shale and he started to ransack the drawers the woman had just arranged.

The little girl, meanwhile, walked over to the box of wood next to the stove, picked something out of it, walked over to me, and held out her hand.

What have we got here? I asked.

To my horror the child presented me with a hand grenade. She was holding it by the pin.

Jesus!!, I cried.

"JUST TAKING A STROLL"

Shale whirled about, and the woman looked at me wide eyed.

Look! Look at what the kid just gave me. A hand grenade, and she was holding it by the pin. I turned to the little girl. *Nix good,* I said. *Nix good. Where did you get this?* I asked the woman.

Other Americans were here.

Nix good, I said. *Nix good. This is a small bomb. Boom. A small bomb.*

The woman started to scream and shrank back. *Take it away, take it away.*

You're a bad girl, I said to the child. *Jesus Christ, she handed it to me by the pin. We could have all been blown to kingdom come. Who the hell could have been stupid enough to give a child a hand grenade?*

Where's the goddamned liquor? bawled Shale.

Take it away, take it away, squealed the woman.

Tell that bitch, if she doesn't cough up with that cognac I'm gonna break that ugly neck of hers.

Ohhh, take it away.

Shale stood over the woman. *Listen you, I'll go out and I'll murder that bastard husband of yours, you hear me? I'll go all the way to Russia and kill the son of a bitch, you hear me?*

Shale, for god sakes...

That's what we're here for isn't it? I'll cut his guts out.

Shale...

I grabbed him by the arm and tried to pull him out of the hut.

That's what we're here for, isn't it? I'll kill the fuckin' bastard. How do you like that?!

I managed to get Shale out of the hut. Realizing that I was still holding the grenade, I looked about for an empty

A NOT-SO-NICE JEWISH BOY FACES WORLD WAR II

area and threw it away with all my strength. I waited for the explosion but none came.

We better get back to the trucks, I said.

When we got back to the trucks they were all loaded and ready to move.

Where the hell ya been? asked Sergeant Garrell. *We almost left without you.*

We were just taking a stroll, I said.

CHAPTER FIFTEEN

I SHED A TEAR

The convoy moved on and we rolled further into Germany. There was a great improvement in the weather. The cold snap ended, and there were occasional glimpses of the sun. We made some half-hearted searches along the way but no Germans were found. From the sound of the gunfire, it appeared that the war was still being fought but, obviously, the Germans were on the run. As we moved on we passed groups of prisoners being herded along. There were also displaced persons trudging by.

It was towards the middle of March when we stopped in front of an impressive mansion.

We're gonna be here for a while, said Sergeant Garrell. *You can get out, but stay in the area.*

We got off the trucks and stretched our legs.

This is quite a place, I said. *Why don't we take a look inside?*

Shale shrugged. He didn't seem very interested. Since his encounter with the woman and the child he'd been rather subdued. He kept complaining about needing to get laid. He fell in behind me, however, and we approached the house.

It was a magnificent structure, two storeys high with gables and leaded windows, the kind that, at night, would have been perfect for a horror movie and, during the day for a period film, a spy movie, perhaps, or an elegant comedy of manners. It had escaped the bombing but several windows had been broken and the shrubbery which, at one time, must have been carefully groomed was now growing wild.

I pushed the door open and peered in. This was obviously the home of someone very important, in the government perhaps, or someone very rich, or maybe an aristocrat.

A NOT-SO-NICE JEWISH BOY FACES WORLD WAR II

I walked through a paneled foyer into a large room. Though the room was in disarray, chairs overturned, a large table shoved against the wall, it was still awesome. A magnificent old tapestry, faded now, was hung on one wall. A huge fireplace on the opposite wall. What sort of people lived here, I wondered. Royalty maybe. Or perhaps a German general and his family.

In my mind a scenario began to take shape. I imagined this impressive officer in his uniform joining his wife for tea. His name, of course, was Curt and he sported a monocle. The wife wore a long gown like in the movies. The woman was full faced. Her hair was light brown and she wore it short. She resembled that English film star, Edna Best.

"And what did the Fuhrer have to say?"

"The usual. He's becoming impossible. Something has got to be done."

"Curt! You mustn't talk like that. You mustn't even think it."

Curt remained silent. He daren't reveal anymore, even to the woman he loved, the woman whose life he'd shared for the past twenty years.

Imagine living in a place like this?, said a strange voice.

I was startled out of my reverie.

Gives me the creeps, said Shale, the strange voice I'd just heard.

It's fabulous, I said.

I walked to the end of the room where I found a circular staircase. There had to be a circular staircase, of course, and the bedrooms were upstairs, of course. That's where they usually were. That's where the family slept. The servants' quarters were probably in the back somewhere. I started toward the stairs.

I SHED A TEAR

Where ya going?
I'm gonna investigate, I said. I started up the staircase.

I was now the young American student, the suitor of the German general's daughter whom I'd met at Yale where we were both studying architecture. No, we were probably studying languages.

"I haven't told my family yet, that you're Jewish."

"But you promised."

"I know, I know and I will. They're really not prejudiced, you know."

"Then why are you hesitating?"

"I've just got to find the right moment. Now, calm down, David. (Or maybe my name was Michael). Not all Germans are anti-Semitic, you know."

There was a room at the head of the stairs. The door was ajar. I pushed it open. I stepped into a small room with two windows overlooking the front lawn. There were a couple of overturned chairs and books. Three of the walls were floor to ceiling book shelves, and there was a ladder on casters. It was a study of sorts. There probably used to be a desk in that empty space over there where the German general sat and did his correspondence.

And books, books, books. Piles of books on the floor which someone, perhaps, had swept off the shelves. Some of the books lay open. I noticed that some were damaged, pages torn. The emotional pain that swept over me was almost physical. What brute would deliberately vandalize these precious objects?

I stepped over one of the piles and examined some of the books that lay helter-skelter on the shelves. Goethe. Heine. Leather bound volumes, the pages tipped with gold. I opened one of the books. It was printed in elaborate Germanic letters, completely unreadable, but these were books nevertheless,

A NOT-SO-NICE JEWISH BOY FACES WORLD WAR II

letters, completely unreadable, but these were books nevertheless, books that could be read by human beings.

Here was a book by...Nathaniel Hawthorne. And here were several volumes of Shakespeare, probably the whole collection. Jack London. Tolstoy.

I sat down on the floor and started to arrange the volumes in a neat pile.

Shale came into the room. *What the hell are you doing? Sitting and reading?*

I was just looking at these books.

Shale kicked one of the piles.

Don't do that!, I snapped.

What's the matter with you? Shale gave the pile another kick, sending books flying across the room.

I stiffened. I was ready to spring at Shale. *I said don't do that.*

Shale gave the books another kick then strolled over to the windows and looked out. *They're unloading the trucks. Looks like we'll be here for a while. I was just talking to Verano. They're sending someone to Paris.*

Oh?

Someone from our squad, said Shale. *Verano submitted your name.*

Who's going? Do you know?

You were turned down.

Who's going?

Sergeant Garrell. They're sending noncoms first. You'll probably be the next one to go.

You think so?

Verano said he'd submit your name again, said Shale. *They may be sending some people to Holland and Belgium. Some guys are going to Brussels.*

I'm gonna hold out for Paris.

I SHED A TEAR

Maybe we oughta go down and help unload the truck, said Shale. *Tell me, what the hell do you see in those goddamned books?*

Books are as important to me as people.

You can't read these, can you?

No.

So what's the difference?

Books contain the best of mankind, I informed him.

You really gonna be a writer when you get out? You think you can make a living at it?, asked Shale.

No. I plan to starve in a garret.

I'm serious.

So am I, said I.

Well, maybe I can say I knew you when.

Corporal Verano came into the room holding a broom. *What the hell are you two doing? Shale, get down there and help them unload.*

Shale jumped to attention and saluted. *Yes, sir!!*

I mean it.

I'm goin', I'm goin', said Shale. He saluted again, winked at me, and left the room.

What the hell are you doing down there?

I was trying to straighten out the room, I said.

We gotta clean the place out. We're spending the night here and some men are gonna be sleeping in this room. Get rid of those chairs. And we'll have to get rid of all these books. Verano started to sweep the books into one pile.

I can do that. I can take care of this room.

Okay, okay. But don't fuck around. Here. Verano tossed the broom to me and left the room.

I put down the broom, picked up the chairs and placed them in the hallway. Then I carefully wheeled the ladder out of the room. I came back into the room, bent down and placed

A NOT-SO-NICE JEWISH BOY FACES WORLD WAR II

some of the books back on the shelf. I started to leaf through one of the books, a book by Thomas Mann. I couldn't read it, but just turning the pages gave me some sort of fulfillment. A tremor of grief started to well up inside of me.

I placed Thomas Mann back on the shelf, sat down on the floor in the center of the pile and pulled the books close around me as if they were a cloak that could warm me. I picked one up and fingered it gently, slowly turning the pages. I couldn't see the print for the tears. I found myself sobbing. I finally pulled myself together and finished cleaning out the room.

CHAPTER SIXTEEN

I EMBARRASS MYSELF

After dinner we took our gear out of the truck and found places for ourselves in the various rooms.

There was a full moon that night. It was a cool night, with a pleasant promise of Spring to come. In one room some of the men were playing poker. Some men were writing letters. I felt restless and decided to explore the area behind the house.

I found my way out the back door and onto a field that looked like it had been plowed recently. The moon lit up the whole area and at the other end of the field I noticed a small building, a cottage perhaps. I made my way across the field, stumbling at times because of the furrows. When I reached the building it turned out to be a crude shed, containing some farming equipment. The door had been torn loose and was supported by one hinge. There was no roof.

I noticed a small wooden box in the corner, half hidden by some straw. I lifted the lid and there lay two bottles of cognac. Wouldn't Shale be pleased, I thought. On second thought, I decided to keep the information to myself. Shale does not hold his liquor well, I reasoned.

I picked up one of the bottles and examined it. It looked quite respectable, a professional label and the cork was undisturbed. I closed the lid and, holding the bottle, sat on the box thinking. I had long ago decided that, if I was to be a writer, I must experience everything in life except, of course, maybe murder. What does it feel like to be drunk, I wondered.

I examined the bottle carefully. It had not been tinkered with. I took out my pocket knife and went to work on the cork, not very successfully. I ended up pushing what was left of the cork down into the bottle.

I smelled the liquor. It smelled awful. I tasted it. It

A NOT-SO-NICE JEWISH BOY FACES WORLD WAR II

burned my throat. It was not very flavorful. How could people drink this stuff, I wondered. I took a healthy swig and swallowed. It was worse than medicine. It certainly warmed you up though.

I took another swig. It didn't taste any better. It sure was potent though. Wow!

I took a third and a fourth.

The liquor began to do its work. Maybe this was not such a good idea, after all.

I set down the bottle. The world was starting to revolve and my stomach didn't feel too good either. I don't know, Beim, maybe you're not too bright after all, I said to myself.

I sat perfectly still, hoping that the world and my stomach might settle down. Apparently the world had no intention of doing so, and I was beginning to feel slightly nauseous.

I tried to stand. The floor came up to meet me.

I got up slowly from the floor, trying to wipe away the dirt and the straw. Holding on to the side of the shed I inched my way toward the doorway. My stomach was struggling to keep its contents down. My head was trying to maintain some sense of who I was, and where I was, and how I was going to get from where I was to where I wanted to go, which was back to the house.

I made it to the doorway.

Three cheers for Private Beim!

Now there was that field to cross. That's a big field, I reasoned. It goes on forever. I looked up at the moon. Shine on, friendly light, and guide me safely to my destination, I said silently.

I took one step forward.

The ground again came up to meet me. It just wouldn't stay put.

I EMBARRASS MYSELF

This was not going to be easy. Maybe crawling was the thing to do. I got down on all fours and began to crawl.

Then I took a chance. I tried to stand. I was able to get to my feet and run a few steps before that vicious ground came up and hit me in the chest. I looked up at the moon. *You're not very much help up, you know,* I said to the moon.

But I was making progress. It looked like I had reached the halfway mark.

I began to crawl on all fours as rapidly as I could. Suddenly I had this irresistible urge to defecate. Oh, no, oh no! I struggled with my belt. I finally managed to get it open. I finally managed to loosen my trousers and pull them almost half way down. It was too late. Oh, God, what a mess! What a goddamned mess! And I passed out.

I woke up, what seemed like, hours later. I found myself looking up into the night.

For a minute I didn't know where I was. Then I remembered. I was still feeling sick to my stomach. The smell reminded me that I had shit all over myself. What a mess! It was still dark, for which I was grateful.

I managed to get to my feet and somehow stagger to the house, holding up my smelly, disgusting looking trousers and falling several times on the way.

Thank God everyone was asleep.

I found my way to the bathroom, got out of my fetid clothing and, standing naked except for my dog tags, went to work washing them. I had no change of uniform and I would just have to wear the wet clothes until they dried. After continual rinsings, I gave up trying to rid my clothes completely of the stench. I found my duffel bag and took out my sleeping bag. Laying my uniform out to dry I climbed into my sleeping bag and closed my eyes. So, that's what it feels

A NOT-SO-NICE JEWISH BOY FACES WORLD WAR II

like to be drunk, I remembered thinking. Well, at least now I know.

C'mon, get up, get up. We gotta help load the trucks. We're moving on. Shale was shaking me.

What?

What's that smell?

That's me. I had an accident.

That meat tasted bad last night, said Shale. *I had the runs too.*

I got dressed, rolled up my sleeping bag and helped Shale load the truck. Sergeant Garrell came by.

Hurry up and get your breakfast. We're moving on.

I thought we were gonna be here for a while, I said.

Don't ask questions and do as you're told.

That wasn't a question, I muttered as Garrell strutted on. Officious little bastard. (And, I remarked, for the first time, that he was shorter than me.)

It had been quiet for a while, but as we ate breakfast the artillery started up in the distance. We climbed onto the trucks and headed deep into the heart of Germany.

CHAPTER SEVENTEEN

I AM A PLAYWRIGHT!

More and more German prisoners were encountered en route. We passed through several towns that looked pretty beat up. In the countryside, however, there were some picturesque villages which had escaped the bombings. I drank in the quaint streets and the buildings and the shops. Some of them were like storybook towns.

It was a cloudy day in April when we stopped near a magnificent castle atop a hill. The castle was said to have been owned by Franz von Papen, someone high up in the government. It was rumored, that Hitler would often stay there.

We got out of the trucks and stretched. Corporal Verano came around with the mail.

Got two letters for you, Beim.

One of the letters was from Ginny. The other was from home. I recognized Rose's handwriting. I opened Ginny's letter first. I read it eagerly, devouring its contents, experiencing vicariously Ginny's experiences in a world I could only dream about.

By this time Ginny had graduated from Ohio State. She had moved, with her family, to the suburbs of Philadelphia. During the day she was working as a social worker. In the evening she was studying acting with Jasper Deeter, the artistic director of Hedgerow Theatre, reputed to be the first real repertory theatre in America.

Deeter had been the original cockney, Smithers, in Eugene O'Neill's play "The Emperor Jones", and had directed on Broadway the Pulitzer Prize play, "In Abraham's Bosom." But Deeter, dissatisfied with the commercial theatre, had left New York and, with some colleagues, including Ann Harding, now a major movie star, had established Hedgerow Theatre in

A NOT-SO-NICE JEWISH BOY FACES WORLD WAR II

an old paper mill in Rose Valley, just outside of Philadelphia. Both O'Neill, himself, and the great George Bernard Shaw allowed Jasper to produce their plays royalty free.

Ginny actually had small roles in the repertory. In the Spanish play, "The Cradle Song," she was playing a nun. The production was brought into New York and played several performances at the Cherry Lane Theatre in Greenwich Village. I replaced the letter in the envelope and sighed. How I envied Ginny. What an opportunity! It was like dying and going to heaven.

I looked up at the sky, at the clouds floating lazily by. Real life, civilized life, was actually going on. People were actually free to do as they pleased. They were able to write, to act, to seek fame and fortune, to go into a bathroom and shut the door behind them. And here I was in the middle of Germany, a nothing. What claim did I have to exist? What purpose was I serving? Helping to kill Germans? Well, I suppose I was helping, in my own **very** modest way, to save the world for Democracy, wasn't I? That was something, wasn't it? It was something that had to be done.

But what about afterwards? If there was an afterwards. The war was still going on. I'd been lucky so far, but that didn't mean that my luck would hold out forever. Well, maybe I ought to be grateful that I was still alive, that I was still in one piece and we were, after all, winning the war. It certainly couldn't go on for very much longer, could it?

I placed Ginny's letter in my inside jacket pocket. I opened the letter from home. Actually there was no letter from home. The envelope contained an unopened letter that was addressed to me at my family home in Newark. It was from The New England Theatre Conference, the outfit that had sponsored the one act play contest.

I tore open the envelope. I unfolded the letter. A piece

I AM A PLAYWRIGHT!

of paper fluttered to the ground. I picked it up. It was a check for twenty five dollars made out to me. I'd won a prize. I couldn't believe it. I was a playwright! Oh God! I couldn't believe it. I was a playwright!! My talent was acknowledged. My future was assured. I was destined for greatness, after all.

I looked at the check again to make sure that it was real. I read the letter again. I had won second prize. Well, not exactly. My play had tied for second place. What difference did that make?

I looked about. Everything seemed different somehow. I looked up at the castle on top of the hill. I looked at the road, at the hedges by the side of the road. The sun was shining, shining more brightly than it had ever shone before. Mother Nature seemed to be smiling down at me. I wanted to memorize this moment, the most important moment, perhaps, in my entire life. This was a day, this was a place I would always remember. Nothing could stop me now! I had to survive. My destiny had been decided. I was going to be a writer, after all. This was just a tiny hint, a little preview of all the wonderful things to come.

CHAPTER EIGHTEEN

A MINOR TRAGEDY

In the middle of April the Lightning Division moved to the German countryside and became an occupational force. We were assigned, rather ambiguously, to "policing the area." For all intents and purposes the war was over. Guard duty seemed to be our main job, that plus overseeing the German prisoners, and keeping the displaced persons in order.

We were housed in a former German barracks and began to live a relatively civilized existence. One could actually sleep in a real bed on a real live mattress. One could take a shower, whenever one chose to, shave in reasonable comfort and, to top it all off, the weather was spring like.

To celebrate our new status the captain grew a mustache, found himself a fancy gun belt, sported two six-shooters, and strutted about flashing a walking cane.

One afternoon Shale was sitting at the table when I came back from guard duty, bursting with the most exciting news. I was walking on air.

You back already? said Shale.

I was on for two hours, I said. *Two hours and fifteen minutes, to be exact. My replacement was late. You sure got it easy.* I could barely contain myself, as I continued. *Well, old man, you'll be on tonight. You'll be taking my place.*

Where you going?

And finally, I revealed the most magnificent, the most exciting, the most unbelievable news. *Why Paris, of course! Where else?*

Yeah?

One guy from our section is going, and my name was the only name submitted. I can't believe it! I've been dreaming about this for years. Of course, the only way to see Paris is with a girl on your arm.

A MINOR TRAGEDY

Well, I don't think you'll have any trouble getting laid.

Oh, Shale, Shale, Shale. Getting laid! I want romance. A magnificent love affair. Can you lend me ten bucks?

Lemme see. Shale examined his wallet and handed me the money. *You taking anything to sell?*

A carton of cigarettes, I said, *in case I go broke.*

You oughta take along some soap...and chocolate. Garrell went there with fifty bucks and came back with three hundred.

The trouble is, this is the only pair of ODs I got. And I need a haircut.

Corporal Verano came bustling into the room. *What are you two doing?*

I just got off guard duty, I said.

I'm writing a letter, if that's all right with you, said Shale.

I've got some prisoners here to clean up the place.

There's nothing to clean, said Shale.

Well, find something, said Verano.

Has my pass come through yet? I asked.

I'll let you know when I get the word, said Verano. He left to bring in the prisoners.

Maybe I oughta start packing, I said.

Did you pass that section with all the women? Some pretty nice babes there...spread out all over the porch. Lots of guys been going out there the last few nights.

Really?

Hell, most of the officers have been regular visitors, including the captain, said Shale.

And we're not supposed to fraternize, said I. *Well, it's no skin off my nose. I'm going to Paris and the hell with the captain. The hell with everything. My dream's come true. Maybe you'll be on the next batch to go.*

375

A NOT-SO-NICE JEWISH BOY FACES WORLD WAR II

Nah, not me. The Riviera, that's where I wanna go, said Shale.

Verano came back with the three prisoners.

Okay, here they are. Let 'em sweep the floor, clean up the place. And when you're through with them send them in to me and they can do the other room.

Yes, sir! said Shale.

When do you think you'll know about the pass? I asked.

Any minute, any minute. Stop pestering me.

What about changing the money? All I got is marks.

All in due time, said Verano, and he left.

Okay, schlemiel, let's go, said Shale. (I'd been teaching him some Jewish words.) He took one of the prisoners to the corner of the room and handed him a broom. *Sweep! Fershtay? Sweep.*

The man nodded, took the broom and began to sweep. Shale took the second man aside, handed him a rag and instructed him to wipe down the legs of the beds. He gave the third man a rag and assigned him to clean the large table in the center of the room, which was perfectly clean.

Where's your post? Shale asked me.

Way out, I responded. *It used to be a barn. One guy came up to me today, said he was Jewish. He was really upset. He was kept together with the Germans, and he begged me to ask the Kommandant to put him in a separate building.*

What can you do?

I dunno, I said. *Speak to the captain maybe.*

He'd ask you how you found out. You know we're not supposed to talk to the prisoners while we're on guard?

What could I do? The man was Jewish, I said. *How could I ignore him?*

Hey! What you got there?, Shale called out. He jumped

A MINOR TRAGEDY

up and approached the man assigned to the table who had just picked up something from the floor.

What you got there? Shale asked.
Cigarette, said the man.
Give it to me.

The man reached into his pocket and pulled out a cigarette stub.

Oh, awright. Keep it, said Shale.
Thank you. I have not had a smoke in days, said the man.
That's just too bad. Go ahead. Get back to work.

The man continued making a show of cleaning the table.

Where'd you learn to speak English? said Shale.
In Russia.
Russia?
Yes. I am Russian.
Are you really? I asked.
If you're Russian, what the hell are you doing here? asked Shale.

I would like to know that myself, said the man. He pointed to the prisoner assigned to the beds. *He is Russian too.* The man reached into his pocket and pulled out a worn document. *These are my papers,* he said, and he handed me the document.

Have you shown this to anyone? I asked.

We have been here two weeks, and have not spoken to a soul. We were prisoners of war and were freed by the English. We were walking down the road and some American soldiers stopped us, and took us here. You see? We have our papers.

They'll probably let you go as soon as they check them, I said.

A NOT-SO-NICE JEWISH BOY FACES WORLD WAR II

Shale offered the man a cigarette. The second Russian joined us, and Shale offered him a cigarette as well. I reached into my duffel bag, pulled out a pack and handed it to the Russian. *You can have this pack if you want. I've got plenty more. How have they been treating you?* I asked.

No worse than we expected. Our fellow prisoners make fun of us though. They say we might as well have fought for them. They ask us if the war between Russia and America has begun yet? Oh, yes. They are convinced there will soon be a war between the United States and Russia.

What part of Russia are you from? I asked.

I am from Moscow. I worked...I covered sports events for the newspaper.

Is that right? I said. *I was studying literature in college. Let me see, I've read "Dead Souls" by Gogol. and "War and Peace" by Tolstoy and Chekhov...*

Your American writers are popular in Russia also. In my apartment I have a good collection. Dreiser. Hemingway.

Have you read "The Grapes of Wrath?" I asked.

That is Steinbeck, is it not? Oh, yes. Very fine.

Corporal Verano came in. *Okay, okay. We need these guys to clean the other room.*

These guys are Russian, I said. *This guy's from Moscow. He's a sports writer.*

Yeah, well they'll still have to clean up the other room.

I'm sorry, I said. *I think you'll get out of here soon.* I shook hands with the two Russians. *Lots of luck.*

Thank you, they said.

Someone called from the other room. *Hey Verano, Two Gun Tommy's out there. He wants to talk to you.*

Okay, okay. Come on, you guys, march.

The three men followed Verano into the other room.

What do you think the captain wants? I asked.

A MINOR TRAGEDY

Who knows? Did you hear the rumor about the peace negotiations? We'll be out of here by summer, said Shale.

Maybe the captain has my pass, I responded. At this point, all I could think about was Paris. Paris, Paris, Paris!

The sound of marching feet could be heard coming from the open window. Shale and I went to the window to investigate. A group of prisoners were milling around. One of them came up to the window. *Hi ya, yank,* he said.

What the hell! Are you Russian, too?, said Shale

Hell, no! I'm a full blooded American.

What are you doing in civilian clothes?, asked Shale.

I'm a veteran from the last war. I stayed over and married this French girl. I'm from Boston...Tremont Avenue, Scollay Square. Believe me I'm gonna say hello to the good old USA and never come back.

How'd you get to Germany? I asked.

Ah, when the Boche came into France they sent lots of Frenchmen back to Germany to work on the farms. The wife was bawling to beat the band. I told her, "Don't worry, kid, the Americans will be here pronto." Hell, I was in the old Fighting 69th. Sergeant in the artillery.

That's what we are, artillery, I said.

Hell, this war'll be over in a couple of days, said the displaced American. *Tell you this, men, it took one war to bring me across and another to take me back to the States and, brother, they'll have a third one if they ever try to get me back here again. Oops, gotta go. Good luck, men.*

The prisoners were being lined up and the American joined the group as Corporal Verano came into the room.

Shale, he shouted, *Get your stuff together. You're going to Paris.*

You mean, Beim, don't you?

A NOT-SO-NICE JEWISH BOY FACES WORLD WAR II

When I say Shale, I mean Shale. What are you deaf, or something?

But...

Am I a moron or something? Am I incapable of expressing myself? Or don't you understand English?

Okay, okay, said Shale. *Calm down. What happened?*

What happened?, snapped Verano. *What do you think happened? I do everything I can for you guys. I cover up for you. I make excuses. I lay my life on the line for you, and what do you do? You screw up, that's what you do.*

Will you stop breaking our hump, said Shale, *and tell us what happened.*

You guys are not supposed to talk to the prisoners while you're on duty. How many times have I told you that? Do not talk to the prisoners while you are on duty! But do you listen to me? Oh, no. Well, for your information, our brilliant linguist here just outdid himself. The captain was around inspecting the posts this morning.

I didn't see him, I muttered.

Of course, you didn't see him. You were too busy...

Why that no good son of a bitch, he's been laying those German broads every night this week, said Shale.

I'm not gonna argue with you, said Verano. *If you don't wanna go to Paris just say so.*

Okay, okay, said Shale. *Take it easy.*

And make sure you hand in your carbine. And report to me when you're ready, said Verano as he strode out of the room.

I'm sorry, kid, said Shale, and he began to get his gear together.

I sprawled out on my bed. I studied the wooden beams in the ceiling. It is not a tragedy, I kept telling myself. It is not a tragedy. You're twenty one years old. You've got your

A MINOR TRAGEDY

whole life ahead of you. You may still see Paris while you're over here. My god, man, you're still alive! You haven't even been wounded. The war's almost over and you are untouched. Think about that!

CHAPTER NINETEEN

THE AFTERMATH

Somehow or other, I survived that mortal blow, and my dream of Paris became even more vivid. I was there. I could see it all. Paris! Montmarte. The Left Bank. Versailles. The Eiffel Tower. Harry's bar where Ernest Hemingway and F. Scott Fitzgerald hung out. A dinner in a French restaurant. Snails, maybe. Frogs legs. I might even meet some lovely French girl. This girl I'd passed on the street one time swam into my mind. I couldn't remember what street it was, or even the city, and there were times when I wondered if I'd just imagined her. But real or not, the image was etched clearly in my mind. She was looking in a store window. I remember that clearly. I saw her back, and her figure was reflected in the glass. She was tall and slim, with fabulous, legs and long brown, lustrous hair. She wore this light green dress. I couldn't see her face but I knew she was lovely, and somehow this image stayed with me.

That's the sort of girl I might meet in Paris, I thought. And Paris would be the ideal place to have a real love affair. I might meet her...at a sidewalk cafe, maybe, or maybe I'd bump into her at some street corner...quite by accident. I'd apologize. She would shrug, and laugh, *Ne pas de quoi.* I would explain that this was my first time in Paris. I had three days to see it all. She would be charmed by my bad French. She would offer to show me Paris. We'd see all the sights and, as the day wore on, I grew much more interested in my companion than in all those historic landmarks. In the evening I would take her to dinner. Obviously the attraction was mutual. One thing would lead to another, and we'd end up having this mad love affair in a room overlooking the moonlit roofs of the Latin Quarter. And afterwards as we smoked a cigarette (even though I really didn't smoke, but this was a

A WILD RIDE

vision) we would talk. We would share our dreams. We would pour our hearts out to one another. She was engaged to be married, and I, of course, was committed to Ginny, so the affair, because it was doomed to be brief, doomed to be over before it had even begun, was all the more poignant...a lovely memory that the two of us would cherish for the rest of our lives, a memory that we would always associate with Paris. Ah well!

******

After my disastrous experience with cognac I thought I'd had my fill, but that evening, the evening of my minor tragedy, when several bottles were smuggled into the barracks I reconsidered. I needed something to take away the bitter taste of my disappointment and, maybe if I didn't overdo it...

I took possession of a bottle that had been left on the table. It was more than two thirds empty. I took a sip, and then another. The cognac didn't taste any better, but it didn't make me sick. As a matter of fact it made me feel rather warm and compassionate.

I decided that, in spite of everything, I loved everyone, even Shale, crude as he was, and Verano, even if he was sort of weak. I even found a warm spot in my heart for poor, misguided Garrell. The fact of the matter is I was above it all. The army, the war was but a trifle, an experience that would soon be a part of the past. I was, after all, a playwright. Why should I be bothered by all this pettiness? This was all grist for the mill. I needed some air.

I wandered out of the barracks into the cool of the night. I strolled down the road. Everything smelled so fresh and green. I stopped in front of a nearby house. An old lady

A NOT-SO-NICE JEWISH BOY FACES WORLD WAR II

was sitting on the steps. Two teen-age girls were leaning out of the window.

Go to bed, the old lady said in German. (By this time, because of my knowledge of Yiddish, I had very little difficulty understanding German.)

I beg your pardon, I said. *Do I know you?*

Go away, said the old lady.

Well, you are certainly unpredictable, I said. *First you try to seduce me and then you cast me out.*

You are bad. You come with airplanes and bombs and big pistols. We don't forget. We don't forget.

Ah, but you see, we came here on a mission, I said. *To save the world for democracy.*

The girls in the window giggled.

Go to bed, said the old lady. *I will tell this American to beat you.*

Yes, yes, screamed the girls.

I looked up at the young ladies. *What light through yonder window breaks? Two lovely Juliets.*

The girls giggled.

Speak again, bright angel. By yon bright moon...or something..something...something. I sat down in the middle of the road, trying to remember more of "Romeo And Juliet." *Ah, to be in England...* No, that wasn't it.

Go away, said the old lady.

I understand your predicament, old lady. But, you see, we are both at a disadvantage. I have only one set of ODs. Not that it really matters, since I'm not going to Paris anyway.

Chewing gum? said one of the girls in English.

Afraid not, I said.

Chocolate? said the other girl.

Sorry. I'm terribly sorry, I continued, addressing the Germans in general, *I'm sorry we bombed your country. I'm*

THE AFTERMATH

sorry you killed all those Jews. And I'm sorry that I'm not going to Paris. Of course, there's still Japan, you know. The war isn't over yet.

Corporal Verano came running down the street. *I've been looking all over for you. Are you drunk?*

Moi?

Jesus! C'mon, get up. Beim, get up. The captain is inspecting all the barracks, and if he sees you like this...

Verano...

C'mon, get up.

Shale says you're a man with a tight asshole, I rambled on. *In his less than poetic way of speaking he means to say that you are uptight. You're afraid of your own shadow. But I prefer to think of you as a man who wants to do the right thing, a man who wants to do his duty.*

That's right. Now c'mon, get up.

Go to bed, said the old lady.

She keeps trying to proposition me, I confided. *We do have a lot to answer for, you know.*

I'm not gonna cover up for you anymore.

But I like you, Verano, in spite of everything. You love music, and anyone who loves music couldn't be all bad. Tell me the truth. Did you really sit in a box at the opera?

I'm very disappointed in you, Beim. I thought you had some class.

Class being...?

You want to go to Paris, don't you?, reasoned Verano. I know, I know. But there's always the next time. You don't want to screw yourself up with the captain. He came back with a case of the clap and he is not very happy. As a matter of fact he is on the warpath.

Tell me this, Verano. Why is the captain such an asshole? Can you tell me that?

A NOT-SO-NICE JEWISH BOY FACES WORLD WAR II

If he catches you like this, you'll never get a pass...to anywhere. Now, will you please get up? Now look, I am responsible for you. Do you wanna get me in trouble?

I heaved a deep sigh and held up my hand. Verano pulled me up.

You are a good man, Verano. You mean well. I'm sure you do.

C'mon, let's go, said Verano.

Not before I say farewell to these lovely young ladies, and ask their forgiveness. I staggered over to the window and addressed the two teen age girls. *You do forgive me, don't you? I may never forgive myself, but that's my problem, a burden I shall carry with me for the rest of my days.*

Go home, said the old lady.

A consummation devoutly to be wished. I peered intently at the old lady. *You are really old. Do you know how old you are? I mean, are you aware of it? Don't look at me like that. It's not my fault. It's our fate, the fate of all mankind. Some day, if I'm lucky, I'll be as old as you are, God help me. Now why do I address an entity whose existence I am skeptical about? Can you tell me that?*

Okay?, asked Verano impatiently. *Have you said your good-byes?*

I don't really want to go back to the barracks, I reasoned. *It's stuffy in there. I mean, after all, I am not on duty, am I? Let's take a stroll down memory lane, down memory lane.* I began to waltz about, and almost fell over. *Oops! Not as graceful as I thought. Talk to me about music, Verano.*

Okay, that's it. You are on your own. The corporal started to walk away.

You don't understand. Where are you going? Are you going to leave me here all alone?

THE AFTERMATH

Verano walked back. *C'mon, Beim, don't make a fool of yourself.*

All right, all right. Far be it from me to get my corporal in trouble. Lead the way. I held out my hand.

Verano took hold of it, placed my arm around his neck and we started to walk back to the barracks.

Jesus! said Verano. *Here he comes now.*

Don't you worry about a thing, I assured the corporal. *I will explain to him. It's not your fault. I am a fuck-up.*

I broke free of Verano's hold. I staggered up the road to meet the captain. I approached the great man and saluted him, rather clumsily, I'm afraid. *Captain Blackburn,* I said. *I salute you.* I lost my balance and fell to one knee. I felt a pair of hands under my armpits. Someone was pulling me up to my feet. I assumed it was Verano.

Take that man back to the barracks, Corporal.

Yes, sir.

The captain walked on. Verano took my arm, placed it around his neck, and walked me back to the barracks.

I don't remember much after that.

I do remember that I spent three days on KP.

As a matter of fact, I was on KP when peace was finally declared in Europe.

CHAPTER TWENTY

A WILD RIDE

A few days after VE Day word came down that the 78th Division was slated for the South Pacific. It was just a rumor, of course, but it did make sense. There were a number of outfits that had seen more action than we had.

The weather, at any rate, was beautiful and so was the countryside, so peaceful and green.

I was seated on the steps of the barracks one day after lunch, when Sergeant Garrell rode up on a motorcycle. The relationship between the two of us had thawed somewhat. There developed a mild form of mutual respect. In some strange way, I actually think there was some sort of mutual admiration.

You feel like going for a ride? asked Garrell.
On that?
C'mon, hop on.

I hesitated. I'd seen Garrell zooming around recklessly on that motorcycle, and I could see myself racing down a hill on the back of that contraption, flying off the road into a tree and lying on the ground, my head split wide open. I did not plan on coming through the war to be killed riding a motorcycle.

C'mon, hop on. I'm going into town for the mail.

Then again, this might be a memorable experience, I decided. After all, as an author, one shouldn't arbitrarily rule out anything. I climbed onto the back of the motorcycle. *What am I supposed to hold onto?*

Me.

I put my arms around the waist of my old enemy.
A little higher.
I grasped his chest.
Hold on tight.

A WILD RIDE

The motorcycle jolted forward. My feet flew up into the air, and I almost fell off the back of that contraption.
Hold on!
I'm holding, I'm holding, I shouted.
The motorcycle flew across the ground onto the road which, luckily, was well paved.
I had no idea how fast we were going but I doubted we could go any faster.
The road was level for a while, but then it became hilly and there were times when the hills were steep. There were times when the motorcycle left the ground, flew through the air and bounced back to earth with a punishing jolt. I became concerned about those vital organs of mine that had not yet experienced their full potential.
You okay? called Garrell.
I'm still here...barely, I shouted into the wind.
After conquering my initial fear I found the ride exhilarating. The breathtaking plunge down the hill, the climb back up towards the sky, racing along, watching the trees fly by.
I looked up at the sky. I became dizzy. I quickly closed my eyes. It was if we were airborne. I welcomed the wind that caressed my face. I could almost feel the clouds all around me. This is why men joined those motorcycle clubs, I thought, zooming across the country. Cares were left behind, responsibility, reality. There was only the vehicle, the fresh air and freedom.
FREEDOM!
We raced through the German countryside. Wouldn't it be wonderful if this could go on forever!, I thought. No future to worry about, no past, just the thrill of the moment. I dreaded the time when this wild intoxication would come to an end. If only one could go through life, never touching the

A NOT-SO-NICE JEWISH BOY FACES WORLD WAR II

ground, flying above all earthly burdens, smelling the green of the foliage, feeling the wind on one's face.

We raced down a hill onto a main road. The nearby village came into view. We drew up at a quaint inn which housed company headquarters.

I'll be right out, said Garrell. He ran inside, and came out a few moments later with the mail bag, which he tied on to the motorcycle. *Ready?* he asked.

Yeah, I said.

Garrell turned the motorcycle around and we headed back. But the thrill was gone. I became aware of my discomfort, seated precariously on the back of this roaring monster. I hadn't been aware of the noise before. Besides, it was getting chilly now. The wind was too brisk, and beginning to sting my cheeks. My arms were beginning to grow numb. I was becoming self conscious about holding on to Garrell.

You okay?

Yeah, I'm fine, I shouted back. But I wished the ride would come to an end. And, holding someone close like that...lets face it, I really needed to get laid.

CHAPTER TWENTY ONE

MAKING FRIENDS

I received two letters that day. One from home, a rather disturbing one. Despite my sister Rose's attempt to sound cheerful I detected a note of unhappiness and disappointment.

Apparently switching universities had not solved her problems, whatever they were. I had the feeling that she was sort of lost, that she didn't really know what she wanted to do with her life. There was a fragility about Rose that really worried me. How I wished I was on hand to advise her, to talk to her, to watch over her.

The second letter was from Ginny. It was full of news about Hedgerow Theatre. It revived the conflict that I was currently facing. I was a writer, there was no doubt about that. That was where my future lay. But what about acting? It was a frivolous occupation, meant primarily for women, for vain, superficial people, egoists. But, god, it was fun! Instant gratification! And, boy, how I needed that! Some instant gratification!

I answered both letters that evening.

I tried to cheer Rose up. I was free now to talk about combat and the dangers I'd faced. I told her how I'd come through the war safe and sound, and how lucky we were in America, not to have gone through the terrible things that the people in Europe have gone through. I wrote nothing, of course, about the possibility of being shipped to the Pacific.

Writing to Ginny I was more open about the possibility of further combat. I wrote how excited I was for her. How thrilled she must have been to appear at a theatre in New York City! I asked hungrily for all the theatre news, and I empathized with her about being saddled with social work in order to support herself; and I thought about how I, too, if I

A NOT-SO-NICE JEWISH BOY FACES WORLD WAR II

survived jungle warfare that is, would some day have to face that dilemma, the struggle for an artist to achieve recognition.

For now, at any rate, life wasn't bad at all. Guard duty. Some perfunctory drilling. And lots of free time.

Shale came back from Paris with not that much to talk about. No, he hadn't taken in many sights. He'd gotten laid, and he'd had some good meals and that was it. I shook my head. What a wasted opportunity! Five days in that glorious City of Light, the romantic capitol of the world, and all that idiot had accomplished was sex and food, which he could have had anywhere. The injustice of it all!

We were moved into town and put up in houses commandeered by the army. The quarters were the most comfortable we'd encountered so far, almost luxurious. In the living room was an upright piano. In the piano bench I found some sheet music, popular tunes, both in French and in German. Every chance I'd get I'd sit at the piano and bang away. I hadn't played in years, and I was quite rusty, which was okay, since the piano hadn't been tuned in quite a while. There was one song, Komm Zurick (Come Back) which really hit home. How I longed to get started with my life, which had been interrupted just before it had really begun.

Shale and I were assigned to guard duty on a small railroad bridge on the outskirts of the town. What we were guarding, we weren't quite sure, but the setting was pleasant enough. Green rolling hills, and a bright blue sky that seemed to go on forever. We took off our helmets and relaxed against the railing of the bridge. To alleviate the boredom I devised different kinds of exercises, knee bends, stretching and running in place.

Shale was debating the thought of marriage. *I was going with this one dame for a while*, said Shale, *but she got too possessive. I mean she'd come into the bar looking for me.*

MAKING FRIENDS

I need elbow room. Then again, the idea of getting it steady is not to be sneezed at.

Two young boys came down the road. They eyed us curiously as they sauntered casually onto the bridge. One of the boys picked up some stones and tossed them over the side.

Shoo, said Shale. *Raus.*

The boys stood there looking up at Shale.

You sure scared them, I said.

Shale glowered at the boys. *You see this gun?* he said. *Watch!* He raised his carbine, aimed at a sign below and fired. The shot came nowhere near the target. The boys shook their heads and smiled.

Boy, look at them run, I laughed.

What have you got there? asked Shale.

The one boy held out his hand which cradled an egg. *Kaugummi?* he asked. *Chocolate?*

Shale turned to me. *You got any chewing gum?*

One pack.

Throw it over. We can have fried eggs for breakfast.

My last pack, I said. I tossed the gum to Shale.

Shale handed the pack to the boy. The boy gave him the egg. Shale tossed the egg to me.

One egg, I said, *for a whole pack of gum? And who's going to cook it?*

A well built young lady with shoulder length blond hair and an attractive rather impish face approached the bridge

Hey, Shale called to the boys. He beckoned them back. He took the pack of gum from the boy, removed a slice, and returned it. The boys ran off before they lost more of their booty. Shale approached the young lady.

Would you like some kowgummi? he asked.

Danke, she said, accepting the gum and putting it in her pocket.

A NOT-SO-NICE JEWISH BOY FACES WORLD WAR II

What's your name? Nahma?
Ushie.
Shale, said Shale pointing to himself.

Ushie seemed interested. She walked over to the railing and leaned against it rather seductively.

Guten tag, she said to me.
Guten tag, I said.
How long will you be here? she asked in German.
She wants to know how long we'll be here.
Tell her, long enough.
You are the first American soldiers in Gartenhausen, said Ushie.
Ask her if she likes American soldiers, said Shale.
Do you like American soldiers? I asked. I kept wondering whether anyone detected that my so-called German was actually Yiddish with a little twist, added in the hope that it sound like German.

I can't say yet, said the girl and shrugged.
Ask her if she lives around here.

Ushie pointed to a house down the road. Shale moved closer to Ushie. Ushie moved away, but not too rapidly. Apparently she didn't want to discourage Shale's interest.

I must go, she said.
Where is she going? asked Shale.

Ushie explained that she had to go home to do some work. *Guten tag,* she said as she sauntered away.

Weederzane, said Shale. *That's a bit of all right. I think I'll drop over there tonight.*

Two other interesting prospects approached the bridge. One was a little on the dumpy side, with short blonde hair and a rather pleasant face. The other was a very pretty young girl, slim, with a peaches and cream complexion, light blue eyes and chestnut hair.

MAKING FRIENDS

Ask them if they have their papers? Shale said.

I approached the two young ladies. *Do you have your papers?* I asked, more self conscious about my Yiddish than ever.

Papers? What papers? asked the short, dumpy young lady in German. *We live down there, right down the road and we went to the village to the shoemaker.* She pulled out a pair of shoes from the bag she was carrying.

They're coming from the shoemaker, I said. *Now there's an interesting young lady.* And I nodded toward the pretty young girl.

Shale, said Shale pointing to himself, and then he pointed to me. *Beim.*

The dumpy young lady was named Erma and the pretty young girl was Anita. Erma put her shoes back in the bag and shook hands with Shale and then with me. *Guten tag,* she said. *Guten tag.*

Step into my office, said Shale. He beckoned the girls to join him at the side of the road.

Mamma saw you come here yesterday. We have large field glasses and we can see everything from our kitchen. You pull guard here and you sleep in the village, said Erma with appropriate gestures.

Not all the time, said Shale.

What did he say? asked Erma.

Nothing, I said.

You're a bad character, said Erma to Shale. She turned to me. *Is he married?* she asked.

She wants to know if you're married.

Nix. Nein.

Nein!? You have three children. I know you.

She's got you married with three children.

Nein, Nein. You got me wrong.

A NOT-SO-NICE JEWISH BOY FACES WORLD WAR II

How many? Five? Six? You're all the same, said Erma. *I saw you talking to that girl. You better be careful. She goes with all the Poles.*
Your friend, Ushie, goes with all the Poles, I said.
Don't you like Americans? asked Shale.
Americans! They chew gum like cows.
What'd she say?
We chew gum like cows. I turned to Anita. *Where do you work?*

Anita smiled shyly. She seemed nervous. I couldn't understand her reply. *What did she say?* I asked as I turned to Erma.

Beauty parlor, said Anita and she pantomimed cutting hair.
Tomorrow, I come to the beauty parlor, I said.
No, said Anita disbelievingly.
Yes, I come...to have my hair cut. Will you put oil on my hair?

Anita giggled, putting her hand to her mouth. *No, no.*
How old are you? Erma asked me.
I'm twenty five, I said, thinking that would be better than twenty. *How old is Anita?*
How old do you think?
Seventeen?
No, said Anita.
Sixteen?
No.
Fifteen?
I am twenty three, said Anita.
She has a child three years old, said Erma.
Is that right? I asked.
Anita nodded.
A dark, sharp featured lady came into view and Erma

MAKING FRIENDS

whispered to Anita, *Frau Fisher.* The two young ladies slowly started to walk away.

Hey, where you goin'? asked Shale.

As the dark lady came near the girls she stopped. *Good day, Fraulein Dorfman,* she said.

Good day, Frau Fisher, said Erma.

So, this is the way you spend your time, said the dark lady. *The next time I see your mother, I shall tell her that you have been consorting with American soldiers.*

My mother knows what I do, Frau Fisher. She tells me to do what I think is right, and to mind my own business.

Frau Fisher snorted and walked on, head held high.

That's Frau Fisher, said Erma. *Her husband is a Nazi. Now the whole town will know that we were talking to the American soldiers.*

Tell her to blow it out, I said.

We must go, said Erma. *We'll see you another time.*

Come by tomorrow morning, I said.

Yes. Tomorrow morning, the same time. Guten tag, said Erma.

You, too, I said to Anita.

I don't know, said Anita.

Wiedersehen, I said.

Weederzane, said Shale.

Wiedersehen, said Anita.

The girls walked away as Corporal Verano came onto the bridge to relieve us.

You know you're not supposed to talk to the civilians when you're on guard, said Verano.

And even when we're not on guard, I said. *But we know better, don't we?*

Okay, okay, said Verano. *It's your ass.*

What's for lunch? asked Shale.

397

A NOT-SO-NICE JEWISH BOY FACES WORLD WAR II

Fried chicken.
A red letter day, I said, and Shale and I headed for the village.

CHAPTER TWENTY TWO

GETTING BETTER ACQUAINTED

Erma came by the next day. Anita couldn't get away from the shop. We made arrangements to meet on Sunday in the field near Erma's house. I learned that Anita's husband and Erma's father had been taken prisoner by the Russians. They weren't sure if either of them were alive.

Sunday afternoon Shale and I appeared at the appointed spot. Erma and Anita were seated on the grass. Anita ran off as we approached.

Guten tag, said Erma.
Guten tag, said Shale.
Guten tag, I said.
Sit down, said Erma and patted the ground.
Where did Anita go? I asked.
Erma shrugged.
Excuse me, I said, and I went looking for Anita. I found her sitting on the grass, looking thoughtful and sort of sad.

I sat down beside her. *You are very pretty,* I said. I took her hand and kissed it. *Do you like me?* I asked. *I like you very much,* I continued. I leaned over and kissed her on the lips. She responded rather tentatively. I put my arms around her and we lay down on the grass. As we kissed my hand explored her body. My heart beat faster as my hand moved up her leg and rested gently on her privates. She put her hand on top of mine, and I stopped.

I was uncertain as to what to do next. What was she thinking, I wondered. Maybe she expected more than a bit of love-making. She was married, I gathered. Or was she really? Then again, she might be a widow.

As I lay pondering my next move Anita rose. She took

A NOT-SO-NICE JEWISH BOY FACES WORLD WAR II

me by the hand and led me back to where Erma and Shale were sitting. We sat down next to them. There was a book lying on the ground next to Erma. I picked it up.

What's this? I asked.

We're going to school to learn English, said Erma. *Study. English.*

I opened the book and read, *Peter is a banker. He rises early.*

Erma took the book from me and read with a thick German accent, *Peter...washes his...face and hands.* She put down the book and looked roguishly at Shale. *Your friend, Ushie. She ran off...she ran away with a Pole.*

Ushie ran off with a Pole, I translated.

No kidding, said Shale.

Now...no fraulein.

She was not my fraulein. You are my fraulein, said Shale.

Nein. I do not go around with married men, said Erma.

What did she say? Shale asked.

Let's go to the house, said Erma. *My mother would like to meet you.*

She led us to her house, which was nearby, and into the kitchen where we found Frau Dorfman, an attractive woman I took to be in her late forties. Erma introduced us and we all sat around the kitchen table.

It's good that the war is over, said Frau Dorfman. *No more airplanes. No more artillery. We had so many air raids we never took off our clothes, waiting for the next one to come.*

The bombs came down all around the fields here, said Anita.

It used to shake the whole house, said Erma.

Yes, war is not good, I said.

GETTING BETTER ACQUAINTED

No, said Frau Dorfman. *Small people like us, we can get along. It's the higher-ups who make the war.*
Six years of war, said Erma. *No dancing, no food, no theatre.*
Well, now you can dance and go to the theatre, I said.
What's that? said Erma.
I said, now you can dance and go to the theatre.
No, not for a long time, said Erma. *Our whole youth is lost. We will never be happy again.*
You are lucky to be alive, I said.
Tell her, tell her, said Frau Dorfman. *Would you like some...?*
I couldn't understand the rest of the sentence. *I don't understand,* I said.
Red. So big. I will bring you some, from our garden, said Frau Dorfman. *Very good.* She picked up a bowl and went out the back door.
We're going to get something from the garden, I told Shale. *I don't know what.*
Do you know if they're letting the prisoners come home soon? Erma asked.
She wants to know if they're letting the prisoners come home soon, I said to Shale.
Her old man? said Shale.
My father was a Socialist and he wouldn't fight, said Erma. *When the army was retreating they took him anyway. Why is Corporal Verano so mean to us?*
Verano doesn't like the Nazis and the German people, I answered, *and he doesn't want to make friends with them.*
But you know us, said Erma. *We aren't Nazis. We're not Nazis.*
We don't really know that, do we? I said.
Is your outfit going away tomorrow?, asked Erma.

A NOT-SO-NICE JEWISH BOY FACES WORLD WAR II

Tomorrow? No. She thinks we're going away tomorrow, I told Shale.

Nein, said Shale. *Nein.*

Some soldiers told us that you were going away tomorrow and that Negro soldiers were taking your place, said Erma. *Ohhhh. Negro soldiers...they say they are very bad.*

She thinks colored soldiers will be taking our place.

Nein, said Shale. *They were kidding you.*

We are afraid of the Negro soldiers, said Erma.

Why? I asked. *They are just like anybody else.*

Ohhh, we are afraid. Thick lips. So black, said Erma.

I have thick lips, I said, trying to eradicate the stereotype. (My lips were full, not really what you might call thick.) *Am I bad?* I turned to Shale. *They're scared of colored soldiers coming. I told them there wouldn't be any trouble.*

Yeah? said Shale. *What about that fight our guys got into with those niggers in the other town?*

That's true, I said.

Then you aren't going away?, asked Erma.

No, we are not going away, I said. I strolled over to a shelf and picked up a German paperback book. *"Love's First Call" Ye gods. Is that yours?*

Yes, said Erma. *It's a very good book.*

Anita, why aren't you saying anything? I asked.

Anita's thinking about her soldier boy, said Shale.

Are you thinking about your soldier? I asked.

No, said Anita.

Frau Dorfman came in with the bowl filled with strawberries.

Let's see what we have here, said Shale.

Sit down, said Frau Dorfman. She proceeded to wash the strawberries, cut the green tops and place them in another bowl. She placed the bowl on the table.

LIEGE

Strawberries! said Shale.

It's better with sugar, said Frau Dorfman. *You understand sugar? Sweet?*

We'll bring you a bagful, said Shale.

I'm going out now and work in our garden. I'll see you later. Eat, eat. And Frau Dorfman went out again.

Your mother is very good to us, I said.

Don't let her know I told you, said Erma, *but she was very good friends with an English soldier after the last war. I think you remind her of him.*

What did she say? asked Shale.

Her mother had an affair with an English soldier after the last war.

That mother's not half bad, said Shale, *come to think of it.*

Speak German, said Erma.

These strawberries are very good, said Shale as he popped one into his mouth.

I followed suit, and then wandered over to the radio. *Let's have some music,* I said and turned it on. A band was playing popular songs. I walked over to Anita. *Come, dance.*

I haven't danced in a long time, said Anita.

Come, come.

I took Anita's hand. She rose reluctantly and we started to dance. I held her close and closed my eyes.

Shale sat next to Erma and they watched us dance.

Before we left we made plans to meet on the weekend.

The next day word got around that some men were being shipped out, but no one seemed to know where. Some speculated that they were being sent to the Pacific. Others heard that they were being discharged. By this time just about everyone in the outfit had been granted a pass except for me.

In the afternoon Corporal Verano came into our house.

A NOT-SO-NICE JEWISH BOY FACES WORLD WAR II

You wanna go on pass? he said to me.
Where?
Liege.
Liege? What's in Liege?, I asked.
You wanna go or don't you?
What about Paris?, I asked.
Liege is what they're offering, said Verano. *You wanna go or not?*

I hesitated. At this point the prospect of getting to Paris looked exceedingly dim. What would I be risking, I wondered, if I did take the pass. *I guess I might as well,* I said, *if that's all there is.*

Thank you, said Verano sarcastically, and left to make the arrangements.

CHAPTER TWENTY THREE

LIEGE

On Friday I shed my fatigues, packed a few things into my duffel bad, and got into my ODs. Along with some other men from the outfit, I climbed into the truck and we started for Liege.

It was the end of July, yet the weather was not very pleasant. The sun seldom shone and it was chilly. Appropriate, I thought. Liege was certainly a comedown from Paris, and I was not too excited about the visit.

It was dark by the time we reached Liege and the appearance of the town was in keeping with the mood of the weather, at least from what we could see at that hour. We were deposited at a small hotel that had been taken over by the American army. Each of us had a room of our own. At this point I was too tired to do any sightseeing, and I was not feeling very sociable. I settled for dinner at a nearby rather nondescript restaurant all by myself. I returned to my room, sat up for a while and did some reading.

I was grateful to the army for one very important thing. During the war they published these wonderful paperback editions of all sorts of books, nonfiction, classics and popular novels. They had rather colorful covers, and were small enough to squeeze into your pocket. I always had one with me. I think it was Hemingway's "Farewell To Arms" I was into at the moment.

I woke up early the next morning, determined to make the most of the day. I was, after all, free for the first time, and in a European town. All right, maybe it wasn't Paris, maybe it wasn't London, maybe it wasn't Rome, but it must have something to offer.

At the desk I picked up a brochure. Liege was

A NOT-SO-NICE JEWISH BOY FACES WORLD WAR II

primarily an industrial town. That figures. Forget romance, forget glamour.

The city had been badly damaged during the Battle of the Bulge, and some of the streets were really depressing. There were two churches, however, which were recommended by the brochure, which looked sort of interesting, and a couple of museums. I dutifully toured the two churches which were, in the final analysis...churches.

I then did some shopping. I found an elegant lace shawl for Ginny, nice smelling perfume for Mother, a pin for Rose, and a tie pin for Daddy. For my little brother, Marty, I found a little replica of a statue called "The Pisser", which showed a little boy urinating. The legend ran that this little prince was lost. When he was found he was in the act of relieving himself. The king was so delighted in having recovered his beloved boy that he ordered a statue made of his son in the position he was discovered.

I came across a photography studio. The pictures on display were not too bad. I decided to have my picture taken. I thought they might have the pictures ready for me that day, but that was impossible. They assured me, however, that they would faithfully mail the pictures to me in Germany. I decided to take a chance. I went ahead and posed for a couple of shots, full length ones, and paid for them. When I left they again assured me they would mail the pictures to me and I would get them the following week.

After a mediocre lunch I visited an art museum which actually had one or two fine paintings.

In the late afternoon I stepped into what looked from the outside like an elegant bar. Inside it turned out to be rather gaudy and cheap looking. I sat on this stool covered in black plastic and ordered a liqueur. When asked what liqueur I'd like I asked the woman behind the bar to recommend one. She

LIEGE

recommended something called Cointreau. As I sipped the exotic liqueur, which had a rather nice orange flavor, I noticed my reflection in the huge mirror behind the bar which was decorated with colored lights. Actually I wasn't bad looking, was I? My spirits rose. Here's this dashing American soldier sipping Cointreau at a bar in Liege, a veteran of the war, a man of the world enjoying a drink in a bistro (is that the right word?) at the other end of the world from Newark, New Jersey. This was an adventure, after all. The drink not only lifted my spirits, but made me feel ready and eager for what the evening had to offer.

I paid for the drink and walked out of the bar. I found myself strolling down a street featuring a number of cheap cafes, with women apparently available and ready to do business. I entered one of the cafes and headed for a small table to the rear of the dimly lit room.

A waitress came over and I ordered a Cointreau. How suave can you get? Even before my drink arrived I was joined by a full bodied, not unattractive woman who appeared to be in her thirties. She smiled, introduced herself and put a friendly arm around my shoulder.

Before the woman could get settled and make her pitch a small, dark intense looking young lady came over and roughly removed the arm from my shoulder. The young lady yanked the woman out of her seat. The woman murmured something but, surprisingly enough, didn't put up any argument. She just shrugged and walked away. Either this aggressive young lady was the proprietor, or she was someone you didn't fool around with.

The waitress arrived with my drink. My new companion sat beside me, and ordered a drink for herself.

I was flattered to be fought over by two women, even if they were two prostitutes. Instinctively, however, I knew that I'd made a mistake. My last encounter with a prostitute back at Ohio State had been a disaster, and left me still a virgin, and twenty dollars poorer.

Then again, hope springs eternal. This was, after all, three years later. I was now a man of the world. Maybe this time the experience might be more rewarding. Besides, what else was there to do in Liege? And, I mean, after all, how long can one remain a virgin?

The young lady caressed my ear, my neck. She couldn't speak English or German. I couldn't speak Flemish. We managed finally to communicate in mangled French, mangled on my part, that is.

The young lady seemed interested in my war experiences. I got the impression that she may have lost a husband or a boyfriend or a brother, I wasn't quite sure which, and she kept saying how much she hated the Germans. She invited me to retire to the back room with her and named her price, which seemed quite reasonable.

We rose from the table and walked through the beaded curtain into the back room. It was like an open lounge where people might just walk on through. There wasn't even a bed. There was just a large divan. We both undressed and climbed onto the divan.

The woman's body was dark, like the complexion of her face and, though her features weren't Negroid, I wondered if she had some colored blood somewhere in her background. Her short body was compactly built with firm small breasts in perfect proportion with the rest of her. She might just as well have been a fellow soldier, however. I felt no desire whatsoever.

She attempted to kiss me. I avoided her lips, and kissed her on the neck. I made a show of placing kisses on her shoulders, her breasts. But nothing. She explored my body

LIEGE

with her lips, attempted to kiss me again. Again I avoided her lips. I was, after all, promised to Ginny and a kiss, after all, signified love. She took my sex in her mouth and I became slightly aroused but, when put to the test, not sufficiently.

We rested for a while. She asked me if, perhaps, this was my first time. Oh no, I insisted. In Germany I had sex with a young lady there, I boasted. My companion froze.

I had sex with a German?! A Nazi?!

No, no she wasn't a Nazi, I said.

She was furious. They're all Nazis. I must be careful. I took my life in my hands when I consorted with a German.

Sex was attempted again, to no avail. We relaxed and Marie, I think that was her name, suggested that I spend the night. Since the cost wasn't that much more I agreed. Besides, I didn't particularly care to spend the night alone.

The night passed slowly. There were intermittent failed attempts at sex, interspersed with respites. Toward the morning Marie persisted orally, and FINALLY...TRIUMPHANTLY...I had an orgasm.

I pulled her towards me and kissed her gratefully on the lips. She kissed me and held me in a vice-like grip. I was amazed at her intensity, her passion. I realized, for the first time, that Marie was actually making love to me. It wasn't just sex, it was love, and my kiss was, obviously, her real reward. How interesting, I thought.

I wondered whether this passion was prompted by the loss of her lover, or was it a form of patriotism? Whatever the reason, I got the impression that my affection was more important to her than even the money.

Afterwards I had a very simple breakfast in the cafe. I kissed Marie good-bye and returned to the hotel. The truck that was to take us back to our post was already parked in front.

A NOT-SO-NICE JEWISH BOY FACES WORLD WAR II

On the ride back, my thoughts kept returning to Marie. What was her life really like? What was her future? Would she find herself another boyfriend, or was it a husband? My heart was filled with gratitude for that unexpected gift of love, a gift of love from a prostitute no less. How interesting!

CHAPTER TWENTY FOUR

NEXT STOP: WALES

The following week my photographs arrived from Liege. I was absolutely delighted. There stood this rather nice looking, stalwart soldier, legs slightly apart, hands casually thrust in his pocket looking directly at you. His quite poetic face was sort of dreamlike, yet sturdy, I noted as I stood admiring it. ("Vanity of vanities...all is vanity.")

Two weeks after my return from Liege an atomic bomb was dropped on the city of Hiroshima. Three days later one was dropped on the city of Nagasaki.

I had mixed feelings about the event. Obviously it meant that the war in the Pacific would soon be over. But this new weapon also meant that the world was changed forever. The estimated dead in Hiroshima was 78,000, according to the United States. In Nagasaki it was 39,000. The Japanese estimated the number of deaths at 240,000. If there was a third World War would it be an atomic one, I wondered. Were we on the eve of destroying ourselves?

The following week Japan capitulated.

Hopes for a swift return home, however, were dashed. The 78th Division was formally designated as an occupational force. How long would it be before I could resume my life, I wondered. How long would I be put on hold?

Then I heard that men were being sent to the Riviera. There was a theatre workshop being set up there, run by professionals, name directors and well known playwrights. Wouldn't that be wonderful!? To get involved in theatre again, on the Riviera to boot!

I told Corporal Verano about my prizewinning one act play, about my acting experience at Ohio State. He knew nothing about the Riviera, but he would look into it. This was said with not much enthusiasm. It didn't sound very hopeful. And Paris seemed just as far away as ever.

How would you like to go to Wales? asked Corporal Verano a day or so later.

Wales?

Yes, Wales, said Verano. *Cardiff, Wales.*

What's in Wales, except for coal mines and singing Welshmen?

They're sending a few men to the University of Cardiff for one semester, said Verano.

A university, no less? The idea of sitting in a classroom did not sound very appealing.

You wanna go, or don't you?

Apparently I seemed doomed to take the leftovers. *Okay, okay,* I said. *I'll go to Wales.*

After all, the island of Great Britain was not that big. How far away could Cardiff be from London? Wouldn't that be something? London! This promised to be an interesting adventure after all.

I had expected to be driven by truck to the French coast, and then sent across the English Channel by boat to England. To my surprise I, along with two other men from my outfit, were driven to a nearby airport. On the way to the airport we discovered that all three of us were headed for the same place, the University of Wales in Cardiff. The plane, we were told, would take us to Heathrow airport, which was just outside of London. From Heathrow we were to take the Underground subway to London. From London we were to take a train to Cardiff.

I had never been on a plane before. I looked forward to the experience, but I was little uneasy. One could recover from a car accident, or a train accident. But a plane crash...? This was the Twentieth Century, of course. Air travel was

NEXT STOP: WALES

quite common and I really should get used to it, I kept telling myself.

With a queasy feeling in the pit of my stomach, I climbed aboard this rather small plane, stowed my duffel bag in a compartment in front and chose a seat by the window. There was an anxious half hour while we waited for some late arrivals.

Finally the door clanged shut. The motor started. The plane taxied around then lined up for the take-off. It moved slowly down the runway and then started to pick up speed...faster and faster and... I felt my stomach drop as we left the ground and climbed straight up into the air.

Looking out the window I saw the earth fade into the distance. This was definitely not the safest way to travel! The plane leveled off, and soon we were flying among the clouds. I was sure we were moving swiftly but, actually, we seemed to be standing still, just floating through the soft, white billows. How the hell do we stay up here, I wondered. (Physics was not my strong point.) The miracles of this modern world. Apparently there were some wonderful things we could do, in addition to being able to blow ourselves to bits.

Trying to forget how far up we were, I settled down, determined to enjoy the flight, and I did manage to relax. It was dusk when the lights of Heathrow airport became visible.

The plane started on a downward path. The earth came closer and closer. We were now racing just a few feet above the ground. The wheels hit something hard and the whole plane shook. My stomach turned.

After a moment I realized that we had landed safely. As the plane came to a standstill I began to feel like a seasoned air traveller. I tried to imagine Mother's reaction to the news that her first born had taken to the air, Mother who

A NOT-SO-NICE JEWISH BOY FACES WORLD WAR II

panicked at the very mention of any sort of a long distance trip, much less flying in an airplane.

The disappointment of missing out on the Riviera, the disappointment of missing out on Paris, slowly faded into the background. I began to look forward to this trip to Cardiff and the University of Wales.

One of the two men traveling with me was a private from Brooklyn. He was quite amiable and outgoing. His name was Steve. The other was a corporal from Boston, rather prim and stiff. I sensed right off that...his name was Matthew...was going to be a wet blanket.

We banded together after we got off the plane. First we searched the airport for a place to change our money into English currency. Then we took the Underground train, which was actually above ground most of the way, to Paddington Station. Paddington Station was not the elegant British structure I expected to find. It was just a very ordinary, rather seedy train station that had probably seen better days.

When we purchased our tickets to Cardiff we found we had over an hour to kill. Since this was our first time in London, I suggested we walk around and see what the city was like. Matthew didn't think that was a very good idea. We might get lost and miss our train. So Steve and I set out alone, leaving Matthew behind to guard the duffel bags.

Make sure you get back here in time, said Matthew. *I'm not going to miss that train because of you two.*

We'll be back. Don't worry, I said.

London had been heavily hit by the Blitz and was just beginning to recover. There were still signs leading to air raid shelters. Here and there were piles of sand bags. In addition to that, the area around Paddington Station was not very interesting, a newsstand, some rather dreary looking shops. Most of them were closed. We walked along the almost empty

NEXT STOP: WALES

streets until we came across a pub. Since neither of us had been inside an English pub we decided to step in and investigate.

We were welcomed warmly by the bartender. Beers were on the house. The beer turned out to be rather flat...and warm, to boot. There were a few patrons, and they were quite friendly. When we mentioned the Battle of the Bulge, the news was greeted with great interest. We were asked where we were from in The States. When I said Newark, New Jersey one of the men said he had a brother in Newark. Did I know so and so by any chance? He lived on Center Street.

No, I said, *afraid not.*

I happened to glance at my watch. *Oh, God,* I said. *We've got about eleven minutes.*

We made a very hasty farewell and raced out of the bar. We looked up and down the street. Which way? We turned left and ran to the corner. That didn't look familiar.

We retraced our steps then ran to the opposite corner. That looked like the right direction. Wasn't that the railroad station down there?

We raced down the street. One block. Two blocks. Three blocks. We must have made a wrong turn. No. No, there it was. Five minutes left.

We ran inside and found ourselves at the wrong end of the station. We raced across the entire length of the station. There we found Matthew, looking fit to be tied.

Do you know what time it is? he asked.

The train hasn't left yet, has it? I said.

Matthew said nothing. He picked up his duffel back and started for Track Three. Steve and I picked up our duffel bags and followed him.

I thought it was supposed to be Track Four, I said.

They changed the track, said Matthew.

A NOT-SO-NICE JEWISH BOY FACES WORLD WAR II

Are you sure?, I asked.

Matthew said nothing.

Well anyway, we made it in plenty of time, said Steve.

Matthew said nothing. He was not about to let us off the hook.

When we arrived at Track Three I approached a uniformed attendant. *Is this train going to Cardiff?* I asked.

Yes, indeed, young man.

Thank you, I said.

Satisfied? asked Matthew.

Steve and I exchanged amused glances.

I just wanted to make sure, I said.

We boarded the train.

As soon as we took our seats, Matthew took out a book and buried himself in it.

The train started right off. It glided quietly out of the station. Steve and I looked out the window. It was dark by this time. Nothing much could be seen.

We tried to nap since we were in for, at least, a two hour ride. I closed my eyes but I was much too keyed up to sleep. Steve did manage to doze off intermittently. Matthew remained buried in his book. I kept peering out of the window, hoping I might see something of the English countryside, but it was just too dark. I finally gave up, and just closed my eyes.

CHAPTER TWENTY FIVE

THE ARRIVAL

It was night time when we reached Cardiff. In the station we compared addresses. Steve and I were staying at one house, Matthew at another. Steve and I exchanged a look of relief.

We found a cab, piled in and drove through the heart of the town, which turned out to be a respectably sized city center. When we reached the suburbs, from what we could make out, the houses were quite charming with carefully tended gardens in front. We dropped Matthew off first.

When we arrived at our address we were relieved to see a light in the front window. We paid the cab driver, climbed out of the cab and, shouldering our duffel bags, approached the front door. I rang the doorbell and we waited.

There was no response.

There must be someone home, I said, *if there's a light in the window.* I rang the bell again.

Finally the door opened a crack and a man's voice was heard. *Yes? Can I help you?*

Mr. Connoly?

Yes?

We're supposed to be staying with you, I said. *We're with the American army.*

Oh, yes, said the man and he opened the door wider. *We weren't expecting you till tomorrow. Come in.*

Who is it, Henry? a woman's voice called from within.

It's the Americans, said Henry.

Steve and I followed Mr. Connoly into the small front parlor where we met Mrs. Connoly. The two of them were sort of a solid looking, middle-aged couple.

Good evening, said Mrs. Connoly. *We weren't expecting you till tomorrow. That's quite all right. Your room is all*

A NOT-SO-NICE JEWISH BOY FACES WORLD WAR II

ready. You're too late for dinner. I could make you some tea and toast, if you like.

That'll be fine, I said.

Steve nodded. *Thank you.*

Except for the K rations we were carrying, which we'd eaten on the train, we hadn't had any food since breakfast. Not wishing to make a fuss we settled for the tea and toast.

You're entitled to breakfast and dinner, said Mrs. Connoly. *We serve breakfast from six thirty to eight thirty, and dinner is served at six sharp. Why don't you show the young men to their room, Henry, while I put on the kettle.*

Follow me, said Henry.

We shouldered our duffel bags and followed Henry up a narrow stairway.

We were ushered into a small, neatly furnished room with twin beds. I had hoped for a room to myself. Growing up I had to share a bedroom with my sister, Rose, and I certainly didn't lack for roommates in the army. Actually the only time I'd had a room to myself was for a few months during my second year at Ohio State, just before I was drafted.

Mr. Connoly turned on a floor lamp. The shade was decorated with flowers. In addition to the beds there were two small bureaus, one tufted chair which was to serve as an easy chair, and a small table with a wooden chair. I assumed the table was supposed to serve as a desk. There was one closet, which didn't look too roomy.

We set down our duffel bags.

I think you'll be comfortable here, said Mr. Connoly.

This is fine, said Steve.

I said nothing. I didn't see myself spending much time in the room anyway. The beds did look comfortable though.

The bathroom's right down the hall, said Mr. Connoly, *You'll find your towels in the drawer there. As soon as you're*

THE ARRIVAL

settled you can come downstairs for your tea. In case it gets chilly, there's the gas heater there. It takes a shilling.

Thank you, I said.

Mr. Connoly left, closing the door behind him.

How much is a shilling? I asked.

I don't know. We'll have to find out, said Steve. *This doesn't look too bad, does it?*

It's small, I said.

Well, it's a place to sleep, said Steve.

That's true, I said. *Shall we unpack or go right down?*

I'm starved, said Steve.

So am I, I said. I opened the door and looked out. *Let's go.*

We trooped down the narrow stairway. In the living room we were greeted by Mr. Connoly.

Right this way, gentleman.

We were ushered into a small dining room.

The table was set for two. Steve and I sat down at the table. Mrs. Connoly entered from the kitchen with a tray containing two pots of tea, four slices of thick white toast, margarine, a small container of milk, marmalade and two cubes of sugar.

Sugar is still rationed, she said. *Meat as well, though there will be meat for dinner. There's milk for your tea.*

Fine, I said.

After pouring a cup of tea I hesitated. I never drank tea at home. Tea was for when you were sick. However, when in Rome... I dropped a lump of sugar into the tea and then a drop of milk, stirred and took a sip. It didn't taste like tea at all, at least not like the tea my mother served. It was really quite good. I spread some margarine and some marmalade on the warm toast and took a bite. I realized, for the first time, how really hungry I was.

A NOT-SO-NICE JEWISH BOY FACES WORLD WAR II

The two of us made short work of the toast.
Would you care for another slice of toast? asked Mrs. Connoly.
That might be nice, I said, trying not to sound too eager.
I'll have another slice, said Steve.
Mrs. Connoly went off the to the kitchen.
What outfit are you with? asked Mr. Connoly.
The 78th Infantry Division, I said. *I'm in the field artillery.*
I'm in the infantry, said Steve.
You were in the Battle of the Bulge, said Mr. Connoly.
That's right, said Steve.
It must have been pretty rough going, said Mr. Connoly.
Half my unit was wiped out, said Steve.
Well, it's over now, said Mr. Connoly. *We were pretty hard hit here too. Not like London, of course.*
Mrs. Connoly brought in the two slices of toast which we promptly disposed of, after which we finished off the tea.
You must be tired after your long trip, said Mrs. Connoly.
We took that as a hint, rose and said good night.
Breakfast is from 6:30 to 8:30, Mrs. Connoly reiterated.
See you then, I said.
We climbed the narrow stairway back to our room, unpacked our duffel bags, used the facilities and stripped down to our shorts. I turned off the lamp and we climbed into our beds.
Do you know what we're supposed to be studying? asked Steve.
I think we can take any course we want, I said. *That was my understanding.*

THE ARRIVAL

Do you know what you're going to take?

Not yet, I said. *I hope they have some theatre courses.*

Is that what you're interested in?

I write plays, I said, *and I did some acting at Ohio State.*

Are you gonna be an actor?, asked Steve.

I'm not quite sure, I said. *I know I'm gonna be a writer.*

What have you written?

Well, I wrote this play that won a prize, said I, trying not to make too much of it, but added, *My first play, my first prize.*

That's great.

Of course, I responded. *it was just a one-act play.*

It's a beginning.

Yes, it is that. What do you do? I asked.

Right now I'm helping my father out, said Steve. *He has a furniture store. When we get back I'm gonna use the GI Bill to study accounting. I wanna be a CPA.*

There is the GI Bill isn't there? That's something to think about.

Well, maybe we ought to try to get some sleep, said Steve.

Yeah.

I drifted off thinking about the GI Bill, and trying to decide what use I ought to make of it.

CHAPTER TWENTY SIX

CARDIFF

We woke bright and early the next morning. It took me a moment to realize we were in Cardiff, and there was a university campus to look forward to. It was seven o'clock when we got down to breakfast. Mr. Connoly was in the living room reading his newspaper.

Good morning, said Mr. Connoly. *Did you sleep well?*
Oh, yes, I said.

The table in the dining room was set for two, with a glass of orange juice next to each plate. Mrs. Connoly brought in the toast and two pots of tea.

How do you like your eggs? she asked.
Sunny side up, said Steve.
I beg your pardon?
Oh, well... I'm not really particular, said Steve.
We usually serve them poached on a slice of toast.
That's fine, said Steve.
Me too, I said.

We gulped down our breakfast. We were eager to face the day, eager to find out what our life was going to be like at the University of Wales.

How do we get to the University? I asked Mr. Connoly as we got ready to leave.

Turn right when you get out the door, then left and keep on going past the castle and you can't miss it.

The castle? I said.

Oh, yes, the Cardiff Castle, said Mr. Connoly. *We're very proud of our castle. You'll pass it on the way to the university.*

A real castle, and we would be passing it every day on the way to the university. Wow!

CARDIFF

We stepped out the door into the bright sunshine. The air was cool and crisp. We looked about. This was Cardiff!

In the daylight the street was even more charming, with the quaint houses and the well tended gardens in front. Maybe Cardiff had been damaged during the war but, apparently, this part of the town hadn't been hit at all.

We walked to the corner, I inhaled deeply the brisk Autumn air. We turned left, walked down one block...and there she was, Cardiff Castle.

It looked immense with the tall stone wall that seemed to go on for blocks. Here and there along the wall were clusters of yellow flowers. And there was the gate and the drawbridge, just like in the movies. The grass alongside the giant wall could have been thicker though. Apparently this wasn't just a story book castle. This was a real building, one that was used by and tended to by ordinary people on a daily basis. This was part of the history of these people. Castles were just a part of their everyday lives. Wow!

It was like a dream. My whole life had become a dream. Here I was half way around the world, dressed in the uniform of a soldier walking next to a legendary landmark, walking next to English history. Here I was the son of a Jewish couple who had emigrated to America from a village in Poland. For years my life had marked time in Newark, New Jersey; an endless round of grammar school and high school, and Hebrew school and homework, a prisoner in classroom after classroom. The drudgery would never end, I thought. I would never become part of the world at large where great things were happening, where people had adventures and life was exciting. And then suddenly high school was over. I severed the umbilical cord and journeyed to a university in Ohio. And there I was in the army preparing to go to war. There I was sweating on maneuvers in the heat of the North

A NOT-SO-NICE JEWISH BOY FACES WORLD WAR II

Carolina sun. The next minute I was in a hospital in Tennessee with a broken toe. The next minute I was rolling through France in the rain on a truck. A soldier whom I admired had been killed during my first day of combat. I was lost in the snow in the Hurtgen Forest. I survived being shelled by German artillery. I was racing down a hill in Germany on the back of a motorcycle. I was lying on the grass with a pretty German girl. I spent the night with a prostitute in Liege. My life, which had been so placid, so mundane, without my even realizing it, had spiraled into the stratosphere. What lay in store for me now, I wondered. What did tomorrow hold?

Because of the war I'd learned to live from day to day. I'd become accustomed to think that each day might be my last. But now, now that I'd survived the war, I could actually think about tomorrow. I could actually think about the future, the future I had blocked from my mind. Now I would **have** to think about the future. The world lay before me, my entire life lay before me with years and years to write my plays or my novels, and maybe...well, maybe...even be an actor. Who knows? Who could tell what miraculous things could happen, now that the threat of sudden death was no longer imminent?

I was determined to make the most of this once-in-a-lifetime experience in Great Britain. Who knows? This might be the highlight of my entire existence. I was free, not only free from the threat of death, but free from all responsibilities...at the moment. Right now, right this very minute I had no one to answer to, no one but myself.

There was, of course, my commitment to Ginny, but that lay in the far distant future. Eventually I'd have to come down to earth, to settle down, to face the burden of making a living, of forging a place for myself in Society, but now was

CARDIFF

not the time to think about that. Now was the time to clasp everything to my bosom..so to speak...to experience it all!

Everything!!

Steve and I walked on past the castle, and there was the university. It wasn't Ohio State, but it was a good sized building. Students were milling about.

As we approached the main building it seemed that all eyes were focused on us. I looked about. Steve and I were the only ones in uniform. What were those intruders, those American GIs doing at their university, I'm sure they were thinking, those savages from across the sea, those "ugly Americans," those yahoos without any of the social graces. And then I thought, the hell with it. We Americans had come to the aid of the English. Without America England would have lost the war. So, whether they liked it or not, the British were in debt to the American GI who fought and died alongside of them. And besides, the young ladies seemed to eye us both with something akin to interest.

After making several inquiries we found our way to the office where we were able to register. I was interviewed by a rather officious looking gentleman who explained to me, rather condescendingly I thought, that I was free to take whatever courses I cared to, and how many I cared to. He suggested, however, that three would be more than enough to keep me busy. I decided to take a course in philosophy and a course in English literature. There were no theatre courses, per se. However there was a theatre group that met occasionally, and the officious looking gentleman thought I might be interested in attending one of their meetings. I was undecided about my third course. There was one in chemistry available. It's true I hadn't learned much in my chemistry course at the University of New Hampshire, but there was nothing here that

A NOT-SO-NICE JEWISH BOY FACES WORLD WAR II

really interested me. Maybe this time something would stick. I decided to sign up for it.

In taking one last look at the curriculum, I noticed that a course in voice was offered. I remembered performing that musical number back at Ohio State. Perhaps, with the proper training, I might turn out to have a magnificent voice.

I'd like to take this course in voice, I said. *Is that all right?*

That's up to you, said the advisor.

Ignoring the irritated look on my advisor's face, I signed up for voice as well. After all, if I decided to be an actor, I should be able to sing as well as act. There was, after all, musical comedy.

After we enrolled, Steve and I took a walk around the campus. We investigated the Student Union which contained a large lounge with easy chairs and a grand piano at one end of the room. We had lunch in the cafeteria and, for dessert, I ate something called "trifle," which consisted of sponge cake mixed in with whipped cream and Jello and fruits and turned out to be the highlight of the meal.

We decided to take a walk to the center of town. On the main street we were pleased to find a large, modern movie theatre which featured both American and British films, and there was a USO center. A dance was scheduled at the USO center for the following evening. Steve and I decided that we would attend.

It was getting on to five o'clock when we started back to the house. On the way I picked up a London paper at a newsstand. London was only two hours away, and a week-end in London was de rigueur, was it not?

As I glanced through the entertainment section I was delighted to find all sorts of exciting theatre to choose from. Laurence Olivier, the magnificent Heathcliff in the memorable movie version of "Wuthering Heights," had, apparently, created a sensation playing the leading roles in a double bill consisting of the Greek tragedy, "Oedipus," and a Restoration comedy entitled "The Critic." This was being produced by an enterprising company called The Old Vic. Also at The Old Vic there was a production of Shakespeare's "Henry IV, Part 1" and "Henry IV, Part 2" both of which had gotten excellent reviews. Ralph Richardson, a popular character actor, was giving a legendary performance as Falstaff in this production, and Olivier was playing Hotspur in Part 1 and Justice Shallow in Part 2. There was also a production of Noel Coward's "Private Lives." Here was an opportunity to see a professional production of this wonderful sophisticated comedy with British actors who could perform it with great style. How would this West End performance compare with the one Ginny and I gave back at Ohio State, I wondered.

We got back to the house just in time for dinner. We were not joined by Mr. and Mrs. Connoly, as I thought we might be. I realized, for the first time, that this was not a private home we were staying at, but a commercial establishment known as a Bed & Breakfast.

Dinner was rather bland, though I continued to marvel at how tea could be made so palatable.

After dinner Steve and I took a walk in the area. When we returned to our room Steve retired early.

I stayed up and read for a while. At the moment I was reading Maugham's charming, off-beat novel called "Cakes And Ale." I was trying to read as much of Somerset Maugham as I could get hold of. There was something compelling about this man's writing. Maugham seemed to have the knack of getting the reader caught up in the story he was telling.

And what a great idea these paperback books were.

A NOT-SO-NICE JEWISH BOY FACES WORLD WAR II

Nothing like this was available in America. Of course, no one in America read anyway. On the bus back in Newark, I would look around and notice that I was the only one reading a book. America really is a barbaric country, I decided.

As I turned off the lamp and snuggled under the covers, I went to sleep warmed by the glow of the story of a barmaid and a royal gentleman. Some day I would write a book at least as charming as that.

CHAPTER TWENTY SEVEN

I MEET A YOUNG LADY

The next day we were up early, even though classes didn't start until the day after. We decided to do some sightseeing.

As we stepped out the door we were greeted by the sight of Matthew approaching the house. He had come to look us up and, surprisingly enough, seemed rather friendly.

Mr. Connoly had boasted that Cardiff was a major seaport and that we really ought to pay a visit to the docks. None of us was really into ships, but we were here in Cardiff, and while we were we here, we might as well see everything we could. So we set out dutifully to visit the docks.

We found our way to the docks, walked about, looked at the ships at anchor, looked at the water...and decided that that was about as rewarding as a visit to the docks could be. Afterwards we stopped off at a little Fish & Chips place for lunch.

Chips I learned were French fries. They were sold wrapped in newspaper, along with fried fish. The food turned out to be a tasty surprise, especially for me, since I wasn't very fond of fish. The proprietor, a chubby, red faced woman refused to take the our money.

The next stop was Llandaff Cathedral, another landmark recommended by Mr. Connoly and, after that, the 15th Century Church of John The Baptist. We were properly impressed, and now we could write home and say that we'd seen what there was to be seen in Cardiff, Wales.

Since we were planning to attend the dance at the USO Steve and I decided not to go back to the house for dinner. Matthew, undecided at first, decided to go to the dance after all. The three of us had dinner at a Chinese restaurant and then headed for the dance.

A NOT-SO-NICE JEWISH BOY FACES WORLD WAR II

******

We arrived at the hall early. The band was just setting up, and two of the local ladies were laying out the punch and cookies. While we were sampling the refreshments I glanced around the room.

The American and the British flags were hung over the platform where the band was tuning up. There were chairs lined up against the wall along the length of the hall. The band started off with a popular British tune of the day. A middle-aged woman came to the center of the stage and, standing in front of the microphone, began to sing in a rather pleasant voice.

"That certain night, the night we met,
There was magic abroad in the air.
There were angels dining at the Ritz,
And a nightingale sang in Berkeley Square."

Three girls came into the hall and sat down. One of the girls caught my attention. She was tall and nicely built with short, brown, wavy hair.

"I may be right, I may be wrong,
But I'm perfectly willing to swear...
That when you turned and smiled at me,
A nightingale sang in Berkeley Square."

I studied the girl's face. It was rather pleasant and had a sweetness about it. She smiled at me. I smiled back.

I'm gonna dance, I said to Steve and Matthew.

I crossed the room and walked over to the girl.

Would you care to dance?

Thank you, she said, and rose holding out her arms. I pulled her to me.

Contact with her body sent a shockwave throughout my

I MEET A YOUNG LADY

entire system. That was the only way to describe it. It was as if a magnet held the two of us together.
My name's Norman, I said.
I'm Clara.
The words didn't seem to mean anything. It was our bodies that were having the conversation.
Are you stationed nearby? she asked.
Actually we're taking courses at the university. We're actually stationed in Germany.
How long will you be here?
Until January, I think. It's very nice, having this dance and all.
It's the least we can do. Were you in combat?
I was in the Battle of the Bulge, in the Hurtgen Forest.
It must have been awful.
It wasn't fun and games, I said. *But I was lucky, I guess. I'm still in one piece, and no harm done, I think. What I mean to say is, it does leave scars.*
I'm sure it does.
The world is a different place. You're different inside.
Does it make you bitter?
Bitter? I'm not quite sure. I don't know. I resent the years it's taken out of my life. But then again, it is an experience. I'm a writer, you see. That's what I'm gonna be, at any rate, and if a writer needs anything at all, it's life experience. What do you do?
I work for Cartwright & Cartwright. It's a shipping company. I work in the office.
That must be pretty dull.
I don't mind.
Do you like to read?
Oh, yes. I read a lot.
Who's your favorite author?

A NOT-SO-NICE JEWISH BOY FACES WORLD WAR II

Oh, I don't know.
She was not a reader, apparently. After a moment I said, *I see you have a movie theatre in town.*
Oh, yes. We have several.
Do you like the movies?
Oh, yes. I go, at least, once a week.
Maybe we can go together some time, I said.
All right.
You live with your parents?
My mother. My father passed away.
The war?
No, before.
That must have been rough, growing up without a father.
We missed him.
We danced through several songs.
By this time the hall was filling up. There were some men in British uniforms and some in civilian clothes, but there were much more women than men.
Would you care for some punch? I asked.
Thank you.
We walked over to the table. I picked up two glasses of punch and handed one to Clara. *L'chaim!* I said. After I'd said it I wondered why. Was I warning the girl that I was Jewish? Did I have a chip on my shoulder about it?
What does that mean?
To life.
To life! said Clara.
Won't you have a cookie? They're very good, said Clara.
Thank you.
I picked up a cookie, handed it to Clara, and took one

I MEET A YOUNG LADY

for myself. *They are good,* I said, after biting into it. *What are you smiling at?*

I made them.

That was sneaky. Suppose I didn't like them?

At that moment a rather pretty girl approached us. *May I have this dance?* she said to me.

I looked at Clara. I wasn't sure what to do.

Clara smiled bravely.

I didn't want to offend the girl. *Okay,* I said. Then I turned to Clara. *Excuse me,* I said.

Clara smiled and nodded. And I danced off with the pretty girl.

I've never seen you here before, she said.

This is my first time.

Are you stationed nearby?

I'm going to the university.

Oh?

The army didn't know what to do with us so they sent a few of us here.

Oh?

The girl didn't really seem that interested. She kept looking around. She was pretty though. Maybe a little too much makeup, and she felt rather bony. When the song came to an end I said, *Thank you.*

My pleasure, said the girl, and she walked away.

I looked around.

I was standing near the chairs, and I noticed a thin, rather plain young lady who looked sort of sad. I walked up to her. *Would you care to dance?* I asked.

The girl looked up, rather surprised. *Thank you,* she said, rose and held out her arms.

We danced in silence. The magic wasn't there. No

A NOT-SO-NICE JEWISH BOY FACES WORLD WAR II

electricity, no nothing. At the end of the song I escorted her back to her seat.
Thank you, she said.
Thank you, I said.
The orchestra started up, and the woman sang:
We'll meet again,
Don't know where, don't know when.
But we'll meet again some sunny day.
I looked around. I spied Clara. She was looking about as she moved slowly towards the door. I caught up with her.
Are you leaving?
I have to catch a bus.
May I walk you to the bus?
If you like.
Just a minute. I wanna tell my friend that I'll be right back. I looked around and spied Steve at the table, drinking some lemonade and talking to a rather heavyset young lady. I walked over quickly.
I'm gonna walk this girl to her bus. I'll be right back. Where's Matthew?
He left.
I'll be right back.
Okay.
I walked quickly back to Clara. We walked out into the street. She led the way across the street to a bus stop.
I have to leave early to catch the last bus, she said.
I hope you didn't mind, I said.
What?
Leaving you like that...when that girl came up and asked me to dance. It was rather embarrassing.
No, of course not. It was perfectly all right.
Would you care to go to the movies Saturday night?
Okay. What are you smiling at?

I MEET A YOUNG LADY

"*Okay,*" I said. *I thought it was an American expression.*
We see American movies all the time.
What time shall we meet?
Well, I have to catch the last bus, said Clara. *It leaves at ten thirty.*
Is seven o'clock okay? Shall we meet at the theatre?
All right.
The Odeon?
The Odeon.
I'll meet you in front of the box office.
Here comes my bus.

Impulsively I leaned over and kissed her on the lips. It took her a moment, and then she responded. The bus pulled up. Clara got on and, as the bus pulled away, she waved to me through the window. I watched the bus drive away and I returned to the dance. I found Steve alone.

Did you meet anyone? I asked.
Not really, said Steve. *Did you?*
I think so. You ready to leave?
Yeah, let's go.

That night, as I crawled into bed and pulled up the covers I lay thinking about Clara. She was rather sweet and certainly responsive. For the first time in my life I felt really dashing, the romantic conqueror.

CHAPTER TWENTY EIGHT

MY FIRST VOICE LESSON

Getting up the next day I was hit with the realization that this morning I'd be back in a classroom. This did not exactly thrill me. I'd attended Ohio State, not because I was anxious to continue with my education. I was just too much of a coward to face life in the raw. And my first class at the University of Cardiff happened to be Elementary Chemistry.

Maybe coming to the university was a big mistake. Maybe I should have held out for Paris or the Riviera, or somewhere more glamorous, more colorful than a university in Wales. Well, it was too late now.

As I entered the classroom I felt very conspicuous, an object of curiosity. The questions floated in the air. What was this American GI like, and what was he doing here at our university? Instead of being uncomfortable or intimidated by the attention I decided to relish it. How nice to be a mystery, I thought. I must capitalize on it.

The professor entered the classroom and the lecture began. *Actually this course should be entitled Inorganic Chemistry, since we will be studying the chemical reactions and properties of all the chemical elements and their compounds with the exception of hydrocarbons and their derivatives.*

My heart sank.

We will touch on the elementary laws of chemistry, its symbols and nomenclature and we will then move on to an introduction to experimental methods.

Well, actually, that didn't sound too complicated, did it? And I really should know something about the matter that surrounds me. After all, one of the characters in one of my plays, or one of my novels, might be a chemistry professor or a scientist.

MY FIRST VOICE LESSON

I sat up, determined to try and follow what was to come. I had purchased a notebook in the university bookstore. I started to take notes. For the first ten minutes or so, I was able to jot some things down. As the professor droned on and on, however, the notes became sparser and sparser. By the end of the hour, my instincts were confirmed. This was a big mistake. Science was not my metier. It never was, and it never would be. In addition to that, this trip was supposed to be sort of a vacation. As I left the room I was pretty sure I would not be returning. Chemistry would have to go on without me.

I met Steve for lunch in the cafeteria. Steve had signed up for advanced algebra and was quite pleased with his first session. Better him than me, I thought. I had heard somewhere that the British were not exactly famous for their cuisine. The food in the cafeteria did nothing to challenge that reputation.

My second course was English literature, the Romantic poets, beginning with Wordsworth and Coleridge to be followed by Byron, Shelley and Keats. Now that was more like it. Byron had always fascinated me, not his poetry per se, at least the poems of his that I'd read. What fascinated me about Byron was the poet's scandalous reputation. Byron, like Oscar Wilde, had put his talent into his work, and his genius into his life. The professor gave a brief summary of the ground we'd be covering in the course, and assigned a book to be bought, which could be found at the university bookstore.

In glancing around the room I noticed a pretty little thing across from where I was sitting. It was Alice in wonderland; shoulder length chestnut hair, turned up nose and lively brown eyes that seemed wise beyond her years. I tried to concentrate on what the professor was saying, but my attention kept returning to the little mouse. Actually that was what she resembled, a pretty little mouse.

A NOT-SO-NICE JEWISH BOY FACES WORLD WAR II

The class was over and the 'little mouse' rose and left the room with a friend, a female friend, I was pleased to note.

I proceeded to the book store and bought the book about the English poets. And there was the 'little mouse' and her friend, just leaving the store. She turned just before stepping out the door. I caught her eye and smiled. Either she didn't see me or maybe she was ignoring me. There was no sign of recognition, or even an acknowledgement of my existence.

I had an hour and a half to kill before my voice lesson. I walked over to the Student Union and entered the lounge. I found an easy chair, settled into it, and started reading about the life of William Wordsworth, which proved surprisingly dramatic. The man who wrote those rather staid, reflective poems about nature and life was actually quite the rebel. In his youth he'd been enthusiastic about the French Revolution, journeyed to France where he took up with a young French lady and produced an illegitimate child.

I happened to look up just in time to see the 'little mouse' pass by, alone this time. I smiled automatically, but she seemed to be completely unaware of my presence. Or was she really ignoring me, I wondered.

Glancing at my watch I noticed I had half an hour to get to my voice lesson. It was to take place a few blocks from the university at the home of the instructor. I found the house without too much trouble.

******

The front of the house was lined with large, grey stones and featured a bay window in the middle. There was a well-kept lawn and, beneath the bay window, a profusion of red and yellow flowers. I walked up the stone path and rang the

MY FIRST VOICE LESSON

bell. It was answered a moment later by a pleasant looking, dignified woman who appeared to be in her fifties. Or was she in her sixties? I was not a very good judge of age.

You're my American pupil. Come in, come in. The voice was low, and mellifluous. Like a cello, I thought, corny as that might sound. There was a certain elegance about the way the woman carried herself. She led me into a small, carpeted living room with a grand piano and period furniture, probably valuable antiques. *Sit down, please. Your name again.*

Norman Beim.

I'm Constance Berganza. It's a Spanish name. My husband is Spanish. I'm Welsh. Are you Hebrew?

I guess I am.

My accompanist was Hebrew. We got on splendidly.

You're a concert singer?

I was up until a few years ago.

That's exciting, said I. *Did you sing opera as well?*

Once or twice. I preferred the concert stage. Would you like some hot chocolate?

Thank you.

I won't be a moment.

Mrs. Berganza left the room and I looked about. Rich-looking drapes on the window, photographs on the piano, a console containing a phonograph and a radio with an elegant vase on top containing red roses. In one corner there was a harp. There were two original paintings on the wall. I walked over to the piano and examined the photographs. Most of them were signed. There was Sir Thomas Beecham, a famous British conductor. "For Constance, your humble servant".

Mrs. Berganza reentered with a tray containing two elegant cups filled with hot chocolate, and a plate containing some biscuits. She set down the tray and the two of us sat down and drank the hot chocolate.

A NOT-SO-NICE JEWISH BOY FACES WORLD WAR II

You worked with Thomas Beecham, I said. *That must have been exciting.*

It was an experience.

Was that good or bad?

Actually he was quite charming, after we got to know one another. Have a biscuit, said Mrs. Berganza.

I helped myself to a biscuit. *You must have been famous,* I said.

I was well known for a period of time. Tell me something about yourself. How old are you?

I'm twenty two. Actually I'll be twenty two next month. I've been in the army for almost three years.

And before?

I was going to Ohio State University. I was going to be a journalist. Well, actually I want to be a writer. I want to write the great American novel. But now I'm not so sure. This one-act play of mine won an award and maybe I'll be a playwright. I'm not quite sure.

Why do you want to study voice?

Well, I took some acting courses at Ohio State and, well, I guess maybe I'm thinking about being an actor too and, who knows, maybe a singer as well. I mean an actor should be able to sing as well as act, don't you think? What I mean to say is there's always musical comedy, and the more one has to offer....

Have you ever sung?

Well, I did do a musical number at Ohio State. A solo, all by myself. Actually it didn't start out that way. I was doing a duet but my partner backed out, so I went on alone.

Were you good?

I don't know. But I was proud of myself, that I had the courage to go on, I mean. I don't know if I can sing or not. I mean I don't even know if I have a voice.

MY FIRST VOICE LESSON

Everyone has a voice.
I mean if I can sing.
Everyone can sing.
Well, I mean... I guess that's what I'm here to find out. How good I am, I mean.

Mrs. Berganza looked at me, looked through me actually, which made me a little uncomfortable. What did she see? She rose and sat down at the piano.

Let's try some scales.

She hit a note and I sang a scale. She hit the next highest note and I sang another scale, beginning at that note. We continued to go higher and higher. I started out quietly, but then as we went on I became more confidant. I sang louder and louder. Mrs. Berganza stopped.

Never louder than lovelier, she said.

What an interesting comment, I thought. How brilliant. Never louder then lovelier. It seemed to open up doors. Never louder than lovelier.

We started the scales all over again. I sang more quietly this time. We continued the scales until we reached my highest note. We then went on to various vocal exercises. This went on for the next half hour.

As we paused I asked, *Do you think I might be able to work on a song, perhaps?*

Do you have one in mind?
Well, there are a couple that I like.
Why don't you bring one along with you the next time.
Okay.
That will be all for today.

What do you think?, I asked. *Do you think I could think seriously about being a singer?*

I'm not prepared to say.
You heard my voice. What do I sound like?

A NOT-SO-NICE JEWISH BOY FACES WORLD WAR II

At the moment, it's uncultivated.
I see.
It takes work.
That's true, it does, doesn't it? Do you think I ought to practice in between?
Not quite yet. I'll see you the same time next week.
Mrs. Berganza escorted me to the door.
Thank you, I said.
You're quite welcome, she said. I could feel her eyes resting on me as I walked down the path. I heard the door close as I reached the sidewalk.

Wouldn't it be wonderful if we could see ourselves objectively, I thought, if I could see myself through Mrs. Berganza's eyes, for example. The phrase kept echoing in my mind as I strolled back to the house. Never louder than lovelier. Never louder than lovelier. What a remarkable woman!

CHAPTER TWENTY NINE

I MEET 'THE LITTLE MOUSE'

The next day was philosophy. I looked forward to it eagerly. At Ohio State my philosophy course had been one of my favorites. The highlight had been the Dialogues of Plato. I vaguely recalled the rather striking image of two wild horses symbolizing the warring elements of human nature, or something to that effect. And then there was Aristotle's Poetics. I'd found both these men challenging and inspiring. I arrived early for the philosophy class and took a seat near the front of the room.

When the lecture began I was surprised to note that, unlike my two other classes, there were a number of empty seats. As the professor droned on I realized why. This was a class in Metaphysics. The professor was going to deal with reality, causality and other esoteric subjects. The textbook we were to purchase was entitled "An Experiment With Time." I did my best to concentrate on the matter at hand but I found my mind wandering. ("Never louder than lovelier. Never louder then lovelier.")

I glanced behind me. There in the row next to mine was 'the little mouse.' The expression on her face, as she listened to the lecture, displayed my own bewilderment. Thank God! I wasn't the only one. I took some notes and resolved to buy the assigned textbook, but really didn't hold out too much hope for the course. As I rose from my desk at the end of the lecture I spotted 'the little mouse' walking out the door. I quickened my step and caught up with her in the hallway.

Hi, I said. *I noticed your expression during the class. Are you as confused as I am?*

I didn't understand a word he was saying.

I'm greatly relieved, I said. *I was really looking forward to this course.*

A NOT-SO-NICE JEWISH BOY FACES WORLD WAR II

So was I.
But I am enjoying the poetry course, I added.
So am I.
My name is Norman. Norman Beim.
I'm Jean. Jean Courbet.
How do you do.
We shook hands.
Courbet? Is that French?
I think so, way back.

What an enchanting creature, I thought. The impish twinkle in her eyes, the surprisingly delightful curves. The face was that of a little girl. The body, though petite, was that of a woman.

Are you enjoying your stay here?, she asked.
I'm beginning to, I said. *Though I don't know how welcome American GIs are.*
Once they get to know you, it'll be much easier.
I was going to have lunch in the cafeteria, I said. *Would you care to join me?*
I was meeting a friend. If you don't mind her joining us.
No, of course not.

We started for the cafeteria.

What is the attitude toward the Americans here at the university? I asked.
You and your two friends are the first. We don't know what to expect.
The Ugly American?
She looked at me blankly.
I mean we are considered rather arrogant, aren't we? And boorish.
I wouldn't worry about it.

I MEET 'THE LITTLE MOUSE'

Then again I guess we have preconceived ideas about the English.

We're not English, said Jean. We're Welsh.

I guess I mean the British.

There's great deal of difference between Wales and England and Scotland, for that matter.

Do you consider yourself British or Welsh?

Actually, I never gave it much thought.

I guess I never thought about myself as American, until I came in contact with other nationalities. What are you majoring in?

I haven't quite decided yet, said Jean. My parents, my father that is, would like me to go into medicine. He's a physician. But I'm not that keen about medicine. And you?

I'm a writer. That's what I intend to be, at any rate.

By this time we had reached the cafeteria and were greeted by Jean's friend, an attractive brunette who appeared to be older than Jean.

This is Helen, said Jean. This is Norman.

How do you do, said Helen, shaking my hand. I can't stay long. I'm meeting Ralph in the music building. He's going to play some of his songs for me.

Helen's friend is a very talented composer.

How interesting, I said.

Norman's going to be a writer, said Jean.

This one-act play of mine won a prize in a nation-wide contest.

That's wonderful, said Helen. You must be very pleased.

It's a beginning, I hope.

A wonderful beginning, said Jean. Are you going to join us for lunch? she said to Helen.

I'd better not, said Helen. I don't want to keep Ralph

A NOT-SO-NICE JEWISH BOY FACES WORLD WAR II

waiting. It's been nice meeting you, Norman. I hope to see you again.

Same here.

And Helen left.

She's very fond of Ralph. I hope she isn't disappointed.

Why should she be?

I think she cares more about him than he does about her. I'm fond of Helen, and I wouldn't like to see her hurt.

She seems like a person who knows her own mind, I said.

When it comes to love, we're all of us vulnerable, aren't we?

I guess so. It continues to amaze me, I said.

What's that?

The surprises that life has in store for us.

Good or bad?

Both, I guess. Do you wonder about the future? What's in store for us?

Do you?

Life, in itself, is a miracle. I sometimes wonder if it isn't all a dream, I said. *I sometimes wonder if I won't wake up in the morning, in my bed in Newark, New Jersey.*

Is that where you're from?

Yes. I'm hungry. Are you?

Let's eat.

We made their way to the food counter.

Don't eat the meat loaf, said Jean. *The baked chicken is usually fresh.*

I discovered trifle for the first time.

It's unpredictable.

We chose our food and approached the cash register.

Let me take you to lunch, I said.

This isn't really a date, is it?

I MEET 'THE LITTLE MOUSE'

Well...
Next time.
That's a bargain, I said.

As we ate our food we chattered on as if we were old friends, eager to catch up on things after a long absence. Glancing about the cafeteria, I noticed a friendlier attitude in the looks I received from the other students. I assumed that speaking to one of their own, on such obviously amiable terms, had earned me, perhaps, a stamp of approval. We left each other reluctantly. Jean had a French class. We agreed to meet the next day for lunch.

CHAPTER THIRTY

AN ARTISTIC PHOTOGRAPHER

After 'the little mouse' and I parted, I was at a loss how to spend the rest of the day. In the evening I was to attend a meeting of the dramatic club at a church nearby.

I decided to have my picture taken. The picture I'd had taken in Liege was fine, but I wanted a head shot, a close-up of my face. If I decided to be an actor I might need one.

As I headed for the photographer's shop I'd noticed on the main street not far from the movie theatre, I wondered if Ginny had received the picture I'd had taken in Liege. She hadn't mentioned it so far. I hadn't written her for over two weeks now, and I felt guilty about it. I really ought to write to her. Up till now, I'd written faithfully at least once a week, and received two or three letters a week from her. But somehow, I just didn't feel like writing. Why? I'd made a commitment and I would probably honor it unless, of course, she changed her mind, and she might if I just stopped writing. Well, I couldn't help it. I just didn't feel like writing, and that was that. The truth of the matter was I was reluctant to face the future, reality that is, surviving from day to day in the jungle out there.

The bell tinkled as I opened the door and stepped into the photographer's shop.

Be with you in a mo', a hearty woman's voice called out.

I examined the various photographs on display. They were quite unique. Very artistic. No ordinary, by the numbers, brightly lit, department store photos with a big smile. These were character studies, with light and shade. That's what I wanted. Something dramatic, something that made me look like an actor, interesting, mysterious, glamorous. Wasn't that

AN ARTISTIC PHOTOGRAPHER

a picture of Reginald Owen, the well known British movie actor? It certainly looked like Reginald Owen.

Yes? Can I help you?

I turned to find myself face to face with a dynamic, middle-aged woman, the sort of gung-ho, no nonsense British types one sometimes sees in English films, like stalwart Margaret Rutherford or quixotic Dame May Whitty.

I'd like to have my picture taken. Something very dramatic, something unusual, I said.

You've come to the right place.

Can we do it now? I mean...are you free?

Well, I do have... She stopped. I guess she may have noticed the eager look in my face. *Well, I don't see why not. The war may be over, but we are indebted to you brave men, our saviors from the Hun. Come. Come into my lair. I'm Hilary, by the way.*

Norman Beim.

How do you do. She shook my hand vigorously.

How do you do, I said.

We entered a dimly lit studio. The walls were covered with black cloth. There was a camera and light stands, a bench, some chairs and a table.

Sit down, sit down. Now, tell me a bit about yourself. I like to know something about my subject before I plunge in.

I spoke about my writing ambitions, my interest in theatre and my war experiences. Hilary studied my face as I spoke and listened attentively. Every once in a while she nodded and made some sort of strange noise like a rumble or a grunt.

I'd like to take one shot in profile, she said finally, squinting at me very professionally.

Profile? But I've got this bump on my nose.

A NOT-SO-NICE JEWISH BOY FACES WORLD WAR II

It's called a bridge, my dear, and that's what makes you distinctive. You're not one of these run-of-the-mill pretty boys.
Actually, I do look better from the front...
Not to fear. We'll take one from the front as well. Do you mind taking off your shirt? I'd like to include the neck and part of the shoulder, perhaps, said Hilary. *You've got a good neck.*
Really? Okay.
While Hilary set up the lights and the camera I took off my jacket and shirt.
You remind me of Michael Redgrave. No, more like Mr. Gielgud.
John Gielgud? Really?
There's a resemblance. A strong resemblance. You're much younger, of course. You might be his son, if he had a son.
He is a fine actor, of course, but he's not very handsome, is he?
Handsome is as handsome does. Now, sit on that chair. Look to your right. Now to your left. Your left profile is your best. Remember that.
Thank you. (I think.) *Do you want me to smile?*
Do you feel like smiling?
Not really.
Then don't. Don't move. Hilary dashed to one of the lights, adjusted it, then dashed back to the camera. *There, that was a good one. Let's take another. There. Well, we are making progress. You're a good subject. Some people just can't sit still. Look this way.*
I faced the camera. Hilary adjusted the lights again and dashed back to the camera.
Let's try a smile. There. That was lovely. Just lovely.

AN ARTISTIC PHOTOGRAPHER

Now let's try a thoughtful.... That's it. Hold it. There. You take direction well.

Thank you.

You're a good actor, I'll wager.

Well, I'm not an actor yet.

You will be.

You think so? I asked as I got into my shirt and jacket. *Is that a picture of Reginald Owen on your wall?*

Why, yes. He was here in Cardiff, on tour. Charming gentlemen. Actually I did have a shot of Mr. Gielgud somewhere. I think someone stole it and, sad to say, I simply cannot find the negative.

Have you taken pictures of many famous people?

I did, when I had my studio in London.

Did you really? That must have been exciting. Who were some of the stars?

My dear boy, stars are people, like you and I. People who never grew up. Mad gypsies. Peter Pan and The Mad Hatter. Delightful children, up to a point that is.

Were they difficult?

The gentlemen were charming, for the most part, that is. The females, however...

Like who?

I never discuss my clients, dear boy. But Mrs. Olivier...Miss Leigh, that is... Hilary, bite your tongue. Oh, dear! What time is it? I must get back to work. I'll have something to show you on Monday, if you care to drop by.

Would you like me to leave a deposit? I asked.

If you like. Three pounds will do. Here, take my card. See you on Monday. Any time. I'm open till six.

The telephone rang and Hilary picked it up. *Hiilary here. What nonsense!*

I handed her the money. Still on the phone, she smiled

A NOT-SO-NICE JEWISH BOY FACES WORLD WAR II

at me and nodded, which I took as a dismissal. As I headed for the door she called out, *See you on Monday.* I nodded, smiled and stepped out the door, and the bell tinkled. It was growing dark. I took in a deep breath of the cold, brisk air. A day well spent.

THE POET

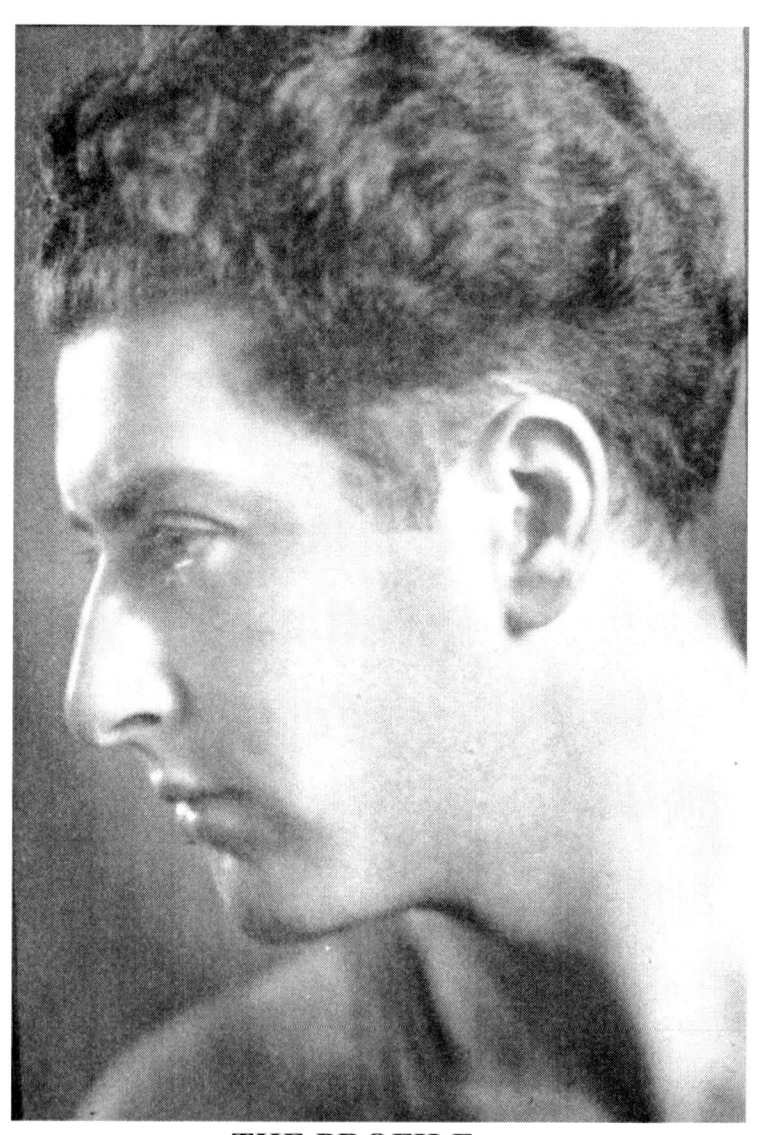

THE PROFILE

CHAPTER THIRTY ONE

THE DRAMATIC CLUB

After leaving the photography studio I headed back to the house. I quickened my step as I realized I would be attending a meeting of the dramatic club shortly. Then I suddenly remembered that I hadn't asked for a receipt for my deposit. I debated about going back but decided against it. Hilary might be absent-minded but I was sure that she was honest.

I was uneasy about attending the meeting of the dramatic club. The thought of facing a group of strange actors, especially British actors, made me very nervous. Suppose I was asked to audition for a role? My American accent would stand out like a sore thumb.

Back at the house I listened carefully to the speech pattern of the Connolys. Their "A"s were broad and their "R"s were soft, almost inaudible. I must remember that, remember that. I dreaded the thought of being the only American at the meeting, and thought seriously about not going.

Finally I asked Steve if he would like to accompany me. Steve had nothing planned for the evening and said he'd be glad to go. After dinner we started out for the meeting.

As we approached the church I grew more and more nervous. There it was, an old, picturesque building. We walked up the three stairs and entered through the main door. In the vestibule a calendar of events was posted. The dramatic club was meeting in a room in the basement.

We descended the rickety stairs. A musty smell permeated the building. There was only one room with a door open and a light shining out of it.

We entered the room. There was a podium at one end and chairs scattered about. It was a room that was probably used for classes and for meetings as well.

A NOT-SO-NICE JEWISH BOY FACES WORLD WAR II

We were greeted by a bespectacled, business-like young lady. *Yes? Can I help you.*

We're here for the meeting of the dramatic club. Is this where they're meeting?, I asked.

Why, yes.

We're attending the university. Actually I studied acting at Ohio State University, and I appeared there in several productions, I said, stretching the truth quite a bit, *and my counselor at the university suggested that I might like to attend one of your meetings.*

Won't you have a seat?

Thank you.

We're a little late getting started. Have you done some acting as well?, the young lady asked Steve.

Oh, no, said Steve. *I'm just a good audience.*

Well, we should be starting shortly. We're trying to decide on our next production. This evening we're going to read, "Blithe Spirit" by Noel Coward. Are you familiar with it?

Actually I played Elyot in "Private Lives" at Ohio State, I said. They didn't have to know that all I did was work on a scene for class.

We did that two years ago, said the young lady. *It was a great success.*

Noel Coward is one of my favorite playwrights, I said.

The young lady said nothing. The conversation came to a halt. There was an awkward silence. Thankfully it didn't last too long since members of the club began to assemble.

Steve and I took a seat. I was pleased to note that most of the members were women. Actually there were only two men, one of them a teenager. The young lady that greeted us seemed to be in charge. She hadn't given her name nor did she introduce Steve and me to her fellow members, who eyed us

THE DRAMATIC CLUB

both oddly. I wondered whether I ought to introduce myself. I thought better of it. Besides there was my American accent. The less I said, the better.

The young lady in charge (I gathered her name was Martha, since she was addressed as Martha) proceeded to hand out scripts. She had one script left. She looked over at me and hesitated.

I smiled at her.

She approached me and said, *Would you care to read the role of Dr. Bradman?*

I'd be happy to, I said, trying not to sound too eager.

He's in three scenes. Two in the first act and one in the second.

I nodded.

Martha handed me the script.

I joined the readers who were sitting in a semi-circle in the front of the room. Under ordinary circumstances I would have preferred a major role. As it was, however, I was grateful that the role was as small as it was. The reading began. I leafed hastily through the pages to find Dr. Bradman.

The characters in the play were gathering for a seance. Dr. Bradman and his wife were friends of Charles and Ruth, the leading characters. I noticed, incidentally, that Mrs. Bradman had more to say than her husband. No matter, no matter. The important thing was to get the accent right.

As the reading progressed I listened carefully to my fellow actors. Broad "A"s, broad "A"s and soften the "R"s, soften the "R"s. There was my first line, and I spoke up.

We're not late, are we? I only got back from the hospital about half an hour ago. Did that sound right, I wondered. I did try to speak through my nose, the way the rest of them did.

I looked about surreptitiously, examining the

A NOT-SO-NICE JEWISH BOY FACES WORLD WAR II

expressions on the faces of the other members of the cast, hoping for some sign of approval. A smile would have been nice. At any rate there was no look of horror at the one line I uttered. I glanced at Martha who was reading the role of Ruth. Her face was a blank. Surely they must all be aware of how phoney I sounded. And, since I was trying to imitate my fellow readers, I was afraid they might think that I was making fun of them. There was no help for it however. I was just doing my level best not to stand out. The first scene ended.

The second scene started right up. There was my entrance, and I pitched right in. *I hope you feel in the mood, Madame Arcati.*

Finally my participation in the first act ended. I sat back and was able to listen to the others objectively. None of the actors seemed particularly brilliant. The leading man was adequate, a bit lifeless, perhaps. Actually Martha was the best of the lot. But I couldn't help admiring the consistency of their British accent. How did they manage it? And how I envied it!

I looked over at Steve. Steve smiled at me. Was that a sign of approval, I wondered. Steve, of course, was a friend. Even if he did approve that wasn't really a fair judgement, was it?

We continued on to the second act without a break. Dr. Bradman didn't appear until the third scene. By this time I felt more comfortable and, as I read, I became more and more aware of the discrepancies between the American and the British accent. That was a good sign, I thought, because if I was aware of it, I could correct it. I stopped trying to assess the reaction to my reading and concentrated on pronouncing the words correctly, as correctly as I possibly could that is.

There was a short break. I was tempted to walk over to Steve and sit beside him, but decided to stay put. The third

THE DRAMATIC CLUB

act, in which Dr. Bradman did not appear, was a relatively short one. Relieved of the responsibility of performing I sat back and, for the first time, listened to the play itself. It was absolutely delightful, funny and clever. If only I could write a play as clever and as funny as that.

At the end of the reading Martha collected the scripts. As I handed her my copy she said, *Thank you.* Was that a sign of approval? Oh, the hell with it! What did I care? I might never see these people again. Then again...

The meeting seemed to be over. The members of the club began to talk among themselves. No one made any attempt to draw Steve or myself into the conversation. I walked over to Steve.

Shall we go? I said to Steve.

Okay, said Steve.

As we headed toward the door Martha called out, *Good night.*

Good night, I said as Steve and I left the room.

No thank you, no come again, no go to hell. Complete indifference. What could be more wounding?

That's a very funny play, said Steve.

It is, isn't it?

Isn't he going to say anything about my reading, I wondered. Finally I could hold back no longer.

It really was strange reading with English actors, I said.

Why?

I mean, the accent.

Nothing. Steve said absolutely nothing. No approval, no criticism. He seemed to take it for granted that I was perfectly at ease during the reading. Maybe I'm a better actor than I think I am. And no, I will not ask his opinion. He is not, after all, an authority. I must trust myself, right or wrong.

A NOT-SO-NICE JEWISH BOY FACES WORLD WAR II

I didn't expect to be invited to the next meeting of The Dramatic Club and, of course, I wasn't. Was it simply indifference, I wondered. Perhaps they resented the American invasion. Or were they, like me, just shy? Whatever the reason, I decided not to make any effort to find out about the next meeting. If they sought me out fine. If not, the experience had been most rewarding, I kept telling myself.

CHAPTER THIRTY TWO

BETWEEN THE DEVIL & THE DEEP BLUE SEA

The next day, though I hadn't planned to return to the chemistry class, I did so anyway. It would be a way to kill the time before I met Jean for lunch. I made no attempt whatsoever to try to follow the lecture, though I did make a show of taking notes.

The lecture seemed to go on forever and I became concerned that I might be late. Suppose I was? Would Jean wait for me? The first meeting went well, and there was definitely a mutual interest, or attraction...or whatever, but that was no guarantee. She might just change her mind. We came from two different worlds. God, that sounded corny. It took great restraint, when the lecture finally ended, not to dash out of the room. I hurried down the hallway. By the time I got to the cafeteria, I was out of breath.

I looked about hastily. There was no sign of Jean. My heart sank. I scanned the room again. There she was! She was sitting at a table, her head bent over a book. I heaved a sigh of relief, and made my way to the table.

She looked up. Those eyes, so wise, and yet so vulnerable. That pixie face. What was it about her that appealed to me so? It wasn't only her looks. A child in a woman's body. What a magnificent combination!

Hi, I said.

Hi, she replied. She smiled. She was obviously pleased to see me. We were old friends and, perhaps, even more. The relationship was so full of promise, so vibrant, so surprising and yet so familiar.

Can I get you something? I asked.

No. I'm fine, she said.

Excuse me. I'll be right back.

I placed my notebook on the table and made my way

A NOT-SO-NICE JEWISH BOY FACES WORLD WAR II

to the food counter. I wasn't really hungry. I settled for the clam chowder, tea and trifle. I was anxious to get back to her, to sit beside her, to be close to her.

How was your chemistry class? she asked as I placed my tray on the table and sat down beside her. She actually remembered that I had my chemistry class this morning. She's been thinking about me.

Chemistry is, obviously, not my metier, said I. *I don't know why I signed up for it.*

You don't have to attend the class if you don't want to, do you?

I thought maybe something might rub off, I said. *I might be writing a novel or a play one day with a chemist as one of the characters. One never knows, does one? Did you have any classes this morning?*

No.

She came here just to be with me! But the joy was short-lived. This wasn't Clara. This was not the sort of girl you went to go to bed with. This was the sort of girl you made a commitment to. But I'd made a commitment already. As far as I knew Ginny was still waiting for me. Or was she? I adored this child, this woman, this girl. And...who knows? Who knows what the future holds? Suppose I didn't go back to America? There was always that possibility. There's just the here, there is just the now. But I had to be very careful. I had to see to it that we enjoyed each others company, and that that would probably be it. I didn't want to hurt her, yet I didn't want to lose her.

I'm writing this thesis on Baudelaire for my French class, she said. *I've got to spend some time in the library this afternoon.*

That's what I should have taken instead of chemistry, I said. *I should have taken French. Why don't we go over to*

the library and I'll do some reading while you do whatever you have to do?
Would you mind?
No.

After I finished my lunch we strolled over to the library. On the way, I found out that she had two brothers. The older brother was a doctor. The younger one was a medical student.

At the library she found some French reference books on Baudelaire and I found a biography of Byron. It was amazing how much pleasure there was in sitting opposite her and just reading. Every once in a while we would look up from our respective books and smile at one another.

After we finished at the library we took a stroll around the campus. We returned to the cafeteria for tea. I knew I'd be seeing her next week in our English literature class, and I decided not to make a definite date. I had to step carefully. A kiss, of course, was a no no. We shook hands when we parted. Her hand seemed so fragile in mine, so delicate. I wanted to hold onto it, to protect it, to cherish it.

******

Saturday evening, on my way to the movie theatre, I stopped at a Chemists (a drugstore, for the unsophisticated) and picked up a package of prophylactics. I arrived at the theatre fifteen minutes early and there was Clara, in front of the theatre waiting for me. She looked tense.

I hope I didn't keep you waiting, I said.
No. I got here early. The next show starts at eight forty five.
I should have checked the schedule, I said. *I'm sorry.*
That's all right, she said.

A NOT-SO-NICE JEWISH BOY FACES WORLD WAR II

You have to leave at ten thirty, I said. *The movie might not be over by then. Do you mind coming in in the middle?*
I don't mind, if you don't.
Next time I'll check the schedule.
She smiled. I bought the tickets. The movie theatre was a large one with a balcony.
Shall we sit in the balcony? I asked.
All right.
We made our way to the rear of the balcony. It was nice and dark and there weren't that many people there. As we took our seats my hand found its way around her shoulder, and I snuggled up close to her.
Is this all right? I said, meaning the seat, of course.
Yes. It's fine.
Did you want any candy?, I asked.
No. I'm all right.
She was so vulnerable, so easy. I had to be careful not to make any promises I couldn't keep. I leaned over and kissed her on the lips. She responded timidly. I placed my free hand on her knee, and waited. She made no objection. I slipped my hand under her dress and began to move up her thigh. She very gently stopped me. I removed my hand. I turned my attention to the screen.
The film was "Gaslight" with Ingrid Bergman, one of my favorite actresses, and Charles Boyer, a romantic star whom I admired; the mysterious, dangerous gangster, Pepe LeMoko, in "Algiers" who seduces the unbelievably beautiful heiress, Hedy Lamarr. Here, apparently, Boyer was the villain. He was in the process of driving Ingrid Bergman mad, and we weren't quite sure why, at least at this point in the film. I'd seen the stage play on which the film was based, and I remembered that Charles Boyer was trying to find the jewels that were hidden somewhere in the house. The jewels

belonged to Ingrid's aunt, whom Boyer had murdered some time ago, unbeknownst, of course, to Ingrid.

I watched the film for a while, then I leaned over and kissed Clara again, this time on the neck. She shuddered. I nibbled gently on her ear. She giggled softly and squirmed and leaned closer to me. The danger and suspense in the movie seemed to be working in my favor.

I saw the play, I whispered.

Oh, don't tell me.

I leaned over and kissed her on the neck. This time my hand found its way to her breast. She almost gasped.

I wish we could find a place, I said.

She sighed. I was beginning to get aroused, and frustrated. I removed my arm from around her shoulder. No use torturing myself.

Are you all right? she asked.

Yes, I'm fine. It would be nice if we could find a place.

Yes, she said. *I know.*

The picture came to an end with the villainous Charles Boyer on his way to prison and Ingrid triumphant. We were even led to believe that Ingrid might find love with the stalwart Joseph Cotten, the police inspector who rescued her.

When the lights came on in the theatre I turned to Clara. *Would you like some candy?* I asked. *How about some chocolates?*

All right.

I climbed over her, making sure my knees rubbed against hers, and went down to the lobby where I bought two chocolate bars.

I hope this is all right, I said as I handed her one.

This is fine.

Are you enjoying the picture?, I asked.

A NOT-SO-NICE JEWISH BOY FACES WORLD WAR II

Oh, yes. It's frightening though. But the acting is very good, don't you think?

Oh, yes, I said. *That's the first time I've seen Charles Boyer play a villain.*

He's very good.

I saw the play on Broadway, I said, trying not to sound too pompous.. *It was called "Angel Street" then.*

With Charles Boyer?

No. That was Vincent Price.

Oh, he's very good too.

We ate our chocolate bars. The coming attractions came on and then the newsreel and then "Gaslight" started again. I placed my arm around Clara, and this time she snuggled up to me and remained there.

Shall we go? I asked when the film reached the part we'd already seen.

All right, said Clara.

In the street I looked at my watch. It was nine thirty.

Would you like some tea? I asked.

I'd love some.

We found a restaurant nearby that was still open. The lady in charge came up to greet us.

We'd like some tea, I said. *Is that all right?*

Yes, of course.

The lady led us to a table in the rear of the restaurant.

The waitress will be with you shortly, said the lady and left.

Thank you, I said. I held the chair for Clara as she took a seat at the table.

Thank you, said Clara.

I sat opposite her. *Did you enjoy the picture?* I asked.

Oh, yes. Did you?

Oh, yes, I said.

BETWEEN THE DEVIL & THE DEEP BLUE SEA

It was rather frightening though.

A young waitress came up to the table holding a pad, ready to take our order.

We'd like some tea, I said.

Would you care for some sandwiches? Scones?

I looked at Clara. *Would you care for some sandwiches?*

I don't think so? Would you?

What are scones?, I asked.

They're little cakes, said the waitress. *They're very good.*

Why don't we have some scones? I turned to Clara. *Would you like a scone?*

All right.

We'll have two scones.

Thank you, said the waitress and left.

The scones were served with butter and jam and were quite nice, crumbly and tasteful and not two sweet, and the tea, again, was flavorful and not like tea at all. I told Clara about my classes and the dramatic club. I told her about my plans to visit London one week-end.

Have you been to London? I asked.

Oh, yes.

Perhaps we can go together some time, I suggested.

That might be nice, said Clara. *I'd have to get my mother's permission, of course.*

Do you think she'd have any objection?

I'll mention it to her.

It might be nice, I said, trying to sound rather casual.

After we finished our tea and scones I paid the check.

I walked with Clara to the bus stop, and waited there with her.

A NOT-SO-NICE JEWISH BOY FACES WORLD WAR II

Will you be coming to the dance on Wednesday? she asked.
Is there a dance on Wednesday?, I asked.
There's a dance every week, said Clara.
Will you be there?
I'm usually there, said Clara, *unless something comes up.*
I couldn't decide whether to meet her at the dance or whether to make a date for the movies next Saturday.
I'm not sure whether I can make it or not. Are you free next Saturday evening?, I asked.
Yes.
Why don't we leave it this way, I suggested, *if I don't see you at the dance, can we meet at the movies? The same time?*
All right, said Clara. *There's my bus.*
Good-night, I said, and I kissed her.
Good-night.
Don't forget to ask your mother about London, I called.
I won't, replied Clara.
She got on the bus and waved to me as the bus rode off, and I waved back. I walked back to the house, the smell of her hair in my nose. My body ached for the feel of her.

CHAPTER THIRTY THREE

CHOICES, CHOICES

When I got back to the house I found it dark, except for a night light in the vestibule. On the small table at the foot of the stairs I noticed two envelopes. Both letters were for me, from Ginny.

I walked into the living room, turned on a lamp and read them. There was news about her classes at Hedgerow Theatre School, about the scenes she was working on for class...a scene from George Bernard Shaw's "Candida" and a scene from Eugene O'Neill's "Beyond The Horizon." She had a job as a social worker and, between the two, her job and the school, she was very busy. And this was in addition to the small role she had in a production at the theatre. The weekends found her exhausted. Both letters ended with "look forward to hearing from you. I hope you're all right."

It was almost three weeks since I'd written to her. Had I decided not to honor my commitment to her, or was it that I didn't want to face the future?

I was in my glory now. There were actually two young ladies and they were both, apparently, smitten with me. I was taking voice lessons from a retired concert singer. I was looking forward to week-ends in London, to say nothing of an affair of the flesh, I mean actually making love to a real live female who wanted me as much as I wanted her.

I was being cruel. I knew that. I knew that Ginny was waiting for my letters, anxiously waiting for them. She'd been waiting for me for almost three years now, and my letters were the only assurance she had that I would return.

I put the letters in my jacket pocket and walked up the stairs into the room. Steve was fast asleep. I used the bathroom, undressed, got into bed and I lay there thinking...thinking about Ginny, about the time we'd spent

A NOT-SO-NICE JEWISH BOY FACES WORLD WAR II

rehearsing. How in tune we were. How close we'd gotten rehearsing that scene from "Private Lives," to say nothing of the scenes from "Medea" and Maxwell Anderson's "Elizabeth The Queen." How we'd supported one another on stage, facing an audience of peers just waiting to find fault.

We were a team. There was no doubt about that. And oh, how sad she looked when I'd said good-bye and left Ohio State for home, left to wait for the call from my draft board. We were simpatico, there was no doubt about that. And the fact that she was Jewish didn't hurt. That didn't hurt at all.

I thought about Clara and this physical thing that existed between us. I was drawn so strongly to her, and she to me. That mutual attraction just had to come to fruition, it just had to. Of course, the relationship was purely physical. Her education and her intellectual interests were decidedly limited. There was no meeting of the minds, there was no common interest, except perhaps for the movies.

And then there was Jean, darling Jean, the child, the woman who, at this very moment, was closest to my heart. Was there a future for Jean and me? Or was I some sort of a monster, leading these women on? I didn't care. Wherever my instincts led, I would follow. I needed this...love...or whatever it was. And if I was a monster, so be it. I decided not to answer Ginny's letters.

******

The next day, in English Literature, the lecture was on Byron, that handsome, dashing poet. that romantic lady-killer. According to one of his lovers, Lady Caroline Lamb, Byron was "mad, bad and dangerous to know." Despite the fact that she was married, Lady Caroline fell madly in love with the poet. In one of her love letters she enclosed a pubic hair,

CHOICES, CHOICES

asking him to send her one of his but "not to cut too close" since she, herself, had drawn blood while procuring the memento she sent to him. Disguised as a boy, Lady Caroline invaded the poet's apartments and wrote in one of his books, "Remember me." He wrote back a now famous limerick:
"Remember thee: remember thee!...
Thy husband too shall think of thee,
By neither shalt thou be forgot.
Thou false to him, thou fiend to me!"
She made a notorious attempt at a public suicide, probably just for show, causing a scandal to end all scandals, and that was in a London accustomed to scandalous behavior. How painful all this must have been for the participants, I thought, but, from an impersonal point of view, how amusing and, above all, how absolutely fascinating.

After class Jean and I adjourned to the cafeteria for lunch. We were joined briefly by Jean's friend, Helen, and her boyfriend, Ralph. Ralph turned out to be a charming, sophisticated man, somewhat older than Helen. He was a composer. The two of them left to attend a concert where one of Ralph's songs was being performed.

What did you think of him? Jean asked, after they'd left.
He seems to be quite nice, I said. *Don't you like him?*
Oh, he's nice enough, I guess.
The conversation turned to Byron and his affair with Lady Caroline.
Who's side are you on? I asked.
Oh, Byron's, of course. He was naive and foolish, and a victim of his own fame.
Do you think so?, I asked.
Don't you?
I don't know, I said. *He's certainly intriguing, isn't he? I wonder how much his lameness had to do with it.*

A NOT-SO-NICE JEWISH BOY FACES WORLD WAR II

A great deal, I should think.

What I find particularly intriguing, I said, *is the fact that he was a misogynist, and yet he continued to get involved with all these women. It reminds me of that song.*

What song is that?

"You Always Hurt The One You Love."

It's inevitable, I suppose, said Jean.

Why do you say that?

I don't know, said Jean. She looked sad and pensive.

I've got to go to my voice lesson, I said. *Would you like to come along?*

May I? Do you think it would be all right?

I don't think she'd mind, I said. *Besides, I'd like to know what you think of my voice.*

Maybe you'd better get her permission first, said Jean. *She might not want me there.*

Maybe you're right, I replied. *Maybe I'd better ask her first.*

******

On the way to my lesson I stopped off at a nearby music store and picked up a copy of a song I'd heard on the radio. Originally it was a French song, but the version I heard was in English. It was called "Symphony." Actually it wasn't the song itself that appealed to me, as much as the voice of the singer. It was deep and resonant and seductive. If only I could sound like that.

Mrs. Berganza greeted me warmly and sat me down for the preliminary hot chocolate. While we consumed our hot chocolate I talked about my classes and the movie I'd seen. I didn't see any point in mentioning that I'd seen it with Clara.

CHOICES, CHOICES

The lesson began with the scales and then moved on to the vocal exercises, which I dutifully performed.

I was impatient to get on to the song. When I asked what category my voice belonged to I was told I was a light baritone, possibly a tenor. It all depended on how it developed. I produced the song I'd brought. Mrs Berganza played it for me once and then I sang it through.

It suits your voice, she said.

I took that as a compliment.

My voice is rather weak, isn't it? I asked.

It will grow stronger, said Mrs. Berganza, *but we mustn't rush things.*

I guess Rome wasn't built in a day.

Mrs. Berganza smiled. *You must learn to be patient. The vocal chords are this little bit of cartilage. This fragile instrument, however, can produce the most magnificent sounds. But this instrument can be easily damaged if pushed too hard, too fast. Actually I have another song I thought you might like to work on.*

She produced the sheet music for a song called "We'll Gather Lilacs In The Spring." *It was written by one of our most popular West End stars,* she said, *Ivor Novello. He's quite the matinee idol. I think this is one of his prettiest efforts.*

Mrs Berganza played and sang "We'll Gather Lilacs In The Spring." She sang it softly in a rather slightly worn contralto. The voice must have been lovely once. It still had a velvety sheen. I sang it through with her once, and then sang it by myself.

It's very pretty, I said. *I like it better than the one I brought. Can I work on them both?*

I don't see why not.

A NOT-SO-NICE JEWISH BOY FACES WORLD WAR II

Are there any exercises you want me to work on by myself?, I asked.

At this point, no.

Before I left I asked if I could bring a friend to my next lesson. *She's a fellow student,* I added. *She'll sit quietly, I promise.*

If you like.

For some reason or other, I left the lesson gnawed by doubts. Did I have the patience to pursue a singing career? Did I have the talent? I certainly wasn't considering opera or the concert stage. Or was I? It would probably be an adjunct to my acting, musical comedy probably. But even so, it would take a lot of patience and time...and money. Where was that to come from? It was the question of money that put an end to my thought of a career as a concert pianist. The future was a frightening challenge. There were so many things to think about, so many choices to make.

CHAPTER THIRTY FOUR

LIFE IS VERY COMPLICATED

The next day in my philosophy class I was able to change my seat and sit across from Jean. The two of us exchanged secret smiles at various times during the lecture. The professor was really pompous.

At lunch I told Jean that I'd gotten permission for her to sit in on my next voice lesson. *I'm going to pick up my pictures now,* I said. *Would you care to come along?*

Yes. I'd love to. Oh dear, I've got my French class.

I'll bring the proofs along tomorrow and you can help me choose.

All right.

I was wondering, I said, *do you think I might be allowed to sit in on your French class?*

I don't see why not, said Jean. *Are you planning to get credit for these courses?*

I hadn't thought about it. There is the GI Bill, but I'm not sure I want to go back to college. I've lost so much time as it is. The war has taken three years out of my life. I've got so much to catch up on. I'll speak to my counsellor and see what he has to say about it. Your French class, I mean.

I've got to go, said Jean.

See you for lunch? I asked.

All right, she said. And she left.

******

When I arrived at the photography shop there was a sign on the door, "Out To Lunch." In order to kill some time I walked over to the movie theatre. The movie scheduled for Saturday was, "In Which We Serve," a war film in which Noel Coward played a sea captain. I'd seen the film, which I'd enjoyed, but it was certainly not the kind of movie that would promote romance. I decided that this coming week-end I would go to London. That meant that this evening I'd better attend the dance to see Clara.

When I returned to the photography shop I found Hilary as busy as ever. There were no customers around and I wondered when and where her business came from. There were four proofs to choose from. I wasn't quite sure how I felt about them. They were not as flattering as I'd hoped they'd be. They were sort of "artsy" looking, just a little too ethereal. Actually I looked better in the picture I'd had taken in Liege by a very ordinary photographer.

Of the four proofs, the most interesting ones were the two profiles. One of them, in particular, had a mythic quality about it, though I wasn't too happy about the bridge on my nose. I didn't look particularly Semitic, I thought. If I did that might limit me in so far as the roles I might be cast in. Actually I looked rather aristocratic. I was curious to see what Jean would say about them. Hilary seemed quite enthusiastic about her work. I tried not to show my disappointment. I left with the proofs, telling Hilary that I'd like some help in choosing which ones to print.

******

That evening I attended the dance at the USO with Steve. I sighted Clara as soon as I came through the doorway. She was serving the punch, and it was obvious that she had her eye on the door. Her face lit up when she sighted me. I brought Steve over and introduced him to her. She poured us each a glass of punch. Steve accepted the punch and then made a point of excusing himself.

LIFE IS VERY COMPLICATED

Have you spoken to your mother about London? I asked.

Not yet, said Clara. She must have noticed the disappointment in my face and added quickly, *I will this weekend. She's been under the weather of late, and I wanted to wait until she was in a good mood.*

Do you think there'll be any problem?

I don't think so, said Clara. *But I will need her permission.*

Oh, I understand, I said. *Would you like to dance?*

Just a minute.

Clara approached one of the older women and asked her to take over the punch bowl, and she joined me on the floor. How nicely our bodies seemed to fit together. She clung to me as we moved about the floor. We danced one dance after another, and then stepped out into the alleyway to get some air.

Are you enjoying your courses at the university? she asked.

One of them, I said. *English Literature. The Romantic Poets. Have you ever read any of Byron?*

Oh, yes. We studied Byron. Actually my favorite poet is Edgar Allen Poe. He's American. He had a very sad life. Clara began to grow more interesting. *I think "The Bells" is very dramatic, don't you?* she asked.

Why, yes. Yes, it is.

We returned to the dance floor. Before we left for Clara's bus, I sought out Steve and arranged to walk back to the house with him.

I'm planning to go to London this weekend, I said to Clara as we stood waiting for the bus. *I thought I'd better go while I still have the chance. One never knows.*

Yes, of course.

A NOT-SO-NICE JEWISH BOY FACES WORLD WAR II

Can we get together the following Saturday? I asked.
All right.
Same time? Same Place?
All right.
As the bus came in sight I kissed her.
I enjoyed the evening. Thank you, she said as she got on the bus. We waved to each other through the window as the bus pulled away.

On the way back to the house I asked Steve what he thought of Clara.

She seems to be very nice, Steve replied.
Do you think she's pretty?
Sort of.
Well, she's not a beauty, I said defensively, *but she's very sweet.*
I'm sure she is.

******

I didn't bother attending the chemistry class the next day. I slept late, and then finished reading "Cakes And Ale." On the way to the cafeteria to meet Jean for lunch, I marveled again at the charm of the writing, the way it flowed, the mood that it set. I wondered if Maugham did a lot of polishing, a lot of rewriting.

In the cafeteria I took out the proofs, which I'd brought along, and showed them to Jean. *What do you think?* I asked.

I like that one, the profile. It has a classic quality to it, she said.

I like that one, too, I said, with not too much enthusiasm. I decided not to bring up the subject of the bridge on my nose.

Might I have a copy? she asked.

LIFE IS VERY COMPLICATED

If you like.
Yes, I would.
On one condition, I said. *You give me a picture of yourself.*
I'm not sure I have one that I like.
Let me be the judge, I said.

She accidentally dropped one of the proofs on the floor. She bent down hastily to pick it up. As she leaned over the hair fell away from the back of her neck. I was surprised to notice that the back of her neck was dirty. I couldn't help but smile. She was a naughty girl. She didn't wash the back of her neck and, somehow, it made her more endearing. I could picture myself washing it tenderly.

I'm sorry, she said as she handed me the proof.
That's all right, I said.
Did I say something funny?
No.
I know I said something funny, said Jean, *or did something. What did I do?*
Nothing, I said. *I swear. I was thinking of something else. I was thinking of Hilary, the photographer. She really is odd. She's like a character in a novel. As a matter of fact she reminds me a little of Margaret Rutherford.*
Oh, dear! I should like to meet her.
If you like we can return the proofs after class and you'll get a chance to meet her.
All right, said Jean.

The subject for the lecture in the literature class was the poet Shelley. Again I thought that the poet's life, like Byron's, was more interesting than his poetry, which I found rather precious. To my surprise I learned that Shelley, like Byron, was quite the rebel, and had all sorts of progressive ideas about Society.

A NOT-SO-NICE JEWISH BOY FACES WORLD WAR II

The professor spoke about the summer Shelley, his wife and her stepsister, Claire Clairmont, who was also Byron's mistress, spent with Byron at his villa near Lake Geneva in Switzerland. That summer they sat around telling ghost stories, and Mary Shelley wrote "Frankenstein." And then there was Shelley's death by drowning during a storm, and the macabre funeral afterwards. How much more colorful and fascinating these figures from the past were, compared to present day celebrities. On the way to the photography shop we discussed Byron and Shelley.

I much prefer Byron, said Jean.

Oh, yes, I said, marveling how similar our tastes were. *I wonder if that villa Byron rented is still standing.*

Have you read "Frankenstein?"

No. Have you?

Yes, said Jean. *It's interesting, but I much prefer "Dracula."*

Really? I must read it, I said.

It was written by Bram Stoker, who was Henry Irving's business manager.

Was he really? I must read it.

At the photography shop I introduced Jean to Hilary.

I was just about to sit down to a spot of tea, said Hilary. *Would you care to join me?*

I looked at Jean.

Jean nodded and said, *Thank you.*

We adjourned to Hilary's flat behind the shop.

The room we sat in served, apparently, as a dining room, living room, reading room and a storage room for various props. There were papers and magazines scattered about, plus various artifacts such as a bust of Janus, the Roman god with two faces and a bust of Shakespeare, in

LIFE IS VERY COMPLICATED

addition to vases and sconces and bits of plaster with Egyptian hieroglyphics.

Hilary cleared off two chairs that were piled with old newspapers, tossing the papers onto another pile of papers. She brought out the tea pot, and cups and saucers, which looked as if they'd seen better days. The tea, however, was fine. There were also little biscuits which had an interesting lemony flavor. Hilary regaled us with tales of the celebrities that she'd photographed in her London shop. She seemed to enjoy the awe her stories inspired.

Before we left I ordered four copies of the profile that both Jean and I favored, and one copy of the full face picture.

I'm looking forward to my trip to London, I said as I walked Jean home. *It'll be my first, except for passing through it briefly.*

Are you planning to take in some theatre?

As much as I can. I've made a list, I said. *I suppose you've been to London a number of times.*

Not really. We have some relatives nearby whom we visit occasionally.

Do you have any suggestions, I asked, *about what I should take in?*

There's the Tower, of course, and Westminster Abbey.

Yes.

Would you care to come in? Jean asked as we approached her house. *My parents would like to meet you.*

I can't stay long. Dinner is served at six.

We entered the living room. It was a large, pleasant room, furnished in good taste, comfortable and homey.

Mother? Jean called. There was no answer. *No one's home apparently.*

Actually, I was sort of relieved. I did not relish being inspected by her parents. *I'd better be going,* I said.

479

A NOT-SO-NICE JEWISH BOY FACES WORLD WAR II

The community theatre is giving a production of "The Misanthrope" next week. Are you interested? she said.

Moliere? He's my favorite playwright, I replied. *They did some scenes from "The Imaginary Invalid" in my drama class back at Ohio State, and I was blown away. Have you read any of his plays? I couldn't believe it. I mean, they were written at about the same time as Shakespeare and they sound as if they'd been written yesterday. They have this breezy, modern quality. Would you like to go?*

I'd love to, said Jean.

It's a date. Don't forget next Wednesday, I said. *You're going to accompany me to my voice lesson.*

I won't forget.

See you next week, I said.

I wanted to kiss her, but I restrained myself, even though I knew the kiss would be welcome. It wouldn't be fair. But then again, who knows? Suppose I decide not to go back? Suppose I decide to stay right here? Wouldn't it be lovely to come home to her in the evening? Then I thought about Ginny, waiting for me back in Philadelphia, waiting and wondering why the letters had stopped. I dismissed the picture of domestic bliss with Jean...for the moment.

It insisted, however, on coming back from time to time. How splendid that would be!

CHAPTER THIRTY FIVE

LONDON!

I had no classes on Friday. Today was the day I would check out London. I wanted to take the first trip on my own. I took a nine o'clock train. At least this time I had the opportunity to view the English countryside in the daylight. The weather was perfect. The sky was a lovely blue with occasional white clouds drifting by.

Looking eagerly out the window as the train sped towards London, I was amazed at the number of meadows and farms there were. Sheep wandering about. Cows grazing. Is England an agricultural country, I wondered.

I'd brought along a book to read. But why read when there were all these new, exciting things to see? Even more exciting things shortly to come. I was actually going to visit London, all by myself. I couldn't believe it. London, the cultural capitol of the world! The London of Queen Elizabeth (the first) and Shakespeare and Byron. The London of Dickens and Sheridan and Henry Irving and Noel Coward and Somerset Maugham.

On the top of my list was the Laurence Olivier tour de force, the double bill consisting of the Greek tragedy, "Oedipus" and the Restoration farce, "The Critic." There was also Ralph Richardson's Falstaff in "Henry IV" parts one and two. And, of course, there was "Private Lives."

As soon as the train pulled into the station I searched out a news stand and picked up a publication that listed all the cultural events. The Old Vic, the theatre company that was producing the first two productions, was ensconced in the New Theatre on a street quaintly called St. Martins Lane.

I hurried out of the station. As I stepped off the curb to cross the street I heard someone cursing. I looked up to find a bus bearing down on me. The bus driver was leaning out the

A NOT-SO-NICE JEWISH BOY FACES WORLD WAR II

window shouting, *YOU DAMN FOOL!* The man was actually shouting at me.

I jumped back, shaken. I stood on the sidewalk trying to catch my breath and collect myself. Good God! I'd almost been run down. That would have been a fine start for the most exciting adventure of my life, to survive the war only to be run down by a London bus. I'd forgotten that the traffic in England bore to the left instead of to the right. What a contrary way of doing things!

I continued on my way still quite shaken, and at a much slower pace. For the rest of the week-end I looked carefully up and down the street before stepping off the curb. To be on the safe side I'd wait until someone started out ahead of me. And, even then, while crossing the street, I looked anxiously about.

I was relieved to find the Underground very easy to get around in. The different lines and stations were marked very clearly, unlike the subways in New York.

When I reached St. Martins Lane and found the New Theatre, I couldn't believe my luck. I was able to get a ticket for that evening's performance of the Olivier double bill. The following day Shakespeare's "Henry IV" parts one and two were being performed, part one at the matinee and part two in the evening. Both performances were sold out. I was encouraged to try for returns just before curtain.

Next I sought out "Private Lives." I was able to get a ticket for Saturday evening.

What next? What next? A tour of the city on a bus. That way I could take it all in.

I boarded a tour bus. I gazed hungrily out the window as the bus wound its way slowly through the streets of the legendary metropolis. I just couldn't believe I was really there, actually seeing these historic landmarks in person. My God,

LONDON!

there were the Houses of Parliament, there was the Thames River, there was the British Museum, there was St. Paul's Cathedral, there was Buckingham Palace and, miracle of miracles, I was witnessing the changing of the guard, and there was the Tower of London and Westminster Abbey.

I stepped off the bus quite dizzy. What next? What next?

Westminster Abbey!

I was absolutely beside myself. Maybe I ought to kneel or cross myself or something. I was entering Westminster Abbey! I wandered into the historic building in a daze. There were the tombs of English kings. There was the tomb of Chaucer, of Darwin, of Isaac Newton. I found the poet's corner. There was a tribute to Shakespeare. But where was Byron? Where was Shelley? And where was Keats, the greatest of them all? I asked an attendant. I couldn't believe it. None of the three were honored there. Talk about injustice! I left the Abbey in a fury. None of the poets honored were on a par with those three immortals. Byron, of course, had led a scandalous life. Shelley as well. Apparently, in England, one is not judged on one's talent alone.

I found a Chinese restaurant near St. Martins Lane and ate a hasty dinner. I hadn't realized how hungry I was. Of course, I was hungry. I'd forgotten to eat lunch.

I headed for the New Theatre agog with anticipation. I was actually going to see Laurence Olivier on stage, in person in a landmark production.

As I was ushered to my seat I held out my hand for a program. I was astonished to find that one actually had to pay for a program! I bought one resentfully. The usher asked me if I would care to order tea. Apparently tea could be ordered ahead of time, and be served in one's seat. Now that is civilized! It was a luxury I decided I couldn't afford.

A NOT-SO-NICE JEWISH BOY FACES WORLD WAR II

My seat was an excellent one. It was slightly to the side, about halfway down. I read the program avidly, devouring its contents. As the houselights came down, I kept marveling at my luck. To see Laurence Olivier in person! The star of "Wuthering Heights" and "Rebecca." The husband of the lovely Vivien Leigh, the star of "Gone With The Wind." Brilliant actor! Great lover! What would he be like on stage? I had butterflies in my stomach. It was as if I, myself, was about to appear on that stage.

The curtain rose on a magnificent set, a building center stage, with great double doors. A procession of priests enter. The double doors open...and there he is, the great Olivier. He enters and addresses the crowd. He does, indeed, look like a Greek god. He speaks marvelously. Yet...yet somehow, as the performance continues... Maybe I was expecting too much. I waited for that, now legendary, animal scream as Oedipus, offstage, puts out his eyes when he discovers he's married to his own mother. The harrowing cry echoes through the theatre, and yet... Maybe because I was prepared for it. That must be it. The curtain comes down. It was a marvelous performance in a marvelous production, and yet...and yet...

I sat through the intermission waiting impatiently for this Greek god to transform himself into a foppish critic. The farce begins, and the transformation is miraculous. Olivier prances and whirls about. He performs with breath-taking atheleticism. He leaps about. He's hoisted into the air on a piece of scenery, supposedly by accident. It's really an astonishing performance. And yet...and yet...the character is almost embarrassingly feminine. And it's all...tricks. The curtain comes down to wild applause.

It was wonderful, yes. Technically the dual performance was dazzling. It was unique. It would take its place in theatre history. But somehow... Wasn't it rather hollow? A

LONDON!

performance distinguished primarily for its pyrotechnics. All surface and glitter, and nothing underneath. I was loath to admit it. It was sacrilege, but I was disappointed. What would his Hotspur be like, I wondered. I had to see it! I just had to see it.

******

I was too keyed up to head for the USO where I planned to spend the night. I walked about leisurely inhaling the night air. What a perfect night! I found my way to Picadilly Circus, the square in the heart of London. There were soldiers milling about. I wondered why. What was the attraction? Oddly enough, they seemed to be eyeing one another.

And then I realized. How naive! I thought back to my experience at the movie theatre in Fort Bragg when that unknown fellow soldier had serviced me so graciously, so thoughtfully.

Good evening.

I was jolted from my reverie.

I turned to find an English army sergeant I took to be in his early thirties, greeting me with a friendly smile. The man was pleasant looking and seemed to be quite cultured.

Good evening, I said.

I'm staying at the "Y" not far from here, said the sergeant.

All right, I said.

My name's Harry, said the English sergeant as we walked along.

Norman.

We shook hands and continued in silence.

I remembered the first time I'd discovered the

A NOT-SO-NICE JEWISH BOY FACES WORLD WAR II

wonderful world of masturbation, what a marvelous discovery, what a relief it was. And, though I gathered sharing this wonderful ritual was not exactly acceptable, I decided back at Ohio state that, if the occasion arose (pun intended) I would definitely follow through.

In the room at the "Y" the British sergeant and I stripped and got into bed, which was a first for me. I was disturbed to find that the sergeant wanted me to turn my back to him and well... This was not what I had anticipated, and I discouraged this more invasive act. The sergeant seemed to be disappointed. However, we did manage to satisfy one another with a less intrusive activity.

You're welcome to spend the night, said the sergeant as we lay smoking a cigarette afterwards.

Okay, I said, since I didn't feel like wandering about London at that hour of the night.

In the morning there was another session. Afterwards the sergeant invited me to have breakfast in the restaurant downstairs. The waitress came over to take our orders. I found myself being particularly charming to the young lady. Was it out of a sense of guilt, I wondered. Was I trying to prove that I was still virile, and that I was interested in the female of the species as well? I smiled at my own confusion. I felt uneasy.

Why? Was it because of what I did, or because what others would think about what I did?

After breakfast the sergeant and I parted, wishing each other luck.

******

I headed for St. Martins Lane and the New Theatre. I hoped and prayed I could get a return ticket for "Henry IV" part one. I went to the box office and was told that they were

LONDON!

still sold out. *There might be cancellations,* I was told, if I cared to wait.

As I stepped away from the box office I was approached by a well dressed, middle aged man who seemed to be part of a group waiting to be admitted to the theatre.

Hi there, Yank, said the stranger. *Are you looking for a ticket to this afternoon's performance?*

Why, yes, I said.

Here you are, said the man and handed me a ticket.

How much? I asked.

That's all right, said the man. *Enjoy it.*

The man walked away and rejoined his group. The army uniform did come in handy at times.

The seat was in the rear of the mezzanine, and when the performance began the seat turned out to be fine.

The production was magnificent; the sets so evocative, the lighting, the costumes. You were actually transported to old London. And above all, the acting. Joyce Redman as Doll Tearsheet. And Margaret Leighton so lovely as Lady Hotspur. And Ralph Richardson's Falstaff! No one could ever play it better. There was that wonderful speech about "honor," delivered center stage, straight front, with such great panache. You knew you were seeing something special, something memorable.

This is THEATRE!

And then there was Olivier's Hotspur. It was a revelation! The dash, the charisma, the passion...and with it all the respect for the language, the magnificent rhythm that seemed to come from the very soul of the actor. Olivier and the character were one, and what a magnificent one! And that death scene! That fall! In full armor, down the stairs. How did he do it? The doubt left by my first encounter with that great actor was wiped away. That's the kind of actor I want to be, I thought.....if I'm going to be an actor, that is.

As I left the theatre I ran across the man who'd given me the ticket. *Did you enjoy it?* the man asked.

Oh, yes! I said. I'm sure that my awe must have been written across my face.

The man smiled. *That's good,* he said and rejoined his group.

******

There was just enough time for dinner at an Italian restaurant near the theatre where "Private Lives" was being performed. In the theatre I waited eagerly for the curtain to rise. How I looked forward to hear the now familiar lines again! I knew nothing about the actors, Kay Hammond and John Clements, who were husband and wife in real life but, according to the program, were major stars.

The curtain rose on the adjoining balconies of a hotel on the Riviera. The scene was just as I imagined it. Elegant. Romantic. There was an orchestra playing softly in the distance, light dance music. Sibyl, Elyot's second wife enters. They're on their honeymoon.

Sibyl: *Elli, Elli dear, do come out. It's so lovely.*

Then Elyot enters (originally Noel Coward, of course) and they speak about Amanda, Elyot's first wife. I knew Amanda would be entering soon on the adjacent balcony, enjoying (?) her second honeymoon. Oh, that witty yet poignant dialogue. I was no longer in the theatre. I was living the lives of these frivolous, endearing, delightful Noel Coward creations. Sibyl and Elyot go off. On the adjoining balcony Victor, Amanda's second husband enters.

Victor: *Mandy?*

LONDON!

Amanda: (Offstage) *What?*
Victor: *Come outside. The view is wonderful.*
Amanda (originally Gertrude Lawrence) enters and they discuss Elyot. Finally Elyot and Amanda are left alone on stage. They are unaware of each other's presence. I couldn't wait for them to come face to face, to fall in love all over again. Finally they discover each other. There's the witty repartee, the flippancy and underneath the heartache. How they loved one another, and how they fought to disguise that love, to ignore it. They banter, they fence and they finally, painfully, admit their true feelings and run off together deserting their current spouses. The curtain falls on Act One.

But not for me. I was still with Elyot and Amanda. Amanda now is Ginny. I remembered the look of love in her eyes as we rehearsed the scene coming up in the second act. I remembered sitting down at the piano in a dressing gown and playing Coward's song, "I'll See You Again," as Ginny sang along in a surprisingly lovely soprano. (Actually the song the script called for was "Some Day I'll Find You," but "I'll See You Again" was easier to play.) I reflected on the performances I'd just seen. Kay Hammond was delightful. John Clements was fine, a little stiff, I thought. I would have brought a little more humanity to it here and there.

As the curtain went up on the second act, I could feel Ginny right there beside me, watching the scene we had performed for the drama class. I was seeing this performance for the both of us. Ginny, dear Ginny. So vulnerable, so sensitive. How I wished she were actually here with me right now. How we would have enjoyed seeing this together, discussing the fine points of the performance. The curtain came down. The play was over. I applauded heartily. No, really, they'd done a fine job. Not, of course, as good as

A NOT-SO-NICE JEWISH BOY FACES WORLD WAR II

Ginny and me, but they were good. And that English accent came to them so naturally. I left the theatre in a cloud of glory. Life was still full of promise, beautiful and exciting.

Suddenly I realized how tired I was. If I planned to visit The Tower of London in the morning, I'd have to get up early. It might be a good idea to get to bed early. I located the USO and was able to get a room to myself.

I read a little of the collection of the two Henry James' stories I was carrying about. I'd finished the first one, "The Turn Of The Screw," a fascinating ghost story and was now into the second, "The Lesson Of The Master." As I read I kept thinking, this would make a great play. That night I dreamt of Ginny. I saw her looking sad and anxious. I felt properly guilty. I really must write to her.

******

In the morning, after breakfast, I joined the line waiting to get into the Tower. With a group of other tourists, I followed the guide. My eyes drank in the historic walls, while I listened eagerly to the guide describe the fascinating events that had taken place within this haunted structure. This was where the child king, Edward the fifth and his brother, Richard Plantagenet, were murdered in 1483. This was where the Duke of Clarence was drowned in a barrel of wine, and this was where Robert Devereux, Earl of Essex (that was Errol Flynn in the movie with Bette Davis as Queen Elizabeth) was held before he was executed. And there were the crown and the scepter and the royal jewels. I stepped out of the darkness into the daylight.

The sky was overcast, in keeping with the mood. And there was the Thames. I was dreaming all this, of course. I'd wake up any minute now in my bed in Newark, New Jersey

LONDON!

and sit down to breakfast in the kitchen and dream about how, one day, I would see the world.

I decided to take a later train, and walked leisurely about the city. There were still the remnants of the war, barbed wire and signs pointing the way to a bomb shelter, but this was still London.

I found my way to Hyde Park and stood listening to a man on a soap box ranting about some tax or other. I wandered about the park, ruminating on my impressions of this visit. There was something so civilized about the English. They seemed to appreciate so much more the finer things in life. Books and theatre and music.

As a matter of fact America seemed so gauche compared to Europe. No wonder Ernest Hemingway and F. Scott Fitzgerald and all of that "lost generation" preferred to live and work, to "find themselves" in Paris.

I didn't really want to go back to America, did I? I remembered that soldier who had remained in Germany after World War I, and married a German girl. No wonder! America was a land of business. The arts, culture was suspect; a frivolity, an indulgence. Making money, that was the important thing. The path I was about to embark on, the struggle to achieve recognition as a writer, would be so much more acceptable here. Artists in America were second rate citizens.

On the train back to Cardiff my mind was so full of thoughts and questions and impressions that I never bothered to open Henry James. I looked forward to sharing my experience with Jean and, of course, writing about it to Ginny.

I would have to write to Ginny about it.

CHAPTER THIRTY SIX

A MUSIC LESSON

I didn't get a chance to talk to Jean before the English literature class the day after my historic London visit. She entered the room just before the class began. I caught her eye and we waved to each other.

Keats, my favorite poet, was the subject of the lecture, and the professor read "Ode On a Grecian Urn." Why did this particular poem seem to speak to me so personally, I wondered.

"She cannot fade, though thou has not thy bliss,
For ever wilt thou love, and she be fair."

Was it because I wanted my time here in Cardiff to last forever? No real responsibilities. The freedom to enjoy the beauty of life.

"Beauty is truth, truth beauty, that is all
Ye know on earth, and all ye need to know."

At lunch Jean and I agreed that Keats was the greatest of them all. I related in detail my visit to London, omitting, of course, my encounter with the English sergeant. I spoke eloquently of my theatre experiences, the plays and the acting. Especially the acting. Jean seemed properly impressed with my pronouncements. How clever she was, I thought, to appreciate my observations, the nuances I perceived in the performances, the pluses and the minuses of my assessment.

After lunch we set out for my music lesson.

Now that Jean was going to hear me sing, I wasn't so sure it was a good idea. I might just make a fool of myself. She might see me for the fraud I really was, and never want to see me again.

All these goals I'd set for myself. What assurance was there that I'd ever achieve them? If I had any sense at all, I'd please my mother and become a teacher. And as far as Jean

A MUSIC LESSON

was concerned, she wasn't even Jewish, whereas Ginny was. Mother would have a heart attack. And what about Jean's family? I assumed she was Protestant, but I wasn't quite sure. Maybe she was Catholic. Whichever, that would certainly be a problem.

But if we really loved each other...

Mrs. Berganza greeted us at the door and ushered us into the living room. She sat us down and brought in hot chocolate for the both of us. I talked about my theatre experiences in London, and how much I enjoyed the trip. Mrs Berganza asked Jean about her courses, and then set her in a far corner of the room while we started on my lesson.

I tried not to be self conscious. Nonetheless, while I sang my scales and went through the obligatory exercises I tried to hear my voice through my friend's ears. There were times when I thought, I wasn't half bad. I began to glory in the sounds I was making.

Never louder than lovelier, said Mrs. Berganza.

I realized that I was forcing, and I pulled back. And then again there were times when I didn't sound too bad. Why couldn't I be a singer as well as an actor and a writer? When we finished with the scales and the exercises, I asked if I could concentrate on the Ivor Novello song. My teacher had no objection.

My heart began beating faster. I was on stage now. The audience, and there was an audience, was waiting to hear me sing. Never louder than lovelier, never louder than lovelier.

We'll father lilacs in the Spring again
And walk together down an English lane
Until our hearts have learned to sing again
When you are home once more.

The song had suddenly taken on more meaning. The words, the music came from my heart. Oh, God, oh God!

A NOT-SO-NICE JEWISH BOY FACES WORLD WAR II

Who was I thinking of? Was it Jean? Or was it Ginny? I couldn't love them both, much less marry them, and I certainly wasn't ready for marriage.

And in the evening by the firelight's glow
You'll hold me close and never let me go
Your eyes will tell me all I want to know
When you are home once more.

My eyes were welling up. I knew I'd sung well, just as I knew I might never sing that well again. How could I possibly duplicate that moment? I was vaguely aware of someone speaking. It was my teacher. What had she said? Was it a compliment?

Same time next week?
Yes.

She had said something before that. What was it?

It was nice meeting you, Jean, said Mrs. Berganza as she escorted us to the door.

Thank you, said Jean.

Had my teacher made a comment on my performance, because that was what it was, or hadn't she? I was certainly not going to ask her, nor did I intend to ask Jean. Why put her on the spot? And actually, I didn't want to know. I didn't even need any comments. I knew I'd sung well.

She's very charming, said Jean.
She's a retired concert singer, you know, I said.
Yes, you told me.
She must have had a lovely voice, I said.
Did she sing for you?
Just briefly, but you could tell. How old do you think she is?
I don't know. I'm not a very good judge of age.
Neither am I.

A MUSIC LESSON

Nothing was said about my voice, but Jean was impressed. I could tell.

I left Jean at the student lounge where she was supposed to meet her friend, Helen. On the way back to the house for dinner I thought back on my performance. I went over in my mind the phrases that I thought could be improved.

******

I had planned to spend the evening finishing the Henry James story, but Steve and I got to talking. As a matter of fact, Steve dropped a bombshell.

I've met this girl, he said. *She's in my mathematics class. Her name is Jessica. And well, I'm not going back to the States.*

You're going to stay here in Cardiff?

Either that, or we'll live in London, said Steve. *That's where she's from.*

You're going to marry her?

Eventually. That's the idea, for now, at any rate.

Are you sure?, I asked.

I think so.

That's quite a decision.

Yeah, I know, said Steve. *I don't know how my family's going to feel about it.*

Have you told them?

Not yet, said Steve.

Wow!

Yeah.

She must be something, I said.

She is to me. I don't know what she sees in me.

What do you mean? She's lucky to get you, said I.

Yeah.

A NOT-SO-NICE JEWISH BOY FACES WORLD WAR II

I turned off the light, but neither of us was ready to turn in.

Are you still going to be an accountant? I asked.

Oh, yes. So is Jessica.

Isn't that something!, I exclaimed.

Yeah. My father's going to be disappointed, said Steve. *He expects me to help out in the store. Keep his books and that sort of thing.*

Maybe you can take her back to the States with you, I suggested.

We talked about that. But I like it here.

Would she be willing to go?, I asked. *If you should decide to go back, I mean.*

I think she'd prefer to stay here. We'd better get some sleep, said Steve.

Yeah.

But I couldn't fall asleep. My head was in a whirl. I soon heard Steve's deep breathing. How in the world can anyone sleep, when all these momentous decisions are being made, I wondered.

CHAPTER THIRTY SEVEN

AN ACT OF BETRAYAL?

Steve's going to stay here in England, was the first thought that came to my mind when I awoke the next morning. If I should decide to stay, I'd have a friend here. That's certainly something to keep in mind.

On the way to our classes we met Matthew, whom we hadn't seen for quite some time. Matthew seemed delighted to see us. I had the feeling that he must be terribly lonely. For the first time he seemed very talkative. He was anxious to hear what we'd been up to. I mentioned that I'd been to London.

You've been to London? said Matthew. *I wish you had let me know. I would have come with you.*

It was a last minute decision, I said.

If you go again, let me know. I've been wanting to go to London.

Steve looked at me slyly and smiled. I said nothing. No way was I going spend a week-end with Matthew, though I did feel sorry for him.

What have you been up to? asked Steve.

Not very much. Except for my classes. There's so much reading to do, said Matthew. *I don't seem to have time for anything else.*

Would you want to take time off to go to London, if you're that busy? Steve asked.

I gave him a dirty look.

All work and no play..., said Matthew, surprisingly enough.

Makes Jack a dull boy, said Steve, making every effort to keep a straight face.

I turned away in order to suppress my laughter.

A NOT-SO-NICE JEWISH BOY FACES WORLD WAR II

Let's get together some time, said Matthew as the three of us separated to go to our respective classes.

Right, right, said Steve.

I said nothing.

After our philosophy class Jean and I walked over to the cafeteria together.

Helen's going to join us. Do you mind?

No, of course not, I said.

As a matter of fact, I liked Helen. She seemed sort of sophisticated. I wondered how old she was. She certainly seemed older and wiser than Jean and myself, or maybe she just gave that impression. We were finishing our meal when Helen appeared.

Sorry, I'm late, she said as she plopped into a chair. *I just came from the lounge. Ralph was going over his new song. He's going to give a little concert in a few minutes. You must come.*

Where is it? asked Jean.

In the lounge.

Would you like to come? Jean asked.

I'd love to hear his song, I said.

C'mon, let's go then, said Helen. *They're going to start any minute.*

Jean and I got up and the three of us started for the lounge.

Who's they? I asked.

A friend of Ralph's, said Jean, *Victor. He's a singer. He has a beautiful voice.*

When we arrived in the lounge, Ralph was seated at the grand piano. A nice looking man, about Ralph's age, was standing beside him. This, apparently, was Victor. They could have been brothers.

There was a small group gathered around the piano.

AN ACT OF BETRAYAL?

Helen waved to Ralph. He waved back. The three of us took a seat on the sofa, where we could get a good view.

The song's called "Memories." It's dedicated to Victor, Ralph announced.

Helen sat up straight. Her eyes shone with pride. Ralph started to play. Victor sang.

I listened in amazement. I looked about. No one seemed to be startled. No one seemed to be surprised. Maybe I was mistaken. I listened carefully to the words. There was no mistaking it. It was a love song, and it was dedicated to Victor. Even the sexual act, unless I was mistaken, was concealed in the poetic verbiage. I looked at Helen. I looked at Jean. They were both listening with rapt attention. Didn't they realize?

The song ended. There was enthusiastic applause. Helen rose and joined Ralph at the piano.

I sat stunned. Should I say something? Helen was Jean's friend. Jean was concerned about her. She'd said so herself. She was afraid that she'd be hurt by Ralph. I thought about my own sexual encounters with men. Yes, but that wasn't love. It was a release. It was comforting to know that if the pressure got to be too much, there was that easy alternative. But romantic love? For another man? It was a territory that felt alien to me.

It was lovely, wasn't it? Jean was saying.
Yes. Yes, it was.

Should I say something to Jean or shouldn't I? How would I feel if someone said something to Jean about my secret encounter? But that was different. There was no emotional involvement. It was nothing more than a...physical act.

You didn't like it? Jean was saying.
No, no.

A NOT-SO-NICE JEWISH BOY FACES WORLD WAR II

What did you really think of it?, asked Jean.

Well, to tell you the truth, I found it rather shocking, I said.

Shocking?

Yes, well. It's a love song, isn't it? And it's dedicated to Victor, I said. *I mean, did you really listen to those words?*

Oh, God! I never thought of that, said Jean.

Maybe I shouldn't have said anything.

No. No, I'm glad you did, said Jean. *That explains it.*

What?

Never mind, she said.

Helen was rejoining us, her face wreathed in smiles.

Maybe I was wrong, I whispered to Jean.

No. No, you weren't.

Is there anything wrong? Helen asked.

Can we talk for a minute? Jean said to Helen. *Excuse me,* she said to me and she drew Helen aside.

I watched the hushed conversation, sorry I'd spoken up. Helen's face turned pale. She looked over at Ralph and Victor. They were engaged in conversation. Oh God, I thought, I've really done it.

Helen left Jean. She walked over to Ralph. She took him aside. Jean rejoined me.

I shouldn't have said anything. I shouldn't have interfered.

No. You did the right thing, said Jean. *I'm so angry. How could he! She's been on the verge of a nervous breakdown.*

Both of us looked over at Helen and Ralph. The conversation was very intense.

You don't understand, we heard Ralph protest.

I began to feel really guilty. Maybe the "affair" (?) with

AN ACT OF BETRAYAL?

Victor was over, a part of the past. But then why was Helen on the verge of a nervous breakdown?

I'm going to spend some time with Helen. Do you mind? said Jean.

No, of course not. I'll see you tomorrow. Don't forget. We're going to see "The Misanthrope," I said.

I won't. I'll see you at lunch.

Yes. Right.

I left Jean and walked out into the open air. I wasn't quite sure where I was heading. One thing I did know. I felt like a heel. After all, there was such a thing as loyalty to one's sex. But then again, if Helen was so unhappy, it really wasn't fair on Ralph's part. Oh, the hell with it, I decided. It's done. I did it. I did what I thought was right. It was not done out of spite, and I put it out of his mind. At least, I tried to.

CHAPTER THIRTY EIGHT

MOLIERE'S "THE MISANTHROPE"

Trying to get the picture of Helen and Ralph and Victor out of my mind, I walked over to the photography studio to pick up my pictures. At the studio Hilary greeted me cheerfully. *Good afternoon, young man. Your photos are all ready.*
Thank you, I said.
I opened the envelope and inspected them. They were mounted nicely, rather artistically.
They turned out very well, chirped Hilary.
Yes, they did.
I knew I didn't sound as enthusiastic as I would have liked. I didn't want to hurt her feelings, but I couldn't be phony. The pictures were rather interesting, I suppose. And I did look sort of...well...regal?
Your friend is lovely, Hilary said.
Thank you.
You make a nice couple.
Thank you.
I paid Hilary the rest of the money. I'd spent more than I'd planned to, but the pictures were...rather classy.
Good luck! Hilary called out as I left the shop.
I headed back to the house.
Today, apparently, was my day for guilt. I felt guilty about exposing Ralph's love affair with Victor. I felt guilty about Jean. I knew she was expecting...or, at least, hoping for more than I probably was prepared to give. I felt guilty about Clara. My feeling for her was purely sexual. I felt guilty about Ginny, getting involved with all these women behind her back, and not writing. I was awash with guilt.
I sat down at the table, determined, at least, to make up for my neglect of the people back home. I brought out my

stationary. I took out my pen and wrote and, as I wrote my self torture eased up a little.

My initial letter was to the family. I wrote in more detail about my participation in the war. I gave some purposely vague details about my experiences in the Hurtgen Forest and afterwards, skimming over the frightening and more graphic moments. I wrote about the good time I was having in Cardiff. I didn't mention Jean or Clara.

I wrote pretty much the same to Ginny about Cardiff and, of course, I went into great detail about the performance of "Private Lives." I knew that would mean a great deal to her. After I finished the letters I walked over to the nearby post office and mailed them.

My thoughts now turned to home, and to the future. I wondered how Mother was holding up. I was sure she was fretting about my safety. I wondered how my sister, Rose, was faring. Was she growing more secure? Was she dating? And my brother, Marty, the child whose hand I had to hold when we were crossing the street. How was he growing up? And I thought about Daddy and our relationship, or lack of it. I loved him, of course, because he was my father. I admired him because he was strong, and brave. He'd stood up to men who tried to rob him. The man was solid, like a rock. I envied that. How I wished that I was anchored like that, that my life was as simple as that. Of course, I didn't really know what went on inside that man. And I was getting tired of regretting the fact that I wasn't that close to him. Maybe when I got back I could remedy that.

The plain fact of the matter was that I was going to have to face the world with nothing but my dreams and my imagination. I was planning to live by my wits or my talent, if I had any talent. One one-act play was not much to go on. However it had won a prize, hadn't it? Surely that was an

A NOT-SO-NICE JEWISH BOY FACES WORLD WAR II

indication of something. Well, the future was still in the future. And now there was the week-end in London with Clara that I had to look forward to...I hoped.

******

The next day at lunch I asked Jean about Helen.
As of now, she's broken off with him. I don't know how long that's going to last.
I was curious about the relationship. Was Ralph interested only in friendship with Helen? Certainly Helen wanted more than that. My mind was filled with all sorts of questions, but I resisted asking them. After all, it was none of my business. Besides, even though Jean and Helen were friends, Helen may not have told Jean everything. After all, there were some things that were private, weren't there?

To add to my discomfort we were joined by Helen. I was relieved when it became obvious that nothing was going to be said about the business with Ralph. Though Helen looked rather pale, there was an air of determination about her, as if she'd been relieved of a burden and was ready to face what lay ahead.

I experienced another pang of guilt. Unfortunately I sighed rather audibly. Jean and Helen looked at me. Finally Helen said, *I'm grateful to you, Norman, for pointing out to me what a fool I've been.* I said nothing because I didn't know what to say. And this made me feel even worse.

Jean left with Helen and we arranged for me to pick Jean up at her house to attend the production of "The Misanthrope."

The community theatre performance that evening was at eight. I arrived at Jean's house at seven. I was admitted by her mother, a charming, to my eyes, middle-aged woman.

MOLIERE'S "THE MISANTHROPE"

I'm so happy to meet you, said Mrs. Courbet. *Jean has told us so much about you.*

I'm very fond of Jean.

As soon as the words were out of my mouth I knew it was the wrong thing to say. Mrs. Courbet was silent for a moment, as the words sunk in. At that moment Mr. Courbet, or rather Dr. Courbet, a rather distinguished looking gentleman, came into the room.

So this is the young man we've been hearing so much about.

Guilty as charged, I said. Oh, God! That didn't sound so good either.

You're going to the theatre, I gather, said Dr. Courbet.

We're going to see "The Misanthrope," I said.

Ah, Moliere. There was a man who could see right to the heart of the matter.

What did he mean by that, I wondered.

We're just finishing our dinner, said Mrs. Courbet. *You're welcome to join us for desert and coffee.*

I don't think we have that much time, I said

Jean's entrance was a welcome sight, a life line, thrown to a man thrashing about in turbulent waters. I was struck once more by the adorable face of a child, on the almost voluptuous body of a woman.

Be sure to dress warmly, Miss, and no hi-jinks, said Dr. Courbet.

Yes, doctor, said Jean.

Our flower is rather delicate, said Dr. Courbet.

Really, Daddy.

Home by midnight, young man.

Yes, sir.

Have a good evening, dear. It was nice meeting you,

A NOT-SO-NICE JEWISH BOY FACES WORLD WAR II

Norman, said Mrs. Courbet, and Dr. and Mrs. Courbet returned to their dinner.

Daddy's rather protective, said Jean. *I had a heart condition and, for a while, I had to limit my activities.*

Oh.

But I'm fine now.

I helped her into her coat and we left for the theatre. On the way I kept thinking about this new information about my friend. A heart condition. For one so young. It was alarming to think about. Actually rather frightening.

It turned out that the community theatre performance was taking place in the church where the dramatic society met. On the second floor there was a large hall with a stage in front. As we walked to our seats a familiar face nodded and smiled at me. Well, it sort of looked like a smile, slightly frozen. It was Martha, the young lady from the dramatic society.

Good evening, I said. *Is this one of your productions?*

Martha looked at me rather enigmatically, as if she had some sort of a secret, one that she couldn't possibly share with me and she walked on...without a word.

Who's that? Jean asked.

She's with the dramatic society.

"*Blithe Spirit?*"

Yes. She's not very friendly, is she? As a matter of fact, she's downright rude, said I. *She didn't even answer my question.*

These are the Cardiff Players. They're rivals.

I said nothing to Jean about being hurt that Martha had not extended an invitation to attend the next meeting. After all I had done a creditable job with Dr. Bradman, hadn't I? Or had I?

Do you know "The Misanthrope?" asked Jean.

MOLIERE'S "THE MISANTHROPE"

No. Do you?
I read it once, said Jean.
And?
It's a masterpiece.
The house lights came down. Three knocks were heard.
That's what they do at the Comedie Francaise, Jean whispered.
Oh?
It's a tradition.
The stage lights came up. The curtain opened on a rather stylized set. It represented a French drawing room. It was not a particularly clever or imaginative set, but it served its purpose. Two friends entered. The costumes and wigs were actually quite nice. The two men were arguing. Alceste, the hero, was accusing his friend of hypocrisy. Why couldn't he be honest and open in his dealings with people? The friend tried to impress on the hero that, to get along in Society, you couldn't always speak your mind. You had to be diplomatic. Alceste is not convinced. He is given a chance to practice his integrity by giving his frank opinion, when asked, about the poem of an acquaintance. The incident results in a law suit. And then there's the lover of the hero, the frivolous, flirtatious Celimene. According to Moliere, most men were hypocrites and liars, and most women superficial or, perhaps, even worse. At least, that was what I thought he was trying to say. At any rate, these characters were drawn with such great compassion, that the human personality in all its variations sprang to life. I forgot the set, the costumes, the wigs, even the actors who were not very polished. I listened to the words and the voice of the playwright, and I was transported. This Frenchman spoke directly to me from a distance of three centuries. The breezy style, the wit, the wonderfully provocative arguments. Civilization itself was on the block. Who was right? Who was

wrong? How did one live in Society? The curtain came down on Act One. Jean was speaking.

Are you enjoying it?
The writing is fabulous, I muttered.
I know what you mean.
Oh, if I could write like that! What did your father say?
"He gets to the heart of the matter."

We got out of our seats and walked into the hallway. Lemonade was being sold.

Would you care for some lemonade? I asked.
Thank you.

I walked over to the table and paid for two cups.

Martha, the dramatic society lady, appeared right next to me and paid for a cup. I was going to ignore her, but decided that would just be rude. *Are you enjoying it?* I asked.

Martha smiled mysteriously and again said nothing, which infuriated me even more.

That woman is really rude, I said to Jean. *I asked her if she were enjoying the show and she didn't even reply.*

She probably thought you were being snide. It is a good production. And this is their rival.

She could have said something, anything. You just don't ignore someone. I don't understand people, I really don't, I said.

And this set me to wondering about Martha. What sort of a woman was she? There was a part of her that was frozen. And yet, when she read the role of Ruth she came to life. Perhaps its easier to live in the world of make believe.

As the house lights dimmed, as the three knocks reverberated through the auditorium, as the curtain parted and the play began I kept wondering, How is this genius going to end it? As the performance concluded, the hero resolved to leave his social circle and seek refuge in the wilderness, where

MOLIERE'S "THE MISANTHROPE"

one could live as an honest man. The curtain closed and then opened for the curtain calls.

The son of a gun. He didn't end it. The story goes on. One is left to solve the issue of who is right and who is wrong for oneself. But what's going to happen to our hero? And what's going to happen to his lover, the flirtatious Celimene? You really cared about these people. They were real. And yet, at the very same time, the play was a work of artifice. And the economy of the writing! I was walking on air as we left the theatre.

Martha walked right past us without a word. I couldn't tell if she didn't see us or she was purposely ignoring us.

Isn't that your friend? asked Jean with a smile.

I chuckled. *Yes. That's my friend.*

CHAPTER THIRTY NINE

CLARA GETS PERMISSION

The following Saturday at seven o'clock sharp I met Clara in front of the movie theatre. I noticed, for the first time, that she had some makeup on, some lipstick. And was there some rouge on her cheeks? I couldn't be sure. Was this something new or was it just that I hadn't been aware of it? Her eyes shone and, though she seemed tense, she was more attractive than I remembered.

As we entered the theatre and found our way to the rear of the balcony, the opening credits were just ending. We snuggled into our seats, and I kissed her.

My mother's given me permission to go to London for the week-end, she whispered.

Wonderful, I said, and my pulse quickened. It's actually going to happen!

"The Picture of Dorian Gray" began to unfold. A handsome young man becomes steeped in corruption. He begins by impregnating an innocent young lady, a lower class show girl, and she kills herself. From there on in Dorian Gray descends into all sorts of unspecified decadence. The young man's features remain as comely as ever, but the face in his portrait, one by one, reveals the cruel, ugly lines representative of all his evil deeds. I began to feel a little uneasy. Although I thought the movie was definitely not conducive to romance, Clara clung to me, her head nestled on my shoulder.

After the movie we walked over to the restaurant. I ordered tea and scones.

What did you think of the movie, I asked.

It was exciting, said Clara.

Exciting?

Well, maybe not exciting, said Clara. *It was certainly dramatic.*

CLARA GETS PERMISSION

It was well done, I suppose.
Didn't you like it? asked Clara.
I don't know. It was certainly provocative. And atmospheric. I'm looking forward to this week-end. Is Friday afternoon okay? To leave, I mean.
I have to work late on Friday, said Clara. *We could leave early on Saturday, if you like. I can't come back too late on Sunday.*

That certainly left little time for romance. And then I realized I'd have to find a place to stay. I wondered if I'd have any trouble booking a room. Since I knew nothing about hotels in London, I decided to play it by ear.

I'm sorry, said Clara.
That's all right. I understand. Well, we do have one day and one night.

While we stood waiting for Clara's bus, I said, *There's a train at nine. Why don't we meet at the train station at eight thirty? By the ticket booth.*

My mother said she'd like to meet you. Can you pick me up?

Yes. Sure.

This was a little hurdle I hadn't counted on. Oh, well. The mother had given her consent. There was probably nothing to worry about.

Clara fished for a piece of paper in her purse. She wrote down her address and phone number.

I'd better pick you up at eight then.
All right.

It's a fifteen minute ride on the bus from here, said Clara. *There's a bakery on the corner where the bus stops. Kingsmith Bakery. You can't miss it. My house is right next to the bakery.*

A NOT-SO-NICE JEWISH BOY FACES WORLD WAR II

As the bus came in sight I took hold of her hands and kissed her gently on the lips.
Your hands are cold, I said.
So are yours, she said. As she boarded the bus she said, *See you Saturday.*
I blew her a kiss as the bus drove off, and she waved to me. On the way to the house I kept thinking about the coming week-end. For one thing, I hadn't counted on meeting her mother. But then again, why should I feel guilty? I'd made no promises. She was an adult. Perhaps she did hope for more than a casual affair. If so, the fault wasn't mine, was it? She was a virgin though. I was convinced of that. For that matter, so was I technically. I mean, here I was twenty two years old and I'd never had a really proper sexual experience, since the experience with the prostitute in Liege was...oral gratification, not the accepted procedure, the real thing, with all that awkward positioning. Come to think of it, Dorian Gray wasn't really that evil, was he?

******

I was tense and uneasy all day Sunday. I was absent-minded during my English Literature class the following day, even though it consisted of another lecture on Keats. I was absent-minded during lunch with Jean. My upcoming voice lesson was bound to be a disaster. My power of concentration was nil.
As I sat drinking the hot chocolate I was vaguely aware that Mrs. Berganza was saying something.
Your friend is charming.
What's that? Yes, she is.
She is in love with you, you know, said Mrs. Berganza.
We're fond of each other, I said..

CLARA GETS PERMISSION

I hope she won't be hurt.

I've never given her any encouragement to think that our relationship was more than...just friendship, I said.

I see.

That's all I needed. Another log on the bonfire of my already roaring guilt.

Shall we start?

All right, I said, with not too much enthusiasm. I hoped my teacher wasn't aware of my indifference.

We set aside our cups and I began my scales. It was impossible to think about singing. My mind wandered as I advanced to the exercises and then to the songs. At the end of the lesson I sighed. I hoped I hadn't offended my teacher by my lack of interest, but I thought it wise not to apologize. Besides, I was not prepared to offer an explanation for my lack of concentration.

That was good, said Mrs. Berganza.

You think so?

Don't you?

I'm afraid my mind was a million miles away, said I.

That's too bad.

I looked at her questioningly.

That you didn't know what you were doing.

But I did it, I said.

Ah yes, but technique is something that you use consciously, at first at any rate. It's something that you must be able to duplicate.

Oh.

There's this story about Laurence Olivier, Mrs. Berganza continued. *His Richard The Third was a triumph. A friend came backstage afterwards to congratulate him and found him looking very despondent.* "What's the matter," *the friend asked.* "You were magnificent." "Yes, I know," *said*

A NOT-SO-NICE JEWISH BOY FACES WORLD WAR II

Olivier. "But I don't know what I did." Mrs. Berganza looked at me and smiled. *You mustn't be impatient, my dear. It takes time.*
How much?
Mrs. Berganza shrugged and smiled.

******

I managed to come down to earth the following day and was more attentive to Jean. I even thought to ask about Helen and Ralph.
I think it's over, as far as any romance is concerned. They will continue to be friends however, said Jean.
Maybe that's for the best.
Are you all right? Jean asked.
Yes, I'm fine. Why do you ask?
You seem preoccupied.
Well, there's lot to think about. The future. I mean I have all these ambitions. I wonder if I can fulfill them.
You can try, said Jean.
I guess that's all one can do. Do you think about the future?
I used to, a lot, said Jean. *But then I've learned to take one day at a time.*
I wanted to ask her about her heart condition, but didn't think it proper. If she wanted to talk about it, she would.
The school choir is giving a concert this Saturday, said Jean.
I'd love to. But I made plans to go to London this weekend.
Good for you.
Is that the only date? For the concert.
I'm afraid so.

CLARA GETS PERMISSION

Are there any other concerts coming up?
I'll check.

******

The rest of the week passed in a haze. All I could think about was London. How should I go about finding a hotel? Would it be difficult to get a room at a decent hotel? I couldn't take her to a flea bag. As soon as we arrived in London I planned to dig up one of those booklets that listed what to do and where. As I recalled they did have ads for hotels.

I cursed myself for not having thought of this before. I'd been there. I knew that I'd have to take her somewhere. Well, there was no use crying over spilt milk. I would just have to make the best of it. I mustn't appear flustered. I wouldn't want to make her uneasy. I was a man about town. This was not unusual. You just picked out a hotel. You phoned them from the train station. After all I was a GI. I was on leave.

Then I thought that perhaps I ought to book the room as a married couple. Then again, she didn't have a wedding ring. Would that pose a problem?

I hadn't seen much of Steve all week. Friday evening I decided to wait up for him. Steve might have some very practical advice. He would certainly be more objective. I tried to do some reading while I waited, but it was no use. I couldn't concentrate, so I just lay there, thinking and stewing.

Steve arrived rather late, and he didn't seem very communicative. I waited until he got into bed and was about to turn out the light.

How you doing? I asked.
What's that? Oh. Okay.

A NOT-SO-NICE JEWISH BOY FACES WORLD WAR II

Anything wrong?

I don't know. She's been acting sort of strange lately.

That settled that. Apparently he was in no mood to give me any advice. *Any particular reason, that you know of?*, I asked.

She's Catholic, you know.

No, I didn't.

And I would have to convert, said Steve. *I said I would, but the more I think about it. Not that I'm religious or anything. But if we have kids they'd have to be brought up Catholic, and that bothers me. I haven't said anything, but I guess it shows. This whole business of religion...*

Tell me about it!

Well, that's my problem. Good night, said Steve and turned off the light..

Good night, I said.

I turned away and sighed. Oh, well. I was certainly not about to burden the poor guy with a very simple little problem like booking a room at some hotel.

CHAPTER FORTY

LONDON REVISITED

I got up early Saturday morning. Steve was still asleep and I was careful not to wake him. I shaved particularly close and doused myself in after-shave lotion. I packed a few essentials, like a change of underwear and my toilet articles. I threw in a book just in case things got boring. You never know. And I gulped down my breakfast.

Off to London again? Mrs. Connoly asked.
Yes. I'm looking forward to it.
Have a nice time.
Thank you, I said.
I certainly intend to, I said to myself.

I wasn't sure where to catch the bus that went by Clara's house so I hiked down to the movie theatre. The bus was a long time in coming. I began to worry about missing the nine o'clock train. When I finally got on the bus I asked the driver if he would let me know when we arrived at Clara's address.

The Kingsmith Bakery is on the corner, I said.
Righto, said the bus driver.
It's about a twenty minute ride, isn't it? I asked.

Instead of answering the driver nodded rather noncommittally. What did that mean, I wondered. Did he or did he not know what I was talking about?

I looked anxiously out the window as we drove through the strange streets. I must have drifted off somewhere because I heard the bus driver call out.

Here we are, son. Kingsmith Bakery.
Thank you, I said.

I got off the bus, took a deep breath and checked the number of the house next to the bakery.

That was it. I took another deep breath, then walked up

A NOT-SO-NICE JEWISH BOY FACES WORLD WAR II

the three steps to the front door. I opened the door and stepped into the hallway. There were the mail boxes. I inspected the names. There were four. What was her family name again? There it was. Dunphy. There was a buzzer underneath the mail box.

I took a deep breath, pushed the buzzer, and waited. And waited. There really wasn't much time to waste. I should have started earlier. The sound of the answering buzzer startled me.

I pushed the inner door open quickly. I stood in the inner hallway and looked about. How stupid! I'd forgotten to note the number of the apartment. Should I go out again and look up the number? I decided to wait. Finally I heard Clara's voice.

Norman?
Yes?
It's up here. The second floor.
Right.

I climbed the stairs and there was Clara standing in the open doorway.

Hi, I said. *I'm a little behind schedule. I had to wait a long time for the bus.*

Come in, said Clara.

She stepped aside. I entered the living room.

It was a neat, uncluttered room, clean, bright and sunny. The furniture had seen better days, but even when new, apparently, had not been very elegant.

Mrs. Dunphy came in from another room, which I assumed was the kitchen since she was wearing an apron.

This is my mother, Norman, said Clara.

How do you do, I said and, impulsively, shook Mrs. Dunphy's hand.

How do you do, said Mrs. Dunphy.

LONDON REVISITED

I tried to ignore the fact that I was being inspected by this rather simple, down-to-earth woman.

Would you care for some coffee, and some toast perhaps? said Mrs. Dunphy.

That would be nice, I said, *but if we're going to make that nine o'clock train...*

I'll get my coat, said Clara.

You've been to London, have you? said Mrs. Dunphy.

Once, I said. *It's quite a city.*

You're from New York? said Mrs. Dunphy.

No, I'm from across the river. New Jersey. Newark.

I see.

My husband, Clara's father, had relatives in Connecticut.

That's not far, from New York or New Jersey, I said.

This was followed by a loud silence. Could she read my mind, I wondered. Did she know that I had every intention of sleeping with her daughter?

You should have good weather, today and tomorrow, Mrs. Dunphy said.

I hope so, I said.

What seemed like aeons later Clara returned, wearing her coat and carrying her overnight bag. I debated about offering to carry the bag, hesitated then decided not to. It might look too intimate, too possessive.

You be careful now, dear, said Mrs. Dunphy. *And give my regards to Mrs. Chester.*

I will, Mother, said Clara. She turned to me. *I'm ready.*

It was nice meeting you, I said to Mrs. Dunphy.

Mrs. Dunphy smiled and nodded. The smile seemed to be rather guarded. I couldn't decide whether to shake hands with her again or not. She didn't seem to want to, so I opened the door and followed Clara into the hallway.

A NOT-SO-NICE JEWISH BOY FACES WORLD WAR II

Good-bye, said Mrs. Dunphy as she stood in the doorway.

Good-bye, I said and followed Clara down the stairs.

I followed Clara across the street to the bus stop. When we looked up there was Mrs. Dunphy standing at the window. She waved to us. We waved back. Is she going to stand there watching us until we get on the bus, I wondered. Which is exactly what she did, waving once more as we boarded the bus.

Is this the bus to the train station? I asked Clara as we took our seat.

Yes. It's only a ten minute ride.

Your mother's very nice, I said.

Yes, she is. We're very close.

I should have booked a hotel, I said. *I don't think we'll have any trouble getting a room though, do you? If you have any suggestions...*

My mother's friend, Mrs. Chester, has a Bed and Breakfast. That's where I'll be staying, said Clara. She must have noticed the look of surprise on my face, to say nothing of the disappointment. *I had no choice,* she added hastily.

I thought we might spend the night together, I said. *I thought that was the idea.*

Oh, we can. After I settle in, I'll come downstairs and let you in. Of course, you won't be able to stay all night.

You think you can? Let me in, I mean.

I'm sure I can, said Clara. *I've stayed there before. My room is right next to the stairs. It won't be a problem, I promise you.*

Are you sure?

I'm positive. I had to agree, otherwise I couldn't have come. I'm sorry.

That's all right, I said.

LONDON REVISITED

I made a valiant attempt to hide my disappointment, plus my concern. Here was a wrinkle I hadn't counted on. The entire venture was nerve-wracking enough. This made it even worse. I could picture myself standing outside the door of the building in the freezing cold, waiting in vain for Clara to open the door. Or I could picture the two of us being discovered by Mrs. Chester as we crept quietly up the stairs. Or I could hear Mrs. Chester calling out just as we opened the door to Clara's room, *Is that you, dear?* Or worse yet, I could picture climbing into bed with Clara stark naked and the door suddenly springing open and Mrs. Chester bursting into the room. Or worst scenario of all, just as we were about to reach a climax the door is opened. *What's going on here?!!* Or just as I was leaving I'm discovered sneaking down the stairs. I rush out the door and poor Clara's left to make up some sort of an explanation.

It's going to be all right, said Clara.

I hope so, I said, trying not to sound too negative.

In the train station at the ticket window Clara insisted on paying her own fare. *That's all right,* she said. *I'm sure your funds are limited, being in the army.*

If you insist, I said.

The gesture made me uneasy. She didn't want to feel obligated in case she should back out at the last minute. Another nail in the coffin.

As we settled on the train I tried to forget the unforeseen complication. I made up my mind to enjoy the week-end, no matter how it turned out.

******

In London we took the underground to Clara's Bed and Breakfast. I waited in the small park across the street while

A NOT-SO-NICE JEWISH BOY FACES WORLD WAR II

she deposited her overnight bag. I decided to keep mine with me. It wasn't that heavy and, besides, I wasn't quite sure how or where I'd be spending the night. While I waited I took out the guide I'd picked up at the train station and studied it. I grew anxious as the minutes passed and no sign of Clara. Finally the door to the building opened and Clara came out and joined me.

I'm sorry, she said. *I couldn't get away. Mrs. Chester's an old friend of the family and she wanted to talk.*

That's okay, I said. *I thought we might visit the National Gallery in the afternoon, and maybe a play in the evening? Would that be all right?*

That sounds lovely.

I took hold of her hand and we made our way to the Underground. I took pride in the fact that I knew exactly where to go, what line to take and what station to get off.

We decided to have lunch first. I remembered an Italian restaurant near Trafalgar Square which was very reasonable. Clara insisted on paying her half of the bill. I began to suspect she was doing all this at her mother's insistence. Don't put yourself in his debt, I could hear her mother saying.

After lunch we walked three blocks to the National Gallery. Clara allowed me to pay her admission fee. I heaved a sigh of relief. We spent two hours oohing and aahing at the sight of the great masterpieces. And then there was tea with little sandwiches at a nearby restaurant.

We consulted the theatre listings in the guide. I would have liked to have seen the second part of "Henry IV" which was scheduled for that evening. I was anxious to see Laurence Olivier play the character role of Justice Shallow.

I decided that Shakespeare might be too heavy going. Instead I chose a play called "Duet For Two Hands." It was a mystery. It had gotten some nice notices, especially for its

LONDON REVISITED

star, Mary Morris. Clara insisted on paying for her ticket. I decided not to make a fuss about it. I bought a program and, as we were being ushered to our seats, I made a great play of ordering tea to be served during intermission. Clara was duly impressed and, I was pleased to note, she made no attempt to share the expense.

The curtain went up on a room in the English countryside. The star of the play ran around barefoot and had this lovely throaty voice. There was some business about a pianist who'd lost his hands in an accident. They were replaced by the hands of a murderer. I was much too keyed up, however, to really concentrate on the play. Clara seemed to enjoy it, and expressed childlike delight at being served her tea during intermission.

It's been a lovely day, said Clara as we left the theatre.
Yes, it has, I said.

Her comment was probably made as a compliment. Instead of pleasing me, however, I found it disturbing. Maybe it was meant as a dismissal. We walked leisurely to the Underground. When we reached the Bed and Breakfast I waited eagerly for instructions.

Why don't you wait across the street. I think we should wait till, at least, eleven o'clock. I think, by that time, everyone ought to be in bed, then I'll come down and get you.

All right, I replied. *I hope there's no problem.*

There won't be. I'm right near the stairway, and the other rooms are to the rear.

All right.

We kissed and Clara left me standing in front of the house. I sighed and looked up at the sky. Thank God it wasn't raining or snowing.

CHAPTER FORTY ONE

AT LAST!

I watched Clara enter the bed and breakfast, then walked across to the park and sat on a bench facing the building. I thought about trying to read. Ridiculous! How could I possibly concentrate? Besides the light wasn't very good. I looked at my watch. Twenty minutes to go. I reached in my pocket to make sure the condom was there. I'd been carrying it around for weeks now. I hoped to hell it was still good. I consulted my watch. Nineteen minutes to go. Time was standing still. I shivered. It was getting colder. I looked up at the sky. There were no stars. There was a quarter moon however. After a while I looked at my watch again. Thirteen minutes to go. This was nerve racking. I sighed and looked around. It was a nice neighborhood. Tall, stately houses, a park. It must be nice to live in a neighborhood like this.

I wasn't sure how long she'd been there. Perhaps I'd dozed off. But the door to the Bed and Breakfast was ajar and Clara, dressed in a bathrobe, was waving towards me.

I walked quickly across the street. I slipped past her and she closed the door behind me.

We've got to be very quiet, she said, and started to climb the carpeted stairs. I tip-toed silently behind her. Her room, as she said, was right at the head of the stairs. We both breathed easy as she softly closed the bedroom door behind us.

I can't see anything, I whispered. *Can we turn on a lamp?*

She turned on a small table lamp next to the bed then placed some clothing over it.

Is that all right?
That's fine.

She took off her robe and climbed into bed. I set down

AT LAST!

my bag and stripped down to my underwear. I took the condom from my jacket pocket, and hopped into bed beside her.

Somehow this was not how I'd imagined it. The whole thing was so stealthy, so hush hush. Where was the romance? The champagne? The music? I turned towards her.

Why don't you take off your nightgown? I whispered.

She did as she was told, and dropped the nightgown on the floor beside the bed. I slipped out of my underwear. I kissed and fondled her. She was not very responsive. I assumed that she was frightened. Good Lord, woman, I said to myself, show a little excitement or, at least, some signs of life. Obviously she was a virgin, but so was I for that matter, and at least I had some vitality. With very little help, or encouragement, the sex act, after many adjustments was clumsily underway.

There seemed to be some problem with the condom, and I wasn't quite sure how far I'd penetrated her. I hoped and prayed that the condom hadn't broken. After many adjustments the act was consummated, on my part that is. I wasn't quite sure about her.

Are you all right? I asked.

Yes, she said. *Are you?*

Yes, I'm fine.

What else could I say? It was not, exactly, an event of great passion, and I wasn't even sure whether or not she'd had an orgasm. I was afraid to ask. We lay beside one another, looking up at the ceiling.

It was a lovely day, she said.

Yes, it was, I said.

In my mind I reviewed the sex act. It certainly could have gone much better, and it would have if I'd gotten some

A NOT-SO-NICE JEWISH BOY FACES WORLD WAR II

cooperation. And, perhaps, it was not exactly gentlemanly to note, but she did have a role of fat around her waist.

What are you thinking? she asked.
Nothing.
I thought the play was wonderful.
Yes, I enjoyed it.
I love the theatre, she said.
Yes, so do I.
It must be wonderful to be able to write a play.
Of course, I've only written one, to speak of. And it is hard work.
Is it?
It was draining.
Was it really?

I didn't respond. I was reluctant to open up too much. After all, the relationship was going to go nowhere. And I certainly didn't want to encourage her to think that it was.

I guess maybe I ought to let you get some sleep, I said.
I think there's time.
I know I won't be able to get any sleep here, I continued.
Are you tired?
Sort of, I lied. *I think maybe I ought to go.*

She said nothing. I started to dress.

Where will you go?
The USO. I won't have any trouble. They have a dorm there. What time shall I pick you up?
I dunno. What time do you think?
I guess you will have breakfast here. Why don't I pick you up around nine o'clock? That'll give us some time to do some sight-seeing. And we can catch a train around five.
All right.

AT LAST!

I finished dressing and picked up my bag, then walked over to the bed, bent down and kissed her.

Good night, I said. *Sleep tight.*
You, too. Can you get out all right?
I think so.

I opened the door, stepped into the hallway and closed the door gently behind me. I tiptoed to the stairs and started down, holding my breath. I thought I heard a noise, like footsteps. I may have imagined it, but I moved quickly towards the outside door, opened it, stepped out closing the door carefully behind me...and heaved a sigh of relief.

The cold air felt invigorating. I looked about and breathed deeply. I thought about Byron. Was this the way the great poet, the great lover felt after an adventure? After a conquest?

Ah, but was this a conquest? Was I, in reality, the conqueror? Or was I but a pawn, a victim of feminine wiles? Clara didn't enjoy the experience. That was obvious. Maybe she wasn't even looking forward to it. Maybe she went through the motions, hoping that it might lead to more than just a passing flirtation, hoping it might lead to...perish the thought...marriage, a home and children.

******

I looked at my watch. It was seven minutes to twelve. Good lord! This earth-shaking experience, this momentous event had taken less than an hour. Actually not much more than half an hour, if that. Surely I had more to look forward to than this hurried, hush-hush assignation. Surely life had more glamorous adventures in store. How much more fulfilling this evening would have been if Jean had been my companion, or Ginny. It would have been delightful. It would have been fun!

I was gratified to find that the Underground was still running. I checked in at the USO, took a shower and climbed into a cot at the dorm. I lay wide awake. Someone was snoring in the cot next to mine. Some romantic evening!

I woke later than I had planned, had a quick breakfast at the USO then raced to the Underground. I found her sitting on a bench across from the Bed and Breakfast. I looked at my watch. It was almost ten after nine.

Sorry I'm late.
That's all right. Did you sleep well? she asked.
Apparently. Did you?
Oh, yes.
No problems? I mean with your mother's friend?
No.
Well, what shall we do? I took the guide from my bag. *Let's see. There's St. Paul's Cathedral. Hampton Court.*
Hampton Court! I understand it's lovely, said Clara.
We'll have to take a train from Waterloo Station. Well, we do have until five fifteen.
Oh, let's.

As we started for the Underground Clara slipped her hand under my arm. She seemed much more relaxed. Apparently the ordeal she'd dreaded was over and done with. Her eyes shone. Her face beamed. She looked almost pretty. Nothing was said about the previous night.

At Waterloo Station I bought some chocolate bars. We sat eating the candy on the train to Hampton Court. Apparently there was quite a crowd visiting the palace.

As we left the train we followed the crowd. And there it was, Hampton Court, an impressive landmark. The former residence of Cardinal Wolsey and Henry VIII. We decided to

AT LAST!

take the tour first, then walk about the magnificent grounds. We listened intently to the tour guide as he led us through the ornate rooms and rattled off the historical significance of it all, including some royal gossip and amusing anecdotes.

We stopped off at the gift shop where I bought some souvenirs to bring home. Clara admired a pill box with a picture of the palace and I bought it for her. We headed for the grounds in back when I happened to look at my watch.

I think we'd better start back, if we're going to make that train.

All during the tour of the palace I'd been thinking how much more fun the visit would have been with Jean by my side. As we boarded the train back to London my teacher's words kept ringing in my ears. *She is in love with you, you know. She is in love with you, you know.* I really had to be careful with Jean. Had I betrayed her with this week-end with Clara, I wondered. This was ridiculous. I've got to stop feeling guilty about everything! Surely Byron never bothered with all this nonsense.

What are you thinking? Clara asked on the train back to London.

I was thinking it's a shame this weekend has to end. Oh God! Wasn't that a stupid thing to say?!

Me too! said Clara and she squeezed my arm.

It was dark by the time we arrived in Cardiff. I walked with Clara to her bus. I was prepared to see her home.

You don't have to come home with me, said Clara.

Are you sure?

I'll be fine.

Inwardly I heaved a sigh of relief. I was not prepared to face Mrs. Dunphy after deflowering her daughter, if you could call it that. As her bus pulled up Clara looked at me eagerly.

A NOT-SO-NICE JEWISH BOY FACES WORLD WAR II

What else could I say? *Next Saturday?* I asked. *Seven o'clock?*

All right, she said.

I could hear the relief in her voice. I kissed her. She stepped onto the bus. I waited till she took her seat and waved to her. She waved back and smiled. As the bus pulled away I sighed. As long as I was here in Cardiff, I thought, I'd have to keep dating her.

CHAPTER FORTY TWO

MATTHEW

After I saw Clara off I boarded the bus that left me off at the movie theatre, planning to walk to the house from there.

As I got off the bus I noticed a familiar figure coming out of the movie theatre. It was Matthew, looking sort of lost and lonely. I debated about making my presence known. Ridiculous, I thought. He is a fellow soldier. Why not give him the benefit of my charming company.

Hi! I called out.

Matthew kept on walking. His mind was obviously somewhere else.

Matthew!

Matthew turned. *Oh, hi.* He looked at my bag. *Are you going somewhere?*

Coming. From London.

Oh!

Actually I went there with a friend, a lady friend.

Oh. How nice for you, said Matthew.

Yes, it was. Would you care for some tea? There's a nice restaurant nearby.

Now?

If you'd care to.

All right, said Matthew.

I led the way to the restaurant. As we sat down at a table the waitress came over and smiled at me.

Good evening. How are you this evening?

Fine. Could we have some tea and scones? I looked at Matthew. *Is that all right?*

Fine.

Thank you, said the waitress as she left to fill the order.

How are you doing? I asked.

All right.

A NOT-SO-NICE JEWISH BOY FACES WORLD WAR II

You don't sound very enthusiastic.
Matthew didn't reply. He fiddled with the silverware. I studied the dour young man.
I'll be glad to get back home, Matthew said. *The English are not very friendly.*
They're Welsh here in Cardiff.
I'm aware of that.
You have someone waiting for you back home? I asked.
What is that supposed to mean? Matthew snapped.
It's not supposed to mean anything. It's a simple question.
Nothing is simple, said Matthew.
The waitress arrived with the food.
I'm glad you're enjoying yourself, Matthew continued, after tasting his tea and taking a bite of his scone.
I'm having the time of my life, I said. *I'll hate to leave.*
Why don't you stay?
I'm thinking about it.
Really?
Of course, it's not the Riviera or Paris, for that matter, but I'm certainly having a better time than I expected to. And we're alive, and the war is over.
Yes, there is that, said Matthew.
So why aren't you enjoying yourself?
I don't make friends very easily, Matthew said.
Neither do I.
Apparently you do.
Well, I'm not a hermit, I said.
I've never been able to make friends, even at school.
Have you tried?
I find people very disappointing.
Maybe you're expecting too much, I said. *Nobody's perfect.*

MATTHEW

Well, I do have my standards, said Matthew.
Aren't you lonely?
I'm used to it.
Are you?
When are you going to London again?
I couldn't afford another trip, said I. *It was exciting though. As a matter of fact...*
What?
Do you ever think about the future? What your life is going to be like? I asked.
I think it's important to plan for the future, Matthew replied.
Man proposes and God disposes. It's a French proverb, I think. What do you plan to do?
I'm going to teach, said Matthew.
What?
History.
It's a noble profession, said I.
What do you plan to do?
Write. I'm a writer. I may go into the theatre, as an actor, I mean.
Really? I ran into Steve. He plans to stay here, too, Matthew said.
When did you speak to him last?
About a week ago, said Matthew. *Has he changed his mind?*
Quite possibly.
Have you ever done any acting?
At Ohio State. It's very exciting. Of course, teaching is a lot like acting. I mean you have to get up in front of the class and keep them interested. I thought about teaching, too.
Well... Matthew shifted in his chair. Apparently he was ready to leave.

A NOT-SO-NICE JEWISH BOY FACES WORLD WAR II

I waved to the waitress to bring the check. We split the bill and left the restaurant. We walked side by side, each lost in his own private thoughts.

I left Matthew at his house. Poor guy, he is a mess, I thought. He reminded me, somehow, of David Jacobs. David was the class whiz back at Hawthorne Avenue School. He and Arnold Pearlman were very tight. They were always together...and rather suspect.

CHAPTER FORTY THREE

UH OH!

Steve was fast asleep when I got in. I was too keyed up to sleep. I would have liked to talk. I lay awake in the dark, my mind spinning. Life was really exciting, and it hasn't even begun. Or has it? Suppose this turned out to be the most exciting part of my life?

I woke late the next morning and almost missed breakfast. Steve was gone by the time I got downstairs.

At lunch Jean was anxious to hear about the trip to London. I was sorely tempted to tell her about Clara, not the intimate details, of course, but the fact that I was seeing someone else as well. That would have made it clear that she was just a friend, one of several. But I didn't have the courage. I clung to the illusion that I knew she cherished as well, that maybe I would remain in Cardiff after I was discharged, and that maybe we did have a future together. So I chattered on and on about the innocent fun I had in London.

I continued to deceive her, and myself as well. It was easier than facing the truth. The truth being that perhaps I had inherited my mother's deepseated mistrust of Gentiles, and I did not have the courage to think seriously about a girl that wasn't Jewish. The truth being that I didn't have the courage to seek a life in a country other than the one I'd been raised in. The truth being that I wasn't larger than life, that I was actually a pygmy, a gutless coward.

But it didn't have to be the truth, did it? I'd been through a war, and I hadn't disgraced myself. There was still time, time to change my mind. I was giving myself a headache, and I just stopped.

The week passed pleasantly enough. The English literature course continued to be fascinating. Coleridge was an intriguing figure, a colorful one. My voice lesson was

A NOT-SO-NICE JEWISH BOY FACES WORLD WAR II

challenging. It would start out well, and then I would get carried away by the sound of my voice and had to pull back. Never louder than lovelier, never louder than lovelier. But I couldn't sing too softly or I wouldn't be heard. I couldn't push because I might hurt my voice, besides which the quality of the sound suffered. Patience, patience I was told.

In the middle of the week Jean and I attended an orchestral concert in the main auditorium, which we both enjoyed.

Saturday evening I walked to the movie theatre. Clara was waiting for me at the usual spot. She looked very tense.

Hi, I said. *I'll get the tickets.*

She nodded.

I walked to the box-office. As I purchased the tickets I glanced at Clara. She didn't look well at all. There were dark circles under her eyes.

All set? I asked.

She nodded.

I handed the tickets to the usher at the door and, as we walked up the stairs to the balcony, she spoke for the first time.

I'm late, she said.

At first I didn't understand what she meant.

My period. It should have started this week.

Is this the first time you've been late? I asked.

It is unusual.

Well, why don't we wait and see? I tried to appear calm. If I appeared worried then she'd worry more. *I'm sure it'll be all right,* I continued.

There was an English film on the screen. Something called "The October Man." It was a spy film.

Nothing registered. My head was reeling. My world was about to collapse around me. Forget Jean. Forget Ginny.

UH OH!

Forget my voice lessons. Forget my writing career. Forget the theatre. What if she were pregnant? I was not going to marry her, that was for sure. But I did have some responsibility. Somehow or other I would have to help out financially. But how? Where would the money come from? I would have to get some low level job and slave away to pay for a child I didn't want. I would have to work as a grocery clerk, the way I worked to earn my college tuition. What a gruesome time that was!

And the thought of Clara being the mother of my child... God! The very thought of living with Clara as man and wife made my stomach do flip-flops. I could see myself getting up in the morning and facing Clara over the breakfast table. I could see myself going to work at the supermarket, spending a miserable day bagging groceries and unloading boxes and placing can after can on the shelf. I could see myself coming home at night, discouraged and disgusted. The baby was crying and Clara looked haggard. She had grown into a nag, vulgar and common. I was disgusted with her and she was disgusted with me.

I could see myself plotting how to murder her, the way the young man in Dreiser's "American Tragedy" had murdered the working girl he'd impregnated. I would take Clara out on the lake in a row boat and drown her. That would solve everything.

I pulled myself together and placed my arm around Clara's shoulder, trying to give her some reassurance, even though I was almost sick with worry. The romance was gone. The glamour was gone. This was for real. How were we going to deal with this crisis? We sat through the film dutifully. After it was over we rose automatically. There was no thought of staying to see the part we'd missed. There was a real life drama to deal with.

A NOT-SO-NICE JEWISH BOY FACES WORLD WAR II

We headed automatically to the restaurant. I ordered the tea and scones and we ate in silence. Finally I spoke up.

You haven't said anything to your mother, have you?

No, of course not.

Do you think she suspects anything? About the weekend, I mean.

I don't think so. She had a long talk with Mrs. Chester, and she didn't seem suspicious.

Do you think she suspects anything...about your being late?

No.

Well, there's no use in jumping to conclusions, I said, *since you say you have been late before.*

She nodded.

I mean I was careful. I did use protection. So I'm sure everything is fine. I didn't add that I had been concerned about the age of the condom, afraid that it might have slipped, afraid that it might have broken.

Clara tried to smile...not too successfully.

We finished our tea and scones. I paid the bill and we waited for the bus in silence.

Same time next week? I said as the bus pulled up.

Clara nodded. I could tell she was relieved at my words. I was not going to desert her. I was not going to leave her in the lurch. She waved to me through the window as the bus pulled away. I waved back.

I walked home in a daze. I had to talk to someone, yet I was afraid to reveal my predicament to anyone. If I should try to turn into a scoundrel, if I should try to deny that I ever consorted with that woman, if I should try to desert her my words could serve to incriminate me.

Steve was reading when I entered the room. *How are you doing?* he asked as I plopped down on my bed.

UH OH!

Ignoring his question I asked, *How's Jessica?*
She's fine. We're friends now. How's Jean?
She's fine.
And Clara?

I now regretted having shared in detail my London adventure. I'd been quite casual in relating all the subterfuge and how I'd carried it off. The man about town. Just another notch in my belt. That's what I'd implied, at any rate.

At this point there was no point in holding back. I'd already incriminated myself. I would just have to reveal the possible dire consequences of my dalliance. Byron, after all, had fostered an illegitimate child. Byron, however, was a lord. Not only a lord, he was a wealthy man.

Apparently there's trouble in paradise, I said. *She missed her period.*

Oh, God! You did use protection, didn't you?

I nodded.

Well...

But you never know.

He was silent for a moment, and then he asked, *Is abortion legal here?*

I don't know. And even if she wanted to... I don't know.

Is she Catholic?

I don't know.

Well, maybe it'll turn out all right, said Steve. *My sister's been late once or twice. You're not thinking about marrying her, are you?*

God forbid!

A friend of mine got hooked that way.

How'd it work out?

All right, I guess. He never complains, said Steve. *And the kid is kinda cute.*

Well, I'm not ready for marriage, that's for sure.

A NOT-SO-NICE JEWISH BOY FACES WORLD WAR II

Especially with Clara. Much less a child to be responsible for. But the idea of an abortion... A distant cousin of mine died that way. They dumped her body on the lawn in front of our high school.

That's because it was illegal maybe, said Steve. *If it's done in a hospital... I mean different countries have different laws.*

It's still murder, isn't it? I'm not gonna think about it. I'll just hope it'll turn out all right.

It probably will, he said. I just wished he'd said it with just a little more assurance.

We got ready for bed. I turned out the lights. I sat up and looked over towards Steve. I kept hoping that my friend might say something, come up with some brilliant solution.

Silence.

After a while I heard Steve's gentle snoring.

Thanks a lot.

CHAPTER FORTY FOUR

THE OUTCOME

I pulled the covers over me, clutched my pillow, closed my eyes and tried to sleep. It was useless. I turned over, then turned over again. This is ridiculous. I sat up, got out of bed and dressed.

I tiptoed out of the room, closing the door gently behind me. I tiptoed down the stairs. The house was deadly quiet. I stood irresolutely. I wanted to talk to someone. Someone who could advise me. Someone who could extricate me from this godawful dilemma. If only I could share this burden with some wise guru who would come up with some brilliant solution. I wished that Mr. Connoly was still up. It might be comforting just to talk to an older man, someone who'd been through the mill.

I heaved a sigh and stepped out the door into the cold night air. It was snowing lightly. I welcomed the gentle drops on my face. Maybe the moisture was a tender caress from Mother Nature, telling me not to worry. Everything would be fine.

I'd never really had a heart to heart talk with my father. I pictured myself confiding in him. Daddy was a man of the world. He'd been through a war. He ran a business. He might not be well educated, or very cultured but he was a gentle man and a strong one. He would know what to say, what to do. He would certainly not condemn me for fulfilling my manhood. He would understand. He would sympathize. He would offer to help. Or would he? Daddy could be very stern. Maybe he would insist that I was now a man, and responsible for my actions. After all, I was a veteran. I wasn't a boy anymore.

And what about Mother? What would she have to say? Would she be disgusted with me?

A NOT-SO-NICE JEWISH BOY FACES WORLD WAR II

And what about Rose? She would understand. She would sympathize. I was sure I could count on her.

But forget Rose. Forget Mother. Forget the entire family, all the aunts and the cousins and the uncles. What about Ginny? Suppose she found out? That might be the end of that!

And what about Jean?

All these thoughts whirled around in my head as I walked rapidly around the block. I was hardly aware of where I was. Where I was, actually, was in the middle of the worst dilemma I'd ever been in.

I looked up at the sky. No, I was not going to appeal to some myth of a god. The solution, whatever it was, lay here on earth. The solution had to come from me and this stranger whom I may have impregnated. And to top it all off, the sex hadn't even been satisfactory. I still didn't think she'd had an orgasm, and if she hadn't had an orgasm maybe it was impossible for her to become pregnant. That was a question that someone could answer. But who? And then there was the question about whether she'd actually had an orgasm or not? She was the only one who could answer that. She was inexperienced however. She might not even know if she'd had an orgasm or not. Was that possible?

I was going to drive myself crazy. I wouldn't think about it anymore. There was absolutely nothing to be done until next Saturday. Then I would know my fate or, at least, if there was a reason for all this concern.

I stood in front of the house. I looked at my watch. It wasn't even one. Determined to remain calm I went back into the house, climbed the stairs, entered the room, took off my clothes and got into bed. I lay down, closed my eyes and fell into a deep sleep.

I dreamt about Ginny. We were appearing in a

THE OUTCOME

production of "Private Lives." This was at Ohio State. It was a great success. The owner of a local theatre was in the audience. He came backstage and wanted to bring the production to his theatre as part of their summer season. Suddenly Clara appeared, holding a baby in her arms. That was when I woke up.

******

Steve was all dressed and getting into his shoes.
How you feeling? Steve asked.
Fine, I said.
I was determined not to think about...what I'd been thinking about, and I was glad that Steve didn't bring it up. It was pointless to try to deal with a situation that might not even exist.
I got out of bed, shaved, got dressed quickly and joined Steve for breakfast. After breakfast we walked together to the university. Steve spoke about Jessica.
She's really a lot of fun. And now that we realize that we're just going to be friends, we're really enjoying each other's company.
We encountered Matthew as we neared the university. He seemed unusually bright and chipper. *Good morning,* he said smiling.
What are you so happy about? I asked.
We're being discharged, Matthew replied.
How do you know? Steve asked.
When? I asked.
As soon as we finish the semester, I guess.
How do you know? Steve asked.
Because men from our division have been arriving in the States, said Matthew. *I got a letter from my family.*

A NOT-SO-NICE JEWISH BOY FACES WORLD WAR II

Steve and I greeted the news in silence.

Isn't that great? Matthew continued. *I sure will be glad to get out of here.*

That doesn't necessarily mean that we'll be discharged, does it? said Steve.

It stands to reason, Matthew replied.

Since when has reason been applied to the army? I said.

You can think what you like, said Matthew, and he walked on ahead.

Apparently we've burst his bubble, said Steve.

How do you feel about leaving? I asked.

I don't know, said Steve.

Neither do I, I said.

For the past two years, almost three, my fate had, for the most part, been in the hands of forces unknown. For the past two years, almost three, I had not been responsible for any major decisions in my life, like where I would go and what I would do. I began to wonder, as I had from time to time, whether one actually is ever the master of one's fate. Was there some mysterious force, like The Fates, those three Greek ladies, who spun the threads of human destiny and snipped those threads when they pleased? Was it already written somewhere, where I would end up and how? Was there any point in pondering the future?

Here we are, said Steve, as we reached the university. *See you later.*

Right, right.

We left one another and proceeded to our separate classes.

******

THE OUTCOME

The rest of the week passed in a haze. There were moments of exhilaration for no reason at all. There were moments of depression for a very specific reason. The voice lesson was a perfect example. There were moments when I knew I was singing well and there was absolutely no doubt in my mind that I would be a major musical comedy star. Then there were moments when I felt lost and confused and knew I would never sing professionally, ever! Mrs. Berganza, as usual, was a soothing presence.

I tried to put off saying anything to Jean about the possibility of being discharged. What was there to say, after all? The news didn't really affect my stay here in Cardiff one way or another. We would probably still finish out the semester. But each time I remembered Matthew's words there was an excitement I just couldn't conceal. Finally I had to say something.

We were sitting in the lounge. It was a cloudy afternoon.

It looks like I may be discharged when we leave here at the end of the semester, I said.

She took the news in silence. My departure was expected, of course, but I could see that my speaking about it so blatantly, so casually came as a shock. What a clumsy oaf I was! Why didn't I keep my goddamned mouth shut! Oh, how I wished I could say, "I'm not going away. I'll be here with you. Don't look so sad. I love you. I will always love you. You're a sweet, darling child and we could make each other happy forever." But I said none of those things. And besides, fool that I was, there was even the possibility of a pregnancy that I might be responsible for. Life was a mess, that was for sure.

******

A NOT-SO-NICE JEWISH BOY FACES WORLD WAR II

Saturday rolled around. It was hard to believe that I was finally approaching the movie house, that I was finally about to hear my fate. Surely, I reasoned, she must know by now whether she was pregnant or not.

She was standing there in the usual spot, and I knew right away, because she smiled at me.

I had my period, she said.

Great!

I bought the tickets and we made our way up to the balcony. I was so exhilarated I didn't even bother to check what the movie was? Who cares!? The weight of the world had just been lifted from my shoulders. I could breathe again. The future looked bright and sunny.

The opening credits were just ending. We took our seats and prepared to enjoy the movie. It turned out to be a Laurel and Hardy comedy. The comedy team were private detectives and traveled to Mexico in pursuit of a criminal. Stan, the thin one with the wide grin, is mistaken for a famous matador. It was not the best comedy this team had made, but you would never know it from the way Clara and I were laughing.

There was no question of sex in our relationship now. We were two friends who had shared an experience, and were fond of one another. How nice to sit and enjoy a movie together! My arm around her shoulder, I felt a special warmth for this young woman who had made me a man of the world. She was a simple person with no pretensions, a woman with a good heart and a pleasant nature. Certainly, one day, she would make some young man a good wife. Or would she? What would she turn out like? Would she blossom into a warm, outgoing housewife and mother? Or would she turn into a sour hausfrau, disgruntled and bitter? That's something I would never know, and I wasn't quite sure that I wanted to

THE OUTCOME

know. But, of course, I did, now that she was no longer a threat.

After the movie we made our way to the restaurant for tea and scones. I escorted her to her bus. We made plans to meet the following Saturday. We waved to each other as she drove off on the bus.

What a pleasant evening! All's right with the world. How could it be otherwise?

CHAPTER FORTY FIVE

THE FIRST FAREWELL

On Monday I was having lunch with Jean in the cafeteria when Matthew passed by. I waved at him. Matthew smiled in recognition and came over to our table. I introduced him to Jean and they shook hands.

Have you received your instructions? Matthew asked.
What instructions? I asked.
On December twenty third we're to report to Southampton, said Matthew. *It looks like we'll be sailing to the States.*

Jean actually turned pale.

I was furious with Matthew, but even angrier at myself for calling our presence to that idiot's attention.

How do you know? I asked. (What a moron!)
Well, it stands to reason, said Matthew.
How do you know we're to report to Southampton?
I received a phone call. They'll be mailing us the instructions. See you later.

Matthew walked away. What a boor! The least he could have done was to say, "Glad to meet you," to Jean.

Well, I suppose it had to come some time, I said.
I don't want you to leave, Jean said. There were tears in her eyes.
We knew it had to come some time, didn't we? We've enjoyed each others company, haven't we?

Jean shrugged reluctantly. It was meant as an acknowledgement.

We've got to enjoy the time we have together, I added. A tired, meaningless phrase, but I didn't know what else to say. I felt like weeping myself.

Jean nodded.

THE FIRST FAREWELL

I took my handkerchief from my pocket and wiped her eyes.

I'm sorry. I am being silly, she said.

I heaved a sigh of relief as Helen came over to join us.

Is there anything wrong? she asked.

Nothing. Everything's fine, I said.

Norman will be leaving soon, said Jean.

Not before the end of the semester, I added.

Helen looked annoyed. I wasn't sure whether she was angry at me or annoyed with Jean. They'd discussed me, I was sure of that, and I wondered what the conversation had been like.

In that case, said Helen, *we've got to throw a party.*

Jean's face lit up. *Yes, we've got to throw a party. We'll have it at my house. Why don't you invite all your friends?* she said to me.

Okay.

Let's make it the twenty first. Since you've got to leave on the twenty third, Jean said.

Okay, I said. *I've got to go. I've got my voice lesson. See you tomorrow.*

I rose. I wanted to bend over and kiss her. Even though I resisted the impulse I could feel her respond to the thought. We could read each others mind. Goddamnit! Why couldn't I have my cake and eat it, too?

******

You look very pensive, said Mrs. Berganza as I sat and drank the hot chocolate.

It looks like I'll be leaving on the twenty third of December.

That leaves us three more lessons.

A NOT-SO-NICE JEWISH BOY FACES WORLD WAR II

Yes.

We shall have to make the most of it, said Mrs. Berganza. *Will you be happy to get home?*

I'll be sad to leave.

Does your friend know?

Yes. She was upset. And so am I.

Ah, yes. She rose from her chair. *Well, let's have a good lesson.*

We got to work. I concentrated on the scales and the exercises. Then I began the song, "We'll Gather Lilacs." I began it automatically. I'd sung it so many times already.

As I sang the second half, in spite of myself, I felt deeply moved.

And in the evening by the firelight's glow
You'll hold me close and never let me go.
Your eyes will tell me what I want to know
When you are home once more.

I knew I'd sung well even before she called it to my attention. *Do you know what you did?* she added.

No, I said. *I just felt it. But I don't know if I'll always feel that way.*

It may come back to you, said Mrs. Berganza, *and eventually it may be yours.*

When I left the lesson I began to feel uneasy. If singing was to take this much out of me, would there be anything left for my writing? Would I have to choose between the theatre and literature?

******

At the house I found two letters waiting for me. I opened the letter from the army first. I was to report to the

THE FIRST FAREWELL

headquarters at Southampton at noon on the twenty third of December.

The other letter was from Ginny. I tore it open and read. "I hope you're all right," she wrote. "I haven't heard from you in weeks. Do please write and let me know how you are." She then went on to tell me about her work in class and at the theatre. She ended with, "I hope to hear from you soon. As ever, Ginny."

Apparently she hadn't gotten my letter yet. I went upstairs to my room. I sat down immediately to write her a letter. I apologized for not writing more often. I'd been so busy enjoying my newfound freedom. The possibility of imminent death had vanished, and I was drunk with life, exhilarated with all the world had to offer. I was sure she understood. I told her all about my trips to London and my voice lessons. I told her that I expected to be back in America some time in January. I hoped that she wasn't working too hard at her job and that she was feeling well.

I wanted to say that I really looked forward to getting together, but somehow I couldn't. I asked myself why. Didn't I love her anymore? Did I ever love her? I had committed myself in a moment of panic, when I thought that I might not live, when I needed someone to think of coming back to. It was Jean that I really loved now.

But then again, how would Jean and I feel about one another, when I was no longer the glamorous Yank from America? When I was just an ordinary young man who was about to gamble on a talent he might not even possess?

Ginny knew me as I really was, my weaknesses and my strengths, and we had so much in common. There was the love of performing. We were both idealistic. We were both insecure. And I knew so well all her insecurities. I knew how self conscious she was about her nose. I knew how

A NOT-SO-NICE JEWISH BOY FACES WORLD WAR II

magnificently talented she was. We bolstered each other's ego. Of course I loved her. What nonsense!

The fact of the matter was Ginny represented reality, and I wasn't ready to face reality quite yet. I was in never never land. I was Peter Pan and Jean was Wendy.

Who would want to leave darling Wendy?
Who would want to leave never never land?
Who wouldn't want to remain a child forever?

Well, unfortunately, I couldn't remain Peter Pan forever. I was just an ordinary human being, with all the problems that all human beings had to cope with. I was over twenty one and the sooner I accepted that fact the better. The trouble was I was a quivering mass of emotions and dreams and ideals without any protective armor to shield those fragile entities from the cold reality of every day living.

And whose fault was that? Was I born that way? Or was it Mother's fault for shielding me from responsibility?

Well you can't blame Mother for everything. You're a grown man.

Grow up!

Easier said than done.

******

I met Clara on Saturday as usual. We were like old friends now. I waited until we were having our tea and scones till I broke the news about my coming departure. Clara looked slightly disappointed, but there were no tears. Her heart wasn't broken. She would miss me for a while, perhaps. Of course, she would miss me. Eventually we would become a memory in each others lives, a bitter-sweet memory perhaps. Clara had a wedding to attend the following Saturday. A friend of hers was getting married. We arranged to meet in two weeks.

THE FIRST FAREWELL

The final weeks slipped by much too fast.

Jean and I went to another symphonic concert in the university auditorium.

I invited Steve and Matthew to the party on the twenty first. Steve asked if he could bring Jessica. I asked Jean and she said of course he could bring Jessica. She was more than welcome.

Clara and I attended a movie on the Saturday before my last Saturday in Cardiff, since the twenty first of December turned out to be a Saturday, and that was the date for Jean's party. We walked to the restaurant together for the last time.

As we sat drinking our tea Clara said, *I've brought you a going-away present.* She took a small parcel wrapped in plain brown paper from her bag, and handed it to me.

Thank you, I said.

Aren't you going to open it?

Yes, I said.

I opened the parcel. It was a pair of woolen gloves, olive drab, the color of my uniform.

I knitted it myself.

Thank you. That was very thoughtful of you.

I stood up, leaned over and kissed her. She blushed.

I hope they fit, she said.

I'm sure they will. I put them on to prove it.

They're a little tight, aren't they? she said.

They're fine.

Actually they were too small.

They should be a little bigger. I should have taken your measurements.

They're fine. Thank you.

I put them in my jacket pocket. As we left the

A NOT-SO-NICE JEWISH BOY FACES WORLD WAR II

restaurant I made a point of putting them on. As the bus came in view I kissed her for the very last time.

Good-bye, I said.

Good-bye, she said.

There was so much more that could have been said. Neither of us could think of how to put into words what we both were feeling.

There were so many things. Nothing was said about keeping in touch, about writing a letter, about letting each other know how things were going. As far as both of us were concerned the interlude was over. As the bus pulled away we waved to each other for the very last time.

I walked back to the house awash with sentiment. Already Clara was a pleasant memory. The harrowing experience of her possible pregnancy was forgotten. We had given each other something...intangible. Perhaps a taste of an intimacy that might eventually become a part of our lives, an intimacy that might be more fulfilling, more pleasurable.

CHAPTER FORTY SIX

WHAT IS THERE TO SAY?

On the eve of the party, my roommate, Steve, left the house to pick up his friend, Jessica. Matthew, as stiff and stuffy as ever, came to the house and we traveled to Jean's house together.

When we arrived we found Jean's friend, Helen, in the kitchen, helping her with the refreshments. Jean wore a blue wool dress which showed her figure to advantage.

You're wearing lipstick, I said. (Jean never wore any makeup.)

I wanted to look pretty, she said.

You don't need lipstick, I said and cursed myself. Idiot! Why do you do that?

I was surprised to see Helen's friend, Ralph, there as well. I wondered if Ralph knew that I was responsible for exposing his...well...not-so-secret love life. Ralph seemed quite friendly and relaxed, so I assumed he knew nothing about my traitorous act. Either that or he held no resentment, which seemed unlikely. Jean's parents were nowhere in sight. Apparently they had left the house in their daughter's care.

While the young ladies busied themselves in the kitchen Matthew, Ralph and I were left in the living room to entertain one another. Matthew sat in a chair nearby erect, prim and silent. Ralph made a futile effort to include Matthew in the conversation. I didn't even bother.

I hear you'll be heading back to the States, said Ralph.

Yes, I said. *We thought we'd be going back to Germany, but it looks like we'll be going straight home.*

You must be relieved.

I can't wait, said I. *I am definitely not army material. Who is?*

The subject turned to our war experiences. I studied

A NOT-SO-NICE JEWISH BOY FACES WORLD WAR II

Ralph as he spoke about having been a pilot in the RAF and flying bombing raids over Germany. I tried to figure him out. He seemed quite charming, with a fine sense of humor, and not the least bit feminine. Was he, or had he really been in love with Victor? I just couldn't picture a romantic relationship with another man. Friendship, yes. Admiration, yes. But romantic love?!

Did you say something? Ralph asked.

No... I really enjoyed your music, I said.

Thank you.

I eyed the grand piano. *Do you think you might play something for us.*

I thought you'd never ask. He sat down at the piano. *What would you like to hear?*

Without waiting for an answer Ralph launched into the popular American tunes of the day; "Deep Purple," "I'll Never Smile Again," "I Walk Alone."

The doorbell rang and I answered it. It was Steve and Jessica. She was a tall, angular girl with laughing eyes and a warm smile. I could see why Steve was smitten.

Sorry, we're late, said Steve

You're just in time, I said.

It's all my fault, said Jessica. *I couldn't find my gloves.*

I introduced Steve and Jessica to Ralph who nodded and continued playing. Steve introduced Jessica to Matthew who rose stiffly, nodded and sat down again.

Jean entered from the kitchen with a tray containing a bottle of red wine and glasses, followed by Helen with cheese and crackers. Further introductions were made.

I'm not very good at hostessing, said Jean. *Please, everyone, help yourselves.* And she sat down next to me. Our hands sought each other automatically.

Jean! Helen said.

WHAT IS THERE TO SAY?

What? Oh! I forgot. There's champagne.
I'll get it, said Helen. She went into the kitchen and returned with the champagne. *Ralph? Ralph!*
Someone's calling my name.
He stopped playing and turned around. Helen held up the champagne. He rose from the piano and opened the bottle quite professionally.
Where are the champagne glasses? he asked.
Just pour, said Helen.
You can't....
Ralph, just pour.
He poured the champagne into the wine glasses and the two of them distributed the glasses.
Who's going to make the toast? Ralph asked.
Norman, said Jean.
I'm not very good at making toasts. Very well, I said. I rose, looked about the room then looked at Jean. I raised my glass, and all I could think of to say was...*To friendship!*
To friendship, everyone echoed.
They raised their glasses and we all drank.
Ralph returned to the piano and began to play some popular British songs, "A Nightingale Sang in Berkeley Square," "We'll Meet Again," mixed in with Noel Coward tunes. Steve and Jessica got up and danced. Helen walked up to Matthew.
Would you care to dance? she asked.
He remained seated. *Thank you. I don't dance.*
You don't or you won't?
He remained silent and blushed. Helen looked over at me. I shrugged. She walked over to the food and ate some cheese.
Jean looked at me. Apparently she wanted to dance. I

had never held her in my arms. I didn't want to hold her close. It would just make things worse, but I couldn't refuse.

I rose reluctantly. She rose and I placed my arms around her. We moved to the center of the floor. She snuggled close and we danced, or rather moved about the floor. She was a very bad dancer, and I kept stepping on her toes, but it didn't matter. We were in our own private world. I didn't know what she was feeling but I was feeling miserable.

Helen came to the rescue. She tapped Jean on the shoulder. Jean looked up bewildered.

May I cut in?

Jean stepped aside. Helen stepped up to me and we danced.

She's in a very bad way, she whispered.

What can I do? I asked.

She didn't reply. I could sense her answer. You've done enough. As I danced with Helen I looked about the room. Jean was nowhere in sight.

Excuse me, I said.

I left Helen and went into the kitchen. She was crying.

I don't want you to leave.

I took her in my arms and held her. Finally she stopped.

I'm making a fool of myself, I know, she said.

You don't want to spoil our last evening together, do you?

No. I won't cry anymore. I promise. Besides, I've got work to do.

She picked up a towel and removed two quiches from the oven where they were being kept warm. She sliced one of the quiches and placed the slices on paper plates.

Can I help? I asked.

WHAT IS THERE TO SAY?

There's a salad in the fridge, she said. *Could you bring that in and place it on the table?*

I did as I was told.

There's food coming, I announced.

Helen went into the kitchen and returned with plates of quiche which she distributed. Jean brought in the rest. There was silence as the food was eaten and wine was poured and drunk. Ralph returned to the piano with a glass of wine and started to play again.

That's your song, said Jean.

It's not really my song, I said.

Do you sing? Jessica asked.

Oh, yes, said Jean. *He sings beautifully.*

You must sing for us, said Jessica.

You don't want me to ruin a perfectly lovely evening, do you? I said.

To my immense relief Ralph began to sing in a pleasant light baritone voice. Jessica joined in followed by Helen.

And in the evening by the firelight's glow
You'll hold me close and never let me go.
Your eyes will tell me what I want to know
When you are home once more.

I gritted my teeth to prevent myself from bursting into tears the way Jean had in the kitchen.

Are you all right? Jean whispered.

Yes, I'm fine.

You don't want to leave. You know you don't.

I never mentioned it before, I said, *and maybe it wasn't fair of me, but I have made a commitment.*

This took her by surprise. After she recovered she asked, *Are you in love with her?*

Yes. After a moment I added, *I'm very fond of you. You know that.*

A NOT-SO-NICE JEWISH BOY FACES WORLD WAR II

Yes, I know.
I shall always value your friendship, I said.
Even as I spoke the words they sounded so hollow, so false and so inadequate.
Ralph stopped playing and took a sip of wine. *Have you heard the one about the two nuns?* he asked.
Do tell! Jessica called from across the room.
By this time everyone was beginning to feel the effect of the champagne and the wine, including Jean and myself. Everyone, that is, except Matthew. He rose.
I've got to be going.
No one protested.
Thank you, he said to no one in particular, and left.
I plopped down on the floor. *I thought he'd never leave,* I said.
What is that man's problem? Helen asked.
He's from Boston, I said. *Let's hear the one about the two nuns.*
Well, there were these two nuns, Sister Pragmatic and Sister Hysteria. They were returning to the nunnery late one night when Sister Pragmatic turned to Sister Hysteria and whispered, "I believe we're being followed." "Let's walk faster," said Sister Hysteria." So they started to walk faster and so did the man. They started to run, and so did the man. "Why don't we separate?" said Sister Pragmatic. "This way he can only attack one of us." So they separated and the man followed Sister Pragmatic." Back at the nunnery Sister Hysteria waited anxiously for Sister Pragmatic's return. When she finally arrived she looked very pleased with herself. "What happened?" Sister Hysteria asked. "Well, I ran as fast as I could and so did he." "Yes?" "But I could see that he was catching up with me." "Oh, dear! What happened then?" "I stopped." "You stopped." "Yes, I stopped and I pulled up my

WHAT IS THERE TO SAY?

skirts." "You didn't!" "I did." "And what happened then?" "He pulled down his trousers." "He didn't!" "He did." "And what happened then?" "Nothing, my dear. Everyone knows that a woman can run faster with her dress up than a man with his trousers down"

There was a burst of laughter. Ralph looked around the room. *"You naughty people! What were you thinking? Shame on you all!"*

Everyone laughed and applauded. Jessica followed with a joke about two monks, and Helen followed with a joke about heaven and hell. Just then Mr. and Mrs. Courbet arrived.

Don't mind us, said Mr. Courbet, *We're just passing through.*

There was some polite laughter and the Courbets retired to another part of the house.

The party began to break up. Steve and Jessica said their thank yous and left. Helen corralled Ralph into carrying dishes into the kitchen and they remained there.

After a moment Jean said, *I've bought you a little present.* She left and returned with a little box, a tie box, which she handed to me.

May I open it? I asked.

She nodded. I opened the box. It was a striped tie, black, red and yellow.

It's the school tie.

Thank you, I said.

I closed the box.

I'd better be going.

I went into the kitchen. I said good-bye to Ralph and shook his hand. I said good-bye to Helen and kissed her on the cheek. I returned to the living room. Jean was standing in the middle of the room looking very small and lost. Our hands met. She walked with me to the door.

A NOT-SO-NICE JEWISH BOY FACES WORLD WAR II

It's cold out, I said.

She ignored my words and walked with me out the door. We stood on the stone steps in the cold winter night.

You'll catch cold, I said.

I leaned over and kissed her on the lips. She clung to me for a moment and then let go. I walked away quickly without looking back. Three days later I was on a ship sailing back to America.

ABOUT THE AUTHOR

Norman Beim was born in Newark, New Jersey attended Ohio State University for a year and two thirds, when he was drafted into World War II. During combat, he learned that his one act play, Inside, had won second place in a nationwide competition. He put aside his decision to become a novelist and decided to become a playwright, while he earned he earned a living as an actor.

After the war he studied and worked as an actor at Hedgrow Theatre, produced and appeared in three plays in Philadelphia, worked as an actor at the Provincetown Playhouse on the Cape, and in the national company of Darkness At Noon.

He settled in New York where he worked as an actor on Broadway, Off Broadway, and on TV. He appeared in the Broadway production of Inherit The Wind with Paul Muni, and later with Melvyn Douglas. He was standby for Van Johnson in the national company of Tribute, and worked with Morgan Freeman at the Public Theatre. He also worked as a director and, all the while, he continued to write plays.

He is a lifetime member of the Dramatists Guild. His plays have been produced nationally and internationally, including the classic, The Deserter. He's written book and lyrics for a number of musicals, including the remarkable Fritz & Froyim.

Twelve volumes of his plays, and three fact-based novels have been published, and he continues to produce novels and write plays which continue to be produced.

A second volume of his memoirs is due out in 2014.